Who Is
That Man?

Who Is
That Man?

In Search of
the Real Bob Dylan

David Dalton

HYPERION

New York

Library of Congress Cataloging-in-Publication Data

Dalton, David.
  Who is that man?: In search of the real Bob Dylan/David Dalton.—1st ed.
    p. cm.
  ISBN 978-1-4013-2339-4
  1. Dylan, Bob, 1941– 2. Singers—United States—Biography. I. Title.
  ML420.D98D34 2012
  782.42164092—dc23

                            2012003490

BOOK DESIGN BY SHUBHANI SARKAR

First Edition

10 9 8 7 6 5 4 3 2

SUSTAINABLE FORESTRY INITIATIVE
Certified Fiber Sourcing
www.sfiprogram.org

THIS LABEL APPLIES TO TEXT STOCK

We try to produce the most beautiful books possible, and we are also extremely concerned about the impact of our manufacturing process on the forests of the world and the environment as a whole. Accordingly, we've made sure that all of the paper we use has been certified as coming from forests that are managed, to ensure the protection of the people and wildlife dependent upon them.

for
COCO PEKELIS
the true fortuneteller of my soul

and

MAX GUARINO
1985–2003
forever young

Contents

Each of us is several, is many, is a profusion of selves.
So that the self who disdains his surroundings is not
the same as the self who suffers or takes joy in them.
In the vast colony of our being there are many species
of people who think and feel in different ways.

—FERNANDO PESSOA

Something Was Happening but I Didn't Know What It Was: *That Afternoon with Bob*

IN THE SPRING OF 1970 I SAW LES BLANK'S LUSH, LYRICAL, AND INTI-mate documentaries about the blues singers Lightnin' Hopkins and Mance Lipscomb (which Les was still editing). They are amazing films—here was the life of the blues itself—and I told whomever I met that summer that they *had* to see them, that they were essential sacred texts of our culture. As it happened I spent the good part of a week in late June and early July on a train with a bunch of blues freaks (the Band, Leslie West, Janis Joplin, the Grateful Dead) and proselytized Les's films to one and all. The Band's Rick Danko asked if Les (who'd by this point moved in with me) might bring the films up to Woodstock so they could all see them. Les and I borrowed a car and drove up to Woodstock to show the films to the Band and assorted Bearsville hipoisie. They were all suitably awed.

A couple of weeks later I got a phone call from Jon Taplin, the Band's manager. Turns out "Bobby" had heard about Les's films and wanted to see them. He was going to be in New York on Friday, and Jon asked if I could set up a screening. No need to ask which Bobby he meant. This was *the* Bobby, Sir Bob himself, my idol, the sublime, inscrutable Bob Dylan. Some years ago Dylan and Howard Alk had taken footage from the Pennebaker documentary of his 1966 European tour and made it into a maddening methedrine-addled antidocumentary called *Eat the Document*. Taplin explained that Dylan now wanted to release *Eat the Document*, but in order to distribute it he needed an extra forty-minute film to go with it. He suggested Bob take a look at one of Les Blank's documentaries.

Les is a large bear of a character—bearded, slow talkin', Southern. He is a man of few words and fewer effusions of emotion, but the idea that Bob Dylan might see his films visibly animated him. But where to screen the films? My walk-up tenement on East 4th Street was out of the question. By chance I had purloined the keys to my publisher's fancy brownstone apartment on a fashionable side street on the Upper West Side while he was on holiday. Just the spot.

The day came. On a swelteringly hot afternoon in late July, Les and I lugged a 16 mm projector, a folding screen, and cans of film uptown on the subway. We set it all up, arranged and rearranged the furniture, and waited. Hours went by. Anxious thoughts attacked us. Did we give them the right address? Was this the right day? Finally they arrived. The Band entered in their cowboy regalia, along with wives and girlfriends in airy summer dresses. And then there was Bob himself. It was as if he had fallen out of the sky from another climate entirely—the dead of winter actually. He was dressed in a long wool overcoat, hat, and gloves (and shades, of course). Low blood sugar, perhaps due to his habit, I thought somewhat uncharitably.

Like a sleepwalker taking his nocturnal stroll, Bob walked straight into the house flanked by Robbie Robertson and Rick Danko and sat down. There were no introductions, no small talk. Even members of the Band who knew him as well as anybody treated him with the deference usually reserved for foreign dignitaries.

While the men retired to the dining room where the projector was set up, the women flipped through European fashion magazines in another room. Les, in a state of alert apprehension, ran the Lightnin' Hopkins film. When it was over Dylan cryptically signaled that he'd seen enough. The lights came up. We all waited for him to say something, but the oracle was silent. Les was now palpably humming with anxiety. I had to do something. I walked over to Dylan, who was still sitting there swaddled in his overcoat and gloves, and asked, "How did you like the film, Bobby?" What was I going to do, call him Mr. Dylan?

He regarded me with a deadpan expression and, passing over my question entirely, asked, "Who's the *architect* of this houuuse?" He spoke the way he sang, leaning on the syllables, the way a cowboy might lean on a bar. I was still listening to the music of the words when I realized he was asking me a question. I froze. He couldn't mean something as literal as this, could he? Dylan being Dylan and all. Of course not. It was code; it was an allegorical question. But about what? I was in a roomful of books and they all had the same title. Like the wicked messenger or Frankie Lee, I was in the presence of the Sibyl but too witless to grasp the message.

The words "architect" and "house" reverberated in my brain. They ballooned into sound sharks and swam eerily through my synapses. They bristled with archaic meanings. They grew huge. They began to fill the room, monstrous dollhouse words that would turn the building inside out if I didn't stop them. All this was taking place in a fraction of a second

I hoped, but it must have been somewhat longer because Dylan spoke again: "Ya know who *built* this place?"

Okay, the only solution now was to play it straight, pretend to take him at face value. "Bobby," I said (after all we'd been through we were now firmly on a first-name basis), "I figure this house must have been built in the nineteenth century."

But centuries and stuff like that meant nothing to Dylan. *He wanted that architect.* "So can we get this guy?" he persisted. For a moment there, I was Bob Dylan's contractor. "This was all a hundred years ago," I said. "Man, the guy is long gone." Mundane matters like the life expectancy of architects or muleskinners didn't enter into it. His idea of history was porous. There were no specific time periods. Everybody who'd ever lived was a contemporary: Noah, Jesse James, Bessie Smith, or St. Augustine himself. They all lived in the timeline of the songs.

And then there was that other matter, the onion-domed Xanadu that Dylan was building at Zuma Beach. Like anyone else involved in building a house he was fixated on the minutiae of wallpaper, carpets, and kitchen cabinets. Enigmatic Bob, it turned out, was seriously into paneling. Bob walked over to the intricately paneled oak walls of the dining room.

"How'd they *dooo* that?" he asked as if it were some lost art.

"Well, you know, with miter boxes, I guess."

"*Miiiter* boxes?" Bob liked the sound of the word. Bishops and carpenters, you know, they all used those things.

No one mentioned the movies or whether he liked them or whether Dylan ever considered using them as part of the thing he was putting together for *Eat the Document.* I went to get a drink of water from the kitchen. When I returned, the Gypsy had gone.

As Les and I walked down the street we wondered how often Dylan encountered situations in which the simplest question could throw his devout followers into a state of paralysis. What if, like some Zen master around whom meanings multiplied like flies, he could never order a cup of coffee or buy a pair of shoes or find a carpenter because no one would believe him capable of such commonplace utterances? Les didn't seem to mind that much that he wasn't going to be on a double bill with Dylan. Dylan had seen one of his movies and that was enough for him.

Who Is

Dylan, the new model hipster, perfect even
to the rake of his cigarette, checks out his
image backstage during his 1965 tour of
England. Okay, Bob—now just grab the
shades and we're done.

Introduction

Those masterful images because complete
Grew in pure mind, but out of what began?
A mound of refuse or the sweepings of a street,
Old kettles, old bottles, and a broken can,
Old iron, old bones, old rags, that raving slut
Who keeps the till. Now that my ladder's gone,
I must lie down where all the ladders start
In the foul rag and bone shop of the heart.

—W. B. YEATS, "THE CIRCUS ANIMALS' DESERTION"

"I HAVE HERE SOMETHING THAT'LL SOLVE ALL OUR PROBLEMS."
"Well, go on, what is it?"
"A bootleg."
"Oh great. That's all we need is another bootleg. What's this one? Copenhagen, April 30, 1966, reel two, second half missing? We've got eight thousand bootleg tapes, man; we're never going to find enough time to listen to them all in our lifetime."
"It's not like that."
"Oh, then what is it?"
[*Looks around apprehensively*] "Bob's brain."
"It's what!?"
"It's one of only three bootlegs of Bob's brain—off a cat scan from when he was, you know, in the hospital in 1997 with, uh, histoplasmowhatever...."
"Sounds a little gruesome."
"But do you realize what this means?"
"Listen ... man ... you okay?"

———

SUCH TAPES WOULD BE USEFUL, NO QUESTION ABOUT IT, BECAUSE IT'S pretty much what we want to know: What goes on in Dylan's brain? How does he think, what does he *meeeaaan*, what are the "keys to the rain," and such? But, hey, what happens in the neocortex *stays* in the neocortex, so we'll have to pursue other means to winkle out the elusive Bob. And this is only fitting since Dylan is essentially a Beat novelist in the manner of Jack Kerouac. The phantasmagoria of his great mid-'60s albums is an expression of his inner turmoil and mirrors the shattering of the culture. The songs on *Bringing It All Back Home*, *Highway 61 Revisited*, and *Blonde on Blonde* are seismic recordings of the conflicts in the streets and in his head, hallucinated autobiographies of himself and his times—the confused signals and psychic static of the '60s.

Dylan emerged just at the moment the counterculture was hatching, his life inextricably connected to the rise of mass bohemia. Dylan's own inner demons meshed seamlessly with its antiestablishment rhetoric, drugs, radical politics, mysticism, and amplified free-floating unrest. Dylan's personal story—whether he likes it or not—is entwined with the '60s and their aftermath.

An agile, subtle, polytropic mind, he registered America's 19th nervous breakdown with hallucinatory precision. Fragmented images and cubist songs replaced the storytelling and ballad tableaux of folk songs and transformed the agitprop of protest songs into a roiling, nightmarish vision in which you couldn't distinguish the chaos outside from the turmoil within.

However far he fled from the front lines, Dylan could never disconnect from the counterculture; he has an umbilical relationship to his time. It is no coincidence that his creative predicament at the beginning of the '70s paralleled a crisis in the culture. The public and private Dylans—his music, his times, and our perceptions of him—are inextricably linked, a sort of Zeitgeist Kid.

And this is where his many shape-shifting personas come in: dust bowl singer, street urchin, son of Ramblin' Jack, Folk Messiah, neon Rimbaud, Old Testament prophet, Amish farmer, howdy-neighbor country boy, whiteface death's-head mummer, Shropshire lad with flowers in his hat, Christlike Bob, born-again Bob, Hasidic Bob, Late-Elvis Dylan with the big WWF belt, Endless Tour Dylan, Jack Fate, Living National Treasure....

Dylan is a method actor who sees his life as an emblematic movie. You make a song real by becoming the character—the voice—who's singing it. Dylan's shedding and adopting of characters (dramatized in the 2007 film *I'm Not There*) is a form of authentic counterfeit—the minstrel as Hamlet. Dylan sees the entertainer as an American hero. His idols are all entertainers (and writers, a subcategory): Blind Willie McTell, Hank Williams, Dock Boggs, Marlon Brando, Elvis, James Dean, Kerouac. They—along with outlaws, drifters, hustlers, and poets—are the American figures Dylan most often invokes. In a country without a past, without a history, entertainers are our psychic guides through the wilderness. Songs are part of the American DNA.

DYLAN CAME OUT OF THE WILDEST, WOOLLIEST, ROWDIEST TALKING tales of all time. When rock 'n' roll erupted in the mid-'50s it was first seen as a novelty. The early singers, including Elvis, were a mythical parade of fantastic and freakish types. Legendary characters roamed the land: the outrageous Little Richard; Fats Domino, the living embodiment of Mardi Gras; Jerry Lee Lewis, the human threshing machine; the shape-shifting Bo Diddley; and Chuck Berry, the raunchy Uncle Remus of rock. And behind them—further back in time and remote from contemporary America—were an even more improbable cast of characters: Appalachian skillet lickers, jug band musicians, and apocalyptic Delta bluesmen like Son House and Skip James.

Dylan's as slippery as Br'er Rabbit but my quest hasn't been to flush him out of his make-believe briar patch. Instead it's to look for Dylan's poetic intention, to read Dylan's biography by the flickering light of songs. I've tried to follow Bob's footprints in the quicksand and have often felt like a fumbling musician trying to keep up with Dylan at a recording session.

When *Chronicles* was published, the complaints about the unreliability of his autobiography as fact seemed farcical. Grumbling that even when he writes his memoirs he's still *making stuff up!* The outrage! He's toying with us! Ping-ponging between fact and fiction—but we expect nothing less of him. After all, who are we dealing with? The mercurial, maddeningly evasive Bob. Smoke and mirrors is Dylan doing what Dylan does best.

His fabrications are the most profound, interesting, and authentic part of his personality. Like Don Quixote, he seems to have walked out of his own fable. And the stuff he makes up about himself is more truthful than any factual account could ever be. However petty, avaricious, cruel, callous, or shrivelingly cynical he may be, the oracular poet who wrote "Desolation Row" and "Visions of Johanna" isn't the same person as the fallible human in divorce proceedings, the sullen, devious interviewee, or the usurper of copyrights. His willful perversity is itself a form of impish magic, a way of keeping his carefully hooded persona animated and untraceable.

Dylan sees America as an endless, unfinishable song, which people add to and change as we go along, altering the rhythm, cutting up the lyrics and patching them back in a different order. He's the classic American type, the confidence man who tells the truth by dissembling and whose presence questions whether there is such a thing as a fixed personality. He is a startlingly unique character who is in fact a composite of American types: the song and dance man, the joker and thief.

His quest has been to cannibalize the great scrap heap of American history—its ballads, tunes, and nursery rhyme fables—and condense the multiplicity of its characters and their stories into a song. The purloining, pilfering, lifting, and outright larceny of songs, books, and images are all part of his magpie nature. He's in the mad American tradition of trying to stuff the Mississippi, the Rockies, Johnny Appleseed, Christopher Columbus, and Orphan Annie all into one whopping tall tale.

I've passed over some periods while slowing others down—suspending time the way Dylan does—so I could see the pictures more clearly and try to keep up with the chameleon as he slithers from one rock to another.

No one has more ingeniously tested the porous border between autobiography and fiction than Dylan; mixing reality and fantasy has always been his witchy brew.

He's the most cunning of self-mythologizers, and he's managed to entangle us in his allegorical character—his persona is so infested with the types he's collected along the way that often he doesn't seem to know where he ends and they begin—which creates an eerie sense of channeling on his *Theme Time Radio Hour* where he'll inhabit George Jones, Skip James, or a refrigerator repairman.

But even if Dylan has frequently gotten lost inside his own labyrinth of prevarications it has made him all the more mesmerizing. There are thousands of possessed fans out there with flashlights searching through his murky skull looking for clues.

Almost everything in Dylan is a re-creation of himself in folklore. America *is* a novel that we make up as we go along. Like Dylan, we are genuine fakes. Genuine like the people who came here, but larger than life, *too* big—fake. So we need stories, the taller the better: Our songs, movies, advertising, pop culture—these are the invented life that binds us together. Dylan's great insight was to see the mythic skin that the great snake America had shed—and put it on himself.

Even the way he came into the world is straight out of a tall tale.

1 Creation Myths

A few toughnecks are still getatable who pretend that aboriginally he was of respectable stemming . . . but every honest to goodness man in the land of space of today knows that his back life will not stand being written about in black and white. Putting truth and untruth together a shot may be made at what this hybrid actually was like to look at.

—JAMES JOYCE, *FINNEGANS WAKE*

"WHEN I WAS TEN I BEGAN PLAYING GUITAR," SAYS DYLAN in *No Direction Home*, the Martin Scorsese documentary. "I found a guitar in the house that my father bought actually. There was something else in there that had mystical overtones. There was a great big mahogany radio, it had a 78 turntable when you opened up the top. I opened it up one day and there was a record on it, a country record, a song called 'Driftin' Too Far from the Shore.' The sound of the record made me feel like I was somebody else. That I was not born to the right parents or something." It's almost as if this character, who became Bob Dylan, had been born in the grooves of a record, and his whole life—imaginary and actual—took place there.

But Robert Allen Zimmerman was born on May 24, 1941, to Abe and Beatty Zimmerman in Duluth, Minnesota. Allegedly. Bobby has other ideas. According to him, he was an orphan—a story he was still telling (to the astonishment of Abe and Beatty) well into 1963. At other times he claimed to be a foundling, the son of an Egyptian king, an Oglala Sioux dancing in Indian festivals and rain dances, a tent-show kid growing up in carnivals—"performing all over the country" on the high wire (and in his spare time taking care of the bearded lady).

In light of Dylan's subsequent mythology, any of these would seem more plausible than the facts. But maybe he wasn't talking about Robert Zimmerman at all; maybe he was talking about the childhood of Bob Dylan (a creation who wouldn't appear until early 1960).

At age five, Dylan gets his first two gigs, singing "Some Sunday Morning" at a Mother's Day celebration and his first paying gig (twenty-five dollars) at his aunt Irene's wedding, where he sings "Accentuate the Positive" in a white Palm Beach suit. Parents' advice: Brush your teeth and don't play with matches.

Although he was only five when the family moved from Duluth, the city left an elegiac trace in his memory: "I like the way the hills tumble to the waterfront and the way the wind blows around the grain elevators," he said in 2009. "The train yards go on forever too. It's old-age, industrial, that's what it is. You'll see it from the top of the hill for miles and miles before you get there."

His brother, David, is born in 1946. Abe gets polio, and loses his job as an office manager at Standard Oil. The family moves north to the mining town of Hibbing in 1947. Poor relatives, they move in with Beatty's parents. Bob's mother is outgoing. Her family has show business connections; they own a movie theater on Howard Street and a local radio station (WMFG).

His father is reserved, gloomy, distant. There's always that fear of the father. Abe, in many ways, resembles Dylan's future manager, the grouchy, sullen, cynical Albert Grossman. After Abe dies in 1968, Dylan says, "I never knew my father."

Hibbing, Minnesota, is the site of the biggest man-made hole in the world, an existential allegory if ever there was one. Like a village in a fairy tale, Hibbing cannibalized itself in search of iron ore, undermining the town itself through relentless excavations. When the ore ran out in the '50s, so did the jobs, and the town underwent a depression from which it never entirely recovered. If the biggest hole in the world had had an effect on him, why hasn't it shown up in any of his songs? Or has it? Is that what he's been doing, filling it up?

Hibbing is bristling with folk motifs, like looking at a scale model, with figurines crossing the square, a railway buff's scale model of a town, an HO-gauge railway set, a cluster of trees, a water tower, a tiny station with signs, a platform piled with suitcases and packages. The woods near Bob's house—the true setting for this idyllic landscape is in the mind's eye. We peer into it through the lens of other people's memories and observe Bobby Zimmerman, Dylan's larval self, attending high school, forming bands. And then there's Hibbing: a stage set of *Our Town*, the urbanite's idea of a small town, a mining town.

In the liner notes to *Joan Baez in Concert Part 2*, Dylan reminisces:

As I waited till I heard the sound
A the iron ore cars rollin' down
The tracks'd hum an' I'd bite my lip
An' hold my grip as the whistle whined
Crouchin' low as the engine growled
I'd shyly wave t' the throttle man
An' count the cars as they rolled past

Describing the small frontier town of Okemah in Okfuskee County, Woody Guthrie wrote, "Okemah was one of the singiest, square dancingest, drinkingest, yellingest, preachingest, walkingest, talkingest, laughingest, cryingest, shootingest, fist fightingest, bleedingest, gamblingest, gun, club and razor carryingest of our ranch towns and farm towns, because it blossomed out into one of our first Oil Boom Towns." Hibbing, too, was a boomtown, but it didn't spawn the wild and woollies of Okemah, Oklahoma. For one thing, as Dylan points out, it was too cold in Hibbing for anyone there to get into trouble.

The real source of Dylan's art is actually in the anti-Hibbing, his reinvention of his past in the imaginary landscape and characters that he created to replace it: Dylan as the miner's son, for instance, in "North Country Blues," or the wistful dreamer remembering his lost love in "Girl from the North Country." He would later mine the imaginary Hibbing for poetic images, not unlike the way Dylan Thomas cast his hometown as Llareggub Hill in *Under Milk Wood*.

"What's dear to me are the Fifties, 'cause that's when I grew up," he remembered in 1997. "Knife sharpeners would come down the street, and the coal man too, and every once in a while a wagon would come through town with a gorilla in a cage or, I remember, a mummy under glass. . . . It was a very itinerant place—no interstate highways yet, just country roads everywhere. There was an innocence about it all, and I don't recall anything bad ever happening. That was the Fifties, the last period of time I remember as being idyllic."

Abe becomes a partner in his brother-in-law's business, Mika Electric, and prospers along with the '50s obsession with the magic of appliances. He buys a house on Seventh Avenue in Fairview, teaches Bobby the value of hard work by having him sweep out the store after school. When Bobby is eight, Abe sends him to repossess appliances from delinquent hire-purchase customers to teach him the value of money.

In 1952, the Zimmermans get the first TV in Hibbing (they're in the appliance business, after all), which coincides with the appearance of the first synthetic folk heroes: Matt Dillon in *Gunsmoke*, Richard Boone in *Have Gun—Will Travel*. Bob's parents wallpaper his bedroom with the cowboy motifs—horses and saddles—that will ultimately mutate into *Pat Garret and Billy the Kid* (and Alias, Dylan's character in the movie) and the mystic West of *John Wesley Harding*.

His childhood and adolescence flash by like the herky-jerky black-and-white frames of a silent film. He joins the Boy Scouts, learns Hebrew for his bar mitzvah, steals apples (just like St. Augustine). Over at WMFG they're playing the Four Lads, Doris Day, and Perry Como as the snow falls on Kresge's on Main Street and on the Mika Electric sign.

"Well, in the winter," Dylan told *Playboy* in 1978, "everything was still, nothing moved. Eight months of that. You can put it together. You can have some amazing hallucinogenic experiences doing nothing but looking out your window. There is also the summer, when it gets hot and sticky and the air is very metallic. There is a lot of Indian spirit. The earth there is unusual, filled with ore. So there is something happening that is hard to define. There is a magnetic attraction there. Maybe thousands and thousands of years ago, some planet bumped into the land there. There is a great spiritual quality throughout the Midwest. Very subtle, very strong, and that is where I grew up. New York was a dream."

When Bob was a teenager living in a little Minnesota town, America for him was still an imaginary country where mysterious things happened and the world could be transformed by a song as he listened to the radio at night, tuning in stations from the ruminating South: blues on KWKH in Shreveport, WSM beaming Hank Williams and Hank Thompson from Nashville, the *National Barn Dance* from WLS out of Chicago. They were all part of a magical sonic landscape, as if music in those places grew out of the soil. "I was always fishing for something on the radio. Just like trains and bells, it was part of the soundtrack of my life."

The forty Jewish families in Hibbing are a kind of north country shtetl. Among the Zimmermans, there's Abe, the son of first-generation Jewish immigrants from eastern Europe; Beatty, the child of second-generation Jewish immigrants; and Bobby, a Jew born in a town full of anti-Semitic Polish and Ukrainian miners' children. The dream of America as the promised land in the little villages in Poland contrasts with the grim reality of Hibbing. It's a remote, isolated place, surrounded by a howling wilderness.

Bob's grandfather, the peddler, reenacts the myth of the poor immigrant entering the promised land. The land of milk and honey or . . . iron ore and sludge. The Zimmermans are more or less assimilated into Hibbing's Christian community, but as Saul Bellow wrote in *Ravelstein*, "As a Jew you are also an American, but somehow you are not."

All of this is partly the origin of Dylan's idiosyncratic point of view: He looks at America with an immigrant's eye, listens with a ventriloquist's ear. A Jew from the hinterlands he was at a double remove from mainstream America—an outsider in a community of outsiders. Dylan would conceal his Jewish origins until the dreaded *Newsweek* article in 1963 exposed them—and then he would deny them.

By the time Bobby was ten, characteristic antisocial tendencies develop, along with writing as a secret parallel life. At first he's just a prolific writer of sentimental doggerel (Mother's and Father's Day poems). At eleven, he is a compulsive, secretive scribbler, arousing a mother's concern. She hopes it's a passing phase, but he never grows out of it. For a misplaced kid, this was a form of disappearing into an imaginary realm. "All I did was write and sing, paint little pictures on paper, dissolve myself into situations where I was invisible," says Dylan.

"Teachers in school taught me everything was fine." Well, he knew *that* couldn't be true. When they try to tell him history is just facts and dates, he doesn't buy that one either. He flat refuses to study it. "There's nothing to figure out in history" would be his attitude from now on. "History is lies!" he wrote on the original liner notes to *Planet Waves*. His would be a folkloric vision of history in which emblematic figures— Tom Paine, Columbus, Jesse James, Captain Ahab, St. Augustine—stride across a haunted landscape.

New Year's Day 1953 marks the death of Hank Williams, the hillbilly Shakespeare (age twenty-nine) slumped in the back of his Cadillac from a drug and alcohol overdose. One of the prime myths of American hipster folklore, this has a profound effect on twelve-year-old Bobby. His first record collection is of Hank Williams 78s. "The sound of his voice went through me like an electric rod." Shortly afterward he takes up music and songwriting in earnest. He sees Hank Williams as a folk chronicler of American myth, a role he will shortly take on himself.

An' my first idol was Hank Williams
For he sang about the railroad lines
An' the iron bars an' rattlin' wheels
Left no doubt that they were real

Bob won't play sports or join extracurricular clubs. He escapes into fantasy. But otherwise he enjoys a normal Midwestern adolescence. He attends Theodore Herzl summer camp and collects pinups: "I dedicated my first song to Brigitte Bardot," he says. He dates the daughters of miners and farmers.

On September 30, 1955, James Dean, the mutant king of American pop culture, dies. The posthumous release of *Rebel Without a Cause* creates the James Dean cult and the romance of teen fatality: cars, fame, speed, death. Bob, age fourteen, collects posters, photos, memorial magazines of Dean. In the 1980s, he twice visits Dean's grave in Fairmount, Indiana.

James Dean's death marks the first fault line in the American teen dream. A year later Elvis appears, an almost occult embodiment of unrealized adolescent fantasies fused onto a chrome-plated R&B chassis. "Hound Dog" and "Heartbreak Hotel" are on every jukebox, beginning Dylan's lifelong obsession with Elvis. In his blurb for Peter Guralnick's *Last Train to Memphis*, Dylan recalls Elvis as an almost supernatural being: "Elvis ... walks the path between heaven and nature in an America that was wide open, when anything was possible, not the whitewashed golden calf but the incendiary atomic musical firebrand loner who conquered the Western world." For Dylan, "the Gypsy" is a conjure man, a genuine folk hero distilling the American grain: gospel, pop, R&B, country. Elvis, like Hank Williams, has a flashy stage persona that seems summoned out of the fabric of the music itself, a prototype Dylan will follow in his many incarnations. More bizarre is Dylan's early and continuing fascination with Liberace.

He begins accumulating rebel prototypes and poses for photographs on his motorbike on the train tracks—like Marlon Brando, the motorpsycho hipster. Along with James Dean (the five-and-dime anarchist) and Elvis (trailer-trash mystic), Brando is his idol. They are standard anti-hero models of the era, but Dylan never completely abandons them. He never entirely abandons anything from his past (including all the easy listening ballads and Andrews Sisters pop/swing stuff he hears on WMFG, which will eventually show up on *Self Portrait*). While fleeing his past Dylan always remembers to grab his sacred icons. His lifelong attraction to outsiders and outlaws will, by the '60s, morph into his fascination with underground freaks and underworld gangsters.

From movie stars and Elvis he learns how to replace himself using mental snapshots. At fifteen Dylan poses in a cowboy hat with a cigarette dangling from his mouth in imitation of the famous Dennis Stock photo of James Dean in *Life* magazine (Dean copped it from an Albert Camus paperback). Dylan will reprise the pose for the publicity shot of *Don't Look Back*.

He gets the moves off in front of the mirror in his bedroom (like many others: Ray Davies, Lou Reed, Pete Townshend, and, of course, Keith) and also clowns (doing goofy hillbilly parodies of "Over the Rainbow"). Dylan also joins his high school pop group, the Golden Chords, as singer, piano player. In photographs he uncannily incarnates the punk Elvis of 1956. They play Moose Lodge events, PTA meetings.

Bob transitions from reclusive, poetry-scribbling introvert ("Bob," says his mom, "was upstairs, quietly becoming a writer for twelve years") to class clown and a show-off onstage. He develops a symbiotic relationship between the two sides of his character: the writer and the performer. He begins his songwriting career by impersonating other songwriters, whose songs he claims to have written himself.

"The mysterious Bob Dylan had a chicken-soup, Yiddishe mama," Allen Ginsberg said of him. Bobby Zimmerman writes poems for special occasions—his mother's birthday, for instance, and Beatty Zimmerman was clearly instrumental in Bob's belief that he was marked out for great things. His mother's love will grant him superhuman powers but also nurture a dark narcissism in him and a deep vein of selfishness, one that will provoke his worst lapses in personal relationships: callous dismissals of old friends and loyal retainers, legendary cruelties, and an often utter disregard for others when it suited him. (Dylan brought his mother along on the Rolling Thunder tour. Whenever Bob sang "It's Alright, Ma (I'm Only Bleeding)," Mrs. Zimmerman would stand up and say, "That's me!")

Bob is always the performer, the busker, the entertainer, demanding the audience to be quiet—even at age four. His life provides the kind of folkloric anecdotes one reads in the lives of saints—of those who know their destiny. Dylan would fulfill that role many times over.

Bobby's teenage record collection: "There Oughta Be a Law" by Mickey and Sylvia, "Baby Blue" by Gene Vincent and His Blue Caps, *Hank Snow Sings Jimmie Rodgers*, the Clovers, Nat King Cole, Bill Haley, Pat Boone, Bobby Vee, Johnny Ace, Webb Pierce, Buddy Holly, Little Richard's "Slippin' and Slidin'" and "Tutti Frutti," Elvis Presley's "Heartbreak Hotel" and "Blue Suede Shoes." Favorite movies: *The Ox-Bow Incident* (cowboy crucifixion, persecution of the outsider), *East of Eden* (lost identity, conflict with the father), *Rebel Without a Cause* (outsider as redeemer), *The Wild One* (rebellion-for-the-hell-of-it), *The Fugitive Kind* (Brando as itinerant guitar player and mojo man). "In those days," the cinema historian Jerry Fagnani pointed out, "fans followed the exemplary lives of the stars in movie magazines. The movies were to me the most important art form in the world. As a preteen I was aware of the movies as a lesson. Current events. They taught you about everything. The Van Johnsons were there, the Ty Powerses were there, the Tab Hunters were there."

WMFG in Hibbing (managed by his cousin Les Rutstein) trickles out pop ballads, dance music, and easy listening potpourri. But late at night the *real thing* pours in over the airwaves from radio stations from Shreveport, Louisiana, and Little Rock, Arkansas—Hank Williams, Johnnie Ray, John Lee Hooker, Buddy Holly, Little Richard, Carl Perkins, Elvis, and Blind Willie McTell. Muddy Waters, Bo Diddley, Chuck Berry, Howlin' Wolf, and Sonny Boy II come booming out of Chicago. A musical geography, a sonic, ideas-as-my-maps America where El Paso and Boston, New Orleans and Duluth are next door to each other. "The radio," says Bob, "connected everybody like Orpheus."

This was how people got their information about what was going on: The radio was a geographical blender. It reflected an imaginary America, a haunted America where all the far-flung places suddenly seemed part of one community, while at the same time their remoteness and inaccessibility added to the mystery. The radio's influence on the dissemination of blues and country music (through broadcasts from the Grand Ole Opry) was considerable. In those days this embryonic family of freaks and future hipsters communicated through the airwaves.

His second motorcycle accident is in 1958. A child runs out in the street holding an orange. "I can still see that orange rolling across the street," says Dylan. He joins his cousin's band, the Satin Tones, and is into Muddy Waters and Jimmy Reed. His new vocal model is Buddy Holly— and he loves imitating Holly's amiable, if-James-Dean-could-sing voice.

On January 31, 1959, Bob goes to see Buddy Holly at the Duluth Armory. That night has gone down in rock 'n' roll history, and a teenage Bob actually made his way to the snowy gig. In Dylan's 1991 acceptance speech for a Lifetime Achievement Award at the Grammys, he would remember the apostolic nod Holly gave him that night. Three days later, Holly dies in a plane crash. The band that takes over Holly's next gig is the Shadows with lead singer Bobby Vee (who then specialized in Buddy Holly imitations). Dylan plays piano with Bobby Vee and the Shadows for two dances in Fargo. This possible alternate career of Bob Dylan ends when, short of funds, they let him go. That doesn't stop him from telling his friends he *is* Bobby Vee.

Bob gets a set of Lead Belly 78s as a graduation present. Lead Belly, a two-time murderer who according to legend sang his way out of prison, was the ideal fusion of singer and outlaw. Recorded by musical anthropologists John and Alan Lomax at the Sugar Land penitentiary, Lead Belly (because he'd been in jail so long) was a living archive of lost black music. After his release the Lomaxes introduced him to New York café society and he became a darling of high society. Fearsome in person, he was also something of an anachronism. Many of his songs had a sweet "folk" quality that was easier for white audiences to assimilate than the raw blues that replaced it. The folk revival began when the Weavers (Pete Seeger was a member) had a hit with his ballad "Goodnight Irene."

Bob has a growing interest in Chicago blues, joins another nameless band playing R&B. While he is playing "Rock 'n' Roll Is Here to Stay" at Hibbing High's Jacket Jamboree Talent Festival, Principal Kenneth L. Pederson shuts off the power.

BY 1959, DYLAN IS A DESULTORY ON-AND-OFF LIBERAL ARTS STUDENT at the University of Minnesota in Minneapolis. Most of his education comes from hanging out in coffeehouses in the Beatnik neighborhood of Dinkytown. Picking up the vibe, he disowns rock 'n' roll for the new thing: folk music. Bob knows which way the wind blows; besides, it's a lot easier for a middle-class kid to find a role in folk central casting than in the hurly-burly, roadhouse raunch of early rock 'n' roll. In any case, he had other ideas.

Rock was breathless from its three-year dash out of Memphis. Compromised by payola, it had been corporatized, and was way too popular, almost kitsch. The college crowd now disdains rock as crass and commercial. This rejection of rock probably also has to do with it being considered Southern and low class (despite the awkward fact that the entire folk canon comes out of the South). The folk craze also allows for elitist "discoveries" of obscure songs, labels, and instruments. Armed with a newly minted ideology (protest), the folk scene shifts from feckless balladeering and strumming into a movement.

With Dinkytown and Minnesota U., Dylan begins his flight from his past. "I never was a kid who could just go home. I never had a home that I could just take a bus to; I made my way all by myself." He saw the future laid out before him as a series of roles he would inhabit. As for his past, he would make it up, inventing sundry biographies more compelling than the suffocating, humdrum background he actually came from. His future selves would all have an undercurrent of fable, folklore, and hobo romance to them.

Of course, you have to leave home if you're going to be somebody else. First thing you need is a new name. According to one story (there's always more than one explanation for everything Dylan does), he begins calling himself Bob Dillon after Matt Dillon, the sheriff on *Gunsmoke*. A Western hero, yeah, but one on TV. In other words, it's an imaginary character (like Bob Dylan), an invention of writer John Meston and producer Norman MacDonnell. *Gunsmoke* was born on September 10, 1955, around the time Dylan decided he didn't want to be Bobby Zimmerman anymore.

Dillon, he claims, was his mother's maiden name (actually, it was Stone). Or he took it from the name of a town in Oklahoma. Or he had an uncle on his mother's side named Dillon. The other showbiz Zimmerman is Ethel, who changed her name to Merman—by lopping off the Zim. But Bob Merman won't do, doesn't have the right ring. At some point this year, Dillon becomes Dylan. "The name just popped into my head one day," he insists. "But it didn't really happen any of the ways I've read about. I just didn't feel that I had a past and I couldn't relate to anything other than what I was doing at the present time." Subsequently Dylan claimed that he'd always spelled it that way or had never heard of the Welsh poet, although Dylan's boyhood friend Larry Kegan distinctly remembered that Dylan "usually had a poetry book in his hand— sometimes [it was] the poems of Dylan Thomas." Over the years he added to the confusion by claiming any number of reasons for the Dylan Thomas spelling, including that it looked better with a *y*. While unlikely, it's possible, because like most of Dylan's choices it's an aesthetic one. Dylan's lyrics are nothing like those of his Welsh namesake, but his talent for obfuscation escalates with the Dillon/Dylan name game. It's also been suggested that one reason for his name change was the rabid anti-Semitism in Minneapolis.

Dylan scans the landscape for folk idols and tries out various Okie-folkie combinations. His ear for mimicry comes in handy, particularly for colloquial expressions, accents, regional American diction—as though these inflections could conjure the people who used them. As far as Dylan is concerned, he is in a foreign country (has always thought of himself as the stranger in town).

Anxious, high-strung, and shy, his knee bounces when he talks. Singing becomes a need; it erupts in him. When he gets nervous, he sings. He plays and sings current folk repertoire in local clubs. Folk music then was union songs, negro spirituals, Appalachian ballads. An indifferent musician, he is slowly incorporating elements of Buddy Holly with the Sonny Terry and Brownie McGhee sound. He briefly emulates current Dinkytown folk hero, "Spider" John Koerner. Onto these folkloric types Dylan fuses the aura of the doomed romantic, walking around cloaked in Byronic melancholy. He gets down first sketches of the early Dylan look. For example, the black corduroy Dutch-boy cap. Even this has roots. It's Raskolnikov's cap from the Classics Illustrated version of *Crime and Punishment*, which Dylan and brother David used to read.

Once a folk devotee, Bob becomes the purest of the pure. He has to have the oldest, most authentic songs. He begins a rabid, quasi-spiritual quest for the obscure, the rare, the core sound. Harry Smith's *Anthology of American Folk Music* is his bible. He's a folk fanatic with a touch of ruthlessness—stealing friends' record collections (it's okay because he is going to be Bob Dylan). Even his victims have to admit he has really good taste.

In Dinkytown coffeehouses, he rehearses his new characters, developing a chameleon's talent for capturing American diction. Like a method folksinger, he has the ability to become the people he identifies with, through imitation of the way they talk and behave. He learns fast—songs, styles, mannerisms—becoming a new person with a new technique every few weeks. Dylan soon has a large repertoire of types at his disposal, but none of them has the mythic weight he needs.

———

IN JULY 1959, HE HEADS TO DENVER, COLORADO, WHERE HE SPENDS the summer playing at a glitzy tourist joint, the Gilded Garter. He meets Judy Collins and, more significantly, Jesse Fuller, the one-man band. From Fuller he borrows the idea for his harmonica rack, as well as his gravelly vocal style. In the fall of 1959, he returns to the University of Minnesota and joins a fraternity, Sigma Alpha Mu. If he was indifferent to college ("pointless and useless knowledge") and the phonies who attended it, he really hated fraternities. He has the self-taught man's derision of academia, tempered by tinges of envy and insecurity ("the old folks home and the college"). The University of Minnesota has little to offer Dylan. Instead he will join a long American tradition of solitary readers through the night, including Melville, Whitman, Hemingway, O'Neill, Kerouac, Ginsberg, Patchen, and Rimbaud. Out of his idiosyncratic studies he will create his own language.

Dinkytown was on the folk telegraph lines between Greenwich Village, Cambridge, North Beach, and other folk epicenters. The folk canon—instruments, look, hip talk, Lenny Bruce, Lord Buckley, black humor, dulcimers—was swiftly transmitted. But the hardcore hipster code hadn't hit Minneapolis yet. For most of the time Dylan spends in Dinkytown, he is essentially your average hooky-playing college boy singing the current folk roster. Jon Pankake (the guy whose record collection he stole) recalls Bob as "a soft-spoken, rather unprepossessing youngster; he was well groomed and neat in the standard campus costume of slacks, sweater, white oxford sneakers, poplin raincoat, and dark glasses, and singing the standard coffeehouse songs." It's not the image we have of the embryonic Dylan or the one he'd want us to have (but even then he had the shades).

He's made his transformation. It's time to move on if he is going to become the character he's been rehearsing for the good part of a year in Dinkytown. That was the other thing he learned from Woody: Keep moving on. Now it's Bob's philosophy: "The important thing is to keep moving, or else to stop on the side of the road every once in a while, and build a house. I guess that's about the best thing anyone can do."

After almost a year of going and not going to college he heads for New York in a snowstorm. Even in Minnesota, people couldn't figure him out, and he was just beginning his serial role-playing. Dinkytown was just a dress rehearsal for Greenwich Village.

Dylan buttons his pants in a Marcel Marceau–like scene on a rooftop in Greenwich Village, 1962. This is the Chaplinesque character he mimed at his early coffeehouse performances.

The Hall of Early Folk Memories

My grandfather used to say: "Life is astoundingly short."
To me, looking back over it, life seems so foreshortened
I scarcely understand how a young man can decide to
ride over to the next village without being afraid—not to
mention accidents—even the span of a normal happy life,
may fall short of the time needed for such a journey.

—FRANZ KAFKA, "THE NEXT VILLAGE"

"THE FOLK MUSIC SCENE HAD BEEN LIKE A PARADISE THAT I had to leave, like Adam had to leave the garden. It was just too perfect," says Dylan in *Chronicles*. In the Hall of Early Folk Memories there will be a diorama devoted to Greenwich Village 1961–64. In it will be waxworks of waitresses in black leotards, with long straight hair and existential mascara; tourists in seersucker suits and crinoline frocks sitting at tables with two-dollar cups of coffee; the overweight club owner counting receipts; some kid from the Bronx wired on crystal meth and reds (okay, Steven Tyler) who's snuck in hoping to catch some unimaginable happening.

The Gaslight, 1961. There's a goofy young hillbilly kid onstage in front of a microphone, with his Dutch-boy cap, striped train engineer shirt, blue jeans, motorcycle boots, guitar, and harmonica rack.

"You had the feeling that he was a total stranger to stage fright," says Antonia, a songwriter best known for "If You Wanna Be a Bird" from the *Easy Rider* soundtrack and a friend of Dylan's. "He was in his element, like a guy sitting in his favorite chair. Offstage he didn't connect with people at all; onstage was where his life was."

Dylan looks around, grins, fiddles with his harp rack, and tunes his guitar, cuts the straggling curly strings off the neck, and jokes. "Even my guitar needs a haircut." In the guise of this stage hobo kid, he's snuck into the inner sanctum of folk. He has defused any ridicule and charmed them with an awkward bumpkin act.

"I thought he was oddly old-time looking, charming in a scraggly way," said his girlfriend at the time, Suze Rotolo. "His jeans were as rumpled as his shirt, and even in the hot weather he had on the black corduroy cap he always wore. He made me think of Harpo Marx, impish and approachable, but there was something about him that broadcast an intensity that was not to be taken lightly."

Flannel shirt, motorcycle boots, blue jeans—outfit of the Beat fellaheen of the world. He'd showcased his persona in tryouts in Minneapolis's Dinkytown. If his impersonation was a bit corny, it was still an entertaining act that had a great long yarn attached to it.

"He used to do all sorts of Chaplinesque moves onstage," says Peter Stampfel of the legendary Holy Modal Rounders. "At the Gaslight he would do these little moves and somebody would wave their hand back and forth in front of the main spotlight so it would flicker like an old-time movie."

"Back then," says Dave Van Ronk, "he always seemed to be winging it, free-associating, and he was one of the funniest people I have ever seen on stage—although off stage no one ever thought of him as a great wit. He had a stage persona that I can only compare to Charlie Chaplin's 'little fellow.' He was a very kinetic performer, and he never stood still and he had all these nervous mannerisms and gestures. There would be a one-liner, a mutter, a mumble, another one-liner, a slam at the guitar. Above all, his sense of timing was uncanny: he would get all of these pseudo-clumsy bits of business going, fiddling with his harmonica rack and things like that, and he could put an audience in stitches without saying a word."

His impersonations verged on vaudeville. He was a practitioner of minstrelsy; that's what he meant when he described himself as "a song and dance man." Sure, it's an act, but the minstrel-boy character is itself part of American folklore. Dylan was a conjurer of atmosphere, a performer, and his delivery of those songs contained the reek and smoke of the rural folk world of the South.

DYLAN SEES LIFE AS A LABYRINTH, A RIDDLE TO BE SOLVED. "IF YOU'RE going to send me something," he writes in *Tarantula*, "send me a key—i shall find the door to where it fits, if it takes me the rest of my life." With

Woody Guthrie he finds that first key. He takes Woody as his patron saint, the first of Dylan's doppelgängers. Guthrie's autobiography, *Bound for Glory*, with its WPA artwork, its hobo idealism—Woody with bedroll and heroic gesture, tramping into the future—had become his bible back in Minneapolis.

Born in Oklahoma in 1912, Woody was an Okie Walt Whitman—a voice against inequality and injustice, champion of the underdog. He had written the national anthem of populism, "This Land Is Your Land," and he glowed with a Depression-era patina. All that great ranting against bureaucracy and fluorescent lighting—"Your red tape and your scary offices!" It was all about solidarity with the workers and belting out "The Ballad of Harry Bridges" to stevedores of Local 10. The sign on his beat-up guitar read: THIS MACHINE KILLS FASCISTS.

He was as close to a biblical prophet in guitar-strumming hobo guise as you could get. Unlike many of the successful folksingers of the day with their trained voices, his was flat and shaky. His point was that anybody could be a singer. You didn't need a trained voice; in fact trained voices were a liability if you were trying to get a message across. The rawness, intensity, and honesty of Appalachian or Mississippi voices made them urgent and utterly believable.

Being short and slight with a physique similar to Dylan's, Woody was an ideal model for Dylan to copy. Overnight he teaches himself the whole of Guthrie's famous "Tom Joad." He is soon affecting an Okie accent. Bob begins honing his rusty barbed wire voice into a subtle and eccentric instrument and develops an aptitude for creating musical hybrids that synthesize American folk music—like singing spirituals to a hillbilly beat. In no time at all Dylan has Woodyized himself.

IN JANUARY 1961, DURING THE WORST SNOWSTORM IN NEW YORK IN twenty years, Dylan—sheepskin jacket, suede boots, jeans, cap—arrives in Greenwich Village wrapped in several layers of impersonations. He wasn't going to show up and say, "Hi, I'm Robert Zimmerman. I'm the son of a Jewish appliance merchant in Hibbing, Minnesota." Of course not. His well-rehearsed principal character, Woody Guthrie Junior, is a good disguise in which to enter the forbidden city, the already formidable Greenwich Village folk scene. The Village is not Dylan's first stop in New York, mind you. According to the version Bob was still telling in 1985, he'd been a hustler up in Times Square before heading downtown.

But this story turns out to be about two gay guys he met in a bar who offered him and his friend a place to stay.

If he prevaricated, exaggerated, and equivocated himself through Dinkytown (Minneapolis's bohemian quarter), he arrived in the Village with some well-honed tales of adventure that were pure Huck Finn: He'd been a carnival barker, a cook, a lumberjack in the great Northwest, and even run a steam shovel in Minnesota. He'd been thrown in jail on suspicion of armed robbery, visited the grave of Blind Lemon Jefferson. He'd lived with four hoboes on the banks of the Mississippi under the Washington Avenue Bridge, jammed with Gene Vincent in Nashville, sat in on Bobby Freeman's "Do You Wanna Dance?" and played piano with Bobby Vee (at least one of these was true).

When they ask him, "Where ya from, kid?" he tells them he calls Sioux Falls home. Ditto Gallup, New Mexico, and Fargo, North Dakota. Dylan finds music in American place names. Granted, the place he was born would've sounded pretty authentic to denizens of Village coffeehouses, many who came from no farther away than New Jersey. A citybilly like Ramblin' Jack Elliott would've been glad to hail from such a place as Duluth.

"Even what we didn't believe was often entertaining," says Van Ronk. "I mean, one night he spent something like an hour, showing a bunch of us how to talk in Indian sign language, which I'm pretty sure he was making up as he went along, but he did it marvelously."

Some thought Dylan a pathological liar, but as Harry Weber, his friend from Dinkytown, says, "Dylan was just a romantic. He remembered what *should* have been." He was just following an old Western tradition in which folks changed their names, changed their pasts, and took on new identities when they lit out for the territory. It's the American way.

Of course, when you tell all manner of different stories about who you are and where you've been, it gets hard to keep it all straight—and there's always somebody in the crowd who'll hear a false note and call you on it. But Dylan, always fast on his feet, had the perfect out. "People listen to his stories," says Cynthia Gooding. "He talks and he laughs, and just when they're about to catch him in a lie, he takes out his harmonica and blows them down." The music confirms the role.

THE VOICE WAS THE FIRST THING MOST PEOPLE MENTIONED, MADE fun of—the dog caught on a barbed wire fence—but we know it as one of the most mesmerizing voices in all of rock. When Dylan said of Van Ronk's voice that it was "like rusted shrapnel" he might as well have been talking about his own. But Dylan's voice has a far spookier range, an intonation capable of inducing some phantasmagoric presences.

Where did that ancient, raspy voice of his come from? A primordial tone that spoke of doom and damnation, out of the mouth of a callow youth barely twenty years old. By mimicking Woody Guthrie, Clarence Ashley, and Son House, Dylan could siphon off the voices that arose from the vinyl surface of Harry Smith's *Anthology of American Folk Music* like restless spirits looking for a home.

Dylan's singing style was at the opposite end of the vocal spectrum of the female vocalists' virginal warble, but they, however inauthentic, were still the most popular style of folksinging. Joan Baez, the queen of the folksingers, had an amazing vibrato, an effect that she had developed by tapping a pencil against her larynx. "The thing about Baez," says Dave Van Ronk, "was that like almost all women on the scene, she was still singing in a style of the generation before us. It was a cultural lag: the boys had discovered Dock Boggs and Mississippi John Hurt, and the girls were still singing to Cynthia and Susan Reed . . . all of them were essentially singing bel canto."

Dylan's early repertoire is filled with dark matter. How could it be otherwise, given the source of his material: Booker White's "Fixin' to Die," Blind Lemon Jefferson's "See That My Grave Is Kept Clean" and "Gospel Plow" with its uncanny death wish. Listening to all the doom and romance of death songs on his first album, you could imagine that you were listening to some octogenarian Delta bluesman, devoid of all hope, pursued into an open grave by malignant spirits.

"Back then I was listening to Son House, Lead Belly, the Carter family, Memphis Minnie and death romance ballads," says Dylan. And death is even an essential part of romance according to Dylan's grim philosophy: "Oh, yeah, in my songs it is. Pain, sex, murder, family." He's more a scavenger than a grave robber, and this is one of his greatest assets. He's not a purist like most folkies of that era.

Eventually all the mythical blues and folk characters would be rediscovered. From the sound of their records they seemed to have come from a remote age, but most of them were in the end found alive and well, running elevators in big hotels, working in mines and sawmills, and pumping gas out on Highway 61. It was a miraculous breakthrough to the under-mind of the scaly original American self. It would have been as if someone had said, "Oh, we just discovered Geoffrey Chaucer living near Brighton." It was a Faulknerian landscape down South, peopled with eccentric, inspired characters not unlike the ones in his mythical Yoknapatawpha County.

"John Hurt is a really interesting story," says Stampfel. "Everyone thought the old country blues guys were dead. Those people quit recording in the Depression. In '63, blues became commercial again. The story goes that a certain speedfreak was going out with an underaged girl and her family was after him to lynch him. They were on the lam then across the South. They ended up in Mississippi in a town called Avalon. He remembered a line from a John Hurt song saying that Avalon was his home. So he went to a local drugstore and asked about Hurt and if anyone knew him. So the guy says, 'Here he goes, over here.' And his playing was just as good ever. All of the country blues fans went 'Gulp!' simultaneously and descended upon the South. They quickly realized that the phone book was their friend. 'Bukka White, where's he from? Booker White, there he is!' One night I found John Hurt in Massachusetts playing at a club. Before the show, I played with him because I knew a song he was doing. Who would have dreamed it possible? But life can be like that."

The South would rise again, but not in the way we usually think of it. This time it would be through music.

"There was a difference in the concept of time, too," says Dylan about the mythic time of the blues. "In the South, people live their lives with sun-up, high noon, sunset, spring, summer. In the North, people live by the clock. The factory stroke, whistles and bells. Northerners had to 'be on time.' In some ways the Civil War would be a battle between two kinds of time."

All blues singers had a story to tell, and Dylan's newly minted character needed a backstory, too, some picaresque adventures, as in *Huckleberry Finn*, where roguish characters, out-and-out scoundrels, con artists, and hucksters constituted a new kind of American hero.

All Dylan's characters come out of the hyperreal landscape where time is suspended and the neon sign outside is always flashing indecipherable messages. The con artist, the impersonation, right down to the name change—well it's an inalienable American right. It's like the riverboat gambler and trickster of conventional morality in Melville's last novel, *The Confidence-Man*. And then with Iceberg Slim and Mezz Mezzrow, you get the hustler, the dope dealer.

But where did Dylan's hobo-kid character come from? Out of the songs, of course—the songs that had obsessed him his whole life. Folk songs, Child ballads. Songs from Harry Smith's *Anthology*—and Woody Guthrie. It wasn't like the well-developed characters in a novel. Just a cursorily filled-in background, the voice itself contained history and geography. If his biographical backstory was abbreviated, it's because his whole personal history came out of the sketchy narrative of a ballad—and the kind of person who would have lived that life and sung that ballad.

The very irrationality of the old weird hill folk songs only added to their sinister appeal. Murders were committed for no apparent reason and without regret or explanation. There were no resolutions, no tidy endings—as in Hollywood movies. The bad guys didn't get their comeuppance and the good guys didn't win in the end. It was all very strange and murky. You didn't have to tell people to stop making sense; it was traditional in the hollers and on the levees. There was more betrayal, murder, and revenge in these songs than in any blood-drenched Jacobean tragedy.

Lives of the Southern mountain people were as mysterious as stories from the Bible or mythology. Some of these tales went back to medieval legends and fused with them in an unbroken oral culture. It was a feudal world transferred to Appalachia, only adding to its authenticity and unfathomability.

The hill-country moon was darker and more foreboding than any moon that shone over Bronxville or Tin Pan Alley. The aspects were grim and the sets gothic and haunted, as if the dire subject matter of the ballads had somehow infected the landscape itself. The moon was a breeder of superstitions, its ghostly orbit and malign influence not far removed from ancient lunar cults. This wasn't the paper moon crooned about in pop ballads. It was a planet that balefully controlled human destiny.

Dock Boggs's life in the Southern mountains, for instance, was violent, eruptible, and capricious. There were blood feuds, rapes, baby killings, suicides, hair-raising stuff. They would kill people just for the hell of it. And this was still going on well into the '70s. Mike Seeger in midinterview had to restrain Dock from going over and killing his entire inlaw family. But all this mayhem, revenge, and murder seemed a lot more appealing than the sanitized suburban society folkies were brought up in, where infidelity, embezzlement, and drunk driving were the most dramatic events they'd encountered.

The rural folk world offered an odd and mouthwatering collection of types. They were legendary, larger than life, from a purer time, a golden age of humanity. Eccentrics loomed large in the folk demographic whose inhabitants consisted of brakemen, miners, muleskinners, moonshiners, bandits, trappers, sheriffs, section hands, train engineers, revenuers, prospectors, drifters, and bootleggers. Also included was a goodly assortment of murderers, arsonists, rapists, and ghouls as you were ever likely to find, all safely bottled in black vinyl.

MOST FOLK SONGS HAD GRIM, MURDEROUS CONTENT (AND SUBTEXT). In "Pretty Polly," a man lures a young girl from her home with the promise of marriage, and then leads the pregnant girl to an already-dug grave and murders her. In "Love Henry," a woman poisons her unfaithful lover, observed by an alarmed parrot that she also tries to kill. So it was a bit bizarre that these songs should become part of the sweetened, homogenized new pop music. While the Weavers, the first successful folksinging group, were unapologetic socialists and outright communists, their hits of the early '40s—"Goodnight Irene" and "Wimoweh" ("The Lion Sleeps Tonight")—hadn't exactly been radical songs. After the Weavers' huge success with "Goodnight Irene," saccharine versions of folk songs continued to make it onto the pop charts with groups like the Tarriers, the Limelighters, the Journeymen, the Brothers Four, the Cumberland Three—wholesome frat-house boys in button-down Brooks Brothers shirts and chinos. Genteel, sophisticated, and lifeless. Your mom liked them. If a folk song did manage to get on the hit parade it was often by someone like Harry Belafonte or Frankie Laine.

The original folk songs were potent, possessed stuff, but the folk trios had figured out how to make this grisly stuff palatable, which only proved that practically anything could be homogenized. Clean-cut guys and girls in crinolines, dressed as if for prom night, sang ancient curse-and-doom-laden tales. Their songs had sweet little melodies, but as in nursery rhymes, there was a dark gothic undercurrent to them—like "Ring Around the Rosies," which happens to be a charming little plague song.

The most famous of these pop folk songs was the 1958 hit "Tom Dooley," a track off a Kingston Trio album, which set off the second folk revival and was Dylan's initial inspiration for getting involved in folk music. And it was the very success of the syrupy folk trios that inspired

Dylan's future manager to assemble one himself: Peter, Paul and Mary. They would make Dylan, the prophet of the folk protest movement, a star and lead to consequences that even he did not foresee. Their version of "Blowin' in the Wind" would become so successful that it would sound the death knell for the folk protest movement. Ultimately there would be more than sixty versions of it, "all performing the same function," as Michael Gray says, of "anesthetizing Dylan's message."

THE FOLK MUSIC SCENE IN THE VILLAGE THAT BOB DYLAN ENTERED IN 1961 was the second-wave folk revival; the first one had taken place in the 1930s and '40s. Folk revivals were created by urban intellectuals and went back to Sir Walter Scott and Rabbie Burns. These card-carrying members of the folk revival movement (part deux) despised the materialistic culture of mainstream America with its commercial bromides and rampant hypocrisy, but they soon created their own set of smug clichés. Of their pieties, the most deluded were that folk songs were, like holy writ, untouchable—and this, in turn, set in motion a misguided quest for the oldest, moldiest version of a song. In *Chronicles*, Dylan described one of the more doctrinaire folkies, his old friend from Minneapolis, as "a folk music purist enthusiast . . . made it his business to tell me that what I was doing hadn't escaped him. . . . He was part of the folk police, if not the chief commissioner [and] wasn't impressed with any of the new talent."

The folk faction was essentially a romantic movement on a quest for a lost, bucolic America, the very America their parents and grandparents had either destroyed or wanted to get the hell out of.

"When Phil Ochs came along he annoyed me deeply at first," says Peter Stampfel. "I thought it was like shtick, plus I had a lot of resentment for the folk scene 'cause as far as I was concerned the folk scene in New York and the folk scene in general was a bunch of rich kids. I mean I was a lower-middle-class kid and the only other lower-middle-class person on the folk scene I was aware of was Karen Dalton and possibly Dino Valenti."

The folk scene was basically a nostalgic agrarian fantasy indulged in by suburban, middle-class college kids and old lefties. The aphrodisiac element in all this was Walter Paterish, the sense of something vanishing, vaporizing, as Shakespeare's history plays were an elegy for the lost world of medieval England, with its folk beliefs, superstitions, and a feudal order that mimicked the cosmic order. Favoring ghosts, nostalgia, and eccentric costumes, a feeling of something gone injected an antiquarian obsession into the folk movement. For folkniks, the phrase "field recordings" had an almost erotic twang to it.

Folk music was organic. The rich loam of the Mississippi Delta or the flinty hills of Appalachia spawned haunting music; things grew out of the ground. The Delta germinated larger-than-life characters. Appalachian hollers spun fantastic figures straight out of American tall tales. These eccentric hill people engaged in bizarre rural activities, as well as playing dulcimers and other exotic instruments. There were jug bands, shape note singing. It was a whole undiscovered world of musty and mysterious presences. They were still out there residing in the vastnesses of the USA—Dock Boggs, Clarence Ashley, the Reverend Gary Davis, Eck Robertson, Kirk and Sam McGee. As odd as these types were, they were also weirdly familiar. We've always had these folk characters around in some form or another, from fairy tales to folktales to witchcraft to tall tales.

The Greenwich Village folk revival was a romantic love affair with an illusion, a world stripped of its grinding poverty and prejudice, one with the vine-covered cottage, the banjo, and the jug of moonshine on the porch. These folkies romanticized a culture that would have hated them. Some parents of folkniks were themselves only a thousand miles and a generation or two away from the rough, hardscrabble lives of these people.

Parents, teachers, preachers, your local rabbi—were nonplussed by these middle-class kids' fascination with such lowly, questionable, aberrant types. What are you doing? We protected you from these ignorant, bitter rednecks and hooch-mad moonshiners, escapees from a chain gang, for God's sake. You want to spend your life doing *what*? These hillbillies and sharecroppers are your *heroes*? Didn't we spend a fortune sending you to college to disabuse you of all this superstitious nonsense about cruel fate and doom? Don't you know what sacrifices we made to shelter you from brutal overseers, mining disasters, and boll weevil infestations?

IT MAY SEEM ODD THAT DYLAN FIRST BECAME ATTRACTED TO FOLK music through the Kingston Trio, a group generally despised by the hard-core folk community, but then that sort of quirky turning point is typical of Dylan's entire career. And their #1 hit, "Tom Dooley," is based on an old North Carolina folk song, itself a bizarre and mysterious tale about the 1866 murder of a woman named Laura Foster. People bought the song for the bouncy tune.

"Folk music, if nothing else, makes a believer out of you," Dylan once said to Greil Marcus. "I believed Dave Guard of the Kingston Trio, too. I believed he would kill or already did kill poor Laura Foster. I believed that he'd kill someone else, too. I didn't think he was playing around."

And there he was, at the very center of the folk universe. He was sleeping on floors, playing for tips. Living was cheap. You could get a two-bedroom apartment for twenty-five bucks a month. Or you could just crash on people's couches and raid their bookshelves as Dylan does in the first pages of *Chronicles*, the fictional library of the fictional couple Chloe and Ray where he claims to have read a nonexistent book by Thucydides called *The Athenian General*. Perhaps he got the Greek historian's *The History of the Peloponnesian War* confused with his other ongoing obsession, the Civil War.

Not that the folk scene in the Village was that big in 1961. It wasn't, for instance, anything like going to Haight-Ashbury during the Summer of Love. It would be Dylan's fame that eventually drew attention to the folk protest movement, made it madly popular, and eventually capsized it—but by then he'd moved on.

Who said you can't clone yourself? Woody Guthrie had the uncanny ability to spontaneously project himself onto other people. But no musician has generated more copies of himself than Dylan.

3 Woody Junior

IN EARLY 1961 DYLAN DOES THE ROUNDS OF THE FOLK RECORD companies—Elektra, Vanguard, Folkways—and they all turn him down. He plays summer gigs in the Cambridge folk scene alongside Jim Kweskin, Eric Von Schmidt. He befriends blues singer John Hammond, son of the legendary Columbia A&R man John Hammond Jr. In his first solo gig at Gerde's, Dylan opens for John Lee Hooker, the voodoo shaman of the blues, with his dark biblical voice and hypnotic repetition. Dylan keeps getting a few small gigs; the audiences are tiny, sometimes only five believers. He develops odd paranoias but thrives in the artificial world of folk clubs and coffeehouses—Gerde's Folk City, the Gaslight, the Kettle of Fish, the Cafe Wha? He sings in the back of the Folklore Center with Izzy Young presiding.

"He seemed attached to his guitar that summer," says Coco Pekelis, who worked at the Folklore Center. "No guitar case, of course, and strings sticking out at jagged angles, no time to wrap the ends neatly around the guitar. And besides, he'd probably need a new set tomorrow. He was obsessed, in his own world. So what if he mistook my straw pocketbook for a waste paper basket, throwing his string wrappers and tired gum straight into it. It didn't occur to me to say anything. That's how intimidating he was even then."

Dylan's repertoire consists of "Dink's Song," "House of the Risin' Sun," "Poor Lazarus," "See That My Grave Is Kept Clean," Woody's songs, some of Jimmie Rodgers's, a few hobo songs ("The Baggage Coach Ahead"), spirituals, country blues, and Appalachian ballads—in other words a cross-section of American folk music.

His performances are travelogues, and each song has a story to go with it. "Dink's Song" he'd heard on the Brazos River when he was down in Texas (or maybe on the radio and he'd never been to Texas). He'd gotten his bottleneck style off a certain eye-patch-wearin' bluesman named Wigglefoot, in Gallup, New Mexico. Some other songs he'd picked up from Mance Lipscomb. Yet another song—"He Was a Friend of Mine"—he got from the Chicago bluesman Blind Arvella Gray, who sang with a tin cup tied to his lapel. He learned a little South Side harp from Little Walter at Theresa's Lounge. Bob's tall tales now fit into the narration; his patter between songs cements the legend. In each set he is retracing Woody's travels in his imagination.

Dylan oscillates between waiflike child and ancient hobo during performances, singing dire and death-haunted ballads in a rusty, world-weary voice. His drawn-out phrasing stretches out the syllables, leaning on them, bending them. His technique reflects a kind of archaeology of folk/blues diction—his phrasing is as original and emotionally effective as Sinatra's.

Early on, Dylan's songwriting specializes in the Will Rogers–type humorous style of songs ("Everybody I seen on the streets/Was all a-running down in a hole in the ground") and the long, rambling Irish pub story ones too. He writes a song to the tune of "Brennan on the Moor" about a boating tragedy on the Hudson (bootleg tickets, boat sank). It's called "Talking Bear Mountain Picnic Massacre Blues." Epic songs, like the old Child ballads—the old songs collected by Francis J. Child in *The English and Scottish Popular Ballads*—are ten, twelve verses long. Even his early songs, the ones he'd written back in Hibbing, were storytelling songs.

DURING THIS TIME PERIOD, DYLAN EXHIBITS HIS PARADOXICAL NATURE. On one hand, he's a reclusive, attic-dwelling scribbler of ancient ballads, and on the other, he's a goofy, basking-in-the-limelight song and dance man. His secretiveness only adds to his mystique in the Village.

"He would withdraw anywhere at any time," says Suze Rotolo. "It could happen in a noisy room full of people or when it was just the two of us alone together. I would observe him mentally go away and then come back. He didn't have to be present all the time. There was something so true about that that I did not feel excluded."

A prolific writer, he stays up all night scribbling, typing, playing his guitar. Often he writes two songs a day; his method is sonic collage. Drawing on overheard conversations, newspaper stories, biblical imagery, dialogue from movies, he "jots down little phrases and things" and sets them to the music of ordinary speech. Early lyrics have both the folksy camaraderie of Woody's talkin' blues and the weird mind turns of the old folk ballads.

IN THE FOLK UNIVERSE THE GREAT WORKS WERE IN THE PAST, HENCE there is almost a taboo about writing new songs. Many folksingers took to backdating their creations and pawning them off as old ballads they'd dug up (the manufacture of tradition is an American vice). Originated by singers fobbing off their own songs as authentic old folk songs, the pseudo or faked folk song went back to at least the eighteenth century, with Bishop Thomas Percy, who composed stanzas of doggerel and passed them all off as genuine. In the Victorian era, the Reverend Sabine Baring-Gould, an outrageous folk song faker, claimed he had gathered "The Gypsy Laddie" (Child ballad #200) from an illiterate hedger. Like other folkniks, Dylan sees folk music as a key to the mystic soul of America—but unlike other folksingers he has no compunction about injecting himself into its fables.

This early Dylan, the retro hobo, dust bowl–singing kid who'd been all over and rode the rails, is one of his greatest creations. He replaces the fixed, traceable Zimmerman, son of a Minnesota appliance salesman, with a persona that is all the more effective for being, for the moment, untrackable. Most people at the time believe his exotic stories. His waiflike look, his mercurial mind, the Okie accent, and the overwrought sensibility create a boggling image that will not stay in focus.

"WOODY WAS MY LAST HERO," SAID DYLAN. "THE GREATEST, HOLIEST, Godliest one in the world." As a teenager in a world of greed and hypocrisy, Bob had to find that one true being, that one incorruptible person, and that was Woody Guthrie. Almost as soon as he arrives in the East he goes to see Woody at the New Jersey state hospital in Greystone Park. Since the early 1950s, Woody had been suffering from Huntington's chorea, a debilitating nervous disease, and is now in very bad shape.

The encounter with Woody is surreal—a scene out of Beckett. Woody doesn't say a word—he is unable to speak—a living, breathing waxwork, an idol that people come and speak to. Dylan looks for a blessing from Woody. Since he is unable to respond you can ascribe just about anything to him. "Woody, just blink twice if I'm to be your true disciple" type of thing.

Woody already knows who he is. Dylan used to get drunk back in Dinkytown and call Guthrie on the phone. Dylan claims to have first heard Woody's *Dust Bowl Ballads* album in South Dakota as a kid and to have met him in Carmel, California, when he was thirteen (back when he was a carnival barker, was it?). Dylan writes "Song for Woody." Woody supposedly calls him "the kid." Dylan claims Woody Guthrie said, "Pete

Seeger is a singer of folk songs, not a folk singer. Jack Elliott is a singer of folk songs. But Bobby Dylan is a folk singer. Oh, Christ, he's a folk singer, alright."

Guthrie's manager, Harold Leventhal, says, "Woody never said anything about anybody visiting him. At that point, he literally never held a conversation. He couldn't."

"I don't think he thought anything of him," adds Pete Seeger. "Woody just sat on the couch, and we weren't sure if he recognized anybody or not. He was already too far gone."

Oh well, maybe the whole Bob and Woody tale is just what *should* have been—which would be in keeping with all the rest of it. In any case the mantle has been passed. The ultimate incarnation of Dylan's Woody obsession is his Guthrie-like pose on the cover of the October–November 1962 issue of *Sing Out!*, the echt folkie magazine.

Dylan's imaginary travels, aside from the exotic background they painted for him, were a way of re-creating Woody's legendary hobo wanderings throughout the '30s. "It was an act but only for about two days, after that it was me." It wasn't a literal impersonation like Ramblin' Jack Elliott's. The ingenuity of Dylan's incarnation was in creating a hybrid of himself and Woody. In "11 Outlined Epitaphs" on the back of his second album, he will parallel his arrival in New York with Guthrie's arrival in the West. MacDougal Street was like the West, mutatis mutandis, as they used to say.

But Dylan's mimicry of Woody has as much to do with music as image; in Dylan's case the two go together. Dylan learns his first great musical lesson from Guthrie. Woody became a great writer of utopian Americana by building his lyrics on existing folk and country tunes, a technique Dylan would take to a high art (and use to jump-start his songwriting career). For Guthrie this had been a way to make his songs sound familiar to a large group of people, but for Dylan the idea provides an additional mythic component. By fusing lyrics onto traditional melodies he can bind himself to the old American folk tradition; his songs will have the uncanny feel of ancient ballads that have grown up out of the earth.

Bob wasn't just a great mimic in that he could do Woody. Guthrie wasn't that hard to imitate (Ramblin' Jack Elliott could do that). Bob could do Woody standing on his head. In "Talking Bear Mountain Picnic Massacre Blues," he does a pitch-perfect imitation of Woody Guthrie's scurrying, world's-a-stirrin', view-from-a-boxcar syntax:

Dogs a-barkin', cats a-meowin'
Women screamin', fists a flyin', babies cryin'
Cops a-comin', me a-runnin'
Maybe we just better call off the picnic

Woody was losing his life, but what would have been the point of handing it over to someone who would just do him faithfully and keep on doing him for the next fifty years? The idea was to take the old Model T Woody and update it.

BOB'S RELATIONSHIP TO WOODY WAS THE CLIMAX OF DYLAN'S FIRST epic story, a story he would continue to tell for a while with quite a bit of embroidery. Since he'd allegorically been anointed to carry on Woody's legacy, he was now part of Woody's story.

Bob had inserted himself into Woody's epic life, as if Woody might've written an addendum to his autobiography, *Bound for Glory*, adding, "Then here come along that Bobby Dylan kid, golldangit! And him carryin' on the sacred ol' torch a Destiny!"

Just to touch Woody was enough. He transmitted. Guthrie had come to stand for a vanished world. He was the last of the legendary voices, a Midwestern prophet, fighting against the capitalist swine as well as being a kind of roué, the kind of guy who would go out to buy a newspaper and disappear for weeks, get rowdy. Good old Woody! He was no saint, like Pete Seeger.

The Beats were much less sanguine about this stuff. That's why they call themselves Beats. They saw the slow, inexorable corporate coach to hell coming into the station, and they weren't getting on that infested train. But Woody was out there riding the rails, hanging out in hobo encampments, inspiring the crowds at rallies, setting up rounds in raucous saloons where cowboys ambled in and shot up the place. A character straight out of *The Grapes of Wrath*, he lived the life of the displaced families in John Steinbeck's novel.

Woody's world, though—like a Grant Wood or a Thomas Hart Benton painting—was gone. Yet he still thought that there was hope for the USA, that the great good-hearted populace could save the land and change the world—a potent myth, and one that once again would be very popular in the '60s. One can imagine just how intoxicating that kind of belief can be. There is sunshine and happy workers are singing in the orange groves.

But the Beats knew what Woody didn't.

Woody, after all, was from the 1930s. The Beats were postwar bohemians; they'd seen the face of the Great Beast of Babylon. In that way Bob was much closer to the Beats than the hippies; he was far more dyspeptic. He was seeing what we were up against and it wasn't pretty. Hibbing was a demoralizing allegory of industrial rape. It made you look ever afterward with a jaundiced eye on slogans about progress, and see instead the horror of "flesh-colored Christs that glow in the dark."

Nevertheless, Dylan believed he had received the apostolic succession from Woody Guthrie, the king's touch, the sort of laying on of hands that in the Middle Ages cured disease and granted fame. The world was a mess, but he had touched Woody, and that was enough for now.

July 1963, Greenwood, Mississippi. Dylan's
first visit to the mythical South of folk
song plunged him into the brutal realities
of the present. At a rally to encourage
black voter registration, he performs "Only
a Pawn in Their Game" (about the murder
of civil rights leader Medgar Evers, only a
month earlier) for the first time.

4   Li'l Abner on Bleecker Street

To be an American (unlike being English or French or whatever) is precisely to imagine a destiny rather than to inherit one; since we have always been, insofar as we are Americans at all, inhabitants of myth rather than history.

—LESLIE FIEDLER, *LOVE AND DEATH IN THE AMERICAN NOVEL*

HERE WAS BOB, IN NEW YORK BARELY FOUR MONTHS, COM-bining, stealing, absorbing—who are we to quibble?—materializing a new Frankenstein's monster out of old bones. Bob the prophet of doom or inspired prestidigitator, the muse of fire who almost offhandedly ignites *all that stuff.* Essentially, he was making combines, like Robert Rauschenberg's combine paintings of the late 1950s—which incorporated stuffed birds, a paint-splattered bed, a goat with a tire around its middle, radios blaring from the surface of the canvas. Because that's the American genius, jamming stuff together—especially things that don't belong. That's what America is: a bunch of people who don't belong anywhere else. His idol James Dean had also made himself up from such diverse types as farm boy, Beatnik, hoodlum, and poetic dreamer.

The Village is the natural environment for a questing loner like Dylan to seek kindred spirits—a sort of folk shtetl of misfits, talented layabouts, college students, and hairy Beatniks. There were folk enclaves in most big cities, and you could go to any of these places and find a group of like-minded people who listened to the same records, read the same heavy books, talked about existentialism, and sipped tea with a cinnamon stick in it. You could find a place to crash and folkie chicks were easy.

Everybody was having a great time, but what bound them together was the great black hole of the '50s, here depicted by Dylan with acid detailing on the original liner notes to *Planet Waves*:

Back to the starting point! . . . I dropped a double brandy and tried to recall the events . . . family outings with strangers—furious gals with garters and smeared lips on bar stools that stank from sweaty pussy . . . space guys off duty with big dicks and duck tails all wired up and voting for Eisenhower.

The military-industrial complex rumbled down the thruways proclaiming its cheerful polymer future: "Better Living Through Chemistry." But children of the middle class wanted none of that. They rejected without pause what their parents and grandparents had struggled their whole lives to achieve. They wanted to get off the freight train of American destiny. They didn't aspire to be captains of industry or executives or doctors and lawyers and such. They'd be cocktail waitresses, Sheetrock hangers, drug dealers—or any other part of the understaffed subterranean economy.

Considering all the fear mongering, corporate greed, and Newspeak blather, this Li'l Abner and Daisy Mae on acid fantasy would seem very appealing. And where they grew up the air had long been sucked out of reality. Life in the leafy streets of suburbia was so bland and homogenized that, by design, not a trace of the demonic menaces of medieval Europe and Celtic superstition remained. But wouldn't you guess, before you knew it these bolshy suburban kids—teenagers filled with thoughts of their untimely and sad demise—began to find these quaint residues of magical thinking, like Doom and Fate, irresistible. Here in the folk hoard was death foretold. Coal mine disasters! Hillbilly suicide pacts! Eternal damnation! All this was thrilling. Doom was cool. But we were as far from the concept of doom as could possibly be imagined. Even sin with its spine-rattling threat of divine retribution had been denied them through the therapeutic eye of psychology. The culture was so sanitized that evil, once a spiritual threat to salvation, was now considered no more than a psychiatric condition. Of course, once the apocalypse had been surgically removed, the military-industrial complex had to find another way to instill fear in the populace (in order to control it). They contrived to create a federally funded doomsday: the bomb.

If the bomb was their big panic button, plastic was their proudest product. With plastic you could eliminate all other elements in the periodic table. It could replace bottles, chairs, nylons, telephones, clocks, plates, cups, billiard balls, radios, and shoes. But it was a miserable miracle, the work of troll-like chemical engineers. It became symbolic of the homogenizing of American culture, and seen through the eyes of idealistic youth it looked like a fiendish invention. Certain ungrateful and college-educated sectors of the youth began to look down on the prosperous, safe, and tidy industrial utopia their parents had created and seek out what was authentic in American culture—which happened to be that of the poorest, most backward, and uneducated people in the USA: itinerant Delta blues singers and redneck mountain folk. There was one place you could find all these people singing their weird old songs. Harry Smith had conveniently stored this treasure trove in his 1952 six-LP collection, *The Anthology of American Folk Music*. If there was a wisp of irony in the fact that the mystic voices of Dock Boggs and Son House were transmitted to them through vinyl, a derivative of plastic, no one noticed.

A SENSE OF URGENCY, MISSION, AND UPHEAVAL WOULD SOON ARISE among the denizens of the Village and other folk shtetls and fuse itself onto the radical causes of the times: civil rights, the Vietnam War, and drugs.

In the Village, as long as you abided by the folk code you were accepted. The early Dylan fit in perfectly with this scene. Everyone from nice middle-class couples to waitresses to old crab-infested folkniks wanted to give the ethereal little-boy-lost shelter from the storm.

The folk fauna consists of a wide range of types: old union solidarity guys, leftover Beatniks, earnest college students, pre-Raphaelite wraiths, the Clancy Brothers peddling Irish blarney, condescending commies like Pete Seeger with his ticky-tacky houses, bluegrass freaks like the Greenbriar Boys, the New Lost City Ramblers, from whom Dylan copped several songs. Then there were the uptown purveyors of glitzy folk memorabilia: the Limelighters, the Tarriers, the Weavers, the Kingston Trio, Harry Belafonte, Theo Bikel, and Odetta. Along with the genuine articles came visiting performers from the hinterland: Doc Watson, John Lee Hooker, the Reverend Gary Davis, and Cisco Houston.

But as far as prestige went, it was an upside-down hierarchy, with those who were most successful at the bottom. On this scale Dylan was in with the in crowd. His mentors in the Village are those two scurvy, ballad-growling dudes: Ramblin' Jack Elliott and Dave Van Ronk, ye old perfesser of the country blues.

These guys didn't care whether he was making it up or not. Only squares believed you are where you come from. Hipster philosophy said you could be whatever you can get away with. It was all in your head anyway. Everybody was living somebody else's life. Ramblin' Jack Elliott was a Jewish cowboy from New Jersey who'd taken on the identity of an old cowhand from the Rio Grande.

By now Dylan had the Woody thing so nailed down that they were calling him a hillbilly singer, which was fine with him. He insists that he's not a folksinger. He's a country singer or a rockabilly singer, he says. He backs Fred Neil and Brother John Sellers onstage.

DYLAN IS SOON A BIG NOISE IN THE VILLAGE. IN COFFEEHOUSES AND folk bars, the nervous, withdrawn exhibitionist is a sight to behold. A precocious hillbilly clown, his legend-generating stories have spun an aura around him that together with his mercurial songwriting creates a fanatical group of followers. Among them is Robert Shelton, a music critic for the *New York Times*. A tall tale is believable only if we want to believe it, and by now there are a lot of true believers. They become complicit in Bob's legend and the spur to his career. His reputation spreads like an underground brush fire. The folk madonnas, Juliette Gréco damsels all dressed in black, are especially crazy about him. The girls— Suze Rotolo, her sister, Carla, and Carla's friend—send a tape of Dylan to the legendary producer John Hammond Jr. up at Columbia Records, along with an impassioned letter.

On September 25, 1961, Bob gets his big break with a two-week gig in which "the sensational Bob Dylan" (that's what the ad says) opens for the Greenbriar Boys. Shelton's article in the *New York Times* the following morning announces the arrival of a new star ("Bright New Face, bursting with . . . ," etc.).

Even providence is with him. That afternoon he goes up to Columbia to play harp on three tracks on Carolyn Hester's album, which is being produced by none other than John Hammond, discoverer of Billie Holiday, Count Basie, and Aretha Franklin. Both men are fantasists, mythologists, and self-mythologists, and Hammond himself is given to apocryphal stories and tall tales (for example, the story that Bessie Smith died because after her car crash a white hospital wouldn't accept her). At the session, Dylan hands Hammond the review and, without ever seeing him perform, he signs Dylan to a record deal (shortly to be dubbed Hammond's Folly). This story becomes part of the Dylan legend. He may not have been a hustler in Times Square, but he did know how to hustle.

Bob was signing with the big time and he knew it. "Out on the street and in the clubs he celebrated with excitement," says Rotolo. "And maybe even displayed a 'drinks on me' joviality, though he was not known for his generosity."

He records his first album, *Bob Dylan*, in November 1961. "Talkin' New York" and "Song to Woody" are the only two originals on the album, along with old Josh White spirituals, Southern white mountain songs, Booker White's "Fixin' to Die," "Pretty Peggy-O," "House of the Risin' Sun," "See That My Grave Is Kept Clean," and "Highway 51." All for $402. Mostly first takes. Doing as few takes as possible will be Dylan's recording habit from now on. Dylan is poised to take the town by storm. Plays harp on Jack Elliott's first album on Vanguard (under pseudonym Tedham Porterhouse). Also plays on Harry Belafonte, Victoria Spivey sessions.

Listening to Dylan's first album today, the astonishing thing is not only how contemporary most of it still sounds, but what a hypnotic singer he is. People make fun of Dylan's voice and imply he made it despite it, but to this day almost no one can cover his songs.

Although only two tracks on his first album were written by Dylan, he so utterly takes over the other eleven songs they might as well be his. He takes possession of each of these songs because he *is* possessed— almost literally. He channels the old blues demons so hair-raisingly you have the chilling sense, especially in the darker songs he covers, that some blues "haint" has grabbed him by the ankles and is pulling him down into an unhallowed grave.

The way he conveys the urgency, despair, and rage of the blues and gospel songs like "Gospel Plow" and "Fixin' to Die" is so intense, and his voice is so amped up, it's as if there's an electrical surge already embedded in his ferocious delivery, which makes it surprising that anyone should have been shocked when he went electric.

It's shattering the way he holds and shudders the notes on muddy river blues like "Highway 51." The oddity and passion of Dylan's graveyard blues on this album—"In My Time of Dyin'" and "Fixin' to Die" with their doomy messages—are sung with such a growling intensity and manic energy it's as if he were speaking in tongues. Only an ancient bluesman like Blind Lemon Jefferson can sing songs like "See That My Grave Is Kept Clean"—or someone very, very young (as in the Huck Finn/Tom Sawyer fantasy of observing your own funeral).

Even on Dylan's goofy version of Jesse Fuller's "You're No Good," or the hokey, faux-yokel "Talkin' New York," a Woody Guthrie talking-blues monologue, he sounds to be having such a good time it's infectious. The folk-grotto standards "Man of Constant Sorrow," "Pretty Peggy-O," and "Freight Train Blues" (where he yodels a long Doppler train whistle) summon up candlelit nights in Village coffeehouses or "the green pastures of Harvard University." He may have borrowed "Baby, Let Me Follow You Down" from Eric Von Schmidt and outright stolen the arrangement of "House of the Risin' Sun" from Dave Van Ronk—much to Van Ronk's irritation—but his impersonations are uncanny.

IT'S THE YEAR ZERO FOR THE FOLK MOVEMENT AND HERE'S BOB DYLAN, come to pull down the pillars of the temple. His audience is already here awaiting him. Well, not Bob exactly, but the Folk Messiah, the one foretold. They are in the coffeehouses waiting for the one who will come and tell them what is written in their souls, why they are here, and what it all means—or at least which way the wind blows.

And he would. He would immortalize the folk movement, make it seem like their noble yearnings were a historical inevitability—but then he'd betray them, and they'd have to topple their little tin god. Half the people in the audience were folksingers or aspiring folksingers themselves, and they were all thinking the mantle might have fallen on any of them—and why not? Who is this squirmy kid anyway?

"Performers who had been on the scene longer and had their niche carved out on the folk circuit were aghast at the audacity of this young upstart punk," says Rotolo. "The malicious underbelly of the folk music beast was revealed, and it was positively an unpleasant sight."

Some in the audience would indeed have careers, although in some cases they would be relegated to a kind of Buffalo Bill's Wild West Show of folk music. Others would go on to be dentists and architects, or even college professors teaching Bob Dylan 101. But in the end it would be up to Bob. They didn't know it then, but it *was* Bob they were waiting for. He's the mysterious stranger who rolls into town and blows everybody's minds, the rainmaker, the seventh son of the seventh son, the self-created mojo man, who, with every breath he takes, whispers, "I'm your Hoochie Coochie Man; everybody knows I am."

AT THE BEGINNING OF 1962 DYLAN MOVES INTO A TWO-ROOM APART-ment in the Village at 161 W. 4th Street over Bruno's spaghetti parlor with

Suze Rotolo. Paul Stookey (of Peter, Paul and Mary) had introduced Dylan to his future manager, Albert Grossman, the year before. With their partnership, Dylan's career begins. Grossman had briefly tried singing folk music himself—sea chanteys and Bulgarian folk songs were his specialty. He made a lot of money for Peter, Paul and Mary with sweetened folk songs ("Lemon Tree" and "If I Had a Hammer") and, a year later, with a soft-core drug song ("Puff, The Magic Dragon"), so when he sees Dylan, Grossman looks at him the way Sylvester looks at Tweetie Pie. He buys out Roy Silver's share of Dylan's management for $10,000. Moody and bearlike, Grossman sees the pot of gold that had been waiting since '59 for whoever could deliver the folk movement's messiah. When asked later on how he and Dylan managed to hook up, Grossman said, "We were both waiting for the same bus."

"The American public is like Sleeping Beauty," said Grossman, "waiting to be kissed awake by the prince of folk music." Grossman has been called "a loathsome evil genius of manipulation and intimidation" and "a miserable human being," but he was great for Dylan's early career and a foil for things Dylan didn't want to do. His first plan, however, is just dopey: to combine Dylan with a Dixieland band.

At the same moment Dylan hooks up with Grossman, the folk scene becomes involved with the civil rights movement—and Dylan gets politicized through his relationship with Suze Rotolo, who comes from a family of union activists. During this time, he writes "The Death of Emmett Till" for a CORE benefit.

In March 1962, *Bob Dylan*—recorded in November 1961—is released. He now considers it out of date, having moved on to hipper, more inventive work, but it has all the qualities of his later selves: intensity, a wide range of regional musical styles, cracker-barrel humor, manic doominess, and an actor's ventriloquism through his use of dialect and phrasing.

Suze Rotolo's mother, Mary, smells a rat from the beginning, despite Dylan putting it around on Mulberry Street that he is an Italian orphan. She becomes increasingly wary of Bob, and when in May, she discovers his real name is Zimmerman, she packs Suze off to Italy.

The apotheosis of Dylan's first role—the dust bowl waif—is his appearance on the cover of *Sing Out!* looking like Woody Guthrie Junior. He'd got the rake of Woody's cigarette down, the way James Dean had copped the existential slant of Camus's Gauloise. The slant of your cigarette was a sign of fatality and stoicism as in Mitchum, Bogart, and Dean.

On December 6, 1961, he had gone back to Dinkytown to show off his new incarnation: "Listen to what's happened to me," he tells friends. But the Minneapolis crowd is not all that impressed with his agitprop folk stance.

Now, in December 1962, he makes his first visit to England—to appear in the BBC drama *Madhouse on Castle Street*, playing an anarchic young student who writes songs. He is also hired to sing two songs—one at the beginning and the other at the end of the play, one of them being "Blowin' in the Wind." Reluctant to read his one line, "Well, I don't know, I'll have to go home and think about it," he wants to sing instead. "Can't I just scat a couple of lines?" he asks the director.

Dylan and Albert Grossman are escorted around London by Andrew Loog Oldham, the Rolling Stones' future manager. "Even that early on," says Oldham, "Dylan and Grossman knew exactly who they were and what they were doing; they were like two sharpies prowling the streets."

While in England, British folksinger Rory McEwen, impressed by Dylan's lyrics, introduces him to the poet and mystical mythographer Robert Graves—whose *The White Goddess* Dylan had been reading. The old Celtic twig reader doesn't think much of him. While in England Dylan runs into Eric Von Schmidt and Richard Fariña and plays harp and sings backup on five tracks on their album (released in '67). Dylan is already busy constructing his persona as the evangelist of Appalachian folk music, telling Brit arts magazine *Scene* that he's "consciously trying to recapture the rude beauty of a Southern farmhand musing in melody on his porch." He flies to Rome with Odetta, where he writes "It Ain't Me, Babe," "Girl from the North Country," and "Boots of Spanish Leather."

ONLY THREE OTHER TRACKS COME OUT THIS YEAR WITH DYLAN ON them; among these is his first single, "Mixed-Up Confusion" (with "Corrina, Corrina" on the B-side), issued at Christmas. Two and a half years before his "betrayal" of the nylon-string cult, he is already playing electric guitar on this manic rockabilly track—and on such tracks as "Rocks and Gravel," deleted from his second album, the forthcoming *Freewheelin' Bob Dylan*.

Dylan is biding his time. The eternal student, he loves riffling through record collections, poring over the Folkways *Anthology of American Folk*

Music—the bible of folknicity—mimicking the vocal styles of Ewan Mac-Coll, A. L. Lloyd, the guitar and drawl of Rabbit Brown.

A voracious reader and autodidact, his reading habits shift from classics of Okie life (*The Grapes of Wrath* and *Cannery Row*) to symbolist poetry (Lorca, Brecht, Browning, Joyce, Melville, Rimbaud, etc.)—all of which Dylan conceals, preferring to affect the role of semiliterate bumpkin.

Dylan in a modified pompadour with his
girlfriend Suze Rotolo. They own
MacDougal Street that winter of 1962,
king and queen of a six-block folk
principality.

5 Folk Messiah

I NTIMATIONS OF IMMORTALITY. IN FEBRUARY 1963 "MASTERS OF War," with illustrations by Suze Rotolo, and an early version of "Don't Think Twice, It's All Right" appear in the folk journal *Broadside*. In March, *Joan Baez in Concert Part 2* is released with Dylan's autobiographical liner notes.

After attacks by *Time* and *Newsweek* later in the year, he will stay away from personal revelations until *Blood on the Tracks*. Sometime this spring he receives a letter from Johnny Cash in Las Vegas telling him how much he likes Dylan's songs. Dylan idolized Cash as a kind of shit-kicking disciple of Hank Williams. "Of course, I knew of him before he ever heard of me," Dylan said of Cash's passing in September 2003. "In '55 or '56, 'I Walk the Line' played all summer on the radio, and it was different than anything else you had ever heard. The record sounded like a voice from the middle of the earth. It was so powerful and moving. It was profound, and so was the tone of it, every line; deep and rich, awesome and mysterious all at once. 'I Walk the Line' had a monumental presence and a certain type of majesty that was humbling. Even a simple line like 'I find it very, very easy to be true' can take your measure. We can remember that and see how far we fall short of it."

Dylan's first pop protest song, "Blowin' in the Wind," injects him into the mainstream, but it's Peter, Paul and Mary who make it a hit. In their suits and dresses, they combine soothing harmonies with a nursery rhyme lilt, and sell 320,000 copies before it appears on Dylan's second LP, *The Freewheelin' Bob Dylan*. The commercial success of "Blowin' in the Wind" will inadvertently lead to the end of the folk movement and Dylan's involvement with it.

As a child of pop culture, Dylan's twin aims in life—to become a great artist and to be famous—would have been contradictory ambitions for, say, the Beats and the abstract expressionists, but Dylan's models would have been more like Hank Williams, James Dean, and Elvis. But as his career progressed he became conflicted. His role as the hobo Woody Guthrie kid had gotten him accepted in the rarefied realm of the

Village, and, in a sense, he had achieved his initial goal to be thought of as an artist by other artists whom he respected. But he knew that this wasn't likely to make him famous (or rich). You could see the high water mark of this old folky road any night on Bleecker Street: Ramblin' Jack and Dave Van Ronk had taken the darn thing just about as far as it could go. He was disheartened by the commercial (and critical) failure of his first album, and while he pondered what to do next, a gaudy angel with glitter on her wings and too much mascara paid him a nocturnal visit.

Dylan's stroke of inspiration was to write a folk song in a pop music idiom—in other words, to fuse (and, essentially, confuse) the two genres. Making folk songs into tuneful pop hits had been the stock-in-trade of commercial folk groups like the Kingston Trio, but Dylan, because of who he was, was exempt from that sort of contamination. Dylan has always been far more accepting in his influences—the Kingston Trio, though despised as selling out the positively 4th Street crowd, remains one of his favorite groups. With the equivocal quasi-kitsch "Blowin' in the Wind" he had achieved his ambition—it was just the sort of song that a group like the Tarriers would sing and was custom-made, of course, for the Grossman-manufactured folk trio Peter, Paul and Mary. None of this, or the more opportunistic of his protest songs that followed, affected Dylan's mojo directly because he wasn't part of a smarmy, harmonizing folk combo—no one would accuse someone who looked like a homeless waif and with a voice like his of trying to accommodate himself to commercial interests—that would be a really perverse thought (and a classic Dylan ploy). And yet, of course, that's exactly what he was doing, as he himself admitted.

With "Blowin' in the Wind" he'd got the fame he sought, made himself a million dollars, but it was a wind that would blow in too much gold dust and too much attention.

Friday, April 13. Solo concert at Town Hall. As opposed to the Carnegie Recital Hall concert organized by Izzy Young in November 1961, when a mere fifty-three true believers showed up, this one is well attended, with raves in the *New York Times* and *Billboard*. On May 12 Dylan is scheduled to appear on *The Ed Sullivan Show*. When forbidden to sing "Talkin' John Birch Paranoid Blues," he walks out. On May 18 he performs at the Monterey Folk Festival with Mance Lipscomb, the Weavers, and Judy Collins.

In May, *The Freewheelin' Bob Dylan* is released—the cover photograph shows Dylan and Suze Rotolo walking through the Village the previous winter—a shot modeled on Roy Schatt's photos of his idol James Dean on the New York streets.

Whereas on his first album only two songs were original compositions, on *Freewheelin'* they're all his own (although many of the tunes and lyrics are traditional, giving his songs the weight and authenticity of classic folk songs). Grafting, borrowing, and wholesale appropriation would become a common practice of Dylan's throughout his career. "Corrina, Corrina" is a traditional ballad but he cobbles it from different versions, plus some lines from Robert Johnson. On "Honey, Just Allow Me One More Chance" he borrows heavily from Henry Thomas, adding lyrics and transforming it into his own. If the first album was an eclectic, eccentric collection sung in a series of Dylan impersonations, here Dylan comes into sharp focus. It's that prairie-dog voice that tells you: Wake up. This is real. This is now. The anthems evolve from the straightforward "Blowin' in the Wind" into the kettledrum *rat-tat-tat* of the antiwar battle hymn "Masters of War," into the apocalyptic symbolist catechism of "A Hard Rain's A-Gonna Fall." The ballads ("Girl from the North Country") and antiballads ("Don't Think Twice, It's All Right") begin drifting into the thought-dream ballads of Dylan's next phase, the Folk Messiah.

This new incarnation fuses Bob I (reclusive poet) and Bob II (charismatic performer), and his election as the crown prince of folk comes from the topical, finger-pointing songs of the year, including "The Death of Emmett Till" (a black teen murdered for whistling at a white woman), "Oxford Town" (James Meredith's 1962 attempt to integrate the University of Mississippi), "Masters of War" (Bay of Pigs), and "A Hard Rain's A-Gonna Fall" (assumed to be about the Cuban missile crisis but written and performed three weeks earlier).

Like Woody Guthrie, Dylan is a master at matching borrowed music to his lyrics so that they appear to be seamless artifacts: "Hard Rain" is based on "Lord Randall," "Don't Think Twice" is from an old folk tune via Paul Clayton's "Scarlet Ribbons for Her Hair," "Bob Dylan's Dream" is from the ballad "Lord Franklin," "Corrina, Corrina" uses the melody of "C. C. Rider," and "Masters of War" comes from a modal English mummer's song via Jean Ritchie's "Nottamun Town."

"A Hard Rain's A-Gonna Fall," his first symbolist "song combine," brings together political and poetic imagery. It's so dense that Dylan claims a new song could be written for every line.

I saw a newborn baby with wild wolves all around it,
I saw a highway of diamonds with nobody on it,
I saw a black branch with blood that kept drippin',
I saw a room full of men with their hammers a-bleedin',
I saw a white ladder all covered with water,
I saw ten thousand talkers whose tongues were all broken,
I saw guns and sharp swords in the hands of young children

Dylan is also incorporating jump-cut images from movies and collage techniques from modern art. Despite the confusing, stream-of-consciousness lyrics, Dylan is rattling everyone's cage. The sign that his time has come is when he starts getting attacked in the press. In late May, *Time* accuses Dylan of making "a fetish out of authenticity," and says his accent "belongs to a jive Nebraskan, or maybe a Brooklyn hillbilly." *Variety* mocks him for using a "deliberately iggerunt" style of writing and delivery.

At the same time, he becomes a symbolic figure in the civil rights movement. On July 6, Pete Seeger and Theodore Bikel take him down to sing at a Student Nonviolent Coordinating Committee (SNCC) voter registration rally in Greenwood, Mississippi. On the edge of a cotton field, Dylan sings "Only a Pawn in Their Game," an intense, chilling performance (included in the D. A. Pennebaker documentary *Don't Look Back*).

Dylan's coronation occurs on July 26–28, 1963, at the Newport Folk Festival, where he appears as a frail, haunted-looking urchin in battle dress: khaki shirt, faded blue jeans. For the finale, the SNCC Freedom Singers, Joan Baez, and Pete Seeger join in a version of "Blowin' in the Wind." Peter Yarrow, of Peter, Paul and Mary, introduces Dylan: "This song was written by the most important folksinger in America today." Two years later, no one would notice the irony that the people booing Dylan at the infamous Newport electric performance were the same folkniks who had made him into a star.

On August 17, the prince and princess of folk unite on the Baez tour, where Dylan occasionally duets with Baez, does guest numbers at selected spots and the odd solo. Dylan has his own agenda. He begins a symbiotic relationship with Baez in which he uses her mass popularity (she'd been a folk star since 1959) to promote himself and give him credibility with her audience, but eventually her association with Dylan would lend weight to Baez as her style of folksinging went out of fashion. At the end of the tour Dylan stays with Baez at her home in Carmel

Valley, California, thus precipitating the imminent breakup with Suze Rotolo.

According to Baez their "affair" wasn't consummated, but rumors in the press magnified it nevertheless. "He was so shy and fragile," Baez told David Hajdu. "We didn't make love. The music seemed enough at the time."

In March 1966, Dylan painted a scathing picture of Baez: "[She] ain't never going to find her people," he ranted to biographer Robert Shelton (who thought it too scabrous to include in his book). "Nobody's going to put up with her. She just . . . hasn't got that much in common with the street vagabonds, man, who play insane instruments. . . . There is no place for her in my music. She doesn't fit into my music. Hey, I can fit into her music, but she doesn't fit into my music—my show. It would have been dumb. It wouldn't have added to me, and it would have been misleading to the audience." In *Chronicles* he redeemed himself by canonizing her as St. Joan: "She looks like a religious icon. . . . Nothing she did didn't work. That she was the same age as me almost made me feel useless."

THE SUMMER OF 1963 IS THE SUMMER OF *THE FREEWHEELIN' BOB Dylan.* Everybody is playing it as Dylan enters the national consciousness. At the August 28 March on Washington, Martin Luther King Jr. delivers his "I Have a Dream" speech, and Dylan performs along with Baez, Odetta, Peter, Paul and Mary, Harry Belafonte, and Mahalia Jackson.

His fame spreads from college crowd to mass audience. Even teeny-boppers show up at his Carnegie Hall concert in 1963. Bob goes pop, developing a new surreal manner of answering questions from the press. "I consider Hank Williams, Captain Marvel, Marlon Brando, the Tennessee Stud, Clark Kent, Walter Cronkite, and J. Carrol Naish all influences." Whereas he'd once thought of the Beatles as bubblegum, he now sees them as the wave of the future, a wave he's about to catch himself. And with Dylan's new pop fame, rumors begin to fly.

As 1963 draws to a close, Bob becomes increasingly unpredictable. On December 13, Dylan outrages attendees of Clark Foreman's Emergency Civil Liberties Committee dinner. He's there to receive the Tom Paine Award. A drunken Dylan, already chafing under his role as spokesman for the New Left, tells the old fogies present that they should be sitting on the beach in Florida. In a final insult a very drunk Dylan tells them that he can identify with Lee Harvey Oswald—an early warning shot that he wasn't going to be living up to anybody's expectations. "I'm tired of hearing that we share the blame for every crime."

He is feeling trapped in "the messiah thing" and suspicious of organizations, causes. The only group he's for is "an organization of disconnected people." And, he claims, "I'm not part of no movement. If I was I wouldn't be able to be anything else but be in 'the Movement.' I just can't have people sit around and make rules for me." It's not just a refusal to become a spokesman; it's an early instance of his innate contrariness and ambivalent relationship with his audience. Still, he never abandons folk music—or protest songs. As with all his other influences, he transmutes it and, throughout his life, returns to it like a touchstone. In October, Dylan appears on the first *Broadside* album, singing three songs under the name of Blind Boy Grunt.

Things begin to go badly between Dylan and Suze Rotolo in the winter of '63, as Suze, once "the true fortune teller of [his] soul," reacts to Dylan's withdrawal from her. His sudden fame and shift in attitude add to her already anguished feelings about Dylan's relationship with Baez (among others). Suze becomes suicidal and moves out of the 4th Street apartment.

"Women rule the world," Dylan says. "I believe that." Not that he has treated them all that well. But they and the often self-generated pain they have caused him are the source of some of the greatest love ballads in all of pop music. From his relationship with Suze Rotolo comes an album's worth of great songs—from the memorable Suze breakup songs ("Don't Think Twice, It's All Right," "It Ain't Me, Babe") to the peevish rewriting of personal history songs ("Ballad in Plain D").

BY 1963 FOLK MUSIC WAS ALREADY SOMETHING OF A JOKE—A SUBJECT of cocktail party comedy albums. With the *Hootenanny* TV show on ABC and Allan Sherman's comedy album, *My Son, the Folk Singer*, nothing much was really sacred about folk music anymore. Although the folk music scene was socially progressive, folk (with its inflexible canon of traditional songs) was musically static. In addition, folk music suffered from a split identity. It was both the collective voice (union songs and spirituals) as well as the high lonesome whine of the isolated razorback—as sung by the children of the middle class.

His previous obsession with Woody Guthrie had been a longing for another age, a more heroic time of camaraderie and adventure. Now Dylan will start to use the life-vision quests of Rimbaud, Dostoyevsky, Kafka, Lorca, and Kerouac as handbooks on how to become his own poet genius. Mythologizing himself as the poet-seer, he converts Woody Guthrie's agitprop into prophetic intuitions, using amphetamines to pry open his imagery. A natural collagist, his musical eclecticism as well as his surreal juxtapositions have their roots in his early radio-listening habits—switching from one station to another.

Dylan writes his songs at the Fat Black Pussycat, transmitting his dense interior life to the page. He's an avid note jotter and notorious eavesdropper, scribbling overheard conversations in his notebook like an informer. His essential secretiveness makes him a riveting presence among the Village floaters. His personality now swings from sweet, shambling, bumbling ragamuffin to an intense, edgy lurker under a dark cloud. He has a fear of crowds and strangers, as well as a pervasive paranoia and morbidity that will bloom into the hallucinatory negativity of *Blonde on Blonde*.

January 13, 1964, *The Times They Are A-Changin'*, Dylan's third album, is released. Dylan's reputation (and sales) gives him complete creative control, and he moves from impersonal, pious protest songs and folk anthems to music in which the complaint becomes a form of personal revelation. The personal soon swamps the anthem/protest song elements to the point where the latter begin to seem arbitrary and hypocritical. The cover of *The Times They Are A-Changin'* shows Bob still doing his Woody Guthrie but by now this is just subterfuge. He's already moved on. (Tony Glover remembers Dylan typing the lyrics to "The Times They Are A-Changin'" and saying, "It seems to be what people want." "Times" being the prototypical Barry "Eve of Destruction" McGuirish protest song.) The album retains remnants of his Folk Messiah incarnation ("Blowin' in the Wind"); news-item songs ("The Lonesome Death of Hattie Carroll," "Only a Pawn in Their Game," and "Hollis Brown"); and love ballads (the missing-Suze song, "Boots of Spanish Leather," and the losing-Suze song, "One Too Many Mornings"). The preachy, somewhat self-righteous us-against-them element is still there in the title song, but the cynicism rises in "With God on Our Side." The radical departure is "When the Ship Comes In," with its thought fragments, apocalyptic visions, and echoes of Kurt Weill and Bertolt Brecht's "Pirate Jenny" in *The Threepenny Opera*. But before you write a great song like this you first have to become the kind of character who would write it. Dylan I had been the Folksinger. Now Dylan II, the Protest Messiah, was about to morph into Dylan III, the Electric God. Much of the impetus for his transformation will come from that damn *Newsweek* article from last November.

Dylan perusing *U.S. News and World Retort*, a parody of the venerable weekly news magazine, put out by the underground newspaper the *California Pelican* as an avoid-the-draft drive. Greenwich Village, 1962.

6   The Zimmerman Letter

"**I** MEAN, WHO KNEW?" SAYS MYRA FRIEDMAN, WHO AT THE TIME worked in the publicity department of Columbia Records and later worked as Dylan's publicist in Albert Grossman's office. "Who knew he was going to be the spokesman of his generation, as opposed to a kind of peripheral very, very compelling kid, just hanging 'round the office. I would often see him up there. Looked like any young kid. Well, one day he goes and tells the whole Bob Dylan Myth story to Billy James, who puts it in Dylan's bio."

The confusion about Dylan's identity had been there from the very start, beginning with the sly, crab-like approach of the bumpkin character who had showed up in Greenwich Village. The folksy, vagabond Bob would have been an obvious act to anyone examining it closely, but if you happened to be a tourist or an impressionable young girl, you might believe all the tall tales he told and they would only add to the patina of the performances. But even if you thought it was just a hokey routine, that was okay too. It worked either way. Dylan would be evasive and funny when people called him on it, but he never got upset about it.

"It was an old showbiz tradition," says Dave Van Ronk. "Everybody changed their names and invented stories about themselves . . . we were all inventing characters for ourselves. Look at Ramblin' Jack Elliott, who had grown up as a Jewish doctor's son in Brooklyn. And then gone out west and become a cowboy and Woody's hoboing buddy."

The bigwigs at Columbia Records, however, didn't realize this was Dylan's way of dealing with the messy issues of personality and identity: Just adopt a persona, and if the literal minded insisted he stick to it for his most recent album, too bad if they didn't get the joke.

What had attracted Dylan to the old weird folk songs in the first place was their biblical belief in Fate. And now this same Fate, in a mundane but devastating form, was going to descend on Dylan himself quite unexpectedly.

"MY JOB WAS TO MAIL LPS AND PR MATERIAL OUT TO NEWSPAPERS AND magazines," says Friedman. "It was a very pleasant job because people were always glad to get records from you. And then one day I got a letter from Hibbing, Minnesota, from the local newspaper. It was written in a large, untidy scrawl on a small piece of paper, not an eight by ten. The person who wrote it was the reviewer for the paper. It began, 'I thought you ought to know. . . .' This fellow was incensed that we were helping Bob promote this false image of himself. The man on the cover of the LP wasn't Bob Dylan, orphan, circus performer, adopted son of some Indian tribe or whatever else he was claiming. No, he was in fact Bobby Zimmerman of Hibbing, Minnesota, whose father owned a hardware store on Main Street. I looked at the letter for a long time and I thought, 'Oh, my goodness! What is this?'

"And it was like a bomb. I was stunned. I can still see myself walking into the office of Billie Wallington, head of publicity at Columbia at the time, with the letter.

"'Billie, would you look at this?' I said. She read the letter with amusement and handed it back to me. I put it in the file and forgot about it.

"The next thing I know it's in *Newsweek*," says Friedman, "under Emily Coleman's byline, saying something like, 'This up-and-coming radical person is actually Bob Zimmerman, and his father owns a hardware store in Hibbing, Minnesota.'

"John Courtland [who also worked in the publicity department] was very tight with Emily Coleman, and I believe he passed the letter to her. It doesn't sound like something that Billie would have done. But I don't remember anybody ever saying, 'He did it,' or 'I did it.' It was more like, 'How the hell?'

"Still, Bob assumed that Billie passed the letter to *Newsweek*, and that not only ended Dylan's friendship with Billie but also began his adversarial relationship to the press.

"I put it back into the file like some moron. We had maybe one Xerox machine in the building. We used carbon paper. So I put it back in the file and when I did go look for it again, it was gone."

The people at Columbia were stunned. It's not that they believed he'd lived with a Sioux Indian tribe or had been a circus roustabout. These stories were obviously childhood fantasies, universal ones almost—like becoming a fireman. But they were colorful and it was part of his image.

Who knows where he came from? They figured he was a Midwestern kid, maybe a runaway.

The *Newsweek* article exhibits more than the usual vitriol, presumably because his early voice in the rising counterculture dismissed slick newsweeklies like *Time* and *Newsweek*. The article begins with his successes, his concerts, and his fanatical following, including "high school and college students to whom Dylan is practically a religion." Then Coleman sarcastically slips into Dylanspeak: "He has suffered; he has been hung up, man, without bread, without a chick, with twisted wires growing inside him."

Coleman catches him out in a series of fibs; perhaps most damaging for a protest singer is his faked life of privation. His audiences, consisting mostly of middle-class suburban kids, envy his hardscrabble upbringing, she says, and then she discloses that he came from the same comfortable middle-class background they did. She questions his name. Isn't he in fact Bobby Zimmerman from Hibbing, Minnesota? He flatly denies this—there must be some mistake—and to prove it, he pulls out his draft card. "Dig my draft card, man. See! *Bob Dylan*." It's true he was now Bob Dylan—he'd changed his name legally a year earlier.

She next catches him lying about his parents. At this point you may have thought Bob would have been a little more cautious about his claims. But, no, he recklessly bluffs it out. He's turned into Huckleberry Finn and he ain't gonna change his story for no glossy rag snoop. Swears he hasn't seen his parents for years. Just completely lost contact. This Coleman exposes as a bald-faced fib. Not more than a few blocks from where Coleman and Dylan are talking, Abe and Beatty Zimmerman are staying at a motor inn. According to *Newsweek*, Bob has sent them plane tickets so they can come to see him perform at Carnegie Recital Hall that very night.

Coleman mocks the poor boy act he struggles to maintain: "Perhaps he feels it would spoil the image he works so hard to cultivate— with his dress, with his talk, with the deliberately atrocious grammar and pronunciation in his songs." He tells her he loves music but despises the commercialism of the music biz. Yet she claims "he has two agents who hover about him, guarding his words and fattening his contracts." Dylan says he disdains publicity but blows it by asking her how long the piece is going to be and if there are going to be any photographs. Just like that, in a series of lethal cuts, Coleman has demolished Bob's ingeniously constructed fable with devastating precision.

Okay, so there are a few discrepancies in his story, but he tells her he's gonna clear all that up in this book he's writing that'll explain everything. And then, always pure contradictory Bob, he adds that the explanations are irrelevant. "I am my words."

Abe Zimmerman, Dylan's dad, was infuriated by his son's earlier claims that he was an orphan and brought up by Indians and carnies. "My son is a corporation," he said, "and its public image is strictly an act. That is what we found so disturbing—and still do. But it's all part of the act."

The Zimmerman exposure was a far more critical assault on Dylan's identity than someone making fun of the Woody Guthrie dust bowl–kid imitations, because it undermined his core personality. Underneath all his hobo-kid stuff was the real Bob Dylan, the vaudevillian poet who had made up this entertaining minstrel character with all his preposterous yarns.

One can imagine how upset he was by the *Newsweek* article, but it was something Suze Rotolo had discovered long before.

"I found out for sure that his name was Robert Allen Zimmerman when I saw his draft card," says Rotolo. "In spite of myself I was upset that he hadn't ever said anything about it.

"We came back to the apartment after a long night out and he was really drunk. When he clumsily removed his wallet from his pocket its contents fell on the floor and that is when I saw his name. We had been laughing, but when I picked up his draft card, my mood changed. So Zimmerman is your real name after all? Yes? Well, why didn't you tell me?

"The discovery of his birth name didn't have to be anything astounding or earth-shattering. I didn't mind us keeping secrets from each other. I was accustomed to that, having grown up in the McCarthy era, when it was necessary to be wary of prying outsiders. But it was suddenly upsetting that he hadn't been open with me. I was hurt."

Ever since he'd left home to go to college, Dylan had been erasing his past and re-creating himself as he went along in a folksy, desultory manner. His impersonations were amiable, droll creations, but after the *Newsweek* piece Dylan was driven to spectacular feats of self-transformation. He became a mercurial T-1000 entity, a shape-shifter capable of turning into whatever his mind touched. And his life, in turn, became this terrible runaway train—a device he created to escape his past but that inevitably forced him to wriggle out of endless ambiguities. Dylan and Jack Kerouac followed a similar pattern of flight from their pasts. Kerouac spent his life hitching, riding boxcars, running away from his hometown of Lowell,

Mass. It was as if the sullen hulk of that Massachusetts mill town shadowed his every move.

"I was just somebody else, some stranger," Kerouac said in a moment of bewildered confession. "And my whole life was a haunted life, the life of a ghost."

Dylan's very success and notoriety as a rebel against society had created the situation in which he now found himself: confronting the Zimmerman letter. But didn't he think that one day someone from Hibbing or Dinkytown was going to show up and expose him? That's the guy I went to high school with; that's the guy I played in a band with.

"It's funny," says Friedman. "The revelation that his name wasn't Dylan but Zimmerman shouldn't have been such a bombshell. This was the kind of thing that was common practice in show business, but not in the folk movement or the protest thing. And for Bob it was a serious issue because, after all, he was Mr. Integrity. A few years later Simon and Garfunkel came along, but back then you never would have had a name like Garfunkel. Or Springsteen! Not to mention the fact that his name being Zimmerman made him a Jewish cowboy from Main Street USA."

As Dave Van Ronk pointed out in his autobiography, many of the people involved in the first folk revival of the 1930s and '40s were Jewish—as were the folkies of the '60s. Van Ronk reasoned that for Jews, belonging to a movement centered on American traditional music was a form of belonging and assimilation.

And no one did a better marginal than Bob because he was from a marginal place, a racial minority—and a changeling. He saw everything through a hole in the fence. He was like a foreigner, an immigrant; he had an alien's view of America. In some ways his distance and his entrancement with American mythologies were similar to that of the musicians of the Brit invasion. Most of America, in the late 1950s and '60s, though, was too submerged in its cultural fog to see its own inheritance.

"The revelation that Jack [Elliott] was Jewish was vouchsafed unto Bobby one afternoon at the Figaro," Van Ronk recalled. "We were sitting around shooting the bull with Barry Kornfeld and maybe a couple of other people and somehow it came out that Jack had grown up in Ocean Parkway and was named Elliott Adnopoz. Bobby literally fell off his chair; he was rolling around on the floor, and it took him a couple of minutes to pull himself together and get up again. Then Barry, who can be diabolical in things like this, leaned over to him and just whispered the word 'Adnopoz,' and back he went under the table."

Here Dylan cracks up in astonishment at finding another musician who is not only Jewish and has changed his name, but is just as involved in self-mythologizing as himself. Jews are also traditionally urban, and Bob was presenting himself as a rural hillbilly character. "I think Dylan initially denied his Jewish background," said Allen Ginsberg, "because he thought it conflicted with the persona he was creating, the Woody Guthrie character. But I don't think he realized how fundamental his Jewishness was to his vision of the world—America in particular."

In America it's a good thing to be an outsider, but to live outside the law you must be honest. His first great pop masterpiece, "Like a Rolling Stone," is all about that. It's a hipster's tale, an outsider's moral stance against the terrible, relentless conformism of American culture, which just swallows you up in its insatiable maw.

Dylan has been one of the great fabulators, both in his life and art. He forms his persona and creates the characters in his songs around the outsider hero, intuitively conflating Robin Hood and Jesse James. To Dylan, all these types—hillbilly, outlaw, rebel, cowboy, outsider—were all really the same character. Arthur Rimbaud = Jesse James = Walt Whitman = Hank Williams = James Dean = Jack Kerouac = Joey Gallo. In a series of American folklore equations, he realigned the American inheritances and invented the cowboy angel hipster. All reflect Dylan's powerful reaction to the Zimmerman letter—denial, rage, and then, eventually, flight.

Dylan with Jack Elliott, two Woody Guthrie
imitators in the last moment when the folk
hegira was still plausible. One of these
guys is going to morph into a Stratocasting
Rimbaud; the other was going to keep the
old, weird flame of folk burning.

7 From a Buick 6

EBRUARY 3, 1964. IT'S THE FIRST TEN SECONDS OF THE BIG Bang. The great freight train of the '60s is lurching into the station. The Beatles are coming. They'll be here in four days. "I Want to Hold Your Hand" is #1 on the charts. It's your last chance to see the USA before it's changed forever, to inhale Kerouac's "charging restless mute unvoiced road keening in a seizure of tarpaulin power." Try doing that in Europe.

Where are we going? Who cares? It's 1964. Just hit the highway: Take the classic Route 66, *On the Road* run across the great divide, the windshield movie that all the Beatniks from Walt Whitman to Saint Jack have to take. Plug into the country, take its pulse, *become* it.

As we head out across the George Washington Bridge, check out your traveling companions. Cat at the wheel is Victor Maymudes, the gentle giant. He's Bob's roadie, companion, bodyguard, chess mate, and fellow pool shark. Guy in the passenger seat, that's Pete Karman, Peter the Scrivener, onetime reporter for the *Daily Mirror* and unofficial chronicler of this twenty-two-day saga. He's a friend of Suze Rotolo's. No one knows how exactly he got to come along on this trip. Maybe it was Suze's idea. Yeah, maybe he's there to keep an eye on her ex.

That bearded Christlike guy in the backseat with the medicine chest is Paul Clayton; sometimes they call him Pablo. He's a folksinger, a scholar, a speedfreak, boyfriend of Carla, and a guy Bob once worshipped—and stole a couple of tunes from ("Don't Think Twice" from Clayton's "Who's Gonna Buy Your Chickens," and "Percy's Song" from "The Wind and the Rain"). Not that Paul minded. He loved Dylan, was likely *in* love with him. And that sullen, brooding guy next to him? Why, that's Bob Dylan, man.

Why is Bob taking this trip and footing the bill for it—all expenses paid out of his own pocket from his newly created Ashes and Sand production company?

REASON #1: Ostensibly to transport himself to various gigs along the way, ending up in San Francisco on February 20. But, hell, we're only talking three shows, so you know there's got to be more to it than that.

REASON #2: The revelations in *Newsweek* three months earlier saying he'd fabricated his own history had vaporized Dylan's carefully invented past and his make-believe Other along with it. This idiot wind had blown down his imaginatively decorated set pieces. The naked truth was that Bob had recently run out of history.

REASON #3 (FOR THE TAX MAN): To promote his new album, *The Times They Are A-Changin'*. You know, chat up deejays, do in-store promotions. Unlikely.

REASON #4: New material. It's out there. Go get it.

REASON #5: Just to get outta Dodge. The folk shtetl was claustrophobic (eight square blocks in Greenwich Village) and provincial in a way real provinces never are. For all the singing about freedom and being free that these folks did, Folkopolis had a lot of rules. In the summer of 1963 he'd been anointed the crown prince of folk at Newport—and he now wanted to escape. But the last four months of 1963 had been really lousy: the Kennedy assassination, his relationship with Suze falling apart, the debacle at the Emergency Civil Liberties Committee dinner, and then the article in *Newsweek*. In his exasperated end-of-the-year letter to *Broadside* he'd been driven to casting spells: "Away, be gone all you demons/An just let me be."

REASON #6: Looking for another style, a newfangled way to express the jangle in his brain, leading to . . .

REASON #7: Go away, come back changed, fulfill the classic need to transform oneself—you know, like Robert Johnson, with the Devil at the crossroads. This new Dylan would be inextricably linked with #5, above. He wanted to escape the folkie princeling image, to make himself mysterious again.

REASON #8: To travel in the footsteps of Beat bodhisattvas Jack Kerouac and Neal Cassady. Dylan and Co. would follow roughly the same route Jack and Neal took on their cross-country trip in '48, New York to New Orleans and then on to the Beat mecca: San Francisco.

"I think it was in everybody's mind that this was a sort of *On the Road* redux," says Karman—just as when Sal Paradise (Jack Kerouac) and Dean Moriarty (Neal Cassady) got into their '49 Hudson and headed west at the end of 1948 hoping to hook into the mysterious circuit board of the American dream/nightmare. Hadn't just such a trip as this given rise to *On the Road*—the hipster's road map of the soul?

And why wouldn't it do the same for Bob? And so it did. On this trip Bob began writing his two breakthrough songs—"Chimes of Freedom," with its flashing chains of images, and "Mr. Tambourine Man," the first of his hallucinated visionary songs.

REASON #9: Possible source for a short narrative concerning "The Adventures of—." And this trip certainly has taken on a mythical aspect in the Life of Bob. What was he up to? You don't bring a chronicler (Pete Karman) along unless you think your journey is going to have some meaning. It's also possible that he intended to rewrite *On the Road* as a symbolist, hipster poem, and this new material would become the germ of his embryonic novel *Tarantula*, which at this point he was calling *Side One* or *Off the Record*.

REASON #10: Troubles with Suze Rotolo and designs on Joan Baez. Bob's apocalyptic visions and his romantic entanglements were becoming fused in some unforeseen manner.

All this would soon be resolved with his next invention: the New Dylan. Up until now Dylan had created a fragmentary self-portrait, partly from his invented autobiography and interviews, but mostly through his songs. His next personification was the young poet (Chatterton, Shelley, Delmore Schwartz) overlaid with the earnest, lefty Jewish kid with a copy of the *Daily Worker* in his back pocket. He would create this new role for himself—the hair, the attitude—the way you write a character in a movie.

In this way, he was much like the original autobiographical singer-songwriters, including blues singers like Robert Johnson and Lightnin' Hopkins, country singers like Hank Williams (the hell-raisin' old lovesick boy himself), and early rock 'n' rollers like Chuck Berry, Little Richard, Bo Diddley, and Fats Domino (Uncle Remus–like singers of their own urban folktales).

On the other hand, most pop performers sang whatever was written for them, so you had to suspend disbelief. Cue: Gary Lewis and the Playboys' "This Diamond Ring" (written by Al Kooper, among others). What ring? Did Gary Lewis's chick stand him up at the altar? Aside from his broken heart and engagement-jewelry-investment problems, you don't really get to know too much more about him from this song. The singer's life began and ended with the song itself—a three-and-a-half-minute disposable soap opera. Aside from the performer's vocal style (and, to a lesser degree, appearance) there was no connection between one song and the next.

With Dylan, we knew we weren't going to get any of this catch-as-catch-can persona business. In Dylan songs, the central character is always Dylan. His albums are seen by his fans as autobiographical, chapters in his ongoing life story. Dylan's sequential persona solved the central dilemma of the pop singer: continuity (especially since his fans tended to buy his albums rather than just his singles).

By the beginning of 1964, Dylan's autobiographical lives were plausible, even looked for. If they didn't exactly form a seamless narrative, it didn't matter; we made the connections in our minds. Dylan was the implied hero of his protest songs: He'd written them, he was singing them, and, given the times, it was reasonable to think he believed what he said. In his love songs, the self-deprecating, whimsical qualities were the most seductive aspects of his character.

But the two Dylans—champion of the oppressed or rueful, lovelorn, yearning swain—could be held in suspension only as long as the situations that called them into being lasted. The very success of his schizophrenic hero had doomed him. As he bewailed in his letter to *Broadside*, the frenzy of renown had taken him unawares: "I am now famous by the rules of public famiosity/it snuck up on me/an pulverized me . . . /I never knew what was happenin'."

Dylan no longer wanted to be seen as a champion of causes; he was a loner, a despiser of hypocrisy and cant. He now found himself in the peculiar position of being an outsider with a fan club. This introverted spokesman and enigmatic teller of truths soon became famous for what he was not—an activist. And fame further complicated his personal life, corroding any hope of maintaining the faithful lover pose. He'd backed himself into a corner. Within a year both sides of the old Dylan had worn out. He needed a new coat.

The lapse between the recording and release of albums has always been problematic for performers and their fans, even when, as in the '60s, albums by major groups came out every six months. Some of the songs on *The Times They Are A-Changin'*, for example, had been written almost a year earlier in the spring and summer of '63. The album itself had been recorded in August and October of the previous year, but when it came out in January 1964, it would be seen as Dylan's latest statement. And since more than half the songs were of the topical, finger-pointing variety, it was assumed Dylan was still *that guy*, the Folk Messiah. Even though in the final verse of the last song on that album, he'd petulantly told "the false clocks" and the "dirt of gossip" that "I'll take my stand/ And remain as I am/And bid farewell and not give a damn."

SPEAKING OF CAUSES, ONE OF THE THINGS DYLAN AND CO. PLANNED TO do along the way was to lend some support to the striking miners of Hazard, Kentucky. A few weeks earlier Bob had attended a rally hosted by the activist and folksinger Hamish Sinclair, secretary of the National Committee for Miners, for the families of the striking miners. But, according to Suze, Bob "endorsed it reluctantly. This was so he could do something privately, without getting involved as a spokesperson." He didn't want to lend his name to any more causes. Instead on this trip they took blankets and clothes to donate.

He was also going to take a bunch of copies of his new album with him, but since the freebies hadn't arrived in time Bob bought a couple of dozen copies of *The Times They Are A-Changin'*, as well as a few copies of *Freewheelin'*, to give out along the way.

Okay, back on the road. Dylan and Co. make a stop in Washington, D.C. It's an odd choice of destination for this bunch of hipsters, but it's on the way, so they check out the national necropolis of hypocrisy and statuary. An Egyptian city of the dead where everything that flows, rumbles, gushes, yelps, and leaps elsewhere in the USA *stops* (except the buck). Here, the whole wild energy of the country congeals: an elephant burial ground, where heroes turn to stone, log cabins are inflated to the size of post office Parthenons, and all the angels' wings are made of marble. Dylan and Co. stop and look at the Lincoln Memorial—Old Abe, the Great Emancipator, carved in marzipan frosting, sitting in his monster chair. It's a little like a class trip, but with a couple of tabs of amphetamine and a few hits of weed, stuff is starting to come into perspective. The sky, for instance. Can anything *be* that blue?

On the night of February 3, they stay in Charlottesville and the next morning head for Harlan County. Outside Abingdon, Virginia, they pick up a miner named Robert Swann. Still in his miner's sooty gear, the guy could be an allegorical figure in a folk song. Bob buys him a beer and gives him a copy of *Freewheelin'*. Whether he'd ever make it into a Bob Dylan song wasn't clear.

Hamish Sinclair is a model character from the radical minstrelsy in the old Woody Guthrie mold. But when Dylan and Co. get to Hazard,

Sinclair is caught up in the strike and can't get together and jam with Bob. Instead he sends them to the picket leader, Jason Combes, but Combes can neither pick nor sing, so what the hell? What's a cause without songs? That's the way Woody would've done it. Picket *and* sing. So they give them the clothes and are on the road again.

Bob set out to have adventures, to meet the people he sang about. If you went by the demographics of the folk horde, the world consisted of brakemen, bandits, cowboys, drifters, and moonshiners. On his journey through the land, however, only one of them did Bob espy. Aside from students and political activists, poets and schoolteachers, the tally came to one miner, one poet, and one grand old man. We want to see Bob interacting with skillet lickers and semi drivers and such, but it's Bob, y'know, so it's not like going on the road with Studs Terkel.

"We hit 46 pool halls from Augusta, Ga. to Berkeley, Calif. We talked to people in bars, miners. Talking to people, that's where it's at, man," Dylan claimed. Actually it was only three shows, Bob, and, as for mingling with groups of people, you've always had an aversion to that kind of thing. When too many fans crowd around him in a record store in Charlottesville, Virginia, he becomes alarmed. Oh well, you don't have to hang out in every roadside joint with lumberjacks and sailors to catch the drift. Dylan absorbs things through osmosis, plucks them out of the air like a coyote sniffing the wind.

At the wheel there's Maymudes, a kinda hipster Lurch, silent, focused in; Pablo (Paul Clayton), with his alchemical pharmacopoeia and his memories; and Karman, parsing sentences and riding shotgun. Back on the road, Bob has crawled into the rear of the station wagon and is hunched over a portable typewriter, antennae twitching, picking up signals like a radio insatiably tuning in to the frequencies of the Great Beast. In a manic phase ("Hey, Paul gimme another of those dexies") Pete Karman tells him he's raving. One of Dylan's lines that particularly irks Pete is: "The birds are chained to the sky. No one's free, even the birds are chained."

The birds-chained-to-the sky thing is a truly horrible metaphor. That's the problem with amphetamine: It's like a goblin's gift. But in a song, well, that's a different story altogether. This particular image ended up in "Ballad in Plain D" where it has a kind of goofy glory:

Ah, my friends from the prison, they ask unto me,
"How good, how good does it feel to be free?"

And I answer them most mysteriously,
"Are birds free from the chains of the skyway?"

They stay the night in a motel in Pinesville, Kentucky. The next day, February 5, they drive to Asheville, North Carolina, but decide against a pilgrimage to the birthplace of Thomas Wolfe, apparently. Bob wouldn't have had much in common with the old literary dinosaur Wolfe, with his sentimental notions and vast inchoate yearnings (well, maybe the inchoate yearnings part). Wolfe came from an age when writers still believed America's vastness could be contained in sprawling, unwieldy volumes (instead of via schizophrenia, hallucinogens, and compact discs). Although, like Dylan and Kerouac, Wolfe's works were ongoing autobiographical narratives, epics of American life as private quarrel. And like them, he too had made adolescent mythologizing into a literary style—the quest of the disenchanted innocent whose illusions are shattered but who goes on to pursue still others because what else is there to write about? Instead of paying homage to Wolfe, they shoot pool and go bowling at a black bowling alley (segregation still rules the South and will for some time). They go to a skin flick. Next day, they move on to Hendersonville, North Carolina.

There they visit Carl Sandburg's 245-acre spread under Sugarloaf Mountain. Goats grazing at the edge of the woods. Bob gets out of the car and announces to an astonished Mrs. Sandburg that he is a poet. He hopes that will get him in the door. Lillian trundles into the house, and out comes the old Cornhusker to see what all the fuss is about. The great man standing there unshaven in his wool plaid shirt and printer's green eyeshade in the front yard, Sandburg had made himself into a character, a gen-u-wine Meriken type. He not only recycled folk wisdom; he embodied it—at eighty-three, his own hero and dupe.

"You look like you are ready for anything. I would like to ask you about forty good questions," he says in the semi-Chaucerian diction of a Lake Superior iron miner. But he doesn't. It would've been a hell of a dialogue, though—a great cover story for *Esquire*: CARL SANDBURG INTERVIEWS BOB DYLAN. One of those crafty, surreal covers George Lois used to come up with—Sandburg and Dylan as *American Gothic*, say—making you take a backward step at the newsstand to check it out.

But there he is, a man of the people, old goat-farmer Carl, a literary Cincinnatus talking in his homespun way, a tumbleweed of a populist. Like a bookish Woody Guthrie, folksy adages, proverbs, and Will

Rogers—like turns of phrase spill out of him. Carl was a poet, biographer, balladeer, folklorist, and had been a housepainter, hobo, dishwasher, newspaperman, coal shoveler, and anarchist too. Now he was a goat farmer and general all-round folksy humbug. "Howdy, and good mornin' to ya, son. What brings you to this neck of the woods?" Even if he didn't recognize in Dylan a fellow genius, he was a genial old fellow.

"On the day God made Carl," said the photographer Edward Steichen, "he didn't do anything else but sit around and feel good."

Like Dylan, Sandburg was a shameless ham actor and impersonator of rustic types. Given the occasion, Carl would recite Norwegian dialect poems. Like Dylan he was an industrious recomposer of his sources. He swung high and low, mixing it up between the poetry of the vernacular—the way folks talked down at the feed store—and the spondeed and dactyled paper poets. Like Dylan, he played guitar and, like Bob, he'd been "submerged all his life in adolescence." Both of them were infatuated with the older, simpler America of legend before everything got so darn complicated—when you could still see the moral issues clear as a prairie dog's eye.

Sandburg had been an anarchist, a pacifist between the wars (I and II), and a lifelong dissenter ("I am with all rebels everywhere all the time and against all people who are satisfied"). He was a collector of folk songs and folklore (*The American Songbag*), a man of the folk, who sang of the lives of the people. "Steel mills slaughterhouses, cornfields, prairies, crowded cities, empty skies" spoke through Carl. His was a widescreen image of America, and he had no compunction about expounding on it. MGM had hired him to write an "epic film about the USA," the raw epic grist that Dylan would mill into his exceedingly fine talking powder. He was the uncoverer, an archaeologist of folklore oddity and intensity, a poetic anthropologist and hypnotist collector, like all the other great American maniacs, identifying himself with America.

Sandburg's poetry had been somewhat demoted and patronized by the time Dylan caught up with him. The New Criticism mocked his quaint verses about Chicago, "City of Big Shoulders," where "the fog comes/on little cat feet." Though he'd spoken to folks who'd spoken to old Abe, his biography of Lincoln wasn't getting much respect either. As Edmund Wilson wrote, "The cruelest thing that happened to Lincoln since he was shot by Booth has been to fall into the hands of Carl Sandburg."

But Dylan wouldn't have cared a fig about literary quibbling of this stripe, and didn't in all probability know anything about it, and in any case had a soft spot for this kind of hokum. He did a fair amount of it himself. But at the same time, Carl's boy-howdy act must've given him pause. He must've felt that, gee, this is what might have become of me if I'd stuck with the Woody Guthrie impersonations. This is what happens when you don't change your act: You end up an octogenarian faux rustic. For someone as mercurial as Bob, that wasn't too appealing.

Bob presents Sandburg with a copy of *Times*, and starts telling Carl about how Woody Guthrie talked him up all the time. Sandburg is gratified to hear it, but he isn't going to let Bob into his study to see where he writes his stuff (Dylan's next request). And that's it; the encounter is over.

Depending on who asked him and when, Karman has different impressions of how it went. To Robert Shelton in 1985, he said that when they left, "We had a definite feeling of disappointment, mainly because Sandburg had never heard of Bobby. As I recall, during the rest of the trip Sandburg's name was never mentioned again. Dylan sank into one of his quiet funks." Three years later Karman tells a revised version to Bob Spitz: "Without looking at each other, I could tell we were equally amazed. I distinctly felt like there was a passage of honor between the young prince and the old king. It was a sincere, no-bullshit, no show-biz moment, and we all noted it respectfully."

In Flat Rock, North Carolina, the group buys fireworks. On the way to Georgia, Bob's sitting in the back of the powder-blue station wagon, conjecturing, free-associating—something he has an uncanny talent for. He could spin words into endless combinations.

The conversation drifts off and they look at the shotgun shacks and the old black women and little kids on the porches with the rusty refrigerators, the piles of tires, and they look back at them just as curiously as Trobriand Islanders must've looked at Malinowski.

On February 6, they reach Atlanta by nightfall. The following day they pick up grass mailed to them at the post office. That night Dylan gives the first of his concerts at Emory University. Everybody is dressed up except for Bob in his tatterdemalion traveling clothes. The students know almost all the songs from their opening phrases (something that would be a little harder to do at Dylan's later concerts).

College towns were Dylan's natural environment, and it was college kids who spread the gospel of Bob. One of the side benefits of these kind of trips was that you got to hang out with like-minded heads in various towns and cities around the country: guitar pickers, bohemians, folk mamas, homegrown existentialists, dewy maidens, and college-educated misfits who read Marcuse and *Pogo*. "One of the feelings of it was that you were part of a very elite special group of people that was outside and downtrodden," Dylan told Doon Arbus in 1997.

"You felt like you were part of a different community," he continues, "a more secretive one. And this community spread out across America. New York had plenty of it, but you go to a city like Philadelphia or, same thing, go to St. Louis, go to Columbus or go to, you know, to Houston, go to Austin, Atlanta, every little city you went to, if you knew who to call, what to look for, you could find . . . like-minded people. That's been destroyed. I don't know what destroyed it. Some people say that it's still there, I hope it is. I know, in my mind, I'm still a member of a secret community. I might be the only one, you know?"

This was the Beat ideal—a community of intellectual outsiders. But it was an ideal that the mass bohemianism of the '60s would blow up and wreck because, for one thing, it wasn't going to be a secret too much longer, and it wasn't the small elite group of insiders anymore. Two, three years, it would all be gone. And Bob would be one of the major causes of its demise.

ON INTO HAUNTED MISSISSIPPI, BIRTH OF THE DELTA BLUES—ALSO home of slavery, segregation (still), and the place where Medgar Evers had been murdered the previous summer.

On their route, they begin to hear loony roadside buzz of American towns with their biblical, industrial, Indian names: Ensley, Arial, Chunky, Cuba/Boligee, Commerce, Dahlonega/Boiling Springs, Demopolis, Walhalla/La Grange, Enterprise, Ponchatoula/Starkville, Villa Rica, Tuscaloosa.

On the radio, Dinah Shore croons, "Drive your Chevrolet, through the USA, America's the greatest land of all." Meanwhile, Kerouac asks, "I mean, man, whither goest thou America, in thy shining car in the night."

And right there in the middle of their journey, on the night of February 9 outside of Meridian, Mississippi, lightning hits the telephone wires. Meridian is the birthplace of Jimmie Rodgers, the singing brakeman, father of country music, whose yodels Bob had used to comic effect on "All I Really Want to Do" and "It Ain't Me, Babe." It is the perfect spot for an epiphany.

Dylan begins to type, "Electric light still struck like arrows. . . ." Lightning is an agent of change in classic American literature; it is the storm after which everything changes—the lightning storm in *Moby-Dick*, the storm in *Huckleberry Finn*, and the one in *On the Road*, just outside New Orleans. "Lightning that liquefies the bones of the world," William Burroughs called it.

The scenes in "Chimes of Freedom" are lit up as if by strobe light—the way the Bible was written, they say, in brilliantly illuminated pictures. Dylan uses a cinematic method of writing, like Kerouac's—with slow motion, jump cuts, and freeze frames.

> *Tolling for the rebel, tolling for the rake*
> *Tolling for the luckless, the abandoned an' forsaked*
> *Tolling for the outcast, burnin' constantly at stake.*
> *An' we gazed upon the chimes of freedom flushing*

The song is a hallucinatory catalog, cast in anaphoric lines, a rhetorical device used by Shakespeare, Dickens, Charles Wesley (and innumerable other hymnists), and long favored by Fourth of July orators. Old Abe Lincoln was partial to it: "We cannot dedicate—we cannot consecrate—we cannot hallow," etc. But in "Chimes of Freedom" the repetition isn't used to hammer home a point (God's or Abe's), instead, like the fading sound of bells in the distance, the tolling lines take on an elegiac quality, like the sad "Bells of Rhymney" by the Welsh poet Idris Davies and set to music by Pete Seeger. It's more of a knell than a chime, really, as he casts a compassionate eye on "the countless confused, accused, misused... /An' for every hung up person in the whole wide universe."

The song is an anthem, if not a hymn—a hymn blessing the meek, the mad, and the lost. It's Bob's last protest song (for a while, at least)—if it can even be called that—and really a catechism linking everything together and fusing it in the tradition of Guthrie's "This Land Is Your Land" and "The Grand Coulee Dam." The prototypes for "Chimes of Freedom" are two songs left off his previous album: "Lay Down Your Weary Tune" and "Paths of Victory," which catalogs images in much the same way as "Chimes" ("the evening train was rollin'/the hummin' of its wheels"), but where these had been personal reflections, "Chimes" is empathetic and inclusive.

A song of transformation, where lightning flashes mutate into pealing bells, electricity fuses Blake, Rhymney, Guthrie, Whitman, and the Sermon on the Mount into a melancholy anthem of the outcast. "Chimes of Freedom" is transitional—a bridge to take him from his previous incarnation to his next one. He drops it from his repertoire by the end of the year—perhaps it sounds too much like an anthem—and with it he dispatches the folk prophet. It's the American way: sloughing off the old—Old Europe, yesterday's papers, last year's model—and growing a new head in its place. Everything is disposable for the transient, the ramblin' man, the drifter, the traveling salesman. Out there on highway 55-N, a new Dylan hatches, one ready to cross over into new territory. Electricity brings this Frankenstein to life.

"Chimes of Freedom" isn't his farewell to folk music as such—that he never abandoned—just his farewell to his role as leader of folk protest as practical solution. And if we're to believe Bob, the whole thing—this singer-songwriter, protest prophet business—got rolling in the first place because he wanted to get his songs published in *Broadside*. That's what he was telling people, anyway.

This, of course, is Disingenuous Dylan Pose #1. What a farce! Contradict everything, even common sense. Even if your responses fly in the face of what you are trying to get across in the song. Not that Dylan has ever been known for giving straight answers to direct questions—but still. At the bottom of it all was a misunderstanding. Dylan isn't so much a political creature as he is the God-haunted seeker after moral truths. And given the temper of the times, moral and political issues were intersecting thick and fast in the mid-'60s. The dissent and rage in his songs wasn't so much a reflection of activism as of an almost biblical sense of morality.

Dylan had moved on into subjectivity, private anarchy, and aestheticism. There were also many other reasons he wished to sever his tethers to the folk movement, the principal one being that it *was* a movement. After all, the idea that there could be a solution—the underlying theme of all protest songs—implied compromise. Dylan no longer believed in causes or political solutions—or in groups. He wasn't going to join their club. They'd have to join his. He opted out, somewhat the way Kerouac had done. He was weary of the folkie rhetoric, the old concessioned images of himself, the smugness of his role as the prince of protest. The humorlessness of those people in the folk movement! Dylan, too, took himself in deadly earnest, but his introspection burned away most of the self-righteousness.

Dylan would henceforth use folk mythology lyrically, draw on the folk vision for its poetry and moral core, as a sort of bible of American lore. Our granary of national mythology teeming with bizarre incident, doomed characters, and strangeness, which Dylan would animate for the rest of his career.

Dylan and Co. pass through Oxford, Mississippi, home of William Faulkner, one of the writers Dylan wanted to meet. However, when they got there he didn't actually seek him out. Perhaps the encounter with Sandburg had soured Bob on meetings with remarkable men. Besides, Faulkner might have proved to be far more ornery than the good-natured Sandburg.

On their way to New Orleans, Kerouac and Co. had stopped in Algiers, Louisiana, to see Burroughs and found his hopped-up wife, the doomed Joan, raking lizards off a dead tree. Dylan and Co. drove right into the city. It is Monday night; the next day is Fat Tuesday. They must've planned their visit to coincide with Mardi Gras, when none of the normal rules applies.

February 10, Mardi Gras eve. They are lucky to find the single room they get, and all four of them pile in together. They wander around for a while and return to the hotel. Pete goes out prowling; the others fall out. Roaming the bars, Karman runs into a stripper who knew Hugh Romney (a.k.a. Wavy Gravy, hipster comedian of the Hog Farm) and brings her back to the hotel. Karman is always depicted as the uptight one of the bunch, but on this particular night he seems to be the only swinger in the group. The others are outraged that he's brought a hooker back with him.

The next day is Mardi Gras. Still groggy from little sleep and the noise of the parade going on from early morning, they pour themselves out onto the street where, by and by, they run into Joe B. Stewart, poet and high school English teacher from Mobile.

"You could see they were exhausted as they tumbled out onto Bourbon Street," says Stewart. "And we were pretty wiped out ourselves. We had been up for five days and nights. It had been sweet and I was open for anything. Standing at the second bar of La Casa, I would not have been surprised if Walt Disney had come through the door. I looked at Dylan's little pale face, which was set in a serious scowl with eyes darting back and forth. . . . Waiting to see if he would be recognized."

This happens a second time. Finally the third time they pass Dylan they have a young girl in tow, perhaps causing him to stop and apologize. "You sure have long hair," she says to Dylan. "Yes," he says, "and I'm going to let my hair grow to the streets and write my poems and shout them from the top of buildings."

New Orleans, home of the House of the Rising Sun (once Dylan's signature song) and the high priestess of voodoo, Madame Laveau. It is the mystic port, the charged space of hoodoo, mojo, and gris-gris, the original magnetic crossroads where demons bearing their mesmerizing cadences poured in from the Caribbean. Here is a witch's brew of musics: Cajun, zydeco, blues, Creole street cries, R&B, jazz, gospel. Fats Domino, Little Richard (teenage Bob's idol), Jelly Roll Morton, Louis Armstrong, Kid Ory, Rabbit Brown (one of Bob's favorite guitar players from *The Anthology Archive*), Guitar Slim, Frankie Ford ("Sea Cruise"), Mahalia Jackson, the Meters, the Neville Brothers, and Professor Longhair. Out of the stew came rock 'n' roll. New Orleans is almost a foreign enclave in Louisiana, but, like everything alien in the USA, it had been assimilated, turned into a kind of Creole Disneyland: the tawdry surrealism of Bourbon Street, the Comus parade, King Zulu, Storyville, juba dancers, cemeteries on tourist itineraries, and streetcars named Desire.

Drunk and a little stoned, you walk outside. Day-Glo Watusis and transvestite tubes of toothpaste are dancing in the street; it's freaky and exotic, but you aren't really that amazed. You've seen all this in dozens of movies; every movie set in New Orleans features a bizarre and grotesque Mardi Gras parade. No, what really twists your head around is finding five guys on five different corners doing five different Bob Dylans.

That's what happens when you get famous; you start running into yourself. Selves you'd discarded, flinging the husks in the wind, are popping up all over the place. You've traveled thirteen hundred miles to get away from the Baby-Let-Me-Follow-You-Down kid, the Blowin'-in-the-Wind boy, the vindictive Masters-of-War prophet, the Corrina-Corrina coffeehouse cat. And here you are pursued by living, breathing, strumming simulacra of yourself. It's like a horror show, and Dylan understands the way Kerouac must've felt, walking down Grant Street and finding fifteen bongo-beating, Gauloise-smoking, wine-jug-guzzling versions of himself sitting on the curb.

The ragtag group goes back to La Casa looking for some local cheap thrills. They're on their way to a Greek bar someone says is cool.

The jukebox gets cranked up (Cue: Lee Dorsey's "Ya Yas"). Soggy dollar bills and quarters on the bar, and the words they're tossing around get slurred. There's a lot of drunken shouting. Bob pulls out a Learn-to-Be-an-Air-Conditioning-Repairman matchbook out of his pocket with an address scrawled on the inside flap—some party he's been invited to. But once outside the bar and out on the street, they get pulled into the wake of the Comus parade, passing around a bottle of wine, watching the black flambeaux carriers floating by and jumping for the beads and doubloons that the paraders are throwing. Bob regales the strangers with tales of all the great Southern writers he's met on his journey. Four days after the encounter and he's already rewriting the Sandburg incident.

The night passes with Dylan careening from bar to bar, wandering into people's houses uninvited, rambling on about Faulkner, flypaper, Tootsie Rolls, and the meaning of life.

As Dylan disappears into the dawn, the schoolteacher thinks, "This guy won't last long; he'll either burn himself out or get himself in some stupid accident the way James Dean did."

Richard Fariña would say much the same thing after Dylan's concert in Berkeley ten days later. What is it with Bob and the rebel without a cause? We'd have to wait another two years and one motorcycle accident to find out. Dean is one of Bob's idols, and he's made two pilgrimages to Dean's hometown of Fairmount, Indiana. But in what way was he like James Dean? Bob wasn't even driving the car on this trip; they wouldn't let him (maybe because Bob constantly talked about Dean). Even Kerouac had compared himself to Dean, calling himself "the James Dean of bebop prosodists." And if there was going to be a James Dean of folk music, Bob would be it.

As for Stewart, he gets a mention in the jacket notes to *Another Side of Bob Dylan* (in which he is referred to as Joe B. Stuart), wherein Bob records his parenthetical Louisiana Baedeker brain-alley ramble:

> (this time. king rex
> blesses me with plastic beads
> an' toot whistles
> paper rings an' things.
> royal street.
> bourbon street
> st. claude an' esplanade
> pass an' pull
> everything out of shape
> joe b. stuart
> white southern poet
> holds me up
> we charge through casa
> blazin' jukebox

gumbo overflowin'
get kicked out of colored bar
streets jammed
hypnotic stars explode
in louisiana murder night
everything's wedged
arm in arm
stoned galore
must see you in mobile then
down governor nichel
an' gone)

The phantasmagoric imagery of Mardi Gras would infest Dylan's songs for the next four years. Mardi Gras, like the medieval twelve days of Christmas, is a festival when the world is turned upside down. Servants become masters; women proposition men. A mock king is elected, along with a Bishop of Fools and an Abbot of Unreason. A charter society forms for Dylan's cast of outcasts, where drifters, hoboes, hookers, and junkies become the unshriven saints of hipsterdom.

Driving west from New Orleans Dylan begins to write "Mr. Tambourine Man." According to Bob, most of his songs arrive fully formed in his head. But "Mr. Tambourine Man" begins on the road and takes weeks to finish—perhaps because it is the polestar song around which he would spin his next persona. No one takes him seriously when he says it isn't a drug song, primarily because of the "smoke rings of my mind" and "take me on a trip" business (even though his first acid trip is a month hence). But while it's unlikely that someone who'd never done drugs (or read Rimbaud) would've *written* this song, to make it into a mere druggy song *about* a drug (marijuana) is, in effect, to dismiss it.

If it's about anything, it's about the self-transforming power of music—an ode to music itself, to its releasing energy. Dylan himself is the newly hatched Mr. Tambourine Man, as he writes and sings himself into his next incarnation. In Dylan's mythology, the song *is* the singer, and it's hard to say which generates which.

The '49 Hudson traveling across the United States, like Huck's raft going down the Mississippi, the *Pequod*, and Rimbaud's drunken boat—all are symbolic craft. Bob sits on the verge, like Ishmael the top man in his crow's nest, surveying the horizon, pondering the "problem of the universe," an epiphany that will change everything. Well, pop music anyway. Which actually is a pretty major shift in the national psyche, given that by 1964 pop had become a parallel universe.

He sings a few songs, and then it's on to Dallas on February 12, only a couple of months after Kennedy's assassination. They do their own Warren report, checking out the Texas Book Depository and the grassy knoll. Sight lines are calibrated, theories are developed, horror expressed. But don't forget that other Dylan: the loner, nihilist, and, of course, agent provocateur Dylan who had stunned the Emergency Civil Liberties Committee by identifying with Lee Harvey Oswald.

On February 15 they arrive in Denver. Dylan hangs out at the Denver Folklore Center, visits the coffee grottoes of his youth, and in the afternoon he plays at the Denver Civic Auditorium, performing "Chimes of Freedom" for the first time.

The following day he takes his friends on an hour's drive from Denver up to Central City, where he'd worked briefly in the summer of 1960 at the Gilded Garter. Now Bob has a chance to demonstrate to his companions that at least a part of his past is true—or mostly. The Gilded Garter was part of Bob's Western honky-tonk legend—Bob Dillon hangin' out at the saloon with galoots and prospectors. But in reality Central City was a Western tourist town and the Gilded Garter no more the genuine West than that Klondike set, the one on the Canadian TV show *Quest* where he'd performed earlier that year.

Dylan's even capable of getting out his box of pastels and sketching a little south-of-the-border medley as in his 1976 "Romance in Durango" straight out of a sightseer's brochure from the '40s: "Past the Aztec ruins and the ghosts of our people/Hoofbeats like castanets on stone." Or is it Dylan's re-creation of a '40s down-Mexico-way song?

That's the funny thing about Dylan: For him, facts don't alter images. Driving across the USA (even in 1964), you're not going to be able to retain too many illusions about the mythic American landscape. A new fast-food joint or a new Holiday Inn room, like some alien pod, is being created every twenty minutes. Look at existentialist photographer Lee Friedlander's urban nightmare landscape *Mobile, Alabama* from the same period, and it's enough to make you want to shoot yourself. It includes all the kitsch of rampant American enterprise: interstates, franchises, suburban sprawl, strip malls.

But none of this highway squalor seems to have made much of a dent in Dylan's mythic America, with its tall-tale characters and sanctuaries of upwelling music and strangeness. Of course, keep in mind that except for New Orleans and the concert dates, Dylan didn't actually get out and *walk* around these places too often. "Bob never wanted to stop," Maymudes recalled. "He was mostly just processing." He just passed through them in his bubble, holding séances with the American past. He would travel through Europe the same way in his mental carriage in *Eat the Document* two years hence.

It isn't that he didn't *see* the brash hucksterism and con-artist counterfeit of the USA; it is precisely what fueled the animus of his mid-'60s rants against the tacky, commodity-crazed American culture. It's just that the numinous geography of the past existed in another dimension.

As they leave Denver, "I Want to Hold Your Hand" comes on the radio. It's already #1 on the American charts. The Beatles had arrived the previous week and caused pandemonium. A group of goofy-looking limeys had built a brand-new rock 'n' roll engine by fusing Everly Brothers harmonies onto a twist-and-shoutish rhythm chassis.

Dylan may have dismissed the Beatles to journalist Al Aronowitz as "bubblegum." A lot of other musicians had made the same mistake—and not just bebop saints either. Tin Pan Alley saw the Beatles as another fad, like coonskin caps. Still, in his heart of hearts Dylan knew the Brits had gone up the mountain and stolen the holy fire of R&B while the Yanks dozed.

"We were driving through Colorado," Dylan said in 1971. "We had the radio on, and eight of the Top 10 songs were Beatles songs.... 'I Wanna Hold Your Hand,' and all those early ones. They were doing things nobody was doing. Their chords were outrageous, just outrageous, and their harmonies made it all valid. You could only do that with other musicians.... I knew they were pointing the direction of where music had to go."

ONE OF THE REASONS FOR TRAVELING ACROSS THE USA WAS TO WRITE the big book, the great American novel that would capture the sullen heart of the woolly mammoth. And Dylan was writing one, and would be writing it for years. It had many names along the way, but *Tarantula* was what it was titled in the end. It was called a novel and still is because it's too long to call it anything else; you can't squeeze the USA into a villanelle or a sonnet. Epic is the only way to talk about the USA. You need widescreen, CinemaScope, VistaVision. Look at Whitman's *Song of the Open*

Road, Guthrie's *Hard Travelin'*, Wolfe's *Look Homeward, Angel*, Kerouac's *On the Road*, Richard Hell's *Go Now*.

Tarantula began in a freaked imitation of *On the Road*, a rambling, hallucinated travelogue (an excerpt appeared in *Sing Out!* in June 1965 entitled *Walk Down a Crooked Highway*). But Dylan's novel would be different from the wanderings of St. Jack. We needed a new book, a new way of interpreting reality, one that would incorporate folktales, movies, characters from the blues, cartoons, and mental history. America being a made-up country, it periodically has to be figured out all over again—retooled, reimagined—and when Americans get serious about themselves as artists they take on the big subject: the USA. It's what every megalomaniacal American artist is after: to swallow the whole continent in one gulp and sound their barbaric yawp over the rooftops of the world.

A few well-known maniacs who've tried: Mark Twain, Walt Whitman, Herman Melville, Thomas Wolfe, Gertrude Stein, Hart Crane, John Ford, Woody Guthrie, John Dos Passos, Norman Mailer, Ken Kesey. They get so far into their subject they end up confusing themselves with it. All of them want to get everything in, to bottle the continent, as in the nineteenth-century San Francisco poem "The Western Man":

Go roll a prairie up like cloth,
Drink the Mississippi dry
Put Allegheny in your hat,
A steamboat in your eye.

Americans always wanted to re-create the promised freedom of the frontier and the cowboy myth—that hypothetical country yet to be inhabited. Even when it's been paved over and malled out, we're all looking to light out for the territory.

Somewhere toward the beginning of 1965, after writing *Tarantula* but many years before publication—at Joan Baez's place in Carmel, in Woodstock at Grossman's, and in hotels in the UK—he realized it wasn't what he really wanted to do anyway; instead, he invented the condensed six-minute mind movie "Like a Rolling Stone." The road-map name poems from *Tarantula* lead to Tiny Montgomery and all those other personification place-name characters, the tall-tale characters, and the underworld monikers—Lem the Clam and Lady Suntan—and fed into the quirky tableaux of *The Basement Tapes*.

But our trip isn't over yet. Our group is on its way to the promised land and travels the covered wagon trail through Grand Junction, Colorado, across the desert to Reno. Then it's over the Rockies where "the wind it was howlin' and the snow was outrageous," across the Sierra Madre to California, and on to San Francisco where Dean Moriarty and Sal Paradise ended their journey in *On the Road*.

Finally they get to the edge of the world: "No more land!" Dean yelled. "We can't go any further 'cause there ain't no more land!" And once you run out of road, there's only one place to go: where Alph the sacred word river runs through caverns measureless to man, down to a sunless sea.

After *On the Road*, all the trips across the USA would be interior. From now on you'd have to travel inside your head through a hallucinated America. The new geography would be an internal landscape populated by Indians, movie stars, outlaws, gamblers—ghost dancers of the delirious continent. If Kerouac had wanted to possess the USA almost physically, Dylan set out to ingest it psychically, an intoxicating brew that would inspire his most sublime songs and almost kill him in the process.

8 The Hallucinated Alphabet

When I began to read an author I very soon caught the tune of the song beneath the words, which in each author is distinct from that of every other; and while I was reading, and without knowing what I was doing, I hummed it over, hurrying the words, or slowing them down, or suspending them, in order to keep time with the rhythm of the notes, as one does in singing, where in compliance with the shape of the tune one often delays for a long time before coming to the last syllable of a word.

—MARCEL PROUST, *CONTRE SAINTE-BEUVE*

I T IS THE SPRING OF 1964 AND SOMETHING IS UP WITH BOB. THE folk police can smell it. Dylan is straying from the flock. Although you could hardly have asked for a more party line protest album than *The Times They Are A-Changin'*—a few of the songs were almost embarrassingly doctrinaire—Dylan himself is already chafing under the obligations it imposed on him. Spokesman of his generation! He wasn't having any of that. Mr. Tambourine Man had been born on that road trip and there was no turning back. By the time folks were singing "The Times They are A-Changin'," Dylan was already singing "Mr. Tambourine Man" in little Village clubs. Even on *Times* there were clear indications of drift: love songs (the sublime "North Country Blues"), existential angst songs ("One Too Many Mornings"), and downright surrealistic dreams ("When the Ship Comes In").

Oh the fishes will laugh
As they swim out of the path
And the seagulls they'll be smiling.

Sure, it's a political song, but not quite in the sense we usually mean. And those stream-of-consciousness liner notes, "11 Outlined Epitaphs"! What did he mean by "there is no right wing"? This was heresy, somewhat buried, but the cognoscenti were worried. The worst part about Dylan's forsaking the sacred folk faith was that the Dylan virus—the genius and energy of his protest songs—had spread the word with more eloquence and imagination than anyone since Woody Guthrie. He'd invaded the campuses and become the voice of the emerging radical left. Dylan was their evangelist, so why these disturbing signs? Though he still looks like a folknik, he is no longer behaving like one. Hard-core folkies see the carpetbagger, the defector coming out in him, and go on the attack. But Bob's got friends in low places. In March 1964, Johnny Cash tells *Sing Out!*: SHUT UP . . . AND LET HIM SING!

On May 17, Dylan performs at the Royal Festival Hall in London. Following a concert in Paris he stays with French singer Hugues Aufray, where he meets Nico, future singer with the Velvet Underground and, later, neomedievalist chanter. Dylan plays her "It Ain't Me, Babe" and writes "I'll Keep It with Mine" for her. He vacations in Greece where he writes many of the songs for his next album, *Another Side of Bob Dylan*.

In a single one-night session starting around seven o'clock in the evening of June 9 and wrapping up at one thirty the same night—Dylan pretty sloshed by this point—he records fourteen songs (many in multiple takes), eleven of which will appear on *Another Side of Bob Dylan*. The session is pretty loose and chaotic, with plenty of wine and children running around. Producer Tom Wilson keeps the takes down to three (or even partial takes, when Dylan would have been happy to redo the entire song), running as tight a ship as possible under the circumstances, and Dylan goes along. He wants to prove the point to friends and invited guests that he could cut an album in one session. Like Mozart or Einstein or somebody, he was capable of superhuman feats.

In July 1964, Bob makes his second appearance at the Newport Folk Festival. His I-couldn't-care-less attitude exudes menacing indifference to the folk oligarchy. He's even too stoned to sing his famous stoned song, "Mr. Tambourine Man." Although his desertion has barely begun, he is already being labeled an apostate. His behavior is seen as self-destructive in the James Dean mode. Still, there are all-night jam sessions with Johnny Cash and Joan Baez at the Viking Motor Inn in Newport, reviving his love of country music.

Later that summer he takes a room over the Café Espresso in Woodstock. With frenzied automatism, he continues writing *Tarantula* and plunges on into his trance-induced lyricism. Dylan is a possessed scribbler, writing on envelopes, napkins, on the backs of cigarette packs. He uses pictures as his inspiration, pinning up postcards, photos torn from magazines, reproductions of paintings, images of jungles burning, and old peddlers.

In August, *Another Side of Bob Dylan* is released. Whichever side you thought he was on, he's no longer there. If you'd signed on to march with Bob in the parade of liberty on his previous album, you could get yourself quite worked up when you put this version of Dylan on your turntable. It wasn't just different from *Times*; it was pretty much its opposite. Not only did it lack one protest song (you could only call "Chimes of Freedom" a protest song in the sense that *Moby-Dick* is a whaling manual), but it also contained a renunciation of protest songs in his letter of resignation to the folk community, "My Back Pages."

On "It Ain't Me, Babe," Dylan fuses the personal and political into a new form of love ballad that is more radical than most political anthems, and makes previous protest songs seem one-dimensional and tinny. And this, as much as his shift in attitude, is what enrages his former fans. It is as if he's vanished into another dimension. It is the stance of the scathing hipster that will signal his next phase. In "Lay Down Your Weary Tune," recorded for *Times* (but not released until twenty-two years later on *Biograph* in October 1985), we can see Dylan departing from the folk curriculum entirely, plunging headlong in his own drunken boat:

The ocean wild like an organ played
The seaweed's wove its stands.
The crashin' waves like cymbals clashed
Against the rocks and sands.

In August he meets with the Beatles at the Delmonico Hotel in New York. His early fascination with them came from his mishearing of "I Want to Hold Your Hand." When they sang "I can't hide, I can't hide," Dylan heard "I get high, I get high." And so when he visits the band at their hotel, he brings along some joints and, so the story goes, introduces them to pot, which leads to World Turning Point #2. Paul, like his New Testament namesake, has a vision: "It's in seven layers. You know, the cosmos. . . ."

Dylan plays a Halloween concert at the New York Philharmonic. By now he's become an avid consumer of amphetamines (his speed diet amps up his natural paranoia). The program notes include his diatribe, "Advice for Geraldine on Her Miscellaneous Birthday," attacking his attackers, real and imaginary:

> needless t' say, these people
> who don't need you will start
> hating themselves for needing t' talk
> about you. then you yourself will
> start hating yourself for causing so
> much hate. as you can see, it will
> all end in one great gunburst.

By the fall of 1964 he's made his first million. George Harrison advises him to get off the street and into a hotel fast. Dylan protests that he doesn't want to become a "rock star millionaire freak," but in that he has no choice.

His two dueling ambitions—to be a successful pop singer and to be taken seriously as an artist—seem to be as incompatible as his fusion of folk music and rock 'n' roll. Anything *that* popular in American culture was by definition debased and a compromise. Folkies defined themselves by their exclusivity and detachment from mainstream society.

That *other side* of Bob really rankled the true believers. In November, Irwin Silber's "Open Letter to Bob Dylan" in *Sing Out!* criticizes Dylan's aesthetic narcissism. In December, Paul Wolfe's attack in *Broadside* accuses him of being a trickster, hypocrite, and exploiter of his audience. He'd sucked out the entire contents of Bleecker Hollow, ruthlessly plundering their paperbacks and hallowed record collections, as well as their chord changes, plaintive tunes, folk music archives, existential jive, underground movies, and avant-garde theater. He'd panned the gold and left the rest.

By the end of 1964 the new Dylan needed a new persona, a new character for the new voice to speak through: the self-created alpha wolf who had neither parents nor precedents.

"DYLAN HAD A GREAT HUNGER," SAYS PETE STAMPFEL. "HE WAS VERY ambitious even when he was impersonating the feckless vagabond singer. That driving ambition had created a revolution in pop music—he'd almost single-handedly made folk songs popular music in America. That would have been thought impossible in 1961: turning a cultish genre—folk singing—into a popular musical form in America by the summer of 1963."

In *Billboard*'s Top 20 of that year there were more folk rock songs—Peter, Paul and Mary's "Puff, The Magic Dragon" and "Blowin' in the Wind," the Village Stompers' (instrumental) "Washington Square"—than there were surf songs ("Surfin' USA" by the Beach Boys and "Wipe Out" by the Surfaris). In the Top 100 there were a couple more: the Rooftop Singers' "Walk Right In" and Trini Lopez's "If I Had a Hammer," but the folk contributions were pretty tame in comparison with the pop hits. They were up against the likes of "He's So Fine" by the Chiffons, "Blue Velvet" by Bobby Vinton, "Finger Tips II" by Stevie Wonder, "My Boyfriend's Back" by the Angels, "I'm Leaving It Up to You," by Dale and Grace, and "Deep Purple" by Nino Tempo and April Stevens. Still, folk rock was the latest fad on the scene, even if Bob was no longer interested.

The Byrds were doing Dylan brilliantly, and even Sonny and Cher were covering his songs, as were dozens of other singers and groups. Dylan had unexpectedly become a pop artist with all its unforeseen consequences, good and bad.

His influence on Brit hipoisie (the Beatles and the Stones) ultimately shifts the direction of rock 'n' roll (and its sinister twin, the music business). With "Mr. Tambourine Man," Dylan opens the door to surreal poetic lyrics in pop music. Bob Lind's "Elusive Butterfly of Love" is an unfortunate example, with its mawkish "Cross my dreams with nets of wonder." Dylan also brings a philosophical melancholy into pop music, from John Lennon's morbid middle-eight verse "Life is very short and there's no time..." to McCartney's breakup-with-Jane-Asher song, "We Can Work It Out." Some other Dylanesque songs include the Beatles' "You've Got to Hide Your Love Away," "Taxman," "Nowhere Man," "I'm a Loser," "A Day in the Life," "The Walrus," and "Come Together," as well as the Stones' "Jigsaw Puzzle," "Get Offa My Cloud," and "Parachute Woman." Feel free to add your own.

The formulaic nature of the pop love song was not that different from the prescribed nature of protest songs. It reduced romance to clichés, "I love you, you love me, ookie dookie do," as Dylan put it. But while the protest movement saw its agenda as a noble cause, its lyrics were often as simplistic and generic as pop songs. Their method depended on rudimentary and repeated causal connections—capitalist greed, war-mongers, racist outrages—between injustice and its social causes. Which is why critics like Jon Landau have seen protest songs, even those of Dylan, as a higher form of kitsch. It was becoming pretty clear that folk rock (that's what the new fusion was being called) had taken folk music from edgy balladry to protest to shameless pop and that was nowhere a coolfry like Dylan wanted to find himself. The popularity of folk rock had led to the demise of the lone acoustic guitar singer; patrons at coffeehouses were now complaining there was no beat!

And the commercialism was rampant. The American Dairy Association even promoted milk products with a full-page newspaper advertisement that depicted a young housewife in her kitchen, strumming a guitar. The headline asked, WISH YOU COULD WRITE A PROTEST SONG ABOUT YOUR FAMILY'S EATING HABITS? Soon there would be folksinger paper dolls, a Bally Hootenanny pinball machine, and a Hootenanny candy bar.

Dylan's success had thrust him from folk and protest into the cycle of pop culture—a world, with its disposable heroes, that was far more brutal than the marginal world of folk or protest. His initial ambition, like that of many other earnest folksingers, had been to immerse himself in the mystery of Appalachian ballads and the country blues. Now he found himself at the center of the despised commercial pop music industry. Dylan had wanted success, but his newfound celebrity involved him in irresolvable complications. With such conflicting motivations he needed to create a new way of expressing these ambiguities—but at this point he wasn't sure what form this would take. Every year or so since Dylan arrived in New York he had molted and shed his former skin, and his shifts coincided with the shifting mood of the times. Along with Dylan, the generation of the '60s was seeking to answer the question of identity, finding a story that would somehow explain who we were, how it all came to be, and what was to come. And how better to find oneself than with a little artificial energy?

"It was during the New York blackout," says Peter Stampfel. "The lights went out in '65. Antonia and I went to the Kettle of Fish and Dylan was there with Grossman. Out of the blue Dylan asked me, 'Have you ever taken any amphetamine?' 'Well, yeah, Bob, of course.' Then he said, 'Well, see, I decided I don't want to write any more songs. I wanna write a book. So I took some amphetamine and decided I was finally gonna write this book, but what came out was "Like a Rolling Stone."'"

It is a compressed novel, a fragmentary rant with biting descriptions of a dizzy socialite. With "Like a Rolling Stone" Dylan notoriously broke the three-minute barrier in rock music, and, though hardly as surreal as his later songs, what it implied would involve a heady brew of innuendo, put-down, menace, and bohemian snobbery.

Dylan was now a novelist who had jumped into his own book, with Bob as the often unreliable, frequently unstable narrator. In Dylan's universe the personality of the singer is central; the narrator of the song is as much a character as any of the people in it. Whenever the style of his songs changed, Dylan created a new persona to sing them. But Dylan's previous incarnations had been either uncanny channeling or that much-resented role, "voice of his generation." His next phase, the newly hatched hipster, would blow everybody's mind.

The Fender Stratocaster (with sunburst finish and rosewood neck) on which Dylan infamously played his electric set at the 1965 Newport Folk Festival—because that was the guitar his idol, Buddy Holly, played.

9 Bob Gets Wired

Open, graves! You, the dead of the picture galleries,
corpses behind screens, in palaces, castles, and monaster-
ies! Here stands the fabulous keeper of the keys to all
times, who knows how to press the most artful lock
and invites you to step into the midst of the world of
today . . .

—GUILLAUME APOLLINAIRE

"THE NEXT THING IS: BOB IS BIGGER, BIGGER, BIGGER," SAYS
Myra Friedman. "I remember him coming down the hallway
in shades and with his hair all curly and the cowboy boots,
and it sure wasn't the kid I'd seen hanging around the office.
He was hot-looking. Sometimes it's really hard looking at stars, whether
it is really coming from inside or whether suddenly this big deal, this
patina, has settled over them. But anyway, he looked great. One of the
great rock looks of all time."

This is the iconic image of Dylan—the shades, the polka-dot fencing
shirts, the curly Gorgon locks—that fused so mesmerizingly with the
music. There he was out there on the street, in some hipster's loft, at a
gypsy's wedding, out on the D train or riding the double-E. And one of
the uncanny things about Dylan is his ability to know how one is going
to look in a photograph as it's being taken, and control the pose.

"Very often (too often in my view) I was aware of being photographed.
So, from the moment I feel I am in the camera's eye, everything changes:
I begin to pose, I immediately create a different body. I change even before the image," Roland Barthes wrote. Given how many photographs
there are of Dylan, it's amazing how good or spectacularly wasted he
looks—anyway, almost always iconically Dylanish. All of his upcoming
album covers—*Bringing It All Back Home, Highway 61 Revisited, Blonde on
Blonde*—are like stills from his inner ongoing movie cycle.

Dylan has a protean shape-shifting capability even in photographs, as if he could conjure up a new form simply by imagining it. "All the great American stars were capable of altering their appearance by an act of will," says Mitch Blank, mystic "deep-taper" of Dylanobilia, "physically transforming themselves into an image that already existed in their minds and transferring it to the photograph that was about to be taken of them—and nobody possessed a more supernatural talent for morphing themselves than Dylan."

A story in *Melody Maker* carries the headline BEATLES SAY DYLAN SHOWS THE WAY. It is January 9, 1965, and he is King Bob, an international pop star, but with edge and attitude. "Everything I did was just for a crowd of people who were on the same wavelength I was on," he claimed somewhat disingenuously. "What I was doing wasn't really for a mass audience."

In March the revolutionary *Bringing It All Back Home* is unleashed on the world. It is the first of Dylan's mid-'6os masterpieces, and with it the decade really starts to roll. Side A is electric with a band; side B is mainly acoustic and solo. On "Subterranean Homesick Blues," Dylan essentially invents rap, using Chuck Berry's "Too Much Monkey Business" as the chassis, much the way the Beach Boys used Berry's "Sweet Little Sixteen" as the soundtrack for "Surfin' USA." Unlike the Beatles and the Stones, Dylan looks on rock 'n' roll and R&B as the Old Testament of rock for which he will write the new gospel. His new hallucinatory style marks the beginning of Cult Bob. On the album cover he toys with us, scattering clues, signs, false trails. Columbia promotes the album with a Dylan doll, an eight-inch, die-cut cardboard, point-of-purchase Bob.

When we first learned of Dylan's early involvement in rock 'n' roll bands—his obsession with Little Richard, Chuck Berry, and Elvis—it was a bit of a shock. Dylan was the living incarnation of the folk griot, the one who would bring that fantastic world to life through a type of transubstantiation. "Folk music was a reality of a more brilliant dimension . . . ," said Dylan. "I felt right at home in this mythical realm made up not with individuals so much as archetypes . . . metaphysical in shape. . . . I had no other cares or interests besides folk music. I scheduled my life around it. I had little in common with anyone not like-minded. . . . I loved all these [traditional] ballads right away. . . . Lyrically they worked on some kind of supernatural level and they made their own sense. You didn't have to make your own sense out of it."

But unbeknownst to us, rock 'n' roll had always been Dylan's model of success; its propulsive momentum matched his nervous energy. As a folksinger his rock 'n' roll adolescence remained a substratum, something he'd buried, temporarily abandoned, but it lay there under layers of the folk song hoard, until it erupted on *Bringing It All Back Home.* By this point his rock 'n' roll legacy had morphed into a new language transformed by its sojourn underground. If he'd stayed on the rock highway from adolescence on, he'd never have found the radiant language that illuminated his lyrics: hillbilly grammar, dust bowl imagery, cowboy vernacular, railroad lingo, mystical geography of place names drenched in history and association, blues argot, and hipster patois. But when the creature awoke in early 1965 it emerged coated in the patina of these ancient woes. Combining the X factor of rock with the mysterious contents of the folk granary would be an act of stunning innovation.

If we'd known about Dylan's Dion DiMucci fixation, for instance, we'd have had a heads-up about how pop-infested he was. In 1965 it would hardly have occurred to anybody that Dion would be any kind of idol to Dylan, Dion being someone who would seem to be far from Dylan's natural grazing ground. But the way Dylan venerates Dion is indicative of his subterranean attachment to pop music; Dion represented hope to Dylan. He was not only a big star at Dylan's label, Columbia, but he was also an early instance of a singer-songwriter, and his profound connection to blues (as on his 2007 album, *Son of Skip James*) shone through whatever teenager-in-love veneer we put on him.

"The voice of Dion came exploding out of what Allen Ginsberg called the 'hydrogen jukebox' in the fifties—the hush-hush age," said Dylan. "Torn right from the start, he had it magically together in the mythic sense—level-headed and trustworthy, rhythmically there's no mayhem—just a sense of wonder, in his voice he tells the untold story in the seemingly secret language. . . . Great singers pass us by like a parade of nobility. There's just something about them that rises above superficial culture. Dion comes from a time when so-so singers couldn't cut it—they either never got heard or got exposed quick and got out of the way."

Dylan's explanation of how his transformation from Folk Messiah to rock star came about sounds straightforward. It was to take "simple folk changes and put new imagery and attitude to them, use catchphrases and metaphor combined with a new set of ordinances that evolved into something different that had not been heard before . . . and [I] wasn't going to take a step back or retreat for anybody."

As to protest songs, he denied he'd ever written more than a couple of them. You must be confusing me with those other guys. "Both Len [Chandler] and Tom [Paxton] wrote topical songs—songs where you'd pick articles out of newspapers, fractured, demented stuff. . . . I wrote a couple and slipped them into my repertoire but really didn't think they were here nor there." As to why he abandoned protest, he claimed that it had become a formula. "After I finished the English tour I quit because it was too easy. . . . It was down to a pattern." However, *Bringing It All Back Home* contains at least four full-blown protest songs (albeit allegorical): "Subterranean Homesick Blues," "Maggie's Farm," "Gates of Eden," and "It's Alright, Ma (I'm Only Bleeding)." He is an enraged visionary, but now taking celestial dictation and railing, like his double, the melancholy Dane, against "the oppressor's wrong, the proud man's contumely, the pangs of disprized love, the law's delay, the insolence of office."

Baez describes Dylan in full genius mode writing the songs that would become *Bringing It All Back Home* up in Woodstock in the summer of 1964: "Most of the month or so we were there, Bob stood at the typewriter in the corner of his room, drinking red wine and smoking and tapping away relentlessly for hours. And in the dead of night, he would wake up, grunt, grab a cigarette, and stumble over to the typewriter again." Bernard Paturel, the owner of the Café Espresso in Woodstock, remembered Dylan assembling his lyrics from images—postcards, photographs, pictures torn from newspapers and magazines—as he paced back and forth in the room above his restaurant, assembling his mental movies.

His first concept for combining words and music came to him when he was eighteen. He had begun reading Allen Ginsberg, Gary Snyder, Philip Whalen, Frank O'Hara, and "the French guys," Rimbaud and François Villon. "I started putting tunes to their poems. There used to be a folk music scene and jazz clubs just about every place. The two scenes were very much connected, where the poets would read to a small combo, so I was close up to that for a while. My songs were influenced not so much by poetry on the page but by poetry being recited by the poets who recited poems with jazz bands."

When Dylan decided to go electric in 1964, he didn't know exactly how to go about it. Producer Tom Wilson's inclination was simply to add an electric backing track to folk vocals and an acoustic guitar as he would do with Simon and Garfunkel's "Sounds of Silence," which he released in September 1965 without even informing them about what he'd done. Putting a Fats Domino–type old rock 'n' roll backing behind an acoustic track of Dylan singing "House of the Risin' Sun" was Wilson's first idea, an approach that would seem somewhat futile considering that in August the Animals had had a hit in the United States with their version—based on the Dylan track on his first album.

Dylan began recording acoustic tracks for *Bringing It All Back Home* on January 13, 1965, but none of these tracks made it onto the final album. His first attempt at recording with an electric band was at Columbia's Studio B on the afternoon of January 14, 1965, when they recorded five of the songs on the album (with another session supposedly that evening introducing another group of musicians). The rest of the tracks were cut at Studio A the following day.

As revolutionary as the album is, you can see that Dylan didn't yet know exactly how to play with a group of sidemen. Bob Hudson describes Dylan's hesitancy when he tried to record with Eric Clapton and John Mayall's band, the Bluesbreakers, in May of that year at Levy's Recording Studio in London: "Dylan haltingly counts it in (with no sense of tempo), the band flubs the entrance, and it all crashes. One of Mayall's people then says, 'Haven't worked much with bands, have ya?' Which must have galled Dylan no end. One month later he was in the studio recording one of the greatest rock songs ever, 'Like a Rolling Stone.'"

There are few takes of songs on *Bringing It All Back Home*, recorded in Dylan's characteristic intuitive manner. "He often recorded his electric songs in fewer takes," Hudson explains, "because he'd tell the band to stop if he didn't like the sound they were getting—even if he didn't always know what to do about it. His customary method involved starting a song, calling off the band if he didn't like the take, then repeating the incomplete takes till they finally made it all the way through the song and got the sound he wanted. The result was that he had few complete takes, since the incomplete takes functioned like rehearsals."

But, as quickly as the tracks were recorded, you can tell the sidemen are trying to figure out what they're meant to be doing, and Dylan is notoriously unhelpful in that department. He will play them the melody on the piano and then they're off and running. As a result, the backing tracks are very busy; everyone is playing full out and all over the track. The guitar player isn't listening to the words; he's just playing a basic jangly backing track, because these are session musicians. Under normal circumstances the lead singer in a group would be saying, "Can we build up to that?" "Don't step on my vocals." It would be arranged. In that sense, this is closer to folk rock as Tom Wilson conceived it: folk lyrics with an electric track.

But, as with many serendipitous incidents in Dylan's career, the flaws became part of his idiosyncratic approach. Dylan played harmonica obnoxiously, but this became an integral part of his style. People appreciated his edginess. The whirling, chaotic backups on *Bringing It All Back Home* create a strange organ grinder effect, something that Dylan would refine—with the addition of pop music melodies—into the wild mercury sound on his following two albums.

When the Byrds made their version of "Mr. Tambourine Man," they would fuse folk music and electric rock more effectively than Dylan had done on his album. Their approach had been based on the Beatles; their producer, Terry Melcher, knew how to absorb folk melodies into a rock song seamlessly. But as sweet as the Byrds' folk rock is, it's now just part of a '60s sound continuum, like "California Dreaming."

On *Bringing It All Back Home*, Dylan is still trying to get the fusion of words and music to gel. When he does, it's epochal. On the first track, "Subterranean Homesick Blues," with its jivey speed-rap paranoia and twangy guitar, it's a mind-altering example of his new approach, essentially Jack Kerouac grafted on to Chuck Berry—Berry's "Too Much Monkey Business" being his inspiration and model. As a protorap song, Dylan's rant ratchets uncannily with the track, the words frequently dissolving into the beat.

> *Maggie comes fleet foot*
> *Face full of black soot*
> *Talkin' that the heat put*
> *Plants in the bed but*

Sometimes it is barely even English, its consonantal clash mimicking Dylan's rock 'n' roll hero Little Richard's *awopbopalooobopalopbamboom* manic attack on "Tutti Frutti." The energy of Dylan's vocals on the R&B-like "Outlaw Blues" is pure rock, inspired no doubt by Brit invasion blues belters, such as Jagger's propulsive singing on the Stones album *12 x 5*, which came out in the United States in November 1964, only a few months before Dylan's first attempt to record *Bringing It All Back Home* in January 1965.

"It's Alright, Ma (I'm Only Bleeding)" is where his metaprotest reaches a toxic pitch; when things are this dark it's obviously no longer a question of which side are you on. All life in America is contaminated. Bebop, the Beats, and film noir had been saying for some time that the air-conditioned nightmare was making people sick and crazy—and this song is a lethal distillation of "I'm in this crazy world, Mama, please help me."

My eyes collide head-on with stuffed
Graveyards, false gods, I scuff
At pettiness which plays so rough
Walk upside-down inside handcuffs
Kick my legs to crash it off
Say okay, I have had enough, what else can you show me?

He's poking at rattlesnakes in the same relentless way he'd done on "Hard Rain." He just doesn't stop. He goes down in his crypt with a candle, has his visions, and then wraps it all up in pop music. The title is a tribute to Dylan's idol, Elvis Presley. In Elvis's "That's Alright Mama," his haunted vocal turns a lover's resignation into a lament for universal loss.

"If my thought dreams could be seen," Dylan sings, but that's astoundingly just what he does. Lyrics were Dylan's way of turning the tables. He was competing with three major bands—the Beatles, the Stones, and the Beach Boys—and the only way he could do it was with the power of his language. The effect of *Bringing It All Back Home* on rock was instantaneous and urgent. Like the archaic torso in Rilke's poem it said to rock's alpha dogs, "You must change!" It tilted the nature of rock. You had John Lennon saying, "I don't want to be Neil Sedaka anymore, I want to be Bob Dylan!" Although, according to Bob, good luck with that. "People who came after me, I don't feel, were ever my contemporaries, because they didn't really have any standing in traditional music. They didn't play folk songs. They heard me and thought, 'Oh, this guy writes his own songs, I can do that.' They can, of course, but those songs don't have any resonance."

Bringing It All Back Home has a wide range of diversity, styles, and attitudes. There are goofy songs: "Outlaw Blues," "On the Road Again," and "Bob Dylan's 115th Dream," delivered as a hillbilly rock, shaggy-dog history of America by a daydreaming pothead. There are love songs such as "She Belongs to Me" and "Love Minus Zero/No Limit"—a kind of prelude to "Sad-Eyed Lady of the Lowlands" on *Blonde on Blonde*. There are mystical songs and the it-ain't-me-babe-so-leave-me-alone songs, which would include "Maggie's Farm" (the old folknik crowd), "Outlaw Blues," and "On the Road Again," with its bitching about *la vie bohème*: "I'm hungry as a hog/So I get brown rice, seaweed/And a dirty hot dog." And, of course, there's "It's All Over Now, Baby Blue," said to be about his old buddy the blue-eyed Paul Clayton but really it's just another of Bob's get-offa-my-cloud put-downs that applies to one and all.

"Mr. Tambourine Man," an acoustic track with minimal backup, introduced the mystical, lyrical writer of his own mind-made Fellini movie. Bob wanted to create his own character, write him into being. "Mr. Tambourine Man," a track left off *Another Side of Bob Dylan*, was a character who was born in a song and then walked on out into the street. And in the mad parade, there's the parabolic parodier himself, Lord Buckley, jingle jangling down the road. The song is both festive and melancholy—like Mardi Gras—and the tambourine, a pied piperish instrument, is the sound of people getting together, a group. The '60s were emerging from the long postnuclear winter. The end-of-the-world party was about to begin again, and the Beatles, fulfilling some atavistic death and re-birth ritual, had arrived in the States on February 4 to bring an end to our mourning for the death of JFK.

We needed a new gospel. Chuck Berry and Jack Kerouac were a good place to start because Chuck had invented the classic motivatin'-over-the-hill engine for rock 'n' roll, and Jack had been in the direct line of apostolic succession beginning with Uncle Walt, the daddy of us all and the great scrivener of Allness and Oneness. His disciple, Thomas Wolfe, a mad encyclopedist of Americanism, was Kerouac's favorite writer. ("I will go everywhere and do everything. I will meet all the people I can. I will think all the thoughts, feel all the emotions I am able, and write, write, write.")

Since the beginning of rock 'n' roll a record album had been just a collection of songs, the hit single plus a bunch of other tracks. The idea of the concept album, in which all the songs connected to a single theme, was a '60s invention sometimes claimed by the Beach Boys for *Summer Days (And Summer Nights!!)*. The role-playing—the Huck Finn/Charlie Chaplin naïf, the doom-laden Blind Lemon Jefferson character on his first album—worked brilliantly for the lone folksinger-songwriter, be-cause, unlike pop music where the single was still king, the standard format for folk music, as with jazz records, was the album; the album is more like a book. Folk music generally consisted of collections of tradi-tional songs by specific artists—Appalachian ballad singers, Delta bluesmen, Breton folksingers—or LPs on specific themes, field recordings, archival collections, anthologies, etc. Music by folkies (i.e., young urban musicians like Dylan, Dave Van Ronk, Paul Clayton) followed the same pattern. Clayton, a big influence and archival source for early Dylan songs, made some albums based on folk themes that mimicked the field-recording style of the old folk musicians down in the Delta and the hollers. Some of these themes stretched the concept to a ludicrous degree, like Clayton's *"Hunt the Cutty Auk" and Other Auk-Hunting Ballads from the Inner Hebrides*. In the sense of the album as a book, *Bringing It All Back Home* is more like a collection of short stories about the narrator's life and impersonations.

Since Dylan's musical output was in the form of albums and the content was either pseudoautobiographical or outright autobiographical, he soon realized he'd created a series of fictional characters and his albums were in effect novels. In some ways, Dylan of the mid-'60s is the final flowering of Beat lit.

Despite the great clangy energy of the rock tracks, it's the surrealist imagery that's at the core of Dylan's new songs.

The cloak and dagger dangles,
Madams light the candles
In ceremonies of the horsemen
Even the pawn must hold a grudge.
Statues made of matchsticks
Crumble into one another

Oddly enough, *Bringing It All Back Home* is in some ways the most realistic Dylan album so far, the lyrics almost a direct transcription of how his mind works. The words arise out of what André Breton's *Surrealist Manifesto* called "Pure psychic automatism . . . the real process of thought. It is the dictation of thought, free from any control by reason."

In Don DeLillo's novel *Great Jones Street*, the protagonist (and narrator) is a rock star and unwilling idol of the counterculture modeled on Dylan. Named Bucky Wunderlick, he becomes dissatisfied with the radical image that has been thrust on him and the unwanted fame that has unhinged his life. He holes up in a bare Village loft to figure out what to do next when his girlfriend brings him a new experimental drug, which has a bizarre linguistic side effect: messing up the centers of his brain that deal with language.

Ah get born, keep warm
Short pants, romance, learn to dance
Get dressed, get blessed
Try to be a success
Please her, please him, buy gifts
Don't steal, don't lift

The words! The words now became manically animated. Like Frankenstein's monster, Baron Bob sent a jolt of electricity through the lyrics. What are these words *on?* Speed for one, and grass. They are words stumbling over each other in brain-dance ecstasy or splenetic rage. He's grabbing images out of the air like somebody in a burning house. Get that and that and that too. Might as well take the clock, a pair of socks, the Bible, and the toaster.

Words were the message, the hook, but the primary instinct of rock had been essentially nonverbal. Some early songs consisted of barely a dozen rebus-like words— "car," "jukebox," "ring," "please," "baby," "please, please, please." Along with its deliberately reductive amputated vocabulary, rock songs presented a limited mise-en-scène, as if (like some avant-garde Frenchman decided to write a novel omitting the letter *e*) you were just going to focus on high school, cars, the hop—the teen genre, in fact. And, as the great originators began to disappear by the end of the '50s— Chuck Berry's in jail, Little Richard's become a preacher, Elvis is in the army, Jerry Lee Lewis is banned—rock became bland. The great storytellers were gone and we were left with what Sasha Frere-Jones calls "the basic Legos of pop music."

But with perverse insight Dylan saw that since rock had gotten rid of the words that meant anything or anesthetized them, it was time to bring them back but now in their crazy hill-country-Delta-blues-modernist glory. Baroque, surreal, haunted language:

Then take me disappearin' through the smoke rings of my mind
Down the foggy ruins of time, far past the frozen leaves
The haunted, frightened trees, out to the windy beach
Far from the twisted reach of crazy sorrow
Yes, to dance beneath the diamond sky with one hand waving free
Silhouetted by the sea, circled by the circus sands
With all memory and fate driven deep beneath the waves
Let me forget about today until tomorrow

"Someplace along the line Suze had also introduced me to the poetry of French Symbolist poet Arthur Rimbaud. That was a big deal, too. I came across one of his letters, called '*Je est un autre*,' which translates into 'I is someone else.' When I read those words, the bells went off. I wished someone would have mentioned that to me earlier. It went right along with Johnson's dark night of the soul and Woody's hopped-up union meeting sermons and the 'Pirate Jenny' framework."

In other words his was a new language composed of mythical, allegorical, folktale, biblical, racing form, comic book, underworld slang, a world populated with Beethoven, Cleopatra, Ma Rainey, Paul Revere, Belle Starr, Columbus, Captain Ahab, Abraham and Isaac, poor Howard and Georgia Sam. When Dylan moved from the political to the allegorical, his new approach would be exotically displayed in songs like "Desolation Row," "Just Like Tom Thumb's Blues," "Bob Dylan's 115th Dream," "Highway 61," "Tombstone Blues," and most spectacularly in "Visions of Johanna."

In Robert Graves's *The White Goddess*, Dylan believed he'd found a way of using the voices in his head as an antenna: "I read *The White Goddess* by Robert Graves, too," Dylan explains in *Chronicles*. "Invoking the poetic muse was something I didn't know about yet. Didn't know enough to start trouble with it, anyway. In a few years' time, I would meet Robert Graves himself in London. We went out for a brisk walk around Paddington Square. I wanted to ask him about some of the things in his book, but I couldn't remember much about it."

"At the very beginning of chapter two of *Chronicles*," says Peter Stampfel, "Dylan mentions that he read some books by Robert Graves in this house that he crashed in. At that time I was deeply into Robert Graves—I'm still into Robert Graves. I believed in *The White Goddess* back then and I'm pretty sure that I'm the person who introduced Dylan to Graves because I would go on about it endlessly—how the culture used to be a matriarchy, and that's when mankind was whole and happy, but then the bad, warlike men came with their blah blah.

"There's even this one early interview in which Dylan says, 'God is a woman, everybody knows that.' Apparently he went to see Graves at one point but Graves wasn't impressed, he thought that Dylan's songs were nursery rhymes. Graves was *very* old school, pre-Socratic, he was obsessed with ancient nature cults and mythical thinking—hence his classic book, *The Greek Myths*. So his attitude was 'Is anybody going to remember his songs in three hundred years?' Personally, I think yes, some of them."

Dylan's use of legendary elements—whether from myth, comic books, or the movies—shifts the plots and sets of his songs into another dimension. In his new incarnation he'd change the play, get a new cast of characters—historical, biblical, fictional figures, mingle the living and the dead—and throw away all the clocks. In this sense he was reinventing and resurrecting the perpetual universe of ballads and the blues.

MIXING IN THE FLOATING WORLD OF INTERNATIONAL POP, DYLAN IS now a cultural synthesizer (whether he likes it or not). He takes the Animals and the Supremes down to the Kettle of Fish and partakes of more Lower East Side adventures with Brian Jones, Al Aronowitz, Allen Ginsberg, and others. He goes on tour in the UK (this is the tour that was the basis for *Don't Look Back*). There are high jinks in the Savoy Hotel with Marianne Faithfull, Dana Gillespie, Donovan, Alan Price, and assorted Brit folkies. He also unsuccessfully attempts to write songs on a tape recorder with John Lennon at his house in Weybridge.

A problem may be that these rock stars with "fronts as big as Harrods" are intimidated by one another's myth. Each one's fame has grown, and everything has become magnified and distorted. As Lennon said, "Whenever we used to meet, it was always under the most nerve-wracking circumstances. I know I was always uptight and I know Bobby was.... I'd always be too paranoid or I'd be aggressive or something and vice versa.... H[e] came to me house ... can you imagine it? ... [T]his bourgeois home life I was living.... I used to go to his hotel rather. And I loved him, because he wrote beautiful stuff. I used to love his so-called protest things. But I liked the sound of him. I didn't have to listen to his words....

"He used to ... say, 'Listen to this, John.' and 'Did you hear the words?' And I said, 'That doesn't matter, just the *sound* is what counts.'"

Dylan records tracks including two takes of "If You Gotta Go" on May 12 at Levy's Recording Studio in New Bond Street. Eric Clapton and John Mayall are in attendance. Dylan complains they only play straight blues. Bob Hudson describes the session as a farcical failure to communicate: "The story of those two takes of 'If You Gotta Go' is that somebody had the idea that Dylan ought to jam with Mayall at Levy's. At the same time, Tom Wilson thought he'd get Dylan to record a 'sales message' to the Columbia sales reps, who were going to be convening in Miami later that year (hence, this whole session with Mayall is called the 'Miami

Sales Message' session). Dylan completely botches the first take of 'Gotta Go' (with the bad count-in, the song doesn't even get off the ground). He then says he doesn't need to count in and just launches into the song. Mayall's band kind of follows behind. After one verse (and the *clunk clunk clunk* of his piano and Mayall's completely uninspired band) Dylan shouts at Wilson, 'Fade it out. FADE IT OUT!' It was a disaster—and although they played together for an hour, I don't think anything further was recorded that day (or ever by Dylan and Mayall's band together). What a train wreck that was."

Dylan also tapes two half-hour shows in June for BBC-TV (see *Don't Look Back* for Grossman's sly negotiation of this deal). Meanwhile, back in the States, "Subterranean Homesick Blues" gets to #39 on the charts.

On July 20, 1965, Dylan's single "Like a Rolling Stone" is released, changing everything. It's not just its epic length: six minutes, eighteen seconds. What's really amazing is the way Dylan combines Kerouac's cinematic narrative with a hurdy-gurdy track that hypnotically follows the rhythm of a hipster-protagonist's inflection. It is a scathing lens for viewing life in the mid-'60s.

The metamorphosis of Bob from protest singer to stream-of-consciousness poet had already taken place by his 1964 appearance at Newport the previous year when he performed "Mr. Tambourine Man." The folk watchdogs had pounced on Dylan at the time for his desertion, but now he had the nerve to go electric. This was what supposedly caused the big dustup at the Newport Folk Festival on July 25, 1965, the so-called incident when Dylan's fans turned against him. Actual booing! That's the story, anyway—a story embraced and propelled by the media—and Dylan himself. Nevertheless, the booing of Bob at Newport (now enshrined in pop music history) is a myth. There may have been murmurs from a few die-hard folkie purists, but most of the objections I heard that day were about the lousy sound system.

The thousands of other kids there had come *because* Dylan had gone electric and written this mind-boggling song. Newport felt more like spring break than a gathering of the faithful. The audience was mainly beer-drinking college kids who'd heard "Like a Rolling Stone" on the radio and come to hear Dylan play rock 'n' roll. However, much of what we believe to be true about that day is actually part of the elaborate Bob Dylan myth.

Dylan opens his set at Newport by playing "Maggie's Farm" (a farewell to the folk work farm). Next he sings "Like a Rolling Stone" (his get-hip-or-get-lost song) and then moves into "Phantom Engineer," an early version of "It Takes a Lot to Laugh, It Takes a Train to Cry" (which would appear on *Highway 61 Revisited*). Dylan and his backup band—Mike Bloomfield on lead guitar, Al Kooper on organ (they'd both played on "Like a Rolling Stone"), plus Sam Lay (drums), Jerome Arnold (bass), and Barry Goldberg (piano)—all left the stage, and that's when the booing and clapping can be heard on the soundtrack. Dylan then returned by himself and played two songs on acoustic guitar: "Mr. Tambourine Man" and "It's All Over Now, Baby Blue." Whomever this final song was actually directed at, playing it as his encore at Newport was provocative, an obvious kiss-off to his folkie contingent. There was thundering applause and shouts for more, but Dylan did not come back; he didn't return to the Newport festival for another thirty-seven years. When he performed there in 2002, he wore a wig and fake beard; what that signified no one knows.

In the 2005 Martin Scorsese documentary *No Direction Home*, Dylan says, "I had no idea why they were booing. . . . But whatever it was about, it wasn't about anything they were *hearing*." A year later he reverted to the martyred artist image of himself at Newport: "Miles Davis has been booed. Hank Williams was booed. Stravinsky was booed. You're nobody if you don't get booed sometime."

Al Kooper, who was onstage, says that the booing wasn't about Dylan going electric at all; it was Dylan *leaving* the stage that caused the animosity, mostly directed at master of ceremonies Peter Yarrow for cutting short Dylan's set: "The reason they booed is because he only played for fifteen minutes, when everybody else played for forty-five minutes or an hour," says Kooper. "They were feeling ripped off. Wouldn't you? They didn't give a shit about us being electric. They just wanted more."

A couple of offstage incidents contributed to the idea that Dylan going electric had been the source of the booing—the Pete Seeger saga, for instance. Because it was about a member of the old guard folkie contingent versus the young genius, the story that Seeger tried to ax the power cable during Dylan's performance has become part of the Dylan legend. It didn't actually happen but could have—and that's close enough for a myth. Seeger said that the story about him cutting the cable probably got started because he'd said to somebody at the time, "If I'd had an ax, I would have cut the damned cable." But as farcical as it seems, a fight did actually take place between two bigwigs over Dylan going electric. The venerable folk music collector Alan Lomax and Dylan's manager, Albert Grossman, got into an actual knock-down, drag-out fistfight, the two of them wrestling each other to the ground and rolling in the dust. What a sight! Lomax was so incensed he tried to get the rest of the Newport board of directors to have Grossman banned from the grounds.

People close to Dylan say that he was oddly both shaken and exhilarated by the experience. Even he apparently didn't know what had caused the booing, but something obviously rattled him because four days after Newport, Dylan recorded "Positively 4th Street," his most poisonous personal assault. But who was the target, the unfortunate character he demolishes in the song? Irwin Silber, who had written his infamous "Open Letter to Bob Dylan" article in the November 1964 issue of *Sing Out!*, is one of the leading contenders, but this piece had been written about Dylan's performance at Newport in 1964, in which Silber criticized him for his desertion—not his amplification. Dylan would not record his first tracks with a band for another three months. As Bob Hudson points out, "From Dylan's perspective, however, so much has happened to him since November 1964 [recording *Bringing*, 'Like a Rolling Stone,' and Newport] that it seems mystifying to me that he even gives two hoots about what Silber wrote eight months earlier in a two-bit folk magazine [Dylan was getting coverage in *Time* and *Melody Maker* at that point], let alone writing a song about him to tell him off." But still, who ever said Bob wasn't one to hold a grudge?

Other contenders for the 4th Street incident include Phil Ochs, Izzy Young, a disenchanted girlfriend (but it doesn't really sound like that sort of confrontation), the whole darn folkie malcontent crowd in general, and anybody else that bugged him. However, the song seems to be directed at a specific person and Dylan loves nothing more than to nurture his resentments and find a suitable target. Whoever it's about and whatever it was over, it's just such a great venting song with that line that swings around and hits you with a left hook:

> *Yes, I wish that for just one time*
> *You could stand inside my shoes*
> *You'd know what a drag it is*
> *To see you*

Nineteen sixty-five is also the summer of Dylan covers. Sonny and Cher—really just Cher, who has the nerve to change the melody—does

"All I Really Want to Do" in go-go-boot style, while the Turtles sweetly defang "It Ain't Me, Babe" and the Byrds send "Mr. Tambourine Man" into the stratosphere. The popularity of these songs leads to the folk-rock fad with entries like Barry McGuire's "Eve of Destruction" and Sonny and Cher's mock Dylan "I Got You, Babe," the alarming clock-radio wake-up song in *Groundhog Day*. It wasn't just the times that were a-changin'; the time signature was a-changin' too. The shift from 2/4 to 4/4 is what makes the difference. They called it folk rock, and Dylan adapted to it fast. But Dylan's new electric style is really amplified Beat-nik blues. Folk rock came more from Dylan's imitators, the Beau Brummels, the Turtles, and the Byrds.

Over that summer, the myth of booing at Newport took on a life of its own. The press couldn't resist the melodrama of irate fans condemning a Judas in their midst for betraying their cause—even if they didn't understand what it was all about. The so-called denouncing of Dylan at Newport was sexy and soon enthusiastically adopted by a faction of youth egged on by the media—and aided and abetted by Dylan himself. What self-righteous fun to yell abuse at the hipper-than-thou Bob now traveling at the speed of sound! Among his disaffected fans the myth of Dylan's perfidy went viral—the self-righteous indignation of youth quick to react to the assumed betrayal. Their former idol had abandoned his sacred role for crass, pop, commercialism. The irony was that Dylan had become a millionaire precisely from his protest song catalog.

By the time he appears at the Forest Hills concert in August 1965, Dylan has embraced the romantic notion of himself as the misunderstood genius jeered at by an ignorant, reactionary mob, warning his backup group (the future members of the Band) to expect harassment from the crowd when they played their electric set. When asked at a press conference in San Francisco, on December 3, 1965, whether he was "surprised the first time the boos came," Dylan said, "That was at Newport. Well, I did this very crazy thing, I didn't know what was going to happen, but they certainly booed, I'll tell you that. You could hear it all over the place. . . . I mean, they must be pretty rich to be able to go someplace and boo. I couldn't afford it if I was in their shoes."

Myths are always more potent than facts and eventually Dylan came to see this alleged incident as essential to his own legend. It was a gripping episode, with a whiff of revolution to it—a classic '60s clash of the hip and the unhip! And the fact that it never happened—who cared? You couldn't ask for a better fable than that. In the documentary *No Direction*

Home—directed by Scorsese and micromanaged by Dylan—the footage focused on his classic '60s career and its pivotal event, the booing at Newport.

But it wasn't just going electric or dressing like a rock star in shades and Beatle boots that indicated things had changed with Bob. He'd gathered around him a sinister cabal of cynical courtiers with their haute drugs, their hip asides, and their vicious put-downs. The chief of these was the ruthlessly witty painter and boulevardier Bobby Neuwirth.

In those days, says Al Aronowitz, "Hipper-Than-Thou was the favorite head game of the Dylan crowd, and Bobby [Neuwirth] was maybe the game's most vicious hardballer, one of those razor-tongued originals who put the dis into disrespect. When he got finished putting you down, you could crawl out the door through the keyhole. He also could slit your throat and you'd never even bleed."

According to Al Kooper, it was Neuwirth who Dylan wanted to be and nightly the two terrible Bobbies practiced the dark arts of character demolition. "By then," says Suze Rotolo, "the multifaceted Bobby Neuwirth, a painter, musician, and very clever wordsmith, was a fixture in Bob's orbit, as was Victor Maimudes [*sic*], Bob's silent and creepy buddy-bodyguard. They were so cool, so hip, so cold. Things got strange. Negative. Bob was thin and tight and hostile. He had succumbed to demons."

Whether it had anything to do with booing or drugs or bad company or fame or haberdashery, who knew? But there was no question that Dylan had changed into something rich and strange.

PLAY MOVIE

SCENES

BONUS TRACKS

COMMENTARY

EXTRAS

SUBTITLES

DONT LOOK BACK BOB DYLAN

10   How Does It Feel? Self-Portrait at 24 Frames per Second

AMERICA THE MOVIE, DYLAN THE MOVIE, DOCUMENTARIES, metadocumentaries—by 1965 Bob felt a sudden desire to be seen. Sure, it was an odd compulsion for the reclusive Dylan, but things had changed. With their flashy mod gear and their politics of delinquency, Brit invasion groups—the Rolling Stones, the Who, and the Yardbirds—were the new cool cats. And Dylan wanted his Stratocaster.

His transformation had been rapid. Between the Newport Folk Festival in 1964, where he was still the crown prince of folk music writing symbolist folk songs, and the release of *Bringing It All Back Home*, he had changed utterly. Eight months after Newport he was the Dada king in shades and floral shirts writing songs for a solid-body guitar about "the geometry of innocent flesh on the bone." This reinvention of himself was so consummate that all previous Dylans would be seen as rough sketches and all his subsequent incarnations as pale reflections. This is the Dylan he would spend the rest of his life trying to escape.

With each new album there had been a new Dylan. Then, just as we would become familiar with the new terrain, he was gone. Not only had he caught the first train out of town, but he'd also completely repudiated his last incarnation, despising everything that this former character stood for.

The odd thing about these changes was that they didn't appear to be mere window dressing, like a new look for Bowie or Jagger might be. This wasn't an act; it was simply Bob, albeit a new, philosophically adjusted Bob.

With the Beatles you could follow their evolution without too much trouble: from Hamburg leather yobs to mop tops to Carnaby Street mods to costume-party hippies to mystic John to just plain blokes. But with Dylan, the shift—because we never get to see the intervening frames—is abrupt and disorienting.

But suppose the chief vampire couldn't see himself in the mirror.

Like a foppish aristocrat, perhaps he said, "Summon someone to paint my portrait." Then changed his mind: "Nah, I think I'll make a movie."

This is not, of course, how it happened. That would be a fairy tale, and this is a story of the music business. If the germ began anywhere, it was in the brain of Albert Grossman, an embittered, wounded "street bear" for whom money and power were the best revenge. But he did have a redeeming taste for fairy tales. And here he was, Dylan—this rare fish he'd caught.

Grossman was a manager of theatrical talent, and he understood Dylan's serial incarnations as performances. After all, he'd first encountered Bob as the folk waif, followed his progress as Folk Messiah, and was along for the ride for Dylan's next act—hallucinatory poet magus. Dylan was, felt Grossman, a consummate performer, and was now a character in search of a play. Grossman would provide one for him. And sell the thing to Warner Bros. Or flog it to ABC as a television special.

Fortunately for us, Dylan has been preserved at this very point in time in not one but three documentaries (a series of self-portraits) filmed during his 1965 and 1966 European tours. Typical of Dylan's secretiveness, paranoia, and mystification, only *Don't Look Back* is now in common circulation. *Eat the Document* has been shown a few times recently but only at the insistence of Dylan's record company, Sony. *You Know Something's Happening*, still unfinished, is not even supposed to exist.

Each one of these films is more dislocated than the next. To watch them in sequence is to witness some twentieth-century self-destructing art form applied to the documentary. By the time you get to *Eat the Document* (Dylan's own version, edited with the help of Howard Alk), you've ended up with a fragmented documentary made to prove something. Or, this being Dylan, to prove the opposite of something.

The vampire of 4th Street wanted to see his new self, and just at that moment—well, maybe a year or so earlier—a new way of capturing reality on film had been invented by a troika of filmmakers who then worked at Time-Life. In the early '60s—while working for Drew Associates, a division of Time-Life—D. A. Pennebaker, along with Ricky Leacock and Albert Maysles, invented a new lightweight 16 mm camera that freed the filmmaker to "float through the world." Their epiphany was to use sound, essentially dialogue, as the organizing principle for documentaries. They developed an ingenious sync-sound system that would allow them to dispense with intrusive narrations and let the interaction of the subjects tell the story.

In the new documentary, the dialogue itself would provide the narrative. No pompous, bromide-saturated narration would intrude here, just the subject as he is, caught on the wing and unaware of the camera—or so it seemed. But, like photography, the new documentary really was another subtler form of manipulating reality, all the more seductive for seeming to be the unvarnished truth. And who better than Dylan himself, the monkey grammarian, to be the protagonist of a new type of documentary that depended on dialogue, on words? The form had found its ideal subject, a spritzer of genius.

Sara Lownds had worked as a liaison between Pennebaker and the powers that be at Time-Life, and had shown Dylan Pennebaker's first film, *Daybreak Express*—a five-minute expressionistic rush inspired by a one-line Ezra Pound poem, set to a Duke Ellington track, and shot from an elevated train. Dylan was impressed. He had found "the Eye," as he called Pennebaker, to materialize his visions.

Ever since Elvis, a movie was a must for any obnoxious little rocker who had reached a certain pitch of stardom. But as the '60s rolled down the tracks this proved more problematic than was at first thought. The old-style, rock-fantasy film—the lads leaping in the air Merseyside—was out of the question for so rare an entity as Dylan. It couldn't be like *Lonely Boy* either, a documentary made about Paul Anka, which cast a cool, sociological eye on the music business. Pennebaker was a true believer; he approached *Don't Look Back* with a fan's indulgent eye. "I think musicians are a strange kind of clergy among us," he says. "They're the closest thing we have to saints."

Only the Beatles had ever solved the rock-star-into-feature-film problem—and only in one movie: *A Hard Day's Night*, a fiction based on the characters of the Beatles themselves. Dylan got the message: It's a play in which you play yourself.

Pennebaker understood from the beginning that *Don't Look Back* was going to be Dylan playing Dylan, a sustained performance onstage and off. The caught-off-guard moments were to be few and far between. Pennebaker's camera is a voyeur, but the scenes are all tableaux. Dylan is always aware of the camera. It's a kind of portable mirror the emperor takes with him; he wants to see how the essence of the vibe operates when he's in a far province.

DON'T LOOK BACK OPENS ON A LONDON WHARF WITH DYLAN CRADLING a stack of cue cards with whimsically spelled words and phrases (PARKING METAWS, SUCKSESS, MAN WHOLE) that he holds up and then tosses away as "Subterranean Homesick Blues" plays. It has become a classic cinematic sequence, mimicked in endless videos and commercials.

"I was in London and I got news that Dylan was in England and going to have a concert at Albert Hall," said Allen Ginsberg. "Got a message through to him at the Savoy Hotel on the Thames. He had a stack of poster boards he'd brought with him. And he and Donovan and Joan Baez wrote words on them from 'Subterranean Homesick Blues.' And that afternoon we went down to shoot it and he sang it." Actually Dylan doesn't even open his mouth during the filming of the song. He just flips the cards while the recorded version of the song plays on the soundtrack.

In all his flashing, chain-smoking, existentialist glory, we watch as he interacts with John Lennon, Donovan, Johnny Cash, Allen Ginsberg, Marianne Faithfull, and Brian Jones, bandying words with heckling students, the sniping press, and generally manipulating reality in bravura, you-are-what-you-think-you-are performances. Then there's the clip-bathe-and-return-your-dog scene (on 65 Revisited), where Dylan exhibits his verbal pyrotechnics on a London street. In Knightsbridge, Dylan spies a sign that reads:

ANIMALS AND BIRDS
BOUGHT OR SOLD ON COMMISSION
WE WILL COLLECT, CLIP, BATH
& RETURN YOUR DOG
KNI 7727
CIGARETTES AND TOBACCO

He carefully reads the words out loud and then in a mind rush begins to spin them into a dozen one-line poems.

I want a dog that's gonna collect and clean my bath, return my cigarette, and give tobacco to my animals, and then give my birds a commission. . . . I'm looking for somebody to sell my dog, collect my clip, buy my animal, and straighten out my bird. . . . I'm looking for a place to bathe my bird, buy my dog, collect my clip. . . . Sell my cigarettes and commission my bath. I'm looking for a place that's going to collect my commission, sell my dog, burn my bird, and sell me to the cigarette. Gonna bird my buy, collect my will, and bathe my commission. I'm looking for a place that's going to animal my soul, knit my return, bathe my foot, and collect my dog. Commission me to sell my animals to the bird to clip and buy my bath and return me to the cigarettes.

This all takes place in under a minute, with Dylan doing a spastic Chaplinesque dance as the words pile up.

Don't Look Back backtracks, ignores chronology, and basically ambles about where it wants to. We're suddenly at the Albert Hall at the end of the British tour with Dylan looking vulnerable and Marcel Marceau–like, singing "The Lonesome Death of Hattie Carroll," his voice searing into that high lonesome whine when it gets to "but you who philosophize disgrace."

Dylan subsequently objected to, among other things, the narrative line of *Don't Look Back.* But the narrative (if you can call it that) is really a sequence of unconnected, grainy tableaux in which Dylan interacts with a series of people and groups: backstage, in hotel rooms, taxis, limos, and trains. The murky graininess of the available-light shots parallels the patina of Dylan's voice.

Dylan in his protopunk haircut enters these scenes like an unstable element, stirring things up, inducing an uneasy disorientation in those he encounters. People are magnetically attracted to him, yet seem to have not a clue what he's about. Nobody knows quite how to take him. The papers throw out fantastic little tidbits. "I'm glad I'm not me," he says when someone reads an item about how he smokes eighty cigarettes a day. Everything gravitates around him. He's the prophet of raw, existential truths; the papers have started calling him an anarchist. "Give the anarchist a cigarette," he says with cool hipster delivery in the last scene of the movie.

"In 1965, God came to London in the form of Bob Dylan," says Marianne Faithfull. "Dispensing the new religion of cool. What struck me about Dylan was that he behaved like some old Beat hipster who'd been around the scene for years. He couldn't have been more than twenty-four. And he was looking down from a great height on dear John Dunbar, my fiancé, who was almost twenty-three. Dylan was cocky and bossy when surrounded by his minions—with Bobby Neuwirth and all those 4th Street hipsters. I remember there were lots of trips to the bathroom, great long amphetamine raps, and eerie silences. The only time I saw him alone was when I was in that hotel room with him and he was there alone because I was meant to go to bed with him and didn't. And it was the only time I ever saw him that he wasn't being Dylan.

"He was courting me, typing up a huge long poem for me—probably things from *Tarantula*. I was in love with Bob Dylan. I was utterly in awe of him. Dylan was one of the absolute necessities for tripping, along with Ravi Shankar and Ali Akbar Khan and . . . Steppenwolf! Dylan was the voice of God, after all. But then a lot of people were the voice of God. Anyway, I was very demure and respectful and I was about to get married—the next week in fact. Dylan became nasty when I refused to go to bed with him. Which turned to pure vituperation when I told him I was going to marry John. 'That jerk? If you're gonna marry someone like that you're more stupid than I thought,' he said. And then, like Rumpelstiltskin, he ripped up the poem he was writing for me and threw me out of the hotel. I was cast into utter darkness, meaning I was also cut out of the movie. Meanwhile, elsewhere in the hotel unbeknownst to me, he's fucking someone else. Dana Gillespie, if memory serves. And so, unceremoniously, ended my brief encounter with Bobby and entourage: Terry Southern, Bobby Neuwirth, Joan Baez, Allen Ginsberg. Allen was my date for Dylan's Albert Hall concert."

In the final sequence of *Don't Look Back*, as the limo speeds away from the Albert Hall concert, an ecstatic Dylan is for once at a loss for words. "I feel like I've been through some kinda . . ."

"Thing," says Bobby Neuwirth, completing the sentence. As fans pursue him, their hands on the window of the car, you understand the meaning of the film's title. *Don't Look Back* had been Dylan's motto for the past four years but it's also the last line of the horror movie *Isle of the Damned*, in which the hero and heroine are escaping in a small rowboat from Dr. Moreau's half-human mutations. But according to *Like a Bullet of Light*, the title came from Pennebaker.

"Because of the way Pennebaker shot and edited it, you get the feeling that he was filming every minute, but not everything got filmed," explains Bobby Neuwirth. "Penny also shot a little bit of film of John Lennon and his wife Cynthia, but the Beatles all got very nervous. They'd just made a film with Al Maysles; they were guys who'd grown up poor and they felt there were certain things you should get paid for. Like when someone takes your picture. It was goofy because they were used to doing *Ready Steady Go!* [a pop music show on BBC-TV] and they did it free because they thought of it as part of promoting a record, but when Penny started pulling out a camera it was clear he was doing this for Dylan. Also, it impinged on their meeting!

"There wasn't much to film anyway. It wasn't as if there was this great dialogue going on—the conversation was about nothing anyway. It was all weirdly formal and uptight—pretty much like what you imagine a bourgeois tea party in Liverpool would have been like. Of all of them, Lennon was the only one Dylan was interested in, and that's why I think Bob probably wanted to shoot the stuff in the limo the following year."

At the center of *Don't Look Back* there's The Encounter, and there are a lot of encounters in the film. There's the plummy-voiced interviewer from the BBC African Service ("How do you see the art of the folk song?"), the probing journalists ("Why are you so angry?"), the kamikaze groupie ("Hey, will you get that girl off our car?"), the drunk who threw the glass out the hotel window, the jerk backstage, Fleet Street hacks dictating their copy over the phone ("the bearded boys and the lank-haired girls, all . . . undertaker makeup"), floaters and fans, promoters, and the High Sheriff's Lady (*and* her three sons). But what we really want to see is our hero mano a mano in the new ultracool mode, squashing some pompous character from the establishment. Just for the hell of it. Hip vs. square. We want to see some existential blood spilled. And, miraculously, there he is—Mr. Jones. In the form of what? Of a reporter in suit and tie from *Time* magazine. Perfect. As Horace F. Judson stands there, Bob hands him a bone. "It's going to happen fast, you're not going to get it all."

In recent years, Horace, the old dodo, has whined that Dylan set him up, that it was all planned for the purpose of the documentary. Well, of course it was. It's Dylan's movie. More significantly, this is a full-length, walkin'-and-talkin', singin'-and-performin' portrait of the artist. Did he really think the ruthless little hipster was going to play fair with him, a hireling from *Time*?

"If I want to find out anything I don't read *Time* magazine," says Dylan with spectacular scorn. "Every word has its little letter and its big letter, man."

You remember the *Time* magazine thing because it is such a symbolic encounter in rock's us versus them mind-set. Dullard reporter versus hipster-princeling Bob takes on the aspects of an epic clash: the confrontation between the rotten, corrupt, aging Henry Luce (slick, smart-alecky) empire and Bob, the little godling bearing rock 'n' roll's Pentecostal message. He won't engage with *Time* magazine on its own terms. Why would he? No, he'll turn it into an absurdist dialogue. Like Muhammad Ali, all whimsy and quick jabs. And hell, maybe he did just do it for the documentary because in a sense he was a sort of Shiva—and the interview, as always in these things, is a battle for who would control reality.

The pretense fostered by cinema verité documentaries is that we are seeing the unguarded self, but with a mercurial and multiphrenic personality such as Dylan's, there's always the possibility that what we're seeing is a Dylan-on-Dylan effect. And, in any case, it's precisely this spin Dylan puts on reality that we want to see. As to whether Dylan's character in these films is a put-on, Pennebaker, for one, could care less.

"I don't think it matters at all. It would be like, after a play, if I told you the whole thing was fake. Does it change your opinion of the play? It's assumed that Dylan was *enacting*. But I think, in *Don't Look Back*, that Dylan's enacting his life as he wishes to enact it. Not necessarily as it *is*, and not necessarily as he wishes it *were*, but just as he wants to act it. *Don't Look Back* is a kind of fiction, but it's Dylan's fiction."

The iconic opening scene of *Don't Look
Back*—a sequence that has been endlessly
imitated in videos and movies—where
Dylan holds up and then discards placards
scrawled with words and freaked phrases
("pawking metaws") from "Subterranean
Homesick Blues." That's Allen Ginsberg in
the corner. London 1965, in the alley behind
Claridge's Hotel.

11 Ballad of a Thin Man

The unspeakable visions of the individual
In tranced fixation . . .
Telling the true story of the world in interior monolog
Composing wild, undisciplined, pure, coming in from
under, crazier the better . . .

—JACK KEROUAC, "BELIEF & TECHNIQUE FOR MODERN PROSE"

IGHWAY 61 REVISITED IS AN ALBUM WRITTEN BY BLUES ghosts, ghosts of the 61 Highway who have infested the brain of a midcentury hipster. "It's like a ghost is writing a song like that. It gives you the song, and it goes away, it goes away. You don't know what it means. Except the ghost picked me to write the song." But it's a haunted house and these are prankish ghosts who even on the darkest tracks squeak, snigger, and sneer.

Delta phantoms rise up, get in the groove, howl at the moon, catch the mailtrain. The title itself referring to the road the blues took, and specifically to Mississippi Fred McDowell's droning slide-guitar lament, "61 Highway Blues."

Lord if I should hap'n a-die, baby
'Fore you think my time have come
I want you bury my body
Down on Highway 61

Dylan comically dabbles in the number magic of the blues:

Now the fifth daughter on the twelfth night
Told the first father that things weren't right. . . .
Let me tell the second mother this has been done

But the second mother was with the seventh son
And they were both out on Highway 61

Underneath it all is the ghost of the blues with its equally outlandish cast of characters and singers. Ma Rainey came to Bob's freak show along with Beethoven, who brought his bedroll. And even Blind Willie McTell showed up here under his pseudonym Georgia Sam, along with Mississippi Fred McDowell and Robert Johnson. You've got Chuck Berry moving like a cool breeze all over the tracks, and there's Ivory Joe Hunter under the plunky piano on "It Takes a Lot to Laugh, It Takes a Train to Cry," a slowed-down country blues shuffle that's a sort of catechism of classic blues lyrics randomly shuffled together.

Well, I ride on a mailtrain, baby
Can't buy a thrill
Well, I've been up all night, baby
Leanin' on the windowsill

It doesn't matter that the verses have nothing in common with each other; it's just pure displaced Delta poetry.

On "From a Buick 6," originally titled "Lunatic Princess No. 3" (we don't know why) we can hear the Yeller Dog rolling down the track to Kokomo Arnold's "Milk Cow Blues"—which is where Elvis comes on board.

The album's title uses Highway 61, which runs from New Orleans to the Canadian border, as an allegory of American crimes. "This land is condemned all the way from New Orleans to Jerusalem," he sang in "Blind Willie McTell" (on *Bootleg Series Vol. 1–3*). It's where Robert Johnson went:

. . . down to the crossroads, fell down on my knees
Asked the Lord above, have mercy,
Save poor Bob if you please

The shrieking slide whistle of the opening of "Highway 61 Revisited" shouts "Wake up!" It's a toxic cartoon denouncing American culture that somehow involves him and his dad, Abe (with whom he had a strained relationship), in a diorama from Genesis. From there the scenario morphs into the American nightmare. With a talent for projecting his personal situation into a mythic dimension, Dylan slyly fuses the political, historical, and personal into a hornet's nest. Dylan is x-raying

American culture, all slick surface and commercial jive promising impossible things, Fourth of July rhetoric, police brutality, and the bomb. He's going into the nightmare's black core.

Now the rovin' gambler he was very bored
He was tryin' to create a next world war
He found a promoter who nearly fell off the floor
He said I never engaged in this kind of thing before
But yes I think it can be very easily done
We'll just put some bleachers out in the sun
And have it on Highway 61

Leslie Fiedler once said that America, the place itself, is a kind of toxic drug—its alienness and vastness a hallucinogen that induces delirium, causing madness, millennial delusions, and imperial maladies. And in the USA of 1965 Dylan knew you needed drugs to be able to penetrate the fog of lies, barbecues, suburbs, and security.

Not that Dylan doesn't believe in America, but his cast of characters don't live in the suburbs. The people who populate his songs are hustlers, wild women of the blues, frontier bandit queens, and former friends who have committed some unnamed transgression. People like Jack the Ripper, Belle Starr, Jezebel, Ma Rainey, Galileo, Delilah, Gypsy Davey, Cecil B. DeMille, Einstein, Robin Hood, Bette Davis, Romeo, Cain and Abel, the hunchback of Notre Dame, the Good Samaritan.

WHEN DYLAN WENT BACK INTO THE STUDIO AT THE END OF JULY TO start work on *Highway 61 Revisited* his producer, Tom Wilson, had mysteriously been replaced by a very laid-back Nashville cat, Bob Johnston. Dylan could hardly have found a more devoted producer than Johnston, who practically worshipped Dylan: "He was freaky to me . . . because I still believe that he's the only prophet we've had since Jesus. I don't think people are gonna realize it for another two or three hundred years when they figure out who really did help stop the Vietnam War, who did change everybody around and why our children aren't hiding under the damn tables now worrying about an atomic war. One day they'll wake up—and they'll realize what they had—instead of asking what kind of album he did and is it as good as the last one. That was always bullshit to me." Johnston claimed all he did was press the RECORD button, but he's a wily old galoot, a character and a half—and that must have endeared him to Dylan right there.

By the time he came to make *Highway 61 Revisited*, Dylan was much more sure of himself in the studio. In the past you could imagine Dylan in the recording studio, the shades, the harmonica rack, the cigarette dangling, the bottle of Beaujolais, the music stand in front of him with his scribbled pages. He's reading the lyrics. This method worked for the folk and protest songs where it was basically him and a guitar—and more or less the way he approached the recording sessions on *Bringing It All Back Home*, with its let-'er-rip arrangements, directed solely by manic energy and high spirits. But, working with session musicians, he needed to propel the songs, to create a sense of spontaneity and the drive—rather than reflection—that a rock song requires. On his acoustic songs—say, "Hard Rain"—Dylan was singing against a chord, which creates an entirely different feeling to working with session musicians, spinning his poetic lyrics around their licks. By the fall of '65 he'd figured out how to fuse his words onto the momentum of a band.

Not that he was going to be any more helpful to the musicians than he'd been on the previous album—after all, it's still Bob.

"He came in and played a song to the band once," Bob Johnston recalled. "And that was how they learned it. He never counted off, just launched right into it, so you always had to keep the tape rolling." Harvey Brooks, who played bass on most of the tracks early on, saw he was on a runaway train: "As I was to learn, this was a case of 'just go for it.' You were only going to get one or two shots, maybe, at each song," he told Clinton Heylin.

In the recording studio, Dylan seems to have followed Jack Kerouac's idea: "first thought best thought," a concept Kerouac didn't exactly always follow himself. The spontaneity of Dylan's method of making his records, his habit of often writing the lyrics to his songs in the studio, his image of recording songs in one take, and the rush of stream-of-consciousness lyrics gave the impression that we were hearing these thoughts as they flew through his brain. But, as Bob Hudson points out, the image of Dylan as an almost supernaturally spontaneous genius who recorded all his songs in one take is actually part of his myth. As Hudson, an observant Dylan sessionologist, points out: "Dylan did not record everything in one take on *Highway 61*. For instance, the released version of 'Just Like Tom Thumb's Blues' is take sixteen (!). Most of the takes were false starts, but there were four complete takes before they got the one they wanted. 'Like a Rolling Stone,' six takes (twenty incompletes). 'It Takes a Lot to Laugh,' ten, with seventeen false starts, 'Desolation Row,' five, with twelve incomplete takes, and so on."

Highway 61 is a druggy, manic, aesthetic crusade: They're all together in a drunken boat, a crank-filled craft on the verge of capsizing and being swallowed up by the maelstrom Dylan and Co. have created. They're kept afloat by the sheer force of will of their Captain Ahab, who manages to maintain his equilibrium through all these unstable songs.

He also had a few nutty ideas. At some point, Dylan wanted Phil Spector to produce the album. Now that's a scary thought! Another plan Dylan had was to bring in a soul sound and actually gets the Chambers Brothers to sing backup on "Tombstone Blues." But in the end Bloomfield's rattlesnake guitar and the scruffy backup sound worked better for the wry lyrics. We'd have to wait another thirteen years to get a gospel backup track on a Dylan record.

"Tombstone Blues" is old-fashioned Buck Owens country rock (overlaid with Chicago blues guitar leads) that chimes perfectly with the mock hillbilly yarn. It wasn't all that laid-back, though. They needed twelve takes to nail it.

Dylan claimed he wrote "Desolation Row" in the back of a cab on the way to the studio, but you know Desolation Row ain't that easy to find and not every taxi's gonna take you there.

> *They're selling postcards of the hanging*
> *They're painting the passports brown*
> *The beauty parlor is filled with sailors*
> *The circus is in town*
> *Here comes the blind commissioner*
> *They've got him in a trance*
> *One hand is tied to the tight-rope walker*
> *The other is in his pants*

"Desolation Row" takes place in a claustrophobic space, in a back alley behind a bohemian crash pad. It's like a circle of hell, but one you wouldn't mind being sentenced to.

Dylan initially did "Desolation Row" with backup musicians, believing he needed a big sound behind it. Bloomfield's guitar and Al

Kooper's organ would seem to be an ideal accompaniment as their quirky instruments were already denizens of Desolation Row. But he wasn't happy. The fact that some of the instruments were out of tune didn't upset him; that was pretty much true of most of the album. It just added that sour jangly sound he favored. Too much precision would kill the vibe.

Just then fate intervened. The Nashville guitar player Charlie McCoy, an old friend of Bob Johnston's, happened to be in New York visiting the World's Fair, and he stopped by the session. Dylan asked him if he'd try playing acoustic guitar on "Desolation Row." McCoy's idol was Grady Martin, who'd come up with the classic guitar riff on Marty Robbins's "El Paso," and McCoy, without being instructed what to do, played a flamenco riff reminiscent of Martin's. McCoy's guitar prances, he makes the words dance. It's far from El Paso and Rosa's cantina but the prettiness of the melody curiously doesn't diminish the phantasmagoria, it only enhances the creepiness and puts all the freakishness in relief.

The title "Desolation Row" combines Jack Kerouac's *Desolation Angels* with John Steinbeck's *Cannery Row*. Al Kooper thought it was about the wildlife on Eighth Avenue—hookers, pimps, drug dealers. The more literary minded said it was T. S. Eliot's *The Waste Land*, but if you went to the movies it was Dylan's eleven-minute, twenty-one-second Fellini movie.

> *Einstein, disguised as Robin Hood*
> *With his memories in a trunk*
> *Passed this way an hour ago*
> *With his friend, a jealous monk*
> *He looked so immaculately frightful*
> *As he bummed a cigarette*
> *Then he went off sniffing drainpipes*
> *And reciting the alphabet*
> *Now you would not think to look at him*
> *But he was famous long ago*
> *For playing the electric violin*
> *On Desolation Row*

Some have theorized it could have been a suicide note, but if you've ever heard Dylan singing in concert, he often turns it into a black humor hymn.

"Just Like Tom Thumb's Blues" is a hipster's weary chronicle of his exotic misadventures in the lower depths of bohemia.

When you're lost in the rain in Juarez
And it's Eastertime too
And your gravity fails
And negativity don't pull you through
Don't put on any airs
When you're down on Rue Morgue Avenue
They got some hungry women there
And they really make a mess outta you

Bob Neuwirth claims to have written this sultry opening scenario—and it does sound like him. The story goes that Neuwirth gave Dylan the first two lines and challenged him to write a song with that opening, and Dylan took him up on it. "Because the cops don't need you/And man they expect the same" also sounds like a Neuwirthism, but Dylan was as cunning an absorber of the vibe as he was a pickpocket of tunes and phrases. By this point he'd got down the hustler's posturing, the drifter's skewed tale, and the pool shark's bag of jaded aphorisms. The tempo slows down to mimic the singer's disillusionment, but Dylan also wants you to hear the midnight-hour melancholy.

Sweet Melinda
The peasants call her the goddess of gloom
She speaks good English
And she invites you up into her room
And you're so kind
And careful not to go to her too soon
And she takes your voice
And leaves you howling at the moon

It is a classic mid-'60s Dylan hipster blend where he stirs up burlesque, morbid introspection, doom, and farce in a witch's brew of emotions.

WHENEVER A NEW LP CAME OUT, IT WAS AS IF BOB HAD CALLED AND left you a message. It's a little enigmatic, but what did you expect? There are coded messages all over these albums. It doesn't really matter what they mean, though Dylanologists pore over them like sorcerers over entrails. You want to know what Bob's up to. What is he *on*? Because you want to be there too.

He tells us what he's doing in that interview with Nat Hentoff: "I wouldn't advise anybody to use drugs—certainly not the hard drugs; drugs are medicine. But opium and hash and pot—now, those aren't drugs; they just bend your mind a little. I think *everybody's* mind should be bent once in a while. Not by LSD though. LSD is medicine—a different kind of medicine. It makes you aware of the universe, so to speak; you realize how foolish *objects* are. But LSD is not for groovy people; it's for mad, hateful people who want revenge. It's for people who usually have heart attacks. They ought to use it at the Geneva Convention."

Well, as always, it's hard to know if Bob means what he says—or says what he means. It is striking, however, that he omits from this rant his drug of choice.

"With his ferocious intake of amphetamine," says Antonia, "he was already such an electric entity, he was *radioactive!*"

It's always been Dylan's claim—at least in the '60s—that he composed his songs in a trancelike state, induced by *whatever*—that he just snatched his songs out of the air. At one time—roughly up to the eighth century B.C.—this kind of channeling was the norm. People heard voices, and one of the things drugs do is let you hear the voices in your head—bat-squeaking sibylline utterances, suppressed by two thousand years of common sense and scientific rationalism.

To twentieth-century minds, everyone before the eighth century B.C. was insane—hence the Bible, mythology, folktales, garden gnomes, little people, water sprites, and Keebler elves. The Old Testament prophets were raving schizophrenics (they didn't know where the voices in their heads came from—and neither do we). Ingesting a god—or a pill from Sandoz pharmaceuticals—led to bringing a lot of old ghosts back to life.

There's even time for a love song on the album—sort of. Naturally, being Dylan, there's a liberal dose of vitriol in his sympathetic offer to help her out.

When your mother sends back all your invitations
And your father to your sister he explains
That you're tired of yourself and all of your creations
Won't you come see me, Queen Jane?

With propositions like this you may want to pass on further offers of help from Bob. "Queen Jane Approximately" is an ode to Joan Baez, set to a very strange melody—essentially roller-skating music—with the accompaniment of Dylan's out-of-tune guitar.

On "Ballad of a Thin Man" the tack piano in a minor key and Al Kooper's *Phantom of the Opera* organ are a perfect setup for the punch line "something is happening here/But you don't know what it is/Do you," with its chilling gong-like "*Mr. Joooones*" hitting you like some terrible obliterating clock. It's a slow-moving horror movie coming at you as you look around the room to see who—other than yourself—might be the target. Kooper's organ howls and groans like a wounded beast dragging its own mutilated carcass away from the psychic bloodbath.

There are many candidates as to whom Mr. Jones might be—too many. It could have been the moronic journalists asking dopey questions, including Max Jones, a jazz critic for *Melody Maker* who wasn't a big fan of Bob's, and Jeffrey Jones, who claimed in *Rolling Stone* that he was the one, and a young reporter for *Newsweek* who pestered Dylan between sets at Newport in '65 about the use of the harmonica in folk music. When Dylan and his cynical courtiers ran into him later on he jeered at him, "Getting it all down, Mr. Jones?" Or it may have been aimed at Dylan's hapless first enthusiast and biographer Robert Shelton, who could never fathom the alien life form he'd made contact with and in the end would destroy his life. The accompaniment is perfect in its frightful, goonish way. That it's Halloween music makes "Ballad of a Thin Man" all the more unsettling; he's laughing at you in the opening verse because to hipster Bob we're all Mr. Joneses. We're the collective Other, the unhip rabble outside the gates of Eden.

Now you see this one-eyed midget
Shouting the word "NOW"
And you say, "For what reason?"
And he says, "How?"
And you say, "What does this mean?"
And he screams back, "You're a cow
Give me some milk
Or else go home"
Because something is happening here
But you don't know what it is
Do you, Mister Jones?

There's not much point in asking Dylan who Mr. Jones is. You know he's just going to keep up the sideshow, but you can't resist, can you? "He's a pinboy," he says. "He also wears suspenders. He's a real person. You know him, but not by that name. I saw him come into the room one night and he looked like a camel. He proceeded to put his eyes in his pocket. I asked this guy who he was and he said, 'That's Mr. Jones.' Then I asked this cat, 'Doesn't he do anything but put his eyes in his pocket?' And he told me, 'He puts his nose on the ground.' It's all there, it's a true story."

The concept of the freak was a drug-induced extension of the anti-hero protagonist of noir movies, and, by the mid-'6os, the freak had become a popular type. Dylan was seen as an antihero ready to lead an army of freaks to pull down the walls of Babylon, and amphetamine is sprinkled over Dylan's mid-'6os albums like volcanic dust.

Rimbaud wasn't just an inspiring literary influence on Dylan; he was also his pharmacologist. Dylan took Rimbaud's advice pretty literally. "It is through the long, endless, unrestrained, and systematic disruption *of all the senses*—madness, torment, poisons—that a poet turns himself into a visionary," the little hashish eater advised. Drugs were the mana of the '6os, the occult substance that altered reality—and by mid-decade reality needed to be seriously tweaked.

THE SESSIONS TO RERECORD "DESOLATION ROW" TOOK PLACE ON JULY 29–30 and August 2 and 4. They were so prolific that Dylan ended up with an hour-long LP. You can't fit all this inspired madness in the micro-grooves of an LP though, so "Sitting on a Barbed Wire Fence," "Positively 4th Street," and "Can You Please Crawl Out Your Window" were cut from the album—the last two becoming the second and third singles off the sessions. But three Dylan put-down songs in a row were too much even for his rabid fans and "Can You Please Crawl Out Your Window" with a bombastic backing track sank like a stone.

But who is this freak he's asking to please crawl out his window and why?

He sits in your room, his tomb, with a fist full of tacks
Preoccupied with his vengeance
Cursing the dead that can't answer him back
I'm sure that he has no intentions
Of looking your way, unless it's to say
That he needs you to test his inventions

Well, who does this sound like? Bob looking at himself in a parabolic mirror. There's always suspicion—even the scathing put-down of Mr. Jones—that it's about him, a warped self-portrait. It's the dreaded self-referentiality of pop-star fame: In the end you're sitting in a room alone gazing into your looking-glass world with room service and a thousand telephones that don't ring.

Alternate titles to *Highway 61 Revisited* dreamed up by Columbia executives—*Yet Another Side of Bob Dylan* and *A Whole New Bob*—suggest how out of tune his record company was with what Dylan was doing. The cover of the album shows an intense, glowering Dylan wearing a Triumph motorcycle T-shirt and a psychedelic blouse borrowed from a local boutique, looking like a 1965 James Dean with a modified pompadour hairdo. At first it seems like the least contrived of Dylan's covers so far. It looks like a casual snapshot, but everything to do with Dylan's image is thought out. This is rock, where the look is consummate. It's a still from a movie, with little clues we can only guess at. Why is Neuwirth standing behind him posing with a Nikon? You'll have to play the album to find out; the movie is in the grooves.

Highway 61 got to #3 in the United States, but its impact was as if a new rock gospel had appeared. Phil Ochs, who had a battered relationship with Dylan, breathlessly described its arrival to Anthony Scaduto: "Every album up to *Highway 61*, I had an increasing lot of secret fear, 'Oh my God, what can he do next?' And then I put on *Highway 61* and I laughed and said it's so ridiculous. It's impossibly good. It just can't be that good. And I walked away and I didn't listen to it again right away because I thought this was too much. How can a human mind do this?"

In some occult way, Dylan became a true mirror of the times—like James Dean in *Rebel Without a Cause*, or Kerouac's *On the Road*—into which the younger generation could see itself and say, "Yes, that's me!"

The USA was a haunted country infested by demons, a country under a spell, a bad dream from which we were always looking for someone to wake us. And there he was! Dylan had created an alternate America, but it wasn't the one envisioned by yippies, hippies, the SDS, the Weathermen, or anyone else.

Dylan was writing in a hieroglyphic language that translated thoughts into visible images. The abrupt transitions, elliptical expressions, abbreviated snatches of dialogue between unknown participants are more like jump cuts in a movie than your average mid-'60s rock song.

Something has changed in the world; some significant shift has taken place: the perception that the world doesn't have to be the way we inherited it. On the contrary, it can be *like this*!

Two aliens from hyphenated galaxies. With
Andy Warhol at the Factory in front of the
double Elvis painting that Warhol gave
Dylan and that Dylan would eventually
trade for a couch.

12 Godzilla vs. Mothra: *Two Icons of the '60s Meet Under False Pretenses*

Bob Dylan and Andy Warhol knew almost nothing about each other before their first meeting in January 1966. Despite his sponsorship of the Velvet Underground—essentially thrust on him by members of his inner circle—Warhol's taste in pop music ran to campy, catchy tunes like "My Boyfriend's Back" and "Da Doo Ron Ron." Then Andy's friends began telling him that Dylan was mocking him (and his relationship with Edie Sedgwick) in "Like a Rolling Stone"—a perfect little nouvelle vague short about a dizzy debutante and her clueless, posturing mentor (Warhol). The diplomat in the song rides a chrome horse, carries on his shoulder a Siamese cat (Andy was a serious cat fancier), and turns out not to be where it's at—which our poor misguided heroine discovers only after he takes from her everything he can steal. Although Dylan and Edie weren't introduced until December 1965, Paul Morrissey, director of the later so-called Warhol movies, points out, "Dylan would run into Andy in the nightclubs with Edie and he wanted her. He just made up his mind he was going to take her away and he did in the end, and then he just threw her away."

Dylan, despite his hip friends and frequent trips to the Museum of Modern Art, seems to have been clueless about pop art. Like many people at the time he probably thought that pop art was a novelty, like Hula-Hoops. But Warhol himself interested him. He wasn't simply a painter; he had become a '60s icon like Dylan. As far as most people were concerned the two of them *were* the '60s. Warhol's image was as indelible as his art, his films were scandalous and inscrutable, and the scene at the Factory had cast an exotic and sinister shadow over him that he had transferred to Max's Kansas City, where he nightly held court in the back room.

Given Dylan's natural curiosity and Andy's giddy pursuit of celebrities, the meeting between them might seem inevitable, but Dylan, who was incessantly touring and recording, needed a specific motive for visiting Warhol—and that was Edie Sedgwick.

The Dylan-Warhol meeting happened to be just around the time that Edie, Warhol's doomed superstar, was wearying of being cast in more and more demeaning roles in his movies—and not getting paid for it. Enter Bob Neuwirth, a charismatic boulevardier, artist, and folksinger, who was Bob Dylan's closest friend and partner in social mayhem. Edie had met Neuwirth just two weeks earlier at Dylan's favorite hangout, the Kettle of Fish. She idolized Dylan but begins a love affair with Neuwirth.

"The joint was atwitter, the denizens agog. Everyone was saying, 'Bobby's coming, Bobby's coming,'" says photographer Nat Finkelstein, on the day in January 1966 that Dylan and entourage paid a visit to Andy Warhol's Factory. The elevator opens, and Dylan, Bobby Neuwirth, and a film crew walk in. "Dylan is acting cool," recalls Warhol's assistant, Gerard Malanga, "pretty much keeping his mouth shut. He had this way of saying, '*Wellll, yeahhh,*' to whatever anybody said."

"The day that Dylan arrived the vibe was so cold," says Billy Name, the Factory's resident photographer and mystic. "Dylan was so cold and unresponsive. Gerard brought him [Dylan] in and introduced him to Andy, and they shook hands actually. And we already had the setup to do the screen test. So we moved right into that." The ostensible purpose of the visit, at least in Andy's eyes, had been the screen test, a three-minute silent film portrait shot with a stationary camera. Screen tests were one of the many ingenious inventions of Warhol's accidental genius. Many famous people visited the Factory, his studio on Forty-seventh Street—Andy encouraged people to drop by—but being shy, inarticulate, and uneducated, his solution to the arrival of daunting guests was to put them in chairs and film them. During the three minutes (the length of a Bolex reel) it took to film the sitters, hidden emotions would unconsciously leak out—paranoia, arrogance, shiftiness—creating some of the most unsettling portraits of the late twentieth century. Among the people recorded in Warhol's screen tests were: Marcel Duchamp, Cass Elliot, Allen Ginsberg, Nico, Lou Reed, and Susan Sontag. They would be screened at sixteen frames per second, giving them an eerie, static quality.

"And then after we did a screen test ordinarily there would be just people laughing and talking about things, but Dylan would not converse," Billy Name recalls. "It was just discomfort and cold and not responsive.

And Andy realizing that he couldn't just do nothing, the way he usually did, and everything would be okay." But it wasn't okay and it wasn't going to be. According to Malanga, Dylan took a dislike to Warhol and his scene almost from the moment he entered the Factory. Not only was he appalled to find himself in a hotbed of gay speedfreaks, he didn't seem to have been aware that Warhol was gay. Many people at the time weren't, in part because he'd been linked with Edie in the gossip columns and in part because of the way he dressed—leather jacket, jeans, boots, shades—an almost identical outfit to Dylan's. Although during the mid-'60s Dylan affected an androgynous image, Neuwirth, Dylan, and their entourage were heterosexual bohemians who amused themselves with macho toys like motorbikes and guns.

For all of its potential as a seminal encounter of two '60s titans, Dylan's Factory visit was, as Malanga describes it, a "non-event." How could it have been otherwise, with the participants focused on maintaining their cool? "It was two totally uncommunicative people noncommunicating with each other," says Paul Morrissey. "Andy was so impressed, because Dylan was such a famous man, but Dylan was so mean and bloody-minded and miserable that he wouldn't talk. His type of drug addiction made him very remote and closed off. He was the withdrawn type of speedfreak, but underneath he must have been resentful and vindictive, as those types of people often are. In his long life in show business, I've never heard that he was a particularly nice guy. Once he hooked up with Bobby Neuwirth, it got worse."

"The circus had come to town," Finkelstein says, "and Andy was in a state of high anxiety. A visit by someone whose personality outshone Andy's, that was huge. No wonder Andy was frightened. These two great beings clashing." Any number of people thought the meeting would turn out to be a classic pop event, even a historic occasion. But like other promising meetings of remarkable men—Edgar Allan Poe and Charles Dickens, James Joyce and Sergei Eisenstein, Sigmund Freud and Salvador Dalí—nothing particularly interesting transpired.

Neither Warhol nor Dylan was a great conversationalist, and as gushy as Andy could be in the presence of another famous individual, he wasn't exactly a warm person. Warhol's chilly aspect, like Dylan's, was part of his image and art. Almost immediately the temperature dropped.

Nat Finkelstein shot the pictures. Even in an awkward meeting such as this you needed photographs. "Their encounter was carefully contrived and well orchestrated," says Finkelstein. "Dylan, Neuwirth, and Andy were sitting together, but their presence there was predicated on being recorded. I told Andy and Bobby to put on shades and look directly into the camera. None of them related to the others. The scene reminded me of three merchant princes done by some Flemish painter, and I shot them that way."

It was the clash of the titans. Who was the hippest? Who would come out of it the coolest? Because Dylan didn't want anything from Andy, and the reason he'd come—Edie—wasn't there, he won the day, but not without making a dumb mistake.

"Once the screen test was over and they'd posed for their pictures," Warhol's friend Robert Heide recalls, "Dylan got up and walked over to one of the panels of Elvis as a cowboy holding a gun [one of several Double Elvises standing against the Factory walls] and said, 'I think I'll just take this for payment, man.' That was only the second time I ever saw Andy blushing, just kind of cringing. Somebody demanding payment!"

But according to Malanga, this isn't what exactly happened. "Dylan didn't simply commandeer the Elvis painting. Andy *offered* it to him. And Andy purposely picked the Elvis. It wasn't as if he had a lot of different paintings lying about. He figured, 'Ah, Elvis Presley, singer; Bob Dylan, singer.'"

Still, as Billy Name explains, it was a little more complicated than a simple exchange: "It wasn't supposed to be just for the screen test; Andy was hoping for an ongoing interaction. Maybe Bob would ask him to do his album covers. Andy made that offer anticipating an ongoing relationship, but Dylan called his bluff, walking off with the Elvis as his pay for three minutes of work. He closed the door and disappeared."

Bobby Neuwirth helped Dylan carry the painting out into the elevator and down into the street. They tied the painting down to the top of their station wagon ("like a deer poached out of season," says Finkelstein) and drove it up to Dylan's Woodstock home. He showed nothing but disdain for it. Depending on who you believe, he hung it upside down, stuck it in a closet, or used it as a dartboard—or worse. According to Morrissey, "A couple of years later, somebody went to visit Dylan in his loft or wherever he lived and there was Andy's painting of Elvis, with a hose coming through his crotch. Andy was really offended. He said in an Andy voice, 'Gee, that's worth a lot of money. He shouldn't have done that.' It was at that point, of course, far more valuable than when he gave it away."

Whether anything like this actually happened, Dylan clearly didn't understand the value of the painting or care for it. "I don't want this," he told Albert Grossman, adding, "Why did he give it to me?" He swapped the picture with Grossman's sofa, but in the end the joke was on Bob. In 1988, Grossman's widow, Sally, sold the painting for $720,000; it is worth far more than that today.

Reasons for Warhol's wanting to meet and film Dylan are not hard to guess. Andy was a promiscuously starstruck character, and clearly in awe of Dylan's celebrity and charismatic cool. He probably thought he might get Dylan to appear in one of his movies, maybe opposite Edie, which would've been a big coup for him. But Dylan had his own ideas for movies, some of which may have involved Edie—but definitely not Warhol.

For a while it was Dylan who held out the possibility of making a movie with Edie. The source of Edie's charismatic energy came from the attraction/repulsion impulse of sexless affairs (which mirrored her relationship with her father), and Dylan saw that Edie might be an ideal foil to play opposite him. As with Andy, her opposing spin and charge would animate them both. But Dylan's attempts to implement his mystical cinematic romances—like *Renaldo and Clara*—have always been problematic. Film, even at its most elusive, is far more explicit than song lyrics (especially Dylan's) and would not fit well with his finely tuned mystique.

The turning point in the Warhol-Edie-Dylan triangle came one afternoon in the Village. Andy was going to be picking up some outfits from the Leather Man and arranged to meet Robert Heide at the Kettle of Fish. Edie by this point was involved with Dylan in some way—a movie project that Albert Grossman was supposedly setting up and so forth, and this had caused some strain between Edie and Andy.

"I get there," says Heide, "and who's there but Edie—Andy hasn't shown up yet—she's sitting there having a glass of white wine and there are tears running down her face. I said, 'What's going on?' And she just starts muttering, 'I can't get close to him. I try to get close to him but he won't respond. I guess it's finished, it's over.' I really didn't know what she was talking about, but it turned out she was upset about Andy, who could be very cold, especially when he felt people were moving away from him. Then Andy comes in with the box and he's actually dressed in a blue suede outfit, and in his whispery voice says, 'Oh, hi, oh, hi!' He's got dark glasses on, and I order a beer, Andy orders a beer, and we're just sitting there.

"A few minutes later, this limousine pulls up, and in comes Bob Dylan—this was around the *Blonde on Blonde* period—Dylan walks over and sits next to Edie. Very little is said, but it's obvious there's this incredible kinship going on between them. Andy's looking over at them—if a look could kill—then he's looking away, and Edie's looking askance, and finally, after about maybe ten minutes go by with no one saying more than a couple of words, Dylan says, 'Let's split!' And out they go and get into the limo. Andy said nothing. He just finished his beer and we left. You know it was that kind of thing around the Factory of always being super-cool, that cold side of amphetamines and not talking too much about feelings. I mean, that was what was unusual about Edie that day because nobody ever really talked about anything personal as far as I could tell. And that moment was the turning point. It was happening right then with her going off with Dylan and then whatever kind of abandonment he was feeling. Andy could be very secretive."

Like most people who only encountered Edie socially, she was a radiant creature—witty, cool, beautiful, and talented. She designed her own clothes, embodied the ultimate mid-'60s hip look, and seemed like someone with infinite possibilities. Dylan, Neuwirth, and Grossman made her think they were going to launch a singing career for her. The problem was she couldn't sing a note. So when she jumped ship and went with the Dylan clan, she had a rude awakening. Nothing was going to happen with her singing career.

"Edie was taken under a management deal with Bob Dylan's hideous manager, Albert Grossman," Morrissey says. "He forbade her to hang out with Andy, and thought Andy should never even *show* her films again, because they would damage her great art career."

"There was the prospect of a movie with Bob Dylan," says Danny Fields, the former Ramones manager and Warhol's friend. "But Grossman never did anything with her. There was talk of it, most of it negative, about Andy. And they would say to her, 'You know you can really go places, you could really be an actress, you're so beautiful, you're getting so thin, why do you hang around with that bunch of dizzy amphetamine faggots? They're not going to do anything for you.' You know she was a new toy for them. So I don't know if she turned her back on Andy in a huff. I think he probably walked on her. But she became more and more absorbed in drugs. It got more and more serious. And she was having this all-consuming affair with Bobby Neuwirth."

Neuwirth says he felt Edie was wasting her time making "fatuous

Warhol movies." So what kind of movie would you make with Edie? Neuwirth made a short, "Chaplinesque" (as he described it) film of Edie pulling her leather rhinoceros on roller skates up Fifth Avenue during the Easter Day parade, with the cops pretending to give her a ticket for an illegally parked pachyderm. As months went by, it was clear that a Bob Dylan film was never going to happen.

"Dylan and Albert Grossman were interested in her as a possible match-up for a film with Bob," says Malanga, "but when they found out she was a bundle of no talent, they dumped her."

Almost everyone who knew them agrees that Dylan and Edie as lovers is a pop myth. "That was a ruse," says Malanga. The fantasized Edie/Dylan love affair is portrayed in the kitschy romance-novel tableaux (logs crackle in the fireplace as Edie and "Dylan" make love at his Woodstock hideaway in the movie *Factory Girl*). "It's a myth, a fabricated myth," Billy Name says. Danny Fields, however, says he has proof of the liaison: that leopard-skin pillbox hat.

"It was said he wrote 'Leopard-Skin Pill-Box Hat' about her," says Fields. "You know she did have a leopard-skin pillbox hat. She also had a leopard-skin coat, which I gather she stole from someone. She left the hat in my apartment. People say there are all kinds of songs he wrote for Edie. Was 'Sad-Eyed Lady' about her or 'Just Like a Woman'? I think if you ask Dylan who he wrote this or that song about he wouldn't know. I think this is all sort of apocryphal now. I think it's one of those things.... There's no truth, there's no history, there's no memory. Especially when you're talking about things from forty years ago."

Dylan himself, a notoriously evasive interviewee and rewriter of history—his own and others—told a 1985 interviewer that "I never had that much to do with Edie Sedgwick. I've ... read that I have had, but I don't remember Edie that well. I remember she was around, but I know other people who, as far as I know, might have been involved with Edie. Uh, she was a great girl. An exciting girl, very enthusiastic. She was around the Andy Warhol scene, and I drifted in and out of that scene."

In a sense, Dylan did make several movies with Edie. His film noir album, *Blonde on Blonde*, with its night world of freaks, the lost, hipsters, and hustlers, seems spun out of the phosphorescent night world that Edie inhabited: all those strange places you find yourself at in the middle of the night with people you barely know doing strange things and you're too stoned to leave. For Dylan, with his attraction to mythical imagery, Edie was an irresistible type: the doomed, elusive damsel seen through his night-vision goggles. As the unattainable, neurasthenic woman, the disturbed lover who takes like a woman but "breaks just like a little girl," the seductive drug geisha holding out a handful of "rain and asking him to defy it," whose infectious gravity could pull him into the underworld, Edie populates *Blonde on Blonde* as its unstable object of desire.

With Dylan, it's always a favorite game to guess who exactly this or that song is really about. In "Stuck Inside of Mobile with the Memphis Blues Again," you've got Ruthie in her honky-tonk lagoon telling Bob that his debutante (Edie) knows only what he needs, "but I know what you want." And then there's the quintessential Edie, the child-woman of "Just Like a Woman." You won't get a better snapshot of Edie than the fog, amphetamine, and pearls in that song, or its refrain about a lover's split personality—all sexy self-possession one moment, collapsed rag doll the next.

Whether they were an item or not, the lyrics from Dylan's 1965–66 streak of songs are littered with mutated Edies. His most haunting line, "The ghost of 'lectricity howls in the bones of her face" from "Visions of Johanna," offers a spectral X-ray of Edie's agitated spirit. In Ivan Karp's perturbed memory of Edie, "There were sparks flying off her brain!"

Warhol's subsequent attitude toward Dylan was dismissive (as it was to most people). "Dylan," said Warhol, "was never really real—he was just mimicking real people and the amphetamine made it come out magic. With amphetamine he could copy the right words and make it sound right. But that boy never felt a thing [*laughs*]. I just never bought it."

Dylan later regretted at least one aspect of the meeting: "I once traded an Andy Warhol 'Elvis Presley' painting for a sofa, which was a stupid thing to do. I always wanted to tell Andy what a stupid thing I'd done, and if he had another painting he would give me, I'd never do it again."

As inconsequential as the Dylan-Warhol meeting turned out to be, its squandered potential has had a long afterlife of speculation and humor, most recently in the *Bob Hates Andy* cartoon strips. In them, Bob makes profound, satiric comments about America while, at the beginning of the series at least, Warhol is presented as a shopaholic ninny who makes fun of Dylan's noble social aspirations. Although cooler looking and more simpatico than the Warhol in the comic strip is, Dylan was in 1966 clearly out of sync with the current avant-garde—he didn't, for one, *get* pop art, and was closer in temperament to the abstract impressionists. Dylan's genius was to fuse the inventions of modernism onto pop music, but by the mid-'60s modernism had been absorbed by bourgeois culture—Kafka and Joyce were taught in high school, toddlers encouraged to paint like Picasso and Miró. The avant-garde had moved on—it mocked the old-school modernist values of originality, passion, and the lone inspired genius (the way we saw Dylan, basically, and he saw himself). Warhol was the avatar of this new aesthetic: postmodernism. Along with all the other pieties postmodernism disposed of was the old bohemian disdain for money. They're artists, that's their job—to irritate self-righteous liberals: *Épater la bourgeoisie!* (Shake up the pretentious middle-class dodoes at any opportunity!)

A comic strip that represents any actual conversation Dylan and Warhol might ever conceivably have had—*as if!* They're an excuse for the creator, Joshua Cicerone, to play with stereotypes of his own devising. In an interview with Kevin Johns, Cicerone admits that, "In a way, they're warring sides of my own psyche."

Essentially *Bob Hates Andy* is about a schizophrenic culture debating itself using Dylan and Warhol as symbolic figures. "I can't help but see these guys as towers of cultural significance," he says. "I love Dylan the musician. I live by Warhol's conceptual revelations. But both artists transcended their craft. They're modern archetypes of genius. I approach them as extreme models of the modern, liberal, volatile, urban intellectual perspective. I definitely look at them as cultural dialogues."

Dylan and Warhol have become caricatures, cultural sacred monsters, and that brief encounter in January 1966 has spawned an ongoing prêt-a-porter cultural confrontation—one naturally not too scrupulous about the facts. Andy never called himself a genius—that would be against the postmodernist playbook. And Cicerone, for instance, seems to believe "Desolation Row" was written about the Factory (really? how would that work?) even though "Desolation Row" was recorded six months before Dylan ever visited it. Well, there was one aspect of postmodernism that Dylan did take away with him. If you were asked to describe postmodernism in one word it would be appropriation, an approach that Dylan in the 2000s would become pretty adept at.

"I have more offenses at my beck than I have thoughts to put them in, imagination to give them shape, or time to act them in." The dark prince of pop in Denmark, 1966.

13 That Wild Mercury Sound:
What Are Shakespeare, Memphis Minnie, Jackie DeShannon, John Lennon, Achilles, Napoleon XIV, Lesley Gore, and Johann Sebastian Bach Doing on This Album?

ORGET THAT YOU BOUGHT THIS ALBUM AN HOUR EARLIER. The disc spins and Dylan comes to life; it's a magical device. He's talking to you (or someone) and you're mesmerized by this tale told in reshuffled verses. *Blonde on Blonde* is a kind of rock bunker hallucination, creating a world in miniature, a sort of self-contained planet inhabited by the dank fantasies that rock projects. Like the Stones' *Exile on Main Street* and Hendrix's *Electric Ladyland* from the same era, these are the kinds of albums you perform séances with on nights when the moon is dark and little children have forgotten to say their prayers. It's a mid-'60s *Tales of Mystery and Imagination* filmed by an androgynous vampire rock star swaddled in fur coats and amphetamine. He's the recluse who rises from his coffin in the crypt of his house on Bleecker Street accompanied by dwarves and monkeys, gypsies, and thieves. You don't have to go to New Orleans to ingest the grotesque tableaux of American life. Mardi Gras, in all its decorative grotesquerie was already internalized into a black light compartment in Dylan's brain.

His actual life wasn't quite as gothic as the scenes depicted in *Blonde on Blonde.* He'd recently entered into that most bourgeois of commitments, getting married in a private ceremony on Long Island—something he'd kept secret even from close friends—and was planning to move into a country mansion in Woodstock. Sara Lownds, the former Shirley Noznisky, was the ideal companion for Dylan, a mystical child he'd met at the Playboy Club. At the time she was married to an older guy and bored, so she started going out on her own and hanging around the Village picking up occult tricks—tarot cards, palm readings, patchouli, and astrology. She wasn't in the folk scene, and she wasn't a fan or a groupie. But she possessed the essential quality of any Dylan partner: she was a mysterious unknown, and through their years of marriage would remain an enigmatic figure.

So, if he was happily married, rich, and living in rural tranquillity, how did all these phantoms and freaks get into the tracks? It's about "a minority of, you know, cripples and Orientals," Dylan explained. "And, uh, you know the world they live in." Where they lived was in Bob's overheated brain.

Blonde on Blonde has a melancholy cast to it, a world-weariness. It was recorded during the American leg of his grueling 1966 world tour, but the jaded mood gives it a ruminative, wistful tone. Exhaustion has turned into a kind of psychic entropy. His nervous system is leaking; the universe to which he's symbiotically connected is winding down. There is a sense of energy draining out; lights flicker from the opposite loft, but there's nothing, really nothing to turn off.

The demons of paranoia pour out of *Blonde on Blonde* like rats from a plague ship: cops, cheating women, swindles, broken promises, double-crosses, phoniness, narcissism (that leopard-skin pillbox hat), sexual vindictiveness. Its atmosphere is claustrophobic. Things are closing in; the oxygen is getting used up. "The room's so stuffy I can hardly breathe . . . and I can't be the last to leave." There's no exit. The album is filled with images of entrapment, being conned, betrayal, the futility of escape. Getting stuck inside of Mobile, the price you pay for going through things twice—or doing fourteen takes of the same song.

The sound of *Blonde on Blonde* is different even from his two previous albums. There's no longer that driving warpath energy of *Bringing It All Back Home* and *Highway 61 Revisited*, with the nuclear momentum of "Maggie's Farm" and the howling vowels of "Like a Rolling Stone." He's not going to lean on the words the way he did on "Like a Rolling Stone." *Howwww does it feeeeel*? His voice is smoother, and he's almost crooning on "Absolutely Sweet Marie."

Like everything else Dylan does and says and sings, *Blonde on Blonde* oscillates between put-on and profundity. The title of the album itself is a double entendre that refers to a rock star's endless harem as well as to Kazimir Malevich's constructivist painting *White Square on White*. Avant-garde art sandwiched between serial blondes. It was "someone else's idea," Dylan says of the title (probably the precociously verbal painter Bob Neuwirth), but still the album's initials spell out "BoB."

On the cover Dylan projects a blurry, haunted image as if he's trying to get away and is moving too fast to stay in focus. It doesn't exactly reflect the sexually sated rock star of the title or, for that matter, the multimillionaire worshipped by legions of recently hipped-up fans. Instead we get an overdressed Hamlet, a tormented-looking spectral Bob, the doomed poet who is starting to evaporate before you even play the album.

Dylan's approach to *Blonde on Blonde* differed from his two previous albums in that he took more care about its production. In the past his song arrangements—such as they were—were typically ad hoc, spontaneous decisions, but on *Blonde on Blonde* they are more sophisticated than on *Highway 61* or any of his previous albums. He's also using better session musicians—the Nashville cats. And unlike Dylan's usual recording MO—his famous boredom with the studio provoking him to try to get his songs down in as few takes as possible—here he did multiple takes: fourteen on "Stuck Inside of Mobile," seventeen on "One of Us Must Know." He clearly thought of it as his '60s masterpiece.

Following his usual approach, he first plays the music on the piano, and then picks up his guitar and plays straight ahead. Not that he wrote charts for the arrangements or anything like that. He's still beaming his codes at the session musicians and they pick up the vibe (and the chord sequences) as best they can.

When they began working with him on *Highway 61*, his producer, Bob Johnston, had warned the session musicians how it was going to go: "I told everybody if they quit playing they were gone. It didn't matter because I could overdub anybody but Dylan. But if you quit with him you'll never hear that song again. And he'd go to the count and play something else. So they came out and got all around. And Dylan said, 'It goes like this. C, D. G.' And then he went over the thing and they said, 'Man, we haven't heard this thing.' I said, 'That's right. The first one who misses just walk out of the room. Don't stop.' And he went out there and started counting off, and that's another thing, too, nobody ever counted off for Bob Dylan. Every other artist in the world that I've been around has a drummer or somebody else counting. He went 1, 2, with that foot and it was gone. When we got through he said, 'Let's hear it back.'"

Al Kooper describes Dylan's manner of operating in the studio as "the roadmap to hell!" But these are seasoned Nashville musicians—they're empaths by nature—and with their hive instincts they tune into Dylan's wobbly wavelength, and after working with Dylan over a period of weeks they all had contact highs.

About the sound of *Blonde on Blonde*, Dylan famously said, "The closest I ever got to the sound I hear in my mind was on individual bands in the *Blonde on Blonde* album. It's that thin, that wild mercury sound. It's metallic and bright gold, with whatever that conjures up. That's my particular sound."

But what is it, this metallic-and-gold wild mercury sound? Some of the alchemy of the *Blonde on Blonde* sound comes from the way Dylan uses freaked Tin Pan Alley, kitsch pop songs, Beatles pastiches, and Euro-trash tunes meshed with blues riffs. When these unlikely elements are juxtaposed with Dylan's surreal lyrics it creates an odd and queasy effect. It's as if morphed by their collision with Dylan's lyrics they turn into a black light version of themselves.

Al Kooper's calliope-like organ curlicues underline the mood of the songs; it tells you where the vibe is coming from. Dylan isn't making fun of the odds and ends of sentimental and cheerful pop music that drift through the songs. He actually likes this stuff, and besides, this is the music of the era.

THE MOST TRANSCENDENT ROCK ALBUM OF THE '60S WITH ITS GNOMIC sayings and mind-jangling lyrics, *Blonde on Blonde* perversely opens with "Rainy Day Women #12 and 35," in other words, a novelty song based on a novelty song. The first ten beats on the drum and tambourine are straight from "They're Coming to Take Me Away, Ha-haaa!" by Napoleon XIV (pseudonym of producer Jerry Samuels), a big hit in 1966.

"They're Coming to Take Me Away" took the metaphor of the lover driven mad from getting rejected by his beloved to its absurd conclusion. He goes berserk and they carry him off to the funny farm. Which of course was what many people thought about Dylan and his lyrics—crazy.

"Rainy Day Women" harkens back to Dylan's goofy early songs and his pastiches of pop. Bob Johnston thought the tune sounded like a Salvation Army band. "Can we get one?" Dylan asked. Instead the trombone, played by Wayne "Doc" Butler, is what gives "Rainy Day Women" its circus atmosphere. It's a parade, more the kind of parade you'd find on Desolation Row. You're going to follow Bob. As in *The Outlaw Josey Wales* he gathers more and more people, types, freaks, ex-lovers as he goes along.

Once Dylan had the "everybody must get stoned" chorus down, he starts singing along (but not in the same key as the band of course). He just riffs his way through the song. You can hear Dylan making up the lyrics on the spot, stumbling over the line, "when you're 'ung and able."

A mood of manic goofiness prevails that seems in keeping with the stories we've been told that everyone playing on the session was drunk and stoned on fancy cocktails and weed. Unfortunately this turns out to be a myth.

Whatever the session guys were on, most people assumed it referred to getting high and that's what made it a hit. Dylan at first (and in a slurred, clearly stoned voice) claimed it was just "vulgar" to call it a drug song, and at a concert in 1991 he slyly introduced "Rainy Day Women" as "one of my early anti-drug songs." We're in Dylanland, where, like Brian Jones, you wear the Nazi uniform to show you are *not* a Nazi.

On a song like "Absolutely Sweet Marie," however, Al Kooper's perky organ keeps reminding you that this is a pop song. You can practically see the go-go dancers in their white boots. Kooper's riffs are the perfect guide to the underlying way Dylan insinuates pop tunes into his songs. Kooper started out in the pop band the Royal Teens, who recorded the hit novelty song "Short Shorts" and worked with the songwriting team of Bob Brass and Irwin Levine, writing "This Diamond Ring," a hit for Gary Lewis and the Playboys.

On "One of Us Must Know," "I Want You," "Just Like a Woman," "Absolutely Sweet Marie," and "Fourth Time Around," the underlying melodies sample from late 1950s/early 1960s pop music. You can hear a ghostly Lesley Gore singing "you don't love me anymore," a subliminal Jackie DeShannon whispering "every time you walk in the room" in the undertones. That was Dylan's genius—to take a Carole King tune, blend in a blues shuffle, and on top of that put lyrics like "Shakespeare's in the alley."

The swirling, giddy calliope momentum of these songs is disorienting, and it gives them a strange torque although you can't exactly say why. The chorus of "Stuck Inside of Mobile with the Memphis Blues Again" could be the guy playing at the bar at the Ramada Inn (where Dylan stayed some of the time while recording *Blonde on Blonde*), but on a stranded hipster travelogue like this, it's the perfect accompaniment.

The lyrics float above the sweet melodies. As on "Desolation Row," the lyrical accompaniment suits his poetic lyrics better than the rock tracks on his previous albums. It also allows him to inject conversational lines like "Aw, c'mon, now" or "Well, anybody can be just like me, obviously/ But, then, now again, not too many can be like you, fortunately." Only Dylan could so casually work lines like these into a lyric and make it sound like verbatim street talk.

The pop music elements roll under the Beat/bluesy lyrics like a wall-to-wall shag rug in an opium den. The jangly melodic tunes all work well against his pool-hall proverbs, his hipster asides ("somebody got lucky, but it was an accident" and "to live outside the law you must be honest"). You don't react to it as a parody because Dylan himself is ambivalent about it.

"Absolutely Sweet Marie" is like Hollywood TV music, underlined by Al Kooper's Europoppy organ. A lot of pop rock sounded like this. It's a scene in a '60s Swinging London movie: There's a girl in a miniskirt walking down the street window-shopping: "That girl with the psychedelic eyes." The "six white horses" lyrics combine incongruously with a *pah pah pah pah pah pah pah*. If you take away the acerbic bluesy lyrics it could be a Cowsills song. It's just the kind of melodic pattern that was in the air, the sound of the day, but with Dylan's words it takes on an unsettling, even ominous aspect.

In "Visions of Johanna" he's in some loft downtown, its occupants bohemians, druggy women, entwined lovers, and assorted allegorical characters. As you get further into the song, the room evaporates, it's an insubstantial space—made out of words and music, and wherever the drugs he's on take him. Phantom peddlers, fiddlers, countesses, and the Mona Lisa mysteriously come onstage. Nothing really happens—communication with other people is reduced to a hand held out tempting him with drugs. Like Sartre's *No Exit*, it's a place that's going to be hard to leave—if ever.

Why is he there? How did he get there? Perhaps, pursued by a mob (his fans), he has taken refuge in a friend's loft, but now feels trapped and threatened even there and retreats further until all that happens takes place in his own head.

One thought leads to another, and as Dylan's paranoia blooms he puts out his spectral tentacles. His sensitivity is so acute he can hear the night watchman click his flashlight. And someone's muttering about him while he's in the hall. Its original title, "Just Like a Freeze Out," bristles with paranoid implications. But is it they who have frozen him out or he who has frozen them out?

We're hearing the song form as we're listening to it—random, floating images materializing as they arise in Dylan's mind. What's uncanny is how he manages to transfer these insubstantial thoughts to us intact, transporting a whole spectral world from his fleeting thoughts into ours.

The industrial space where it takes place—a loft—resembles the lab-like atmosphere of the recording studio where these thoughts will be embedded in the microgrooves of vinyl LP and wake up when we play the record.

Who is this Johanna? Could be Joan Baez, but unlikely. More likely Sara. The title, perhaps the song itself, is spun out of the rhythm of that name. It's one of those names that comes with its own music, like Lolita or Cabiria. Dylan's publicist Myra Friedman says that one afternoon Dylan was up at Grossman's office and heard someone there call out the name of the accountant, Johanna. He began repeating "Johanna, Johanna, Johanna," as if it were a mantra.

In "Visions of Johanna" Dylan is the Prince of Denmark at his moodiest. As if Hamlet just imagined the whole play he's in—it must be something like Elsinore on endless winter nights—with sexual tension spiking between the murders, suicides, poisonings, plots.

"Visions of Johanna" is Dylan's hallucinatory masterpiece with its fantastically spectral "The ghost of 'lectricity howls in the bones of her face." His alternate current surges through the song, black-lit images brilliantly illuminated like stroboscopic flashes: "the skeleton keys and the rain" and "jewels and binoculars hang from the head of the mule" (illustrated on the cover of the Stones' 1970 live album *Get Yer Ya-Yas Out!*).

"Obviously 5 Believers" is one of the few songs on *Blonde on Blonde* that has the explosive energy of his two earlier electric albums. It could easily be a track on *Highway 61*. And part of the reason for this is that it's a Beatles pastiche. Dylan has always been very competitive, and his principal rivalry, at this point, was with the Beatles. This song with its jumpy fifteen jugglers is Bob doing his version of a Beatlesy pop song. The Beatles wrote this song in at least ten different versions but when they sang it they weren't being ambivalent about it; it was that pure infectious Beatles rush of joy. Dylan isn't just parodying the Beatles the way Zappa or the Fugs might; he manages to parody them and take them seriously at the same time. There are other Beatle-inflected tracks on *Blonde on Blonde*, like "I Want You" taken at a Beatlesy, "Ticket to Ride"–style gallop.

And of course there's "Fourth Time Around." The title itself refers to the multiple Dylan-Lennon back-and-forth borrowings. At some point in 1965 Dylan's listening to *Rubber Soul* and thinking, "Jesus, this isn't 'I Want to Hold Your Hand' anymore!" And then he comes to "Norwegian Wood," and he's stunned. "What *is* this? It's me, Bob. He's doing *me*! Even Sonny and Cher are doing me, but, fucking hell, I *invented* it." It's like hearing himself through somebody else's voice and he wants to repossess it, which he did pretty literally on "Fourth Time Around." Al Kooper thought Dylan's parody imitated Lennon's song too closely. "Aren't you worried about getting sued?" he asked. Dylan said it was his song first.

By 1965 John Lennon had developed a phobia about being a pop musician in a mop-top pop group and wanted to break out of it. Dylan was an obvious direction to go in. But there was another reason for writing "Norwegian Wood" in Dylanese or "gobbledegooky," as Lennon put it. He was having an affair and wanted to write about it as obliquely as possible:

"I was very careful and paranoid because I didn't want my wife, Cyn, to know that there really was something going on," he told David Sheff. "I was trying to be sophisticated in writing about an affair. But in such a smoke-screen way that you couldn't tell."

While "Norwegian Wood" is warm and wistful, Dylan's version is stone-cold. Also, you get involved with the story of the affair in "Norwegian Wood." In "Fourth Time Around" you don't care; it seems mean-spirited as well, and not just toward the girl in the song (whom he seems to have crippled into the bargain). And who, other than the unfortunate girl, are the last two lines—"I never asked for your crutch/Now don't ask for mine"—directed at? John Lennon? Or us?

OF ALL THE TRACKS ON *BLONDE ON BLONDE*, THE ODDEST AND MOST mesmerizing is "Sad-Eyed Lady," which was recorded on the night of February 16, 1966. "We went down there [the Columbia studios in Nashville] for *Blonde on Blonde*," Bob Johnston recalled. "And the first thing [he did] was beautiful. He said, 'Well, I got an idea.' . . . He stayed out in the studio 10 or 12 hours. He never left it. He'd eat candy bars and drink milk shakes and all, and nobody does that much. I sent the musicians away and told them to do anything you want to and be in phone contact. Don't go home . . . you can be in the studio down here if you need some beds or something. About 2:00 in the morning Dylan came out of the studio and said, 'I got a song I think. Is anybody left here?' First thing we did was 'Sad-Eyed Lady of the Lowlands.'"

The melody of "Sad-Eyed Lady of the Lowlands" isn't like American pop music; it's coming from another place entirely: It's Dylanized Euro-pop; it has a French cabaret vibe to it.

Here Al Kooper's organ is somber and reverential, in tune with the worshipful mood of the song. Like a medieval troubadour Dylan is professing a mystical bond with his beloved, the abject, worthless lover on bended knee, pledging his troth to Sara, who is presented as a Joan of Arc–like figure.

Its hypnotic tone comes from the mix of the sweet pop melodies and the compacted intensity of the lyrics against a long, droning vespers chant. Dylan described "Sad-Eyed Lady of the Lowlands" as "a piece of religious carnival music," whose religious tone is based on Johann Sebastian Bach's "Jesu, Joy of Man's Desiring."

At eleven minutes, twenty-three seconds, Michael Gray calls it "beautiful fur wallpaper" and after a while the song's singsongy repetition induces a hypnotic trance. But the point of it isn't to put you to sleep; it's to mesmerize you. It's Bob the existential spider of Bleecker Street spinning a cocoon into which he would encase himself for seven and a half years. "Sad-Eyed Lady" is the track on *Blonde on Blonde* that would seal in the four A.M. Nosferatu vampire Dylan. The Egyptian embalmers are closing up the sarcophagus with beeswax and honey. After the 1966 world tour (which would end in May) he would hibernate for almost eight years, during which his mystique would bloom. On the other side of this track, the Dylan of the '60s would vanish as if in a premature burial.

Dylan wore that polka-dot shirt as if it were his own portable solar system. Denmark, May 1966, at a press conference with Richard Manuel (future lead singer of the Band) in the background.

14 After the Ambulances Go

DYLAN'S WORLD TOUR HAD BEGUN IN THE FALL OF 1965 when he decided to take his show on the road with his electric touring band, the Hawks—the future members of the Band. They include Robbie Robertson (lead guitar), Richard Manuel (keyboard), Rick Danko (bass), Garth Hudson (organ), and Levon Helm (drums). Originally part of Ronnie Hawkins and the Hawks, a Canadian rock band playing raunchy gutbucket gigs, they were recommended to Dylan by Mary Martin, who worked in Albert Grossman's office and knew how to get in touch with them.

Dylan had first seen them at a club in New Jersey performing as Levon and the Hawks. On August 28, they play their first gig together at Forest Hills Stadium in Queens, New York, and for the first half of the show Dylan plays an acoustic set by himself—a practice he would follow on the rest of the world tour. The audience applauds Dylan's old songs, but as soon as the electric set begins, fans who've read about the "riot" at Newport start booing on cue. Dylan splits after "Like a Rolling Stone."

And the next thing he knew he was on a plane to LA with his entourage, now including his intuitive organ player, Al Kooper, who picks up the tale from here: "So we took off and I was between Bob on the window and Neuwirth on the aisle. Dylan said, 'Boy, you better keep your seat belt on, this is the worst flight I've ever been on.' I'm a little nervous. I looked around and everyone was having their drinks and laughing, and I thought, 'Oh, let's put Al on! Everything's fine.'"

None of them (except Neuwirth, apparently) knew that the kind of life-threatening level of fame they were heading into would require actual trick-store disguises (as opposed to the existential kind), especially Kooper: "When we got there, Neuwirth handed me a pull-over-your-head Halloween mask and said, 'Put this on and follow me, we're gonna move fast.' All three of us put our masks on, got off the plane and ran from the gate to the limo." Wow, that's like get-your-picture-taken-in-the-airport fame, like the Beatles. Bob was escalating into stratospheric celebrity.

They play the Hollywood Bowl on September 3, 1965, and the audience is enthusiastic. After the show Dylan meets his idol, Marlon Brando. They discuss possible movie projects. Brando, as both antihero and movie star, is the ideal model for the new Dylan, portraying outsider types, specifically the guitar-playing drifter/malcontent in *The Fugitive Kind*.

While in LA, Dylan and Phil Spector hang out. A more unlikely pairing of performer and producer is hard to imagine: Dylan, whose reputation is that he records many of his songs in one take—often without even rehearsing with the band—and Spector, the wall-of-sound sorcerer who can cook a single for months on end. They share a few similarities nonetheless: eccentricity, isolation, genius, paranoia. "I love to read letters that call me sellout, fink, fascist, red," says Dylan.

For the American tour (October through December) Dylan and the Hawks tour in an old air force Lodestar troop transport plane. Ed Freeman from *Twin City a Go-Go* magazine catches the shock of the new Bob playing his black-and-white solid-body electric guitar: "Dylan used to sound like a lung cancer victim singing Woody Guthrie. Now he sounds like a Rolling Stone singing Immanuel Kant."

In February 1966, Dylan's *Playboy* interview with Nat Hentoff appears.

"What happened," Nat Hentoff recalls, "was that I did the interview with Bob—we did a standard one that was okay but nothing special—and sent it to the *Playboy* offices in Chicago. An editor there must have cleaned up the interview—you don't clean up Dylan! They sent the fixed-up version to Bob, because they had a rule at *Playboy* that the interviewee had to give permission for content of the interview. And all of a sudden on a Saturday morning I got a call from Dylan saying, 'I'm not going to give permission, they changed things.' I said, 'It's okay, Bob, you have a right to say no.' 'I have a better idea,' he said. 'We're gonna do a new one right now,' and he just started talking at an immense rate. I didn't have a tape recorder, so for the next hour and a half I had a pen and pencil and I just wrote down everything at a furious rate. By the end of the day my hand ached from taking all these notes down. He just composed it right over the phone. Dylan did the whole interview—questions and answers—I was just the straight man. That's how that fantastic tall tale thing about How I Chose My Career came about":

Carelessness. I lost my one true love. I started drinking. The first thing I know, I'm in a card game. Then I'm in a crap game. I wake up in a pool hall. . . . I move in with a high school teacher who also does a little plumbing on the side, who ain't much to look at, but who's built a special kind of refrigerator that can turn newspaper into lettuce. I hit the road. The first guy that picked me up asked me if I wanted to be a star. What could I say?

"This was in the days before he became aloof and evasive with the press," Hentoff says. "He used to stop me on the street: 'When's it gonna run? When's it gonna run?' Not long after that he became a recluse!"

The 1966 US tour begins in Louisville on February 4, then moves on to Nebraska and up through the heartland to Denver, then over to the Pacific Northwest, over to Hawaii.

PERTH, AUSTRALIA, APRIL 23, 1966. YOU'RE IN A HOTEL ROOM ON THE forty-first floor. There's a room service tray with uneaten food on it, a guitar on the couch, a TV on with the sound turned off, and a Charlie Rich cassette playing. His mutinous crew, the Hawks, are lounging about and smoking foreign cigarettes, and some girl in a miniskirt and halter top is talking too loud in Strine—that malignant form of Australian English, a churlish revenge on the mother tongue, a payback for her ancestor getting deported for stealing a loaf of bread.

There's a man standing in the middle of the room, ranting, speaking in tongues as it were. It's Dylan. He's just like one of his songs. You've no idea what he's talking about but he's . . . *brilliant!* You've read all about him in the press; you really wanted to meet him. He sounded so interesting—and, well, *odd*. You tell him you want to interview him—that's the last thing Dylan wants, of course, but it's the all-purpose excuse for getting your foot in the door—but what would you call him? Maniac? Genius? Now they're saying he's a traitor. That sounds sexy. Either way, you just had to see him for yourself.

The moment you step into the room he's on a roll (and a number of controlled substances). He's been on a roll, as it turns out, for days. He's done seven concerts in nine days since he got to Australia, hasn't slept a wink for the last three—and isn't planning to sleep until he "gets that wasted feeling" and climbs aboard the Lodestar.

His world tour began in Australia, and he has exasperated, insulted, and confounded the Australian press. They haven't a clue what to make of him. We expect no less. Aside from being accused of causing civilization to fall apart and musical schizophrenia (DYLAN'S MANY HATS COME TO TOWN), the Australian response is relatively positive.

This is Bob in high mid-'60s mode just before the crash, shifting between manic outbursts and sweet reasonableness. One minute he's saying people should be who they are, as they see themselves, which sounds perfectly sensible, even banal. And, for a moment, you think, "Oh, he's not crazy at all, like people say. He's just talking common sense." But, just then, he crosses the room and comes toward you. He has something important to tell you. He's discovered the truth! He knows what *it* is:

"This should be their religion—if any—the Self!" he declaims with Pentecostal urgency. "You go down into the deeper self and go through it all and come out the other side. Go back into your own self, deeper than the surface world—you won't need religion or philosophy anymore because you will *know*. Do you see, it all makes perfect sense. It's just as real to me as this . . . *ashtray!*"

"Wait a minute," you think. "Where have I heard this rap before?" It's the methamphetamine wormhole rant—in other words, the raving sulfate Theory of Everything—which Dylan seems to have hit on this very instant, the very moment that you entered the room with your notepad in your hand.

And then he's on a bat about the Gospel of Compassionate Cruelty. He admits he can be quite cruel. His cruelty by this point is legendary. But now he's developed a theory about it: "We should all be cruel—to show someone what was wrong with her life." In the blink of an eye he's turned into Ayn Rand.

"There were these two conflicting points about him," said Rosemary Garrett, the astonished twenty-year-old Australian actress who'd just met him that day. "He changed radically from one to the other. Almost like dealing with two people. I'm not saying there was anything like schizophrenia, understand, but something was happening to him that was beyond his control."

Well, yes. That mid-'60s image was high maintenance. He was burning up, synapses crackling, consuming his vital natural resources at an alarming rate, and clearly on a collision course with himself. The two Dylans were programmed to crash and self-destruct any minute—in this very room, perhaps. How would he ever be able to escape his fate? Other '60s icons weren't that lucky. They lacked Dylan's wariness about being swallowed up by the maelstrom and had paid for it with their lives: Joplin, Hendrix, Morrison.

The great Beat, bebop, ab-ex heroes, all the hipster icons, had died young. Jackson Pollock never made it to 45; Lenny Bruce OD'd at 40; James Dean, dead at 24; Neal Cassady (model for Beat hero Dean Moriarty in *On the Road*), 41; Charlie Parker, 35; Hank Williams, 29; Hart Crane, 32; Billie Holiday, 44; John Coltrane, 40. When you die young, you don't get to spoil your own legend. Dying young was proof of authenticity—a disregard for convention, the highway code, schedule A drugs, and accepted ideas. But Bob didn't want that fate for himself.

But if he didn't end up destroying himself—by drugs, suicide, insanity, physical collapse, or disintegration—there were freaks out there, driven to psychotic pitch by Dylan's genius, who harbored dark homicidal thoughts about him. They could hear the hypnotic hum of "Desolation Row" pounding in their ears.

And the only way they could silence that reproachful voice was to kill the messenger. His songs had done something to the wiring of their brains. As Phil Ochs in an interview morbidly predicted:

Dylan is LSD set to music. . . . I don't know if Dylan can get on stage a year from now. I don't think so. I mean that the phenomenon of Dylan will be so much that it will be dangerous. One year from now I think it will be very dangerous to Dylan's life to get on the stage. Dylan has become part of so many people's psyches and there are so many screwed up people in America, and death is such a part of the American scene now I think he's going to have to quit.

Youth cultures demand blood. They require burnt offerings, the death of their idols—to show they really *meant* it. And if they don't do it themselves their fans might just do it for them. Rock itself was fertilized by the blood of martyrs. The death of James Dean had set off rock 'n' roll itself in the '50s; in 1963, the assassination of President Kennedy, the first viable rock 'n' roll president, in a blood-drenched Lincoln Continental, had brought on the '60s. The Beatles had given up Stuart Sutcliffe; the Stones had sacrificed Brian Jones.

According to Rosemary Garrett, "I think [Dylan] was frightened by what people expected of him, what they had begun to think of him, what place they had put him into as to what he could tell them about truth, and I think he wanted to escape. It seemed, almost, that he courted a way of escape through doing anything that he could do to himself, such as drugs."

There was no exit, no way out. Escape was futile because another gigantic world tour was looming, a huge concert at Shea Stadium (just like the Beatles), more dates in August, and then on to Moscow and on and on. The omens were accumulating. On April 30, 1966, Richard Fariña would be killed riding on the back of a Harley-Davidson, doing 90 in a 30 mph zone. Two days earlier his book, *Been Down So Long It Looks Like Up to Me*, had come out. He was twenty-nine years old. "Using a blowtorch on the middle of the candle is less aesthetic than burning it at both ends," Fariña had written perceptively about Dylan's (and his own) headlong plunge, "but more people see the flame."

Dylan had been coming to these critical points throughout his career. Talking to Studs Terkel in 1963, he told him about a book he was writing about his first *week* in New York, taking the risk of becoming a musician. "It's about somebody who has come to the end of one road, knows there's another road there but doesn't exactly know where it is, and knows he can't go back on this one road." And here he was again at that same point.

It was probably then that he decided to kill Bob Dylan off—*that* Dylan—in some Australian hotel room. He'd thrown his body out a tenth-floor window—like that scene in *Eat the Document*.

By 1966 a number of Dylans are on the loose, all in one way or another engendered by him but now out of his control. From here on in, the imaginary characters start multiplying, interbreeding. His life is one of constant flight, and once spotted he escapes down the railway tracks on a long-gone train.

ON THAT LAST LEG OF THE AUSTRALIO-EURO-BRIT TOUR DYLAN AND the Band were pushing all the buttons, amping up the sound, deliberately provoking the raging folkniks as the groundlings hissed, booed, and slow clapped at Bob, the betrayer of the folk ministry. They're the peasants with torches and pitchforks in a Frankenstein movie, grumbling, cursing—the terrible chant of the crowd. Bob, an angst-driven metamorph, pursued by a predatory entity, in this case—what irony!— his own frenzied fans and their addled image of him. But Dylan had no intention of placating them. Of course not. He was going to stir it up and shove it in their faces on the doomed and triumphant days of the 1966 so-called Judas Tour.

In May he gets to Paris. In the morning he buys a ventriloquist dummy at a flea market. Some of the most amazing images of Dylan are pictures taken of him with this dummy on his knee. An earnest bald man with a microphone is asking Dylan questions, and Dylan in turn asks the dummy. His Other, his doppelgänger, supplies the answers. At the concert that night the French, who knew that when you went to a Dylan performance you were meant to boo about something, call him a traitor. *"A bas le traiteur!"* But they boo his acoustic set as well. (Of course it might have also been the gigantic backdrop of a huge American flag—mid–Vietnam War.)

In England we find a new kind of agitation. The idiots are still out there, but there's a twist. Keith Butler at the Manchester concert calls out "Judas!" To which Dylan replies with iambic lilt—like a line from one of his songs—"I don't *believe* you. You're a liar." In the following years John Cordwell also claimed to be the Judas brayer, but both Butler and Cordwell have left us, so we'll have to extend the Order of Folk Indignation to them both posthumously. When asked subsequently why he'd done that, Cordwell couldn't remember. He had no agenda; the word just poured out of his mouth unbidden—which only confirms that Dylan had somehow hypnotized the guy, telepathically put the word in his mouth. He was just another essential actor in the Dylan diorama.

Later on we see Dylan looking out a taxi window, wearing shades and smoking. "I heard you booing out there," he says to some kid. "I heard you booed. Let's go. . . . This guy here *booed*." But it isn't Keith Butler or John Cordwell. The kid tries to defend himself, mouthing, "It wasn't me." But Dylan doesn't believe him and shouts, "No, you booed!" He loves teasing the kid, making him feel bad, while telling members of his band he loves the booing (although it eventually drove Levon Helm crazy and forced him to leave). Why not?

Press conferences at the Savoy Hotel May 3 and Paris May 23 are, as usual, fatuous. But one interviewer stumbles through his questions in a foreign accent toward what is the sorest point of all: "An image is projected about . . . about something which is . . . which we feel is . . . particularly serious." He eventually gets to the point: "And then if you became cynical about it, then one begins to doubt sincerity."

"I'm not sincere at all," Dylan says. "I'm not any more sincere than you are." This is the most lethal cut of all, since it repudiates the entire credo of the folk movement, its vaunted authenticity—his denial undermining his protest songs as well as anything else he's stood for. Unrepentantly Dylan repeats, "I ain't any more sincere than you."

When asked why he isn't singing protest songs anymore, Dylan deflects the wearisome question with "I don't want to talk about protest songs." Then, when they persist, he delivers his classic ambivalent retort: "That's all I do is . . . uh . . . protest." And that, at least, is true.

Dylan strenuously objects to their assumptions about his involvement in protest songs as if it had been thrust on him, whereas his involvement in writing these anthems had been a pretty calculated strategic shift on his part. The equivocal "Blowin' in the Wind" had made him rich and famous. His first manager, Roy Silver, immediately recognized its commercial potential as did the far wilier Albert Grossman, with whom Silver shared an office.

Another interviewer at that same press conference in Paris zeroes in on what was to become a far more troubling question for him: "Don't you ever come offstage?" he asks. "Are you ever yourself at any time?" To which Dylan affectlessly gestures no.

IN LONDON, DYLAN MEETS WITH JOHN LENNON.

"We were trying to make a story which consisted of stars and starlets who were taking the roles of other people, just like a normal movie would do," Dylan explained to *Sing Out!* magazine in 1968. "That's not what anyone else had in mind, but that is what myself and Mr. Alk [editor, with Dylan, of *Eat the Document*] had in mind. And we were very limited because the film was not shot by us, but by the Eye [Pennebaker], and we had come upon this decision to do this only after everything else had failed. . . . If we had the opportunity to re-shoot the camera under this procedure, we could really make a wonderful film."

The prime example of Dylan's reenacting concept is the footage shot on Friday, May 27, 1966, with John Lennon in the back of a limo driven by Andrew Oldham's criminal chauffeur, Tom Keylock, as they tool around Hyde Park.

Although they don't exactly fulfill our expectations of such an encounter, it's still a sight to behold the two sharpest minds in rock as they play with words from which all trace logic has been surgically removed. Even if the parody sketches they pull out of thin air don't always work, it's amazing to watch them as they engage in mock-voice patter and surreal quips, running through absurd routines, scrambling up and down fan-tastic flights of fancy as if they were syntactical staircases, language tee-tering, like a drunken acrobat, on the edge of nonsense.

> **DYLAN:** Someone said, "You wanna be on Northern Songs," and you laughed and Paul McCartney looked the other way and talked to Ringo. . . .
> **LENNON:** And Rob Roy leapt into the room with a big kilt on and said, "Hey, Bobby, have you heard this one?"
> **DYLAN:** Haha! You haven't lived in Texas, man. . . .
> **LENNON** [*In Brit deejay voice*]: Tell me about the Mamas & Papas, Bob. I believe you're backing them bigly.
> **DYLAN:** I knew it would get to that. I knew it would get to that. Naw. You're just interested in the big chick, right? She's got hold of you, too. She's got hold of everybody. Everybody asks me the same thing. You're terrible, man. . . . Barry McGuire tells me he's a great friend of yours. . . .
> **LENNON:** I did have a letter from his manager saying he was very close to you, being on the bosom of the current folk-a-rock-boom.

Dylan, though sick, gamely tries to maintain the repartee. He seems uncharacteristically skittish and jaunty, playing the court jester to a deadpan Lennon. Lennon, although in fine "Scarborough-is-a-scarf-that-covers-Yorkshire" form, also seems stoned and edgy. As he admit-ted in a 1979 interview with Jonathan Cott, he was "Frightened as hell, you know, I was always so paranoid. He said, 'I want you to be in this film,' and I thought, 'Why? What? He's going to put me down. It's gonna be . . .' You know and I went all through this terrible thing. So in the film I'm just blabbin' off, just commenting all the time like you do when you're very high and stoned. But it was his scene, you know, that was the problem for me. It was his movie. I was on his territory."

But what we see in the scene is the opposite, a Dylan we've never seen before and are unlikely to see again, a Dylan sucking up to someone (even if it is John Lennon), unable to hit the ball back across the net, a Dylan talking too much out of nervousness and a cool John Lennon to-tally in charge.

We see a couple of instances of Dylan directing the film. At one point he insists Pennebaker film something *real* outside the window—"Get those two lovers over there"—and at another point he tries to get Lennon to go back to the beginning of a piece of nonsense about Barry McGuire, saying, essentially, take two.

Since we seem to be watching Dylan and Lennon acting out some sort of unfinished play, it's easy to wonder if Dylan and Lennon were trying to re-create the sort of hyper rap they engaged in off-camera.

"They had a funny relationship to begin with," says Pennebaker. "In this particular scene it was as if they were trying to invent something for me that would be amusing in some way, but at the same time they were doing it for each other. It was not exactly a conversation by any means. Dylan was so beside himself and in such a terrible state that after a while I don't think he knew what he was saying. We hauled him up the stairs of the hotel and when he got to his room he was really sick."

At one point Lennon prescribes an extraterrestrial-sounding patent medicine that sounds like Dylan's given surname: "Do you suffer from sore eyes, groovy forehead, or curly hair? Take Zimdon!"

In a 1980 interview Lennon explained the reason they were sick as dogs was that Dylan, who'd introduced the Beatles to marijuana two years earlier, brought some heroin with him on this visit, which they'd both snorted and gotten violently ill. "We ended up in the hotel lobby throwing up in those Victorian flower pots. This being England, nobody turned a hair."

Back in Woodstock after an eight-month world tour, summer of '66, Dylan is in bad shape. He is drugged, exhausted, and cranky. His creeping megalomania is fast turning into paranoia. Everyone wants something from him—a situation partly of his own devising. His overweening ambitions have created unrealizable expectations. Not only is he a brilliant songwriter and singer, but he's also now trying to be a cutting-edge film director, an avant-garde novelist, and an art brut painter.

But things are closing in. He owes his record company, Columbia, a fourteen-track LP. His novel, *Tarantula*, for which he had taken a large advance, is long overdue. ABC is clamoring for their film. Besieged and at his wit's end, in mid-July Dylan has his motorcycle accident.

There were some very strange hypotheses
about what happened to Dylan after his
1966 motorcycle accident. Had he been
abducted by aliens? His brain siphoned off
by the CIA? Almost any of these supposi-
tions would have seemed more likely than
that he'd decided to give it all up and
become a family man. Dylan at the piano
in Hi Lo Ha, his house in the old Woodstock art colony of Byrdcliffe.

15 Somebody Got Lucky but It Was an Accident

SCENE 129. EXT. STRIEBEL ROAD—DAY
A quiet, leafy stretch of two-lane blacktop near Woodstock, New York. The booming sound of a motorbike engine erupts in the quiet morning air. Coming right at us is DYLAN in goggles on his Triumph motorcycle. Close-up of Dylan's face, hair blown back by the wind. He's leaning forward with a slightly maniacal gleam on his face. In a medium shot we see the bike and a car following him with a female driver, his wife, SARA DYLAN. Reverse angle from Dylan's POV: the road ahead, sun glancing sharply through the leaves, flaring the lens. Close-up of Dylan's face, he's squinting, his face contorted. The sun in his eyes is blinding him. Close-up of Dylan's boot as he slams on the rear brakes. The bike lurches, skids, and slides out from under him. Medium shot of Dylan as he slides across the road behind the bike. Close-up of Dylan's face with a stricken look. Medium shot of Striebel Road as the camera pans, looking for Dylan. Silence, then the sound of crickets, a dog barking in the distance. Camera pans revealing motorbike on its side in the middle of the road, front wheel ominously spinning. Camera looks behind the bike and finds Dylan sprawled on the road. Flies buzz around his bloodied face and neck. It's not clear if he's alive or dead. Sound of car door opening and slamming, woman screaming. Shot of trees, telephone poles going by seen from Dylan's POV in backseat of car. FADE TO BLACK.

IN THE YEARS FOLLOWING THE CRASH, THE STORIES ABOUT HOW SERIous the crash was would vary greatly. According to Dylan, "[My wife] was following me in the car. She picked me up. Spent a week in the hospital, then they moved me to this doctor's house in town. In the attic. He had a bed up there in the attic with a window lookin' out. Sara stayed there with me."

Dr. Ed Thaler's attic in Middletown is where he claims he abided for six weeks. Cynically some have speculated he was holed up there in an attempt to get off drugs, but given his subsequent habits this seems un-charitable. After the crash his imbibing of pharmaceuticals doesn't seem to have abated all that much. Robbie Robertson remembers him being "up all night, smoking a million cigarettes."

Dylan's friend, the journalist Al Aronowitz, claims that he's one of the first people Bob told about the accident. "Bob said, 'I'd been up for three days—I was crashing from speed. I was disoriented. I think there was something up ahead of me and the shadows of the leaves on the back of it were moving. When the sun came flashing through the leaves I couldn't see a thing. I slammed down on the rear brakes and went flying over the handlebars. As I flew through the air my whole life passed in front of me. I saw myself outside the movie theater in Hibbing. . . . I was in the Folklore Center talking to Izzy Young.'

"Stuff like that. And he went on recounting scenes from his life, de-tailing the life-flashing-before-his-eyes scenario. I felt he was pulling my leg a bit, but with Bob you want to hear the story—*especially* if he was making it up. You don't say, 'But, Bob, if you hit the rear brakes on your bike you wouldn't be thrown over the handlebars, the bike would fall over and you'd skid on the ground.' Because obviously that's what hap-pens. I felt he wanted me to believe him and believe that the accident had been more serious than it actually was and that it had all happened just like he'd said it had—how he almost died and how seriously he'd been injured—even though he was sitting there looking no different from any other time except for the neck brace, which looked a little like a prop. He wasn't trying to play it down, that's for sure. I got the feeling he wanted me to go around and tell the story just as dramatically as I'd heard it from him. He survived with barely a scratch, but I think he was enjoying the fact that his accident had taken on such hair-raising pro-portions in people's imaginations, that there were people coming up with bizarre speculations about his physical and mental state, stories like about Elvis and James Dean."

Despite the rumored seriousness of the accident, it was reported some-what offhandedly in the local newspaper as: CYCLE MISHAP, the sort of thing you read in the *PennySaver*. Nobody who saw Dylan after the accident found him seriously injured or even incapacitated. Except for the neck brace, a few scratches were the only sign that an accident had happened at all.

In fact, it's pretty clear by now that the accident was actually a minor incident—little more than a nasty spill. If it had been the life-and-death incident that Dylan claimed, an ambulance would have been called.

There would have been a police report, specialists would have been summoned, and he would have been put in intensive care in the hospital. If he'd had a serious spinal injury or broken his neck, putting him in the attic of a country doctor's house for six weeks would have been criminally negligent.

But a motorcycle crash was something Dylan wasn't about to downplay for any number of reasons. First and foremost was it got him out of a lot of stuff—touring and *Tarantula*, just for starters. In true Bob fashion, it also gave him the opportunity to live the scene in *Tom Sawyer* in which Tom and Huck Finn observe Tom's funeral service peering down from the gallery of the church—an experience Bob would get to "re-live" in 1997 when he had that blood disease and got to read his own obituaries, complete with rows of pictures of all the Bobs in all their incarnations.

Dylan had a talent for exploiting the underlying mythology of events. The crash was another incident loaded with potential resonance and Dylan managed to spin that brilliantly too. If Dylan had been knocked down by a bicycle on Bleecker Street, he wouldn't have been able to take advantage of it in quite the same way. Eddie Cochran, the 1950s rebel rock 'n' roller, for example, had the misfortune to die in a London taxicab. Not exactly a legendary fate for a wild child. Events in American popular history involving emblematic types, machines, and death—Jackson Pollock, James Dean, Jayne Mansfield, Hank Williams—were symbolic events. Dylan's two earliest heroes, Hank Williams and James Dean, both died in cars (even if Hank wasn't actually driving).

In 1987 Sam Shepard (in the form of a play) interviewed Dylan for *Esquire* about the deaths of Williams and Dean:

SAM: Did he [Hank Williams] mean the same thing to you as James Dean?
BOB: Yeah, but in different ways. They both told the truth.
SAM: They both died in cars.
BOB: Yeah.
SAM: A Cadillac and a Porsche.
BOB: He was on his way to Ohio, I think. Some gig in Ohio.
SAM: I saw the car he died in. Cadillac coupe, convertible. I looked in the backseat of that car and this overwhelming sense of loneliness seized me by the throat. It was almost unbearable. I couldn't look very long. I had to turn away.
BOB: Maybe you shouldn'ta looked at all.

Dylan would later tell Al, "That accident came like a warning and I heed warnings." Needless to say it provided an ideal plot point, an opportunity for rebirth.

SIX WEEKS—AND PROBABLY SOONER—AFTER THE ACCIDENT, DYLAN was back home at his Woodstock house, Hi Lo Ha, beginning his eight-year retreat. No one knew what he was doing. He was up there somewhere—a black hole, situated somewhere off Route 28. His fans pulled out their old LPs, reread his liner notes, and examined the pictures on his album covers for clues.

The fuzzy nimbus around the photo of Dylan and a beautiful young woman on the cover of *Bringing It All Back Home* seemed to invite speculation into his private life. We look at him through a greased lens, peeping through a keyhole down on our knees. And there he is, glaring back at us, sitting with his cat in a forest of symbols: LPs by Eric Von Schmidt, Lotte Lenya, Robert Johnson, the Impressions, and Dylan (cover of *Another Side*) are displayed like Russian icons. There's a fallout shelter sign, a copy of *Time* magazine, Dylan's sculpture, *The Clown*, made out of pieces of colored glass.

That was the closest we were likely to get to how he spent his days (and this photo was already a year and a half old). We were peering into some intimate scene we'd interrupted. He was just begging us to read stuff into it, titillating us with an intimate glimpse of his home life. What were we to think? Who was the beautiful woman? What was her relationship to Dylan? Was she the Miss Lonely from the song who once threw the bums a dime and now, thanks to Bob, really knew where it's at? *Was* she a woman? Given the hothouse world of his albums, she could easily be a transvestite. She could be Dylan in drag! In a way that made perfect sense: Here was Dylan in the solipsistic universe of his songs where all the characters are him (the woman is actually Sally Grossman).

We were by now far too hip (thanks in large part to Bob) to read fan magazines with their dating dos and don'ts or stars' dopey responses to the Proust questionnaire ("I like steaks well done and long drives at night") to find out for sure. But maybe we'd have liked a peek into his life at Hi Lo Ha—an at-home-with-the-stars feature on Bob, like they had in the old movie magazines, where stars do all the things other people do: have barbecues, go shopping, putter around their gardens, and generally indulge in their main off-set activity—redecorating.

Celebrities will do anything to keep their name in the public eye, including hire publicists, indulge in bizarre tabloid behavior, get themselves on Page Six, go into rehab, fake scandals, license their songs for commercials (by the 1980s Dylan would shamelessly follow). But none of this anxiety about being forgotten applied to Dylan at this point. He was a legend and "nothing so perpetuates a legend as the disappearance of its subject."

Dylan and his wily manager, Albert Grossman, knew something about the value of mystique that others didn't—and in any case this was Bob Dylan, the most elusive rock star of all. Not a word went to the press, not even a cheery PR bulletin from Myra Friedman saying, "Bob is recovering nicely and will be back with us soon. He sends his best wishes to all his fans and thanks them for their very welcome get-well-soon cards."

Instead of forgetting about Dylan in exile, his fans became even more obsessed. Absence further generated mystique. John Lennon, then living in the Dakota, was so impressed by Dylan's reclusive magic that he tried to emulate it. But no one could master inscrutability like Dylan. Such was Dylan's charisma that three years later Xeroxes of the cover of *Nashville Skyline*, showing a beaming, howdy-neighbor Bob, were used at colleges to calm protesters and to stop demonstrations from becoming violent. All they needed to do was hand out pictures of that face.

After the crash, sightings of Woodstock Dylan began to trickle in. Bob sitting by his woodpile, taking his daughter to the school bus stop, buying bread at the Woodstock Bakery, drinking cappuccino at the Café Espresso. This was the strangest image yet of Dylan. Reports of the mundaneness of Dylan's domestic life in the woods with his family suggested a Dylan enacting the role of a suburban husband and father.

In *Chronicles* Dylan wrote, "I had very little in common with and knew even less about a generation that I was supposed to be the voice of.... I was fantasizing about a nine-to-five existence, a house on a tree-lined block with a white picket fence, pink roses in the backyard."

"IN THE LATE 1960S, UNTIL HE BEGAN TO DECONSTRUCT HIMSELF with *Nashville Skyline*, Bob Dylan was still the hippest person on the planet." So said Michael Gray, the supreme Dylan exegete, and we fervently believed it.

You're at a party in the Village, just say at some rich guy's duplex. *He's* the reason everybody's here. When he walks around people tug on his sleeves—old friends, old folkies, people who begin with the terrible line, "You may not remember me, but . . ." But when he sits down, a glass of wine in one hand, no one bothers him except for a few pretty girls who kneel before him as before a roadside altar.

You look at him across the room. He sits there, arms folded, a wooden box on his knees—what's in there? Probably a set of harmonicas but we won't ask. He's as motionless and hieratic as a pharaoh. He has a vision- ary's eyeball that could x-ray all that was corrupt and phony, and who knows what he sees when he looks at you.

He has the destiny gaze of saints, dictators, and mental patients. He'd taken up wearing shades indoors, hipster style. In *POPism*, Warhol saw Dylan's enigmatic posturing as part of a cultivated mystique: "At Sam's party Dylan was in blue jeans and high-heeled boots and a sports jacket and his hair was sort of long. He had deep circles under his eyes, and even when he was sitting he was all hunched in. He was around twenty- four then and the kids were all just starting to talk and act and dress and swagger like he. But not many people except Dylan could ever pull that anti-act off—and if he wasn't in the right mood, he couldn't either."

Dylan became such an obsession for the counterculture because he so immaculately embodied its newly hatched mythologies: From folk music he brought the authenticity of a crusade, from rock the idea of a revolutionary momentum that could change the world, and from the Beats the fusion of drugs and attitude that made hipness seem like an enlightened state of being.

Dylan took the concept of hip from the Beats, hustlers, dope dealers, and crazy wisdom jazz musicians—and redefined it. With him it took on a quasi-religious fervor for the new mass bohemia. How intense *was* this obsession? Well, needless to say, the quest for Dylan's prophetic in- tuition goes on unabated to this very day, but here's an example from 1969. It's been three years since Dylan stopped being *that* Dylan, the liv- ing icon of the counterculture and the hipoisie, but here is Jann Wenner, the creator of *Rolling Stone*, asking him the questions you've been want- ing to ask him since, say, 1965. All right, so it's now November 1969, but you still want to know. The question in a nutshell is how does it feel to be Bob Dylan. After fifty frustrating years of trying to get him to answer this question we know it's a futile undertaking, but, in 1969, it was still worth trying to winkle out a response from the sphinxlike Bob, even if it makes you sound like a credulous hippie.

But Jann didn't care if it made him sound a little foolish. He was just asking the questions to which we all wanted to know the answers but would've been too afraid to ask.

"Many people . . . all felt tremendously affected by your music and what you're saying in the lyrics," Jann tells him in *Rolling Stone* in 1969. Dylan pretends to be astonished that Jann's saying stuff like this.

"Did they?" says Bob disingenuously. But this is a classic Dylan ploy. Jann, bless his heart, presses on: "Sure. They felt it had a particular relevance to their lives. . . . I mean, you must be aware of the way that people come on to you." Well, the second time around Dylan can't exactly pretend that he doesn't have a clue what Jann's talking about, so he says, "Not entirely." Then he delivers a mocking coup de grâce: "Why don't you explain it to me?" Jann realizes he's in a sand trap but won't give up. "I guess if you reduce it to its simplest terms, the expectation of your audience— the portion of your audience that I'm familiar with—feels that you have the answer."

"What answer?" asks Dylan.

Jann tries again: "Like from the film *Don't Look Back*—people asking you 'Why? What is it? Where is it?' . . . Do you feel responsible to those people?" Bob comes back with: "I don't want to make anybody worry about it." This seems perfectly reasonable—even if a total fib.

Here's where the host of unbidden Dylans begins to fill the room. Suddenly Dylan's talking to you as if you were no more than a line in one of his songs. It's—what is it? Hell, you can't place it, is it some Delta blues griot, a line from a Pentecostal sermon? Whatever it is, it's perfect, delivered with a kind of iambic grace: "If I could ease somebody's mind," he says, "I'd be the first to do it. I want to lighten every load. Straighten out every burden. I don't want anybody to be hung-up . . . [*laughs*] especially over me, or anything I do. That's not the point at all."

Jann, probably stung by the voices Dylan is manifesting, doesn't know that he's been transported to a whitewashed tabernacle choir in Lula, Mississippi, midsentence, and he proceeds, as any journalist would, with the list of questions on his yellow pad. Dylan has evaded his question, so Jann asks it again: "Let me put it another way. What I'm getting at is that you're an extremely important figure in music and an extremely important figure in the experience of growing up today. Whether you put yourself in that position or not, you're in that position. And you must have thought about it—and I'm curious to know what you think about that."

"What would I think about it?" Dylan responds. "What can I do?"

What Jann doesn't understand—and, really, who would at that point—is that he isn't talking to *that* Dylan, which is why he next asks, "You wonder if you're really that person."

Dylan doesn't know what he's talking about, and his answer sounds just like a line from "Ballad of a Thin Man": "What person?"

"A great 'youth leader,'" says Jann. To which Dylan responds: "There must be people trained to do this type of work."

But Jann wasn't the only person confused by the change that had come over Dylan. The disappearance of the mid-'60s messiah of rock had become the obsession of an entire generation.

Like Marlon Brando, Mick Jagger, Muhammad Ali, Dylan turned the concept of fame upside down. Fame was no longer a vulgar condition to be disdained by the pure artist. It was the divine right of genius, something to be toyed with and subverted through put-on and self-parody. Dylan made the artificial state of the star a personal value. He loved folk-based archetypes out of the old ballads, the outrageous names of blues singers—Howlin' Wolf, Muddy Waters, Lightnin' Hopkins. Why not just manufacture one for yourself whenever you needed it? Bob always had sticky fingers. When he needed a new name, he took it from a Welsh poet. When he needed a new personality, he just borrowed one. According to Al Kooper, "Bob wanted to be Bobby Neuwirth" and simply absorbed Neuwirth's caustic manner into his own persona when the occasion arose.

That Dylan had also raised rock to the level of literature was proof that the counterculture could achieve anything it set its mind to, and do it better and hipper and have more fun doing it than conventional culture was capable of. We were going to change all culture in our image.

His fans believed he was a visionary in the literal sense, sort of an Old Testament prophet in houndstooth trousers, like, you know, Isaiah or Ezekiel. Even Robbie Robertson, who'd been around Dylan's academy of cool long enough to know better, was still asking him the same kind of question in a taxi five years later: What is the next direction in music going to be? Dylan is astounded—but also perplexed. By 1974 even he doesn't know the answer. He's as lost as anybody else.

WHOEVER ROBERT ZIMMERMAN IS OR WAS, "DYLAN" HAD GOTTEN AWAY from him—and it was his own fault. Kerouac may have moaned, "There's that terrible moment when you lose control of your own image." But Dylan knew from the very first that he was playing with a devil doll and one day it would come back and ask him to pay the price.

He had created a fantastic image—the stratocasting Rimbaud—a creature so fantastic, an act of supernatural invention so far beyond earthling capacity it was something you yourself could not have done, even on a lot of drugs.

Dylan's album covers moved from portraits to posed tableaux, to a still from a movie, to the ghostly out-of-focus cover shot on *Blonde on Blonde* where he has become a blur. As you tear off the shrink-wrap he's fading, already gone.

Then one day the wild mercury Dylan *was* gone, despite Jann Wenner's brave attempts to retrieve him. Where did he go?

It was as if he had walked off into the woods never to be seen again—which he sort of did—off into the manicured woods of Woodstock. And in his place was an utterly different Dylan, an earnest rabbinical student—conservatively dressed, glasses, and short curly hair. His hair was still curly only because he was unable to find a bottle of Ouzo (his preferred method of hair straightening) to relax it.

Bob's brain. We already know quite a bit
about what goes in his cerebellum—
that's what his records are—but what we
want to know is *how* it works. One possible
cross-section—and that's just for starters.

16 Fifty-Four Minutes Inside Bob's Brain

INTERVIEWER: Why are you here?

DYLAN: I take orders from someone on the telephone, but I never see him. He calls up and tells me where to go.

—EAT THE DOCUMENT

"*T*HUNK!*" [*SOUND OF DEAD BOLT ON SAFE OPENING*]

"We're in!"

"What do you see?"

""Hold on ... um ... a beagle on a zebra crossing ... Glasgow train station ... sandwich board guy ... looks like sign says END OF DAYS! or something ... dog barking ... long goods train trundling through sheep-grazing fields ..."

"Where the hell is he?"

"Oh, here's something ... view of drab rainy street, must be looking out a window ... ghastly wallpaper, a portable TV set with rabbit ears ... yellow flowers .... bottle of Jack Daniel's ... newspaper ... hotel restaurant ... could that be Bob at the piano? God, it is! He's writing something on the back of an envelope!"

"Freeze-frame it!"

"What are you talking about? This isn't a DVD, it's Bob's brain."

"Oh, yeah, I forgot. Can you see what he's writing?"

"Shit, screen's gone black."

"Fuck. Catch anything?"

"I see a man walking into the room ..."

"*Like a camel and then he frowns ...*"

"He's folding something, some papers, maybe ... or rolling a cigarette ... or counting change."

"What does he look like?"

"Can't see his face yet, but he's got on these hideous blue trousers."

"Oh, that's gotta be Albert Grossman."

"Wait a minute, there's something very strange going on here. Dylan is getting up from a chair and walking over to a girl with short dark hair. He's saying something. 'You're not the type to be hypnotized. You must be the type to do something else.'"

"Naughty man!"

"She's pushing him away . . . she's saying 'wee,' 'ouee,' 'oee,' or something."

"Maybe '*Oui, oui, oui*'—y'know, French."

"I'm very tired . . ."

"Never mind, keep going!"

"Not me, you idiot, that's Bob talking to the girl. 'I just have to be entertained before . . . before lunchtime.'"

"Well, that's an original approach, I'll grant him that."

"Jesus Christ, the girl . . . she's crawling to the edge of the balcony as if about to jump . . . Bob's freaked out, he's shouting something, trying to stop her. Dear God, it looks like she's hanging from the edge of the balcony . . . Bob looks over the edge of the balcony and walks away."

"What happened? Did she jump?"

"People below staring at the ground, a news vendor, some people outside the Albert Hall . . ."

"But can you see the girl?"

"Nope. But here's Robbie Robertson looking down from the balcony. 'Just like that,' Dylan says to him. 'Oh boy,' Robbie says. He's aghast at the situation, you can tell. 'That's one thing,' says Dylan. The heartless bastard!"

"Hold on, I know what that is, it's a scene from, y'know, that nutty Dylan, uh, documentary, whaddayacallit? Where did you say you got this bootleg of Dylan's brain again? This sounds to me like one of those cheap copies of *Eat the Document* from Taiwan."

"Damn."

D. A. PENNEBAKER HAD FLOWN TO STOCKHOLM AT THE END OF APRIL 1966 to film Dylan's European tour and followed him until the end of the tour a month later. Dylan's friend Howard Alk was the second cameraman and Alk's wife, Jones, was the sound recordist. As if mimicking a Dylan lyric, chaos broke out the day they landed in England when sea-men went on strike while Mary Quant and Peter Sellers were receiving their OBEs from the Queen in Buckingham Palace.

Although beloved of Dylan fans, and arguably *the* classic rock documentary, you can see why Bob wouldn't have been all that happy with *Don't Look Back*, the film made the previous year by Pennebaker. Not only was its intention (to show "what Dylan's really like") something Dylan avoided at all costs, but also its narrative—the story of Dylan's tour of England—was out of sync with his current cubist manner of composition.

Odd as it may be, Dylan considered *Don't Look Back* something of a plodding self-portrait. "After *Don't Look Back* was finished," says Penne-baker, "Dylan came to me and said, 'You've got your film'—which he called *Pennebaker by Dylan*—'now I want you to help me make my film. But this time there's gonna be none of this artsy-fartsy documentary cinema verité shit. This is going to be a *real* movie.' For Dylan, a real movie meant 'people acting'—even if it involved them playing themselves. And only Dylan really knew what that meant."

Incredible as it now seems, *Eat the Document* began as a sort of Bob Dylan network special. Two years earlier you wouldn't have caught Dylan making any kind of TV show, never mind the special that ABC had in mind when they gave him a hundred-thousand-dollar advance for a one-hour documentary of his upcoming 1966 world tour for their series *Stage 66*. A Joan Baez special, maybe. An evening with Peter, Paul and Mary, perhaps—but it wouldn't have been in the cards for Dylan. Still, something was needed now, a *filmed* something that would in some way parallel the Dylan style. ABC, of course, had not a clue what they were getting themselves into.

"This time Dylan got more involved in the actual filmmaking, meaning he'd say things like, 'Shoot this' or 'Did you get that?' He would occasionally get people to say things or set up situations," says Pennebaker. "For instance, he would get rooms filled with strangers who appeared out of nowhere and get them all into the scene. I don't know what he was smoking, but he was pretty far up in the air." Improvised scenes out of a Pirandello play—five-characters-in-search-of-a-scene type of thing—would follow. On tour there was always a readily available troupe of actors, but not everybody was as good at playing themselves as Dylan.

"There was one scene up in my hotel room in Paris," says Pennebaker. "There was this huge mirrored clothes cabinet and he had people going in, closing the doors, and then coming out. There would be a succession of people. I don't know where they came from. There would be strange women and guys and I would just film these little scenes."

Some of the most spectacular footage of Dylan shot on the 1966 tour comes from the concerts filmed at Glasgow, Paris, Dublin, Manchester, and London. At the Glasgow Odeon, May 18, there's Pennebaker crawling around the stage, hovering over Dylan's shoulder, lying at his feet and pointing the camera directly at his face. The performance footage of Dylan singing (an unreleased) "Tell Me, Momma" and "Ballad of a Thin Man" is wildly chromatic and strange. Light shatters into spiky arc-welded halos, colors bleed, light fizzes, images break up. There are gravity-defying moments as when the camera momentarily turns upside down to direct its gaze at the piano keyboard (so that Pennebaker can focus on the black and white keys), and then, like some sort of light-seeking bug, hovers around Dylan, the flaring light turning his head into a celestial sparkler.

The atmosphere Dylan and Co. generated was contagious, and Pennebaker soon got into the psychotropic swing of things: "About the second concert I really got totally bored looking through that lens at him 'cause I wanted to go out there on stage with him.... So I just got out there and he didn't know what I was gonna do.... I was standing there with my camera and Dylan came out, saw me and he just really broke up. He totally cracked up, it killed him, because it was such a funny idea.... I had a very wide-angle lens and I could just stick it right in front of their faces, and it was so amazing to get that close. You know, that was a homemade lens. I made that lens. There was no lens like it then, it made marvelous distortions."

This was the stuff that excited Pennebaker. Dylan, however, was more interested in his little set pieces. So he proceeded to organize his own one-act plays. Dylan wanted to be his own scriptwriter and director, to make the audience experience how chaotic life on the road is.

AFTER FILMING THE CONCERT FOOTAGE, BACK IN THE STATES, PENNE-baker spent the early part of June syncing up the sound. Dylan looked at the raw footage and still didn't have any clear idea what should be done with it. "Dylan was in a really drained state of mind.... He was up in Bearsville and didn't want to get into it. We were supposed to deliver this thing to ABC and they kept calling me because they kept thinking I was the director/producer." Through the end of June and on into July,

Dylan ran the footage over and over again, trying to picture in his mind how the pieces they'd shot could fit into the film he *thought* they'd shot.

Shortly after Dylan's motorcycle crash, Pennebaker again went to visit him: "Albert [Grossman] got pissed at me because he said I wasn't helping [Dylan] edit enough. And I explained to him that I was never supposed to be editing it. I had another film to make. [Dylan] didn't appear to be very knocked out by the accident, so I never quite knew what happened, or talked to him about it."

By this time, ABC was beginning to bear down on Dylan to produce a finished film. According to Pennebaker, "Dylan told me, 'Why don't you guys do a rough edit of all this stuff so we can see what all we got?' So Bobby Neuwirth and I made a first version from the footage. It was all guessing. We didn't figure out what to do with any of these things. We just stuck them together quickly as a kind of a sketch. It's called *You Know Something's Happening*. To jump-start the editing process, because nothing was being done. . . .

"And one day Greil Marcus came in and saw it," says Pennebaker. "He thought it was a finished film—I had a hard time talking him out of it—and wrote a review saying what a great film it was. And Dylan happened to read it and said: 'What the fuck is this? Whaddaya doing? You're not supposed to be making this film.' And I *wasn't* supposed to be, you know. I just said, 'Hey, it's only a rough cut.'" But whatever state it was in, Dylan hated it.

"They'd made another *Don't Look Back*," said Dylan. "It was obvious from looking at the film that it was garbage. It was miles and miles of garbage."

According to Pennebaker, "The film Dylan wanted to make wasn't bereft of ideas, it's just that they were *all in his head*. What we were going to get on film wouldn't be that! I think he thinks I'm somehow shooting this thing the way he wants it to be shot. I wasn't opposed to the film he wanted to make; I just didn't know how to do it. So I started making the same old kind of film—the only film I know how to make, actually.

"But he was very pissed at everybody, and I don't know whether it was because they were putting pressure on him to get the film ready for TV and he didn't want to do it, or whether he felt he was in some kind of film competition with me, which I certainly never wanted to get into. So he just tucked away the film that Neuwirth and I had worked on. He just buried our version, and they went on and made a film."

If, in Dylan's mind, Pennebaker had failed in his attempt to follow the quark-like track of Dylan's thought processes, the 1966 footage is far from being a "newsreel." The opening shot of *You Know Something's Happening* is hallucinatory. As the band moves down the highway, the sky pulsates to a Dylan track, as if the day itself is astonished to see such goings-on. Indoors (where most Dylan life takes place) the wide-angle lens creates the distorted perspective of medieval rooms in paintings of the Annunciation. The quality of the film stock, like the raking light of a sky before a thunderstorm, sheds an eerie radiance on everything.

DYLAN NOW DECIDED HE WOULD MAKE HIS OWN FILM. IN LATE JULY 1966, with the help of Howard Alk, Dylan began to edit footage from the tour to make his own antidocumentary. Pennebaker sent two editors to help him and Dylan brought in Robbie Robertson to offer suggestions. Dylan edited his version in the manner of the Burroughs cut-up technique, splicing short film clips together, abutting unrelated scenes into bizarre sequences—in the manner of his mid-'60s songs.

This was *Eat the Document*, a little under one hour of fragments flashing, with Dylan and Howard Alk manically splicing pieces together on the Moviola (from the footage Pennebaker shot of Dylan's 1966 European tour), thus creating their own antidocumentary.

The camera lurches, careens, crashes into things, gets distracted, wanders off, interrupts itself. Right there in the first scene Dylan tells Pennebaker: "Rick Danko and I are going to snort some methedrine. This is what it's like. This is life on the road. Film it, let the truth be our judge."

Dylan rises up from behind a piano, cupping his hands over his nose. There's manic laughter and then there it is—Rick Danko snorting meth out of a snuffbox, right before our eyes. And we're off. It's a euphoric dopamine rush: high-speed, frenetic, disjointed, and disorienting.

We're only thirty seconds into *Eat the Document* and our cerebral cortex is jammed. We've got a serious contact high. Synapses firing randomly, snatches of dialogue, incoherent scenes, odd activities are thrown at you. The camera leers at the world through its wiggy 10 mm fish-eye lens and registers it on phosphorescent film stock. The piano has been drinking, the furniture is restless, the wallpaper is changing its spots.

Eat the Document consists of fifty-nine separate scenes, some lasting less than a minute, as if some cinematic tease is constantly tantalizing you with an amazing scene and then, just as you become involved, yanking you away to get a cut of something else, a series of unrelated scenes told through a frantic eye. One odd sequence after another unfolds, alternately manic and curious.

There are bizarre impromptu theater-of-the-absurd pieces like the brief interlude in Paris with the French actress Zuzu. Others include Bob in a white matinee idol jacket, drawing a filigree mustache and beard on his face with a pen and crawling onto the ledge of the George V Hotel in Paris, floors above the street. There's Richard Manuel from the Hawks trying to procure a blond girl with Australian currency. A man with a sandwich board appears; on the front panel it reads: IT IS APPOINTED UNTO MEN ONCE TO DIE. When he turns around we see the other side: AFTER THE JUDGMENT.

There's Dylan in the hotel bedroom reading a music paper, an almost life-size picture of his face on the cover. Then we see that iconic Hamlet-like image of Dylan stroking his chin and looking out the window onto railway tracks. Ethereal and androgynous in his shades and always with a cigarette as if he lived on smoke, he looks a little like a ghost looking out on a world he's about to disappear from.

Eat the Document is also hallucinatory in the use of sound: Dreamlike fragments of speech and overheard dialogue pop spookily out of the soundtrack. The disembodied voices come loose from their sync moorings. Like bicameral chatter or schizophrenic feedback, these voices often don't always connect with the things we're seeing on-screen. Dylan's aim is to disorient you, to make you feel the way he did. There are no clues, no explanations.

It's shot in some pretty spectacular locations: Copenhagen, Glasgow, Paris, London (although we don't get to see too many of the sights). So what is this group going to do in a foreign country? Sightseeing is out of the question. It's uncool and, besides, psychically impossible for Dylan and Co. They're in their own bubble. We see repeated images of travel—but at one remove as seen through a dining car window, a train steaming and whistling across country, car windshields, hotel windows. He's constantly looking at life, people, places through panes of glass. It's as if Europe has become a series of exotic rides—a hipster's version of Disneyland except that they are time travelers from the future. Of course they're not going to go see the Eiffel Tower, the Tower Bridge, the Little Mermaid statue. They've come from the future—just catching snapshots of the present.

The natives seem straight, and from another age altogether in comparison to Dylan and his entourage who, in C. P. Lee's words, "appear to have descended on an unsuspecting Europe like exotic animals from an intergalactic zoo." People look back at Dylan as if seeing him in an exhibit, and Dylan looks back at them like someone trapped in a snow globe.

The only things they're interested in aside from performing and parrying with journalists and fans naturally are the bizarre and grotesque. According to Dylan, "We went out to see a haunted house, where a man and his dog were supposed to have been burned up in the 13th century. Boy, that place was kooky."

When in Copenhagen, how could he resist visiting Elsinore, Prince Hamlet's castle? "Without the strain of having to be a 'public figure,' he became less reserved and strolled around asking plenty of questions," Garsten Grolin wrote in the Danish magazine *Ekstra Bladet*. "He wanted to know everything about the history of Kronberg— if Shakespeare had ever been there, where was it that Hamlet had met his father's ghost. All the time the film crew were shooting the episode for the TV film, which will be called, *The 20th Century Hamlet*." If only!

In *Eat the Document* it's as if the images of people and places were somehow siphoned off telepathically by Dylan. The illusion that we are watching these scenes from inside Dylan's brain is created by a fusion of Dylan and Alk's methedrine-like editing style and Pennebaker's intentionally freaked version of Direct Cinema. In an attempt to simulate the effects of Dylan's amphetamine-saturated brain, it distorts the world and the stage as if adapting to Dylan's skewed perspective. In contrast to the black-and-white cinema verité of *Don't Look Back*, the look of *Eat the Document* is positively trippy. Some of this has to do with the uncoated 7242 reversible color film stock used, one of the first fast films that Eastman Kodak brought out. But it's the advantage Pennebaker took of it—intuitively playing on its distortions and technical shortcomings—that makes the footage so electric.

This was Dylan's farewell to the '60s, a full-on experimental work into which he inserted clues (or so we tell ourselves) about where he's going next. Toward the end of *Eat the Document*, Dylan—mugging, goofing, doing bizarre and humorous readings of his own song (and clearly high)—sings "Mr. Tambourine Man" with its great chord-dominated harmonica solo as his face fills the screen. According to C. P. Lee in *Like a Bullet of Light*, by ending the film with a performance of "Mr. Tambourine Man" and a cover of Gordon Lightfoot's classic "Early Morning Rain," he was implying that he was at the end of a cycle, that he was going back to his acoustic roots—the ancient folk music that he will reawaken in his next musical mutations: *John Wesley Harding* and *The Basement Tapes*.

While it may seem churlish of Dylan to dismiss the Pennebaker footage out of hand, it's not difficult to see why he disdained the ersatz reality of the documentary (which in essence claims that you are seeing someone as they really are). Dylan's entire life and art have consistently questioned such naive ideas about identity—not to mention reality. Dylan saw documentaries as he'd come to see folk music, a form that exuded authenticity, but was almost as much a work of fiction as your average Hollywood movie.

But Dylan is a mythmaker, a collector of folk truths, legends, and revelations, for whom the garden-variety realism aspired to in most documentaries is toxic. So *Eat the Document* might be seen as Dylan's poetic journal of the 1966 tour—how it *felt* to him, its arbitrariness mirroring the way memory is reconstituted from fragments.

According to Pennebaker, the title means "Eat shit!" but "Cannibalize it!" may be more accurate. When Dylan complained of working on a documentary about himself, his friend Al Aronowitz said, "Documentary? *Eat the document!*" Which is pretty much what Dylan did—chew up the footage and spit it out. *Eat the Document* has fifty-nine scenes in fifty-four minutes of choppy, maddeningly cut edits. Jonathan Cott in *Rolling Stone* described the bizarre editing of *Eat the Document* as "quasi-methedrine logic suggesting a self-consciously disintegrating structure."

"What we were trying to do," Dylan explained, "was to make a logical story out of this newsreel-type footage . . . what we tried to do was to construct a stage and an environment, taking it out and putting it together like a puzzle. And we did. That's the strange part about it."

What he was dealing with was far from "newsreel footage," and as for making it into a "logical story," that's the last thing *Eat the Document* is. The film is often slyly witty, clever, sometimes dazzling. He'd essentially invented a mad version of an MTV video fifteen years too early—if it weren't, that is, a film about Dylan, and if thousands of feet of great performances hadn't been left on the cutting room floor.

"We cut it fast on the eye," says Dylan. Yes, but looking at it today after three and a half decades of MTV jump cuts, YouTube, speed dating, texting, and Twitter, it doesn't seem quite the headlong gallop of a headless horseman it once did. Its juxtapositions now look almost quaint, old-school avant-garde.

In late 1967 Dylan and his friend the filmmaker Howard Alk showed

ABC-TV a thirty-minute work-in-progress print of *Eat the Document*. If Dylan hadn't thought much of Pennebaker and Neuwirth's version of the footage, ABC's reaction to Dylan's version was apoplectic. Officially ABC said, "There was some disagreement over the format of the show," but in reality they were so outraged at what they saw that they wanted the film *destroyed*. They wanted to hack up the footage, incinerate it, and scatter its ashes in the executive washroom. According to Jon Taplin, the Band's future road manager, it was only by sneaking into ABC and smuggling the film out in a shopping bag that it escaped being incinerated.

Bizarrely enough, Dylan and Alk didn't think they were being deliberately provocative, or even making something unacceptable for commercial television. They intended to conform with the television format and even inserted pauses for commercial breaks. "It was a little too freaky for ABC at that time, I guess, and they rejected it," Jonathan Taplin says. No kidding. Eventually Dylan had to pay ABC back the advance, but now the film was his and he could do with it whatever he wished—which he did with a vengeance.

WHAT DID DYLAN WANT FROM HIS DOCUMENTARY? WHAT KIND OF film *would* come out of a head like his? Jonathan Cott suggested in *Rolling Stone* that Dylan wanted to make an "anti-documentary that uses the 'star' image in order to demystify and decompose it." In other words Bob deconstructing Bob, dismantling the monumental Dylan effigy he'd so brilliantly created.

Aside from his lyrics, there are other clues as to his bizarre editing technique on *Eat the Document*, and they can be found in his liner notes and his novel, *Tarantula*, both of which teem with surreal scenes, bizarre tableaux, and a cast of sideshow freaks, outlaws, characters from folklore, literary saints, and straw dogs—akin to the assemblage of eccentric types on the cover of *The Basement Tapes*.

Was he trying to cast the characters from his songs in a movie? Give them legs and set them loose on the world? In a sense Dylan's songs are short surreal film sequences, his lyrics a form of cinematography complete with tracking shots, extreme close-ups, and reverse angles.

Maybe one day Dylan will paint his cinematic masterpiece. In the meantime we have his spectral movies in our heads; they run every time we hear "Visions of Johanna," "Desolation Row," or "Positively 4th Street."

The Band stand before an endless road—in the woods near Woodstock, 1969—or 1869. This was to be the original cover of the Band's second album. From left: Richard Manuel, Levon Helm (facing away), Rick Danko, Garth Hudson, Robbie Robertson.

17   Who Is Tiny Montgomery?

He had the tradition in him, deep, in his brain, his words. . . . It enabled him to draw up from Shakespeare. It made Noah, and Moses, contemporary to him. History was ritual and repetition, when Melville's imagination was at its own proper beat. It was an older sense than the European man's, more to do with magic than culture . . . . It gave him the power to find the lost past of America, the unfound present, and make a myth, *Moby-Dick,* for a people of Ishmaels.

—CHARLES OLSON, *Call Me Ishmael*

What's going on up there, man?
You mean with Bob and the Band?
Yeah, what's up with these guys?
Hell, they've seceded.
They've *what*?
I don't know how else to describe this exactly . . . but
   they're beginning to look like something out of a
   Mathew Brady Civil War photo.
You're kidding?
Nope. It's like they're into some kinda time-travel type
   thing.
What are they using as a time machine?
Bob Dylan.
Oh, okay, I get it.
You do?

S OMETIME IN THE SUMMER OF 1966 AND CONTINUING FOR THE next year and a half Dylan and the Hawks (the future Band) fell into a time swoon. Maybe it was the accident. He certainly didn't want to go on another tour like the one he just finished. For all the progressive experimental drive of Dylan's mid-'60s rock, it was time to go elsewhere. Having resigned his role as the commissar of revolutionary acts, where was he going to go next? There *was* only one place left to go: the past. Dylan's always had a confusion about time—when things happened—along the lines of Louis B. Mayer's "1812, when was that?"

If you were looking for Dylan in 1967 you weren't going to find him up in Woodstock, not the living, quivering soul of Bob, anyway. For that you'd have to go back to, say, 1860 or so. Soon everybody would be spelunking into their own stalagmite-infested pasts. The Rolling Stones had their blues readymades on *Beggar's Banquet*, and the Beatles released their last studio album *Let It Be* (recorded in January 1969, before *Abbey Road*). Originally titled *Get Back*, it contained one of the Beatles' earliest compositions, "One After 909."

The Basement Tapes, like a lot of things in Dylan's career, got started in an unlikely manner. He invited two members of the Hawks, Richard Manuel and Rick Danko, to come up to Woodstock so he could film them in some scenes for *Eat the Document*. They already looked like a pair of Civil War veterans, two guys at the bar in a saloon in Dodge City. And this fit in perfectly with Dylan's next time-traveling stage.

In *Chronicles*, Dylan says that the Civil War is central to everything he writes. He studied it in the New York Public Library, poring over old newspaper accounts. He's got nineteenth-century DNA, from his interest in poets like Henry Timrod to his dedication of albums to Herman Melville. Up in Woodstock you could indulge in this kind of reverie.

By inviting Danko and Manuel—two guys who weren't actors, but who were in a band—up to Woodstock, Dylan clearly had something in mind other than his feckless filmmaking endeavors. Eventually the other members of the Hawks moved up to Woodstock too, and, uncannily in tune with Dylan's Civil War obsession, they consciously formed their image around daguerreotypes of Confederate veterans. As the Band, they would revolutionize what rock music could be.

Between June and October 1967 (and again in November, after the *John Wesley Harding* sessions), Dylan and the Band record demo tracks on a two-track home tape recorder in the garage of the Band's house, Big

Pink, in West Saugerties, New York. Altogether they recorded more than one hundred tracks, sixteen of which would be released in 1975 as *The Basement Tapes*. On these sessions Dylan goes back to his folk roots, no longer referring to it as folk music—which he says "is such a shuck." Instead, he now calls it the authentic stuff, "historical traditional music." Later called Americana and alt-country, it featured a whimsical cast of folk characters and their sense of seeking salvation, community, joy, and everyday life. As such, *The Basement Tapes* is as remote in time and place (as well as attitude) to the cynical, hipster nightmare blues of *Blonde on Blonde* (1966) as it is to *John Wesley Harding* (1967) that followed. At the same time there's a feeling of claustrophobia, desperation, and the need to escape in songs written around this time, including "Too Much of Nothing" and "I Shall Be Released."

The origin of *The Basement Tapes* was very basic. Dylan's "mailbox money" (his royalties) was running out and Grossman essentially said to Dylan: Well, if you're not touring and not recording, you better go write some songs, make some demos, and we'll sell them. "No, they weren't demos for myself," Dylan explained to *Rolling Stone* in late 1969. "They were demos of the songs. I was being PUSHED again . . . into coming up with some songs. You know how those things go."

And Grossman did in fact sell a bunch of these songs to the limeys (as well as to a few other people). Julie Driscoll covered "This Wheel's On Fire" and Manfred Mann had a hit with "Quinn the Eskimo." When Dylan's demo was played for Manfred Mann, he asked, "Who is the terrible singer?" These demos were the source of much that got onto the world's first bootleg album, *The Great White Wonder*.

But why the return to the past for these tracks? Well, Bob never did believe in chronology in the history book sense, and living up there in that spooky house like something out of *The Shining*, you could wander through time at will, flipping through Emerson—with whom Dylan had a lot more in common at this point than, say, with Abbie Hoffman. He also absorbed books of poetry Ginsberg had sent him: Sir Thomas Wyatt, Campion, Emily Dickinson, Lorca, Blake, Whitman, Rimbaud.

Dylan seemed to feel a certain repulsion to his own era: ". . . too much of nothing . . . the waters of oblivion . . . it's all been done before, it's all been written in the book. . . ." Dylan and the Band repudiate "that psychedelic shit," along with rock, protest, flower power. They don't acknowledge that the Vietnam War is raging—or they do it indirectly by transposing it to the Civil War or biblical battles. It's the retreat into folk, legends, history, timelessness. As Robbie Robertson put it, "We were rebelling against rebellion."

The whole episode of Dylan and the Band might have been a short story written by Melville: "Being Some Account of a Chronicle of a Traveling Troupe of Players—Who for the Time Being Ain't Goin' Nowhere." They were saying, "Hell, we'll create our own reality, anyplace, anyhow, anytime, using only the tried-and-true materials—Whitman, Melville, Lem Motlow, and Mother's Best Flour—just as long as it ain't here 'n' now."

Even if he'd wanted to go back to folk music, it wasn't going to be the same egg he'd hatched out of; it wasn't there anymore. So the only solution, since simply playing and singing the old ballads was no longer an option either, was to reinvent folk music from original sources, one of these being Dylan's uncanny ability to pull wacky characters and saucy scenes out of his teeming imagination. Dylan is a master gleaner, picking up the faint emerging frequencies of times past and present, and amplifying them. Commonplace sayings, stuff off police blotters, heard at a coffee shop counter, in the bus station. Where he had once fed on '60s energy, momentum, and ignition, he now drew on America's eerie word mound.

The folk hoard was the great greasy gumbo tome in which the experiences in the New World were recorded. Dylan would take some of the grudges, broken promises, and a few stolen horses from the mad dream book and summon up personifications of place, like Tiny Montgomery—the place names in American geography being themselves boastful, Bible-thumped, careless, commemorative, and plain nutty. American speech, D. H. Lawrence said, "contains an alien quality, which belongs to the American continent and nowhere else."

Bob had already been through this territory earlier in his career as a folksinger, but Dylan, unlike many who'd sung old folk songs before, refused to become frozen by the folk conservancy. He knew that you had to take this material and reanimate it. If you don't put your own humor and pathos into these songs and marinate them in your own peculiar times they were just relics in formaldehyde. All this haywire energy and these crazy wisdom yarns had been like a Poe story, prematurely buried under the avalanche of industrial urban society and waiting to be unearthed. And Dylan knew that profoundly. These songs were calling to him: "Hey, there, Bob, come jump into the swamp and wake us the hell up!" He wasn't just a troubadour, or the other names he self-deferentially uses to describe himself. He was a sort of musical idiot savant.

A communal exchange of musical energy through music, no one listening just playing for their own joy. "You know, that's really the way to do a recording," Dylan told *Rolling Stone* in 1969, "in a peaceful relaxed setting, in somebody's basement. With the windows open and a dog lying on the floor."

Most days Dylan would show up at noon, make coffee, and then type out lyrics on a typewriter, writing seven, eight, nine, ten, sometimes fifteen songs a day. He introduced the Band to weird old American folk music, and the Band taught Bob how to play in a group. "He damn sure didn't know how it was supposed to sound, either," as Levon points out, "which is what made it so interesting."

The band could follow Dylan as he meandered, jettisoned logic and syntax altogether, and moved through nursery rhyme verses and neologisms. From the contact with Dylan, the Band morphed from a funky R&B group into folk rockers, and through that time-weighted molasses music they transported themselves into their Civil War veterans gravitas.

"*The Basement Tapes* were incredibly different from what we did with Ronnie Hawkins and from what we did with Bob Dylan," Robbie Robertson explained. "When the band became *this character*, this kind of sound and music, it had nothing to do with what we had done with either of those two. This was not done on purpose. It is just what came out."

Much of the invention came straight out of the loose improvisational atmosphere, doing it on the spot. Scat, nonce words, and filler words led to surrealistic phrases, like Paul McCartney using "scrambled eggs" for "Yesterday." For example, in "I'm Not There (1956)" the words are jumbled and the sense of the song is just floating:

> Thing's all right and she's all too tight
> In my neighborhood she cries both day and night
> I know it because I was there
> It's a milestone but she's down on her luck
> And she's daily salooning about to make her hard earned buck
> I was there

Some of these songs were made for other people, but clearly a few were intended for Dylan himself and earmarked for the Band to record.

In essence the Band's sound, although very different from much of what they did on *The Basement Tapes*, evolved out of this process.

The very inscrutability of many folk songs was mesmerizing. Mystery, Dylan said, is "a fact, a traditional fact." But, as Bob Hudson points out, sometimes urban-dwelling Northerners attribute mystery where there really is only muddle, misunderstanding, and often pretty down-to-earth explanations:

> I was thinking about Greil Marcus's liner notes to *The Basement Tapes* (and his later book), and I remember him discussing, with great passion, the mystical surrealism of old folk songs like "I Wish I Was a Mole in the Ground" and how those shaped *The Basement Tapes*. True enough—but this week, I heard an album by old-time fiddler Christian Wig (from Ohio), and he sings an old version of "Mole in the Ground." But his version makes sense of the odd lyrics in a way Marcus hadn't thought of. Wig's older version goes like this:

> > Tempe she lives up on the hill
> > Her daddy owns the biggest moonshine still
> > He won't let me come up
> > He won't let her come down
> > I wish I was a mole in the ground

> > I wish I was a mole in the ground (x2)
> > If I's a mole in the ground
> > I'd root that mountain down
> > I wish I was a mole in the ground

> Wishing to be a mole in the ground was meant to be funny! It's a joke—and is only as mystical as a lot of humor is. The singer wants to root the mountain down to get to his true love! Pretty practical really. (And sort of sexy as well.) Marcus has a tendency to romanticize and mythologize the folk tradition to a certain extent. But then, so does Dylan.

> It's curious that most of us who were raised *outside* a strongly traditional folk culture tend to view it as romantic/mystical. But those within the culture see the internal logic of that culture in a way the rest of us don't—and even find the culture pedestrian. Or put it this way: Dylan (and Marcus) are fascinated by African-Americans and Appalachians because in a sense they're really tourists in those cultures.

DYLAN WAS UNBELIEVABLY PROLIFIC IN 1967, WORKING WITH ROBBIE Robertson, Rick Danko, Richard Manuel, and eventually Levon Helm (who'd left the Hawks during the 1966 world tour because he couldn't take the constant abuse from fans—the very abuse Dylan thrived on).

Over five and a half months Dylan and the Band recorded 107 different versions of songs, including 32 covers. The range and variety of songs is incredible: "Quinn the Eskimo," "Tears of Rage," "This Wheel's On Fire," "You Ain't Going Nowhere," "I Shall Be Released," "Too Much Of Nothing," "Nothing Was Delivered," "Million Dollar Bash," "I'm Not There (1956)," "Sign On the Cross," "Clothes Line Saga."

The pleasure in listening to *The Basement Tapes* comes, in part, from the songs' rawness and sheer jumping-out-of-their-skin delight. Listening to them we get involved in the process of Dylan's creation, the spontaneity of the rough draft. Even the mistakes are fascinating. Unfortunately when Robbie Robertson edited the tapes for the released version he overdubbed instruments (piano, percussion, guitars) on five of the songs, which took away from the authenticity of the performances. He also included Band songs, which interrupted the flow of the tracks.

One of the things that holds Dylan's little packets of images together on *The Basement Tapes* (and maintains what momentum there is in *Tarantula*) is Dylan's lunch counter rhythmic flow of speech, the lope of vernacular phrases, expressions.

> *Grady O'lady comes in—gives everybody the nod & wants to know*
> *where she can get a maid—"dig henry miller?" she asks kind of*
> *snaky like—"you mean that fantastically dead henry miller?*
> *the real estate agent henry miller?" "what you mean?"*

Dylan is a sensitive radio tuner—hence his fascination with Bobbie Gentry's "Ode to Billie Joe," which he refashioned into "Clothes Line Saga."

> *The next day everybody got up*
> *Seein' if the clothes were dry*
> *The dogs were barking, a neighbor passed*
> *Mama, of course, she said, "Hi!"*
> *"Have you heard the news?" he said, with a grin*
> *"The Vice-President's gone mad!"*

"Where?" "Downtown." "When?" "Last night"
"Hmm, say, that's too bad!"

Dylan is the original human radio, randomly tuning in signals from just about anywhere. Like the schizophrenic housewife in John Cheever's story "The Enormous Radio" who hears conversations two backyards away, Dylan can seem to pick up what's going on in people's heads through his phantom radio antenna. It makes everybody nervous—even Dylan. For a couple of years—roughly 1964–66—he'd turned himself into a telepath. Now he was channeling crazed old hill-country banjo pickers, the sounds of Appalachian ballads and blues. He could fly through time and be back by morning. Perhaps that's what happened in Australia when he was channeling, metaphorically getting into a doublet and hose if that's what it took.

"It was amazing to see him work on a song," Rosemary Garrett recalled about that hotel room in Australia. "He would have the poetry of it worked out in his head and he would say to Robbie: 'Listen, Robbie, just imagine this cat who is very Elizabethan, with garters and a long shepherd's horn, and he's coming over the hill in the morning with the sun rising behind him. That's the sound I want.' And then they would begin to play and out of this would come some kind of rhythm, and then the music would take shape. They did this for hours and hours, Dylan setting a scene and everybody playing music to create the sound of that scene."

This may have been one of his more eccentric moves but it shows a ferocious dedication to method songwriting. While working on *Infidels* in 1983 he would explain the feel he wanted on a song by saying to guitarist J. J. Holliday, "Buddy Boy Hawkins [a blues singer from the '20s with a dirgelike sound] combined with a striptease act: that's the vibe we're looking for."

He's an animator, an underground cartoonist, infatuated with nicknames—a technique that worked well in *The Basement Tapes* but capsized a lot of the paper boats in *Tarantula*. On *The Basement Tapes* Dylan pulls out of the ether an eccentric cast of characters with colorful names—*personages*—what else would you call them? He let loose a pack of American archetypes: Mrs. Henry, Tiny Montgomery, Turtle, Silly Nelly, RoseMarie, Skinny Moo, T-bone Frank, Mouse, Moby Dicki, and Quinn the Eskimo. Also, images from blues, hipster chronicles (Mezz Mezzrow, Iceberg Slim), pool-hall lingo, mafioso nomenclature, characters with names from hop joints, William Burroughs–type characters

(Salt Chunk Mary, the Sanctimonious Kid), and Damon Runyon's gangsters (the Lemon Drop Kid, Last Card Louie).

Some of the tracks on *The Basement Tapes* would eventually turn into great tracks by both the Band and Dylan. So why didn't he record them subsequently in the studio? Well, he tried; these were the sessions for *Self Portrait* and the tracks that ended up on the supposed throwaway album *Dylan*. He didn't use the Band on these sessions because by then they were *the Band* and had their own career and character. In any case, Dylan never wants to record with musicians who are already too familiar with the material. Without spontaneity and surprise you aren't going to capture the sense of abandon of *The Basement Tapes*. As Billy Bragg told Sid Griffin, "They caught lightning in a bottle."

Dylan as the character Alias in *Pat Garrett and Billy the Kid*, a fantasy Western concocted out of panoramic landscapes, cowboy hipspeak, and Dylan's lyrical soundtrack.

18 The Cowboy Angel Rides:
John Wesley Harding

Since these mysteries are beyond me, let us pretend to be
the organizers of them.

—JEAN COCTEAU, *WEDDING ON THE EIFFEL TOWER*

W E'RE IN AN APOCALYPTIC WASTELAND, CAR PARTS, OLD
tires, oil drums, red sky, smoke rising in the distance
over an endless burnt-out landscape. A ragtag group of
bearded old men, young women with babies, teenagers,
dogs, and children are gathered around a junkyard fire. An intense youth
in glasses and short, curly hair, dressed in torn and ragged clothes, is sitting in a plastic beach chair. He begins to strum his guitar, singing in a
husky, strangled voice, as if barely able to get out the strange tale he's telling. It's a ballad about an obscure cowboy saint, John Wesley Hardin.

Cowboy songs, *High Noon* Manichean confrontations between good
and evil, are always going to be popular especially in a postnuclear age.
We're addicted to morality tales because even in these badlands, the USA
is this big geographical machine we're still trying to figure out how to
operate.

Hardin—or Harding as Dylan calls him—isn't quite as famous an
outlaw as Jesse James or Billy the Kid, although there had already been
three country songs about him, including one by Johnny Cash. From the
first few lines we know this cowboy. He's the generic misunderstood,
good-hearted gunslinger—even if the real John Wesley Hardin was
something of a homicidal psychopath. Still, he's the mythic cowboy, so
what he was actually like doesn't concern us and doesn't concern Dylan
long either. He's a Western Robin Hood like Woody Guthrie's "Pretty
Boy Floyd," who left Christmas dinners and thousand-dollar gifts for
poor folk in his travels. That's the kind of story we like in the US of A.

The gunslinger of the title track from Dylan's next album, *John Wesley Harding*, is straight out of the Woody Guthrie bag of sanctified bad

guys. It is the Book of the Outcast, an outsider's album full of losers, drifters, martyrs, radicals, and immigrants. The ghost of Hank Williams hovers over it—specifically his alter ego, Luke the Drifter, the name Hank used for his cautionary, humorous, and religious songs. These songs sympathize with the plight of the misunderstood, the hard done by, the put-upon rural dude.

Dylan's mode of communication circa late 1967 was allegory—basically saying one thing while meaning something else. Bob's gotten serious since we last heard from him. *The Basement Tapes* won't be released for another seven years, and even the bootleg *The Great White Wonder* won't appear for another two.

Everything for Dylan is now on another level—spiritual, moral, dark, and doomy. He speaks in parables and fables. "John Wesley Harding" is an allegory, but of what? On one hand, he's the cowboy as a Christ figure, an idea Dylan himself seemed to endorse. Still, it's hard not to read the last verse without thinking of Bob:

All across the telegraph
His name it did resound
But no charge held against him
Could they prove
And there was no man around
Who could track or chain him down
He was never known
To make a foolish move

As with other tracks on this album, you can see each layer—historical character, mythic outlaw, saint, and self-portrait—transparent through the other. Dylan says that originally he planned to write a long, many-versed ballad, but we don't need that. The cowboy is an American cultural artifact, and he arises spontaneously in our minds from Levi's jeans ads, cigarette commercials, and Waylon Jennings albums. We visualize John Wesley Harding in the flickering light of the projector at one of the movie theaters run by Bob's uncle in Hibbing. "John Wesley Harding" might be a trailer for an epic Western.

When *John Wesley Harding* comes out in January 1968, the oracle has been silent for a year and half. It is startlingly unexpected, as if somebody has abruptly changed the channel. You were just listening to *Blonde on Blonde* and now *this*! When Dylan emerges (on vinyl at least) from his retreat, it is as the grim figure of an Old Testament prophet who speaks in riddles that are now parables, the images stripped bare. His new style is epitomized in the chilling vision of "All Along the Watchtower." The emptiness and terror of the present has ballooned and is now seen as a heroic space into which the imagination can rush. He communes with history, the Bible, Hank Williams, Blake, Gimpel the Fool.

John Wesley Harding has a sepia-tone, nineteenth-century quality to it, underlined by the monochrome cover, which shows a black-and-white photo of Dylan, two singers from the Indian group the Bauls of Bengal, and a local handyman, Charlie Joy. They look timeless, like frontier types—but without any context they could almost be medieval figures. What exactly is going on in this enigmatic picture? Dylan's inscrutability had reached such a pitch that people even began finding faces in the tree. After I heard that you could make out the faces of the Beatles in the bark—well, I saw them too. Who knew what this meant or why Dylan had put them there or if they were there at all. Even without the bark-decoding element, the album cover resonated with mysterious implications as though something momentous had occurred, but we are all—including Dylan—affecting that nothing was really going on.

The austerity of the album had an instantaneous effect on the hothouse climate of psychedelic music. "Nothing is revealed" was the catchphrase that summer (this might just as well be applied to Dylan himself). The phrase was bandied about so shamelessly in London in 1968 that local ordinances against its gratuitous use had to be enforced.

On the album, Dylan's voice is a spirit from the beyond admonishing the frivolities of the age. The unflinching moral tone was utterly unlike the tracks on *Blonde on Blonde* or anything else around at the time. In 1967, psychedelic monsters roamed the land from the Beatles' *Sgt. Pepper* to the Stones' *Satanic Majesties* with its 3-D cover. Dylan was the lone gunslinger riding into town and evaporating the psychedelic pyramid (one he'd helped to build) and now sang to us from the ruins. In an instant he made obsolete their trippy toys—their wah-wah pedals, twenty-four-track recording studios, tapes playing backward. All the hip young dudes at their control panels were wringing their hands in despair. "He's ruined us! He's bloody making records at Woolworth's!"

Dylan's tone on *John Wesley Harding* is that of someone stunned by a traumatic experience that has affected his coherence and memory. The stories are stripped of detail, which has turned them into little enigmatic tales, and the storyteller feels no need to explain, except, of course, in the diversionary liner notes.

You have to fill in the gaps yourself. On *Blonde on Blonde* the confusion came from the noirish atmosphere. Here we are being told dense, contradictory stories with pieces missing, songs with narratives so condensed they're difficult to follow. The play, by the time you arrive, has been going on for some time. The tales have been overheard on a train or in the next room. When someone comes in and asks you what just happened you can't really say.

Dylan is reinventing the folk ballad, reassembling the parts so that they mimic the haunting phrases and troubling stories of the folk hoard. They're disjointed, just the way Mark Twain, that old Southern yarn spinner, said they should be in "How to Tell a Story": "to string incongruities and absurdities together in a wandering and sometimes purposeless way."

The folk song gospel is made up of fragments, just like the United States. It's all cobbled together, knitted together, like a patchwork quilt. The discontinuity, the incongruity between one thing and another is just what made the old ballads seem so mesmerizing and profound.

So what's Dylan been up to since *Blonde on Blonde*? He's been playing cards with Tom Paine, hanging out with St. Augustine, running his fingers along the words in the Bible, watching the verses ignite like that "burning ring of fire" that June Carter and Merle Kilgore found in Carter's granddaddy's Bible, a song Dylan would later record with Johnny Cash on February 18, 1969, and again, without Cash, on a rare outtake from the *Self Portrait* sessions.

Alleged historical figures pop up. St. Augustine isn't the North African shaman of guilt and redemption; he's more a plaster saint, he's emblematic. He's all saints, and saints traditionally end up martyrs. Tom isn't Thomas Paine the American revolutionary (or even an Emergency Civil Liberties Award statuette). He's more like a crossing guard.

But it doesn't matter; their names are loaded with collective associations. They awaken images, give off sparks. St. Augustine's wearing a coat of solid gold; we understand that. But what is he doing with a blanket underneath his arm? Has he, too, joined the rootless band of other sanctified hoboes on the album?

The album's liner notes present a comic *Tarantula*-like tale, very different from the dark tales within (except for the goofy "Frankie Lee and Judas Priest" pseudoparable on the album). The liner notes are allegedly there to explain what we're about to hear but instead lead us into a typical Dylan Möbius strip. Frank is a Dylanologist and the three kings are trying to decode Bob.

> "Frank," [the first king] began, "Mr. Dylan has come out with a new record. This record of course features none but his own songs and we understand that you're the key."
>
> "That's right," said Frank, "I am."
>
> "Well then," said the king in a bit of excitement, "could you please open it up for us?"
>
> . . .
>
> "All right," said Frank, "I'll see what I can do," and he commenced to doing it. First of all, he sat down and crossed his legs, then he sprung up, ripped off his shirt and began waving it in the air. A light-bulb fell from one of his pockets and he stamped it out with his foot. Then he took a deep breath, moaned and punched his fist through the plate-glass window. Settling back in his chair, he pulled out a knife, "Far enough?" he asked.
>
> "Yeah, sure, Frank," said the second king. The third king just shook his head and said he didn't know.

The album track "Frankie Lee and Judas Priest" (no relation, apparently, to Frank and the three kings) borders on pastiche even when it comes right out and shamelessly states its moral ("Don't go mistaking Paradise/For that home across the road").

With *Another Side*, Dylan had supposedly given up moralizing ("Fearing not that I'd become my enemy/In the instant that I preach"), but some of the homilies on *John Wesley Harding* are so literal only Bob could pull them off: "One should never be where one does not belong." They would have seemed hackneyed and smarmy coming from, say, Paul McCartney—or Paul Simon. But when delivered with Dylan's junkyard-dog rasp the words remain believable, if wobbly. With Dylan they come off like barfly pool-hall aphorisms and vernacular folk wisdom chestnuts. Through Dylan's tormented vocals and wailing harmonica, even the banalities of the fragmented lyrics are raised to a transcendent level.

Sure, there's a lot of moralizing on *John Wesley Harding*, but then most of American literature consists of how-to and self-improvement books—and folk music does too. "A folk song," Woody opined, "is what's wrong and how to fix it."

Dylan says he was plagued by fear and tormented by the Devil while working on the album. It's a mysterious, troubled, Bible-haunted record, spooky, stark, and dark, saturated in Old Testament dread dealing with a desolate, bankrupt America. It's infected with Puritan guilt, related by a teller of folk song history, steeped in the nineteenth century. You read the King James Bible long enough and that Jacobean prose is going to bleed through.

Also interesting is the mode of storytelling. Dylan's songs usually emanate from inside that fitful head, but on *John Wesley Harding* he's the humble scrivener, relating things that have happened offstage. He's the scribe, the court recorder, the witness on the battlements, saying, "This thing I saw and that, and also. . . ."

Dylan has always claimed to live on another plane—and we believe him, especially when he starts talking in that spooky Cotton Mather voice:

The age that I was living in didn't resemble this age, yet it did in some mysterious and traditional way. Not just a little bit, but a lot. There was a broad spectrum and commonwealth that I was living upon, and the basic psychology of that life was every bit a part of it. If you turned the light towards it, you could see the full complexity of human nature. Back there, America was put on the cross, died and was resurrected. There was nothing synthetic about it. The godawful truth of that would be the all-encompassing template behind everything that I would write.

As unexpected as the appearance of *John Wesley Harding* was in the climate of rock in the late '60s, it did have one thing in common with the mood of the counterculture: the sense of an impending apocalypse. The counterculture narcissistically focused on a number of incidents that seemed to confirm that a day of reckoning was at hand—when actually what was about to end was just our youth.

Dylan's ethereal and otherworldly voice, along with the wounded animal howl and the whine of the harmonica, laid a disturbing tone over the entire album. Who but Dylan would have thought that three-verse fables (with acoustic guitar, harmonica, drums, bass, and Peter Drake's steel guitar) would be the perfect accompaniment for the end of the world?

FANS HAD BEEN READING THINGS INTO ALBUMS BY THE BEATLES, THE Stones, and Dylan—Dylan especially—since the mid-'60s. Initially this began when listeners began tuning into albums to catch the vibe of these preternaturally hip creatures (rock stars). But as Charlie Watts said of the Stones, "We were only 15 minutes ahead of our time." As the '60s wore on and fans started getting higher and higher and weirder and weirder, they began reading things into absolutely everything: obscure lyrics—and there were plenty of those—album covers, playing tracks backward. Messages were everywhere you looked. There was only a short step from this to believing their albums could divine the future. The Stones' "Let It Bleed"—which eerily seemed to anticipate Altamont, Watts, the Manson murders, and the chaos at the end of the 1960s—was a classic example. The Beatles' *White Album* was notoriously misinterpreted by Charles Manson, who psychotically read his own demonic parables into "Helter Skelter" and "Piggies."

Rock stars were ahead of their time, but they weren't prophets or fortune-tellers. For the most part they'd just conflated their personal traumas with the world around them. And we'd turned Dylan's meltdown and crash, the Beatles' disintegration, and Keith Richards's anguish over Mick sleeping with his girlfriend, Anita Pallenberg, into epic fantasies (rock's principal mode of expression being hyperbole).

The pivotal song on *John Wesley Harding* is "All Along the Watchtower," around which the other songs on the album revolve. With its biblical imagery and its end-of-days shudder it has become an anthem for teenagers' solipsistic fantasies of impending doom ever since. It is also Dylan's most played song on the Never Ending Tour. Jimi Hendrix brilliantly latched on to Dylan's eerie sense of foreboding and amped it up, his howling opening chords electrifying the words and bringing out the terror of the song. In creating a menacing rhythm for his fateful warning, Dylan had inadvertently invented heavy metal. The opening licks—the iv-v-iv *chuck-a-chuck chuck-a-chuck*—are the power chords behind Led Zeppelin.

Hendrix's telegraphic semaphore at the end of the song is like an ominous extraterrestrial code beaming from outer space. We can't decipher the baleful omen the riders are delivering—but we feel it in our bones and know it does not bode well for us. It's just a shot away.

> Outside in the distance a wildcat did growl
> Two riders were approaching, the wind began to howl

In Isaiah's prophecy, the horsemen who are approaching the watchtower to bring good news—"Babylon has fallen!"—would be cause for rejoicing among eighth-century B.C. Jews. Isaiah is foretelling the destruction of an evil empire. So why are Dylan's and Hendrix's versions so apprehensive and terror ridden? Dylan has catastrophically reversed the point of view—the riders are coming to tell us not of an oppressor overthrown but of our own doom—because now *we* are Babylon.

Among his shifting chameleon-like postures we can no longer pinpoint Dylan. In the coming years he will juggle these Dylans on a high wire without a net. He'd always told us he was a juggler; we just didn't realize it was us he was juggling.

The juxtaposition of Bob Dylan, the dark prince of rock, and Johnny Cash, the good ol' boy of country music, seemed an unlikely pairing. But that only went to show how little we knew about Bob— or Cash. On the set of *The Johnny Cash Show*, 1970.

19 The Invisible Man Goes to Nashville

S OMEWHERE BETWEEN THE CRASH AND 1968 DYLAN HAD GONE country. Around 1969 Dylan cynics explained this unexpected move by saying that "country music was the last area of authentic American music left for us to rip off." The story as far as Dylan is concerned is obviously apocryphal. Dylan has always recognized country as the genuine legacy of white folk music—not to mention his long friendship with his shotgun-riding buddy, Johnny Cash, who was a kind of latter-day Hank Williams. Up until the House Un-American Activities Committee witch hunts of the 1950s, country was also labeled "folk music." But with the association of folk music with Village lefties and out-and-out pinkos like Pete Seeger the term was dropped like a hot skillet.

But how had Dylan caught his recent country bug in the first place? The explanation for his new attraction to country music was that he was returning to his roots. According to Dylan it was through country music that he had first come into the world. Not only had he been born to the sound of a hillbilly gospel record, "Driftin' Too Far From the Shore," he claimed that "the people who shaped my style were performers like Elvis Presley, Buddy Holly, Hank Thompson." And, of course, Hank Williams had always been his talisman: "I used to sing his songs way back even before I played rock as a rock 'n' roll teenager." We knew that this was the first music he'd gotten hooked on—and that was before rock 'n' roll even existed—if such a thing can be imagined. While *Nashville Skyline* was hardly a tribute to Hank Williams—aside from the lament "I Threw It All Away," there's nothing on the album that remotely harkens back to Hank—it was undeniably a country pop record.

Supposedly his country undercurrent got reawakened when he started recording in Nashville. He'd been working with these two Nashville musicians, Kenny Buttrey (bass) and Charlie McCoy (guitar, etc.), since 1966, all the way through *Blonde on Blonde* and *John Wesley Harding*. Instead of Dylan giving Kenny Buttrey and Charlie McCoy a case of the existential flu, he'd picked up the honky-tonk fever from them. Like the transmute that he is, Dylan's hyperabsorbent personality had gotten a serious country contact high. What he'd got wasn't the shit-kicker blues—more an easy-listening Nashville martini infection. But before he'd gone down there he'd neglected to get inoculated and now he had the pedal-steel blues. It was in part Dylan's influence that pedal steel became so popular in '70s rock. When he got back home up in Woodstock he'd be listening to Buffy Sainte-Marie or Bartók and suddenly that Nashville metronome would click through his brain. It was like he'd been bewitched. He found he couldn't write the wild stuff anymore.

In one sense, it was as if Dylan had come full circle. After all, they'd called Dylan a hillbilly when he first came to Greenwich Village, but what did they know of hillbillies? There weren't any Rimbaud-reading, foreign-flick-watching Jewish hillbillies, were there?

Clearly the fault line between North and South created by the Civil War a century earlier still rankled. Northerners treated country music with scorn. And while the folksingers in the Village had idolized Appalachian hollow dwellers, the contemporary urban progeny of these mule-skinners and moonshiners were a lot less appetizing. In turn, these descendants hated the pinkos, the homos, and the negro-loving, sandal-wearing residents of Greenwich Village with a distilled passion.

The hybridizing, mongrelizing, merging, rockifying Nashvillization of country music into rock was a recent phenomenon. While country was one of the natural-born daddies of rock 'n' roll, it had generally been held in contempt until Gram Parsons, the ambassador of rhinestone hipness, came along. And that in turn led to the Byrds doing their sweet harmony country covers of Dylan songs. During that time, country quickly caught on as a colorful, rural second home for rock—with a whole new wardrobe to go with it: boots, hats, capes, and Nudie cowboy glitter. All this would eventually lead to the Eagles and one of the best-selling albums of all time.

Dylan had been coming to Nashville for three years before he appeared on the stage of the Grand Ole Opry with Johnny Cash, but he had made the trip mainly under the cover of night and only to record. The first sessions for *Nashville Skyline* were in February 1969, but as smitten as he was with country music, he hadn't come to Nashville with a fully thought-out concept album in mind (not that forethought about cutting records has ever been a characteristic of his). He showed up with only four songs.

It was the beginning of Dylan's dry season. Even the fact that he'd bizarrely tacked two country songs on the end of his previous album,

John Wesley Harding, a record of biblical, doom-laden songs, might be seen as a sign that he was having a hard time coming up with new ideas. Clive Davis, head of Columbia Records, was at first hesitant about Dylan's move into the country field but must have felt that anything new might help because Bob just wasn't delivering. And the beast needs product. "I knew he'd been having some difficulty coming up with his own material . . . so I encouraged him." His producer, Bob Johnston, had also seen that Dylan was going through a hard spell, and country seemed the likely place to go hide out for a hermit crab in need of a new shell. Johnston hoped that the clash of the titans—some kind of collaboration between Dylan and Johnny Cash—would prod Dylan into action, but even this didn't provoke Dylan into a particularly fanciful new phase of creativity. *Nashville Skyline*, the album he recorded February 13–18, 1969, is barely twenty-eight minutes long (including an instrumental and a duet of an old song), half the length of *Bringing It All Back Home*.

Nashville Skyline was released in April 1969. The cover shows a beaming Dylan holding an acoustic guitar and tipping his hat in a howdy-neighbor gesture. He looks happy and friendly, but maybe this wasn't especially directed toward us. If he was trying to reach Middle America, which was one theory about Dylan's new musical direction, he wasn't going to get through to them with his characteristic scowling, sullen poses from the past.

"We didn't know what to do," says the photographer Elliott Landy who took the cover photo. "We had no concepts, we just winged it. It started out terribly painful and hard. We couldn't get anything good. He was uncomfortable being photographed, and I was uncomfortable. We just stayed with it and we got a moment that was very special."

The idea for this pose may have been pure happenstance, but it pretty much duplicates the cover of Eric Von Schmidt's *Folk Blues*, which you can see right behind Dylan on the cover of *Bringing It All Back Home*. It's unlikely given the inventiveness and coherence of Dylan's image bank that this was a coincidence.

For a songwriter as prolix and profound as Dylan, the simplicity and simplemindedness of *Nashville Skyline* were puzzling. It was as if he'd been dealt a limited vocabulary and banal sentiments and told, "Bob, let's see you try to make music out of this." Which was sort of the way we reacted to it at the time—as if Dylan were saying, "Okay, now watch me pull this out of my hat!" *Nashville Skyline* seemed to be Dylan doing a kind of country vaudeville: Here his claim that he was really just a "song and dance man" is no joke. It was light and entertaining, and it showed that he was allowed to produce a minor work, a divertissement, now and again, like, say, Mozart's *A Little Night Music*. But back then we didn't know what was coming next.

On *Nashville Skyline* Dylan was actually crooning—like Bing. Was he next going to tell us Bing was his real role model and he was only kidding about Woody 'cause it sounded so authentic? For a magpie collector like Dylan and someone who was an unabashed admirer of Tiny Tim and Liberace, anything was possible.

Not only was he doing a country album and not really saying anything cryptic, prophetic, biblical, or otherwise interesting at all, his snarly tone had also vanished. Even that he'd taken from us. His former girlfriend Bonnie Beecher said it was his sweet old voice back again. And that was true; it's a voice that can be heard on a tape he'd made in St. Paul before setting off for New York. But this new voice had the disconcerting quality of reinforcing the easy-listening country sound and the attitudes expressed in the songs—the same complacent middle-class values he'd taught us to suspect. Did he mean that there was nothing wrong with the world now, that it was all fine and we didn't need to worry about the My Lai massacre or Buddhist monks in flames?

Dylan had two explanations (modest by his standards) for his new voice: (a) he'd given up smoking or (b) he was no longer nervous in the recording studio and could therefore sing in his relaxed normal voice. But then with Bob, there's nothing more suspicious than a straight answer.

Nashville Skyline was filled with clichés like "Love is all there is." It well may be that clichés, as Freud said, are the profoundest form of communication—that's why they become clichés—but for Dylan to be retailing platitudes seemed almost spiteful.

"These are the type of songs that I always felt like writing when I've been alone to do so. The songs reflect more of the inner me than the songs of the past." So who was the guy in the shades and polka-dot shirts we'd gotten hooked on? And then he changed his story. In 1978 he told us there were hidden clues buried in the album: "On *Nashville Skyline* you had to read between the lines." This was plain perverse since the album— at least without a secret decoder ring—had an eerie and off-putting lack of depth. It was all surface and that surface was so glossy and reflective as to preclude other levels of interpretation. As Robert Christgau said of the lyrics, "They are so daringly one-dimensional they seem contrived."

Dylan apparently had a new method: "Now I can go from line to line, whereas yesterday it was from thought to thought." There's a sort of *Manchurian Candidate* quality to this explanation, which brings up the alien nature of the album. As Christgau went on to say in his review: "Dylan wasn't singing, it was somebody else, some cowboy tenor who sounded familiar." Exactly—that only confirms what we thought all along. This cowboy singer is a substitute for the real Dylan, held under observation somewhere.

Could Dylan, like Lonesome Rhodes in *A Face in the Crowd*, really be making a record for "rednecks, crackers, hillbillies, hausfraus, shut-ins, pea-pickers"? Whatever his motivation it was too sweet even for *Billboard*: "The satisfied man speaks in clichés," their reviewer said, "and blushes as if every day were Valentine's Day.... So goodbye, Bob Dylan, I'm glad you're happy though you meant more to me when you were ... confused like everybody else."

IN MAY 1969 JOHNNY CASH INVITES DYLAN DOWN TO NASHVILLE TO appear on his TV show. The next day he takes him out fishing on the lake to relax him, but it's going to take more than that to calm him down. Dylan's scared to death, giving off sparks, ready to bolt, a nervous wreck. "The string is taut" was one description of Dylan backstage at the Grand Ole Opry where Cash's special is being recorded. No cameras allowed. It is as if his barely materialized new persona is unstable, so fragile it might be demolished by a glance, a flashbulb, a question that might worm its way into the motherboard. Dylan is barricaded. He says he will answer questions only with written responses. Red O'Donnell, the reporter from the now-defunct *Nashville Banner*, is asked to slip them under Dylan's dressing room door. But how do you ask a question on paper along the lines of, "Why are you so weird?" which is basically what O'Donnell wants to know. Red's standing outside the door and the little freak won't even come out and talk to him. When O'Donnell finally does get to speak to him, he's so rattled he ends up almost insulting him. "Do you have any friends?" he asks.

The Opry audience would have been utterly dumbfounded by Dylan's problem—the conflict between being a star and wanting to be left alone. What in tarnation! This was when the Opry used to take place in the Ryman Auditorium in downtown Nashville, a rough old converted tabernacle with wooden seats. Filled with pure pandemonium and country bunkum raised to the level of great spectacle, nothing quite encapsulates the democratic folksiness of country music in the same way. In front of a huge Hot Rize Flour sign showing a country boy and his dog going fishing, there's Hank Snow and Pat Boone (the Opry is nothing if not all-inclusive) in the spotlight getting into a somber duet of that old Hank Williams airport-hallucination number, "I Saw the Light." Guests, friends, family, and fans would wander about backstage and visit, holding conversations, eating, drinking, selling used cars, and joking while a mother changed a diaper. Even the Avalon Ballroom in the high hippie days never approached the Opry for sheer looseness. Nobody was hassled, no star trips, no backstage passes even. It was a sort of Noah's Ark with music. All of creation seemed to be there, swirling about in mass confusion, with the whole event being broadcast live to five million listeners. And all this was happening right *onstage*.

Then, in the midst of this, was this weirdo telling the locals he's just folks like them, looking pale in a black jacket with an open collar, a week's growth of beard, resembling, as Peter Doggett put it in *Are You Ready for the Country*, "a defrocked priest or a salesman on the skids."

"That was the first live performance Dylan had done [since the Guthrie tribute]," said Kenny Buttrey. "He was more or less a recluse." And when the red recording light came on Dylan looked back at his backing band in helpless terror. "I've never seen anybody that scared. He was like a kid at a talent show who was so frightened he was getting ready to run off stage to mommy."

"How hard it was sometimes," Dylan told David Amram, "to be stared at or treated like some kind of person from outer space." But to the Grand Ole Opry crowd he *was* an alien. Just look at any photograph of Dylan circa 1965–66 (still the most widely reproduced image of him forty-five years on) and you can imagine what an average country music fan might have thought about that character.

The Opry audience was one generation away from outhouses, possum huntin', moonshinin', kin courtin'—and maybe not even that. These were the descendants of the very muleskinners and holler dwellers Dylan had idolized.

The emcee at the Opry has to explain to the perplexed audience the odd situation of his reluctant star. "Bob just doesn't really believe who he is," he tells them—an observation truer than he knew. The audience had come to see Johnny Reb along with this strange phenomenon, Bob Dylan.

On the set of the Grand Ole Opry they've rigged up an old shack suspended on wires—this was standard hokum for the Opry—but Dylan insists they take it down, that it's going to freak out his fans. This is not the country approach to life or entertainment. Country stars of this era are make-believe royalty whose very flamboyance and over-the-top gaudiness are a kind of acknowledgment that this is all just dressing up. Nobody would have thought it was demeaning to have an old shack as a prop at the Grand Ole Opry.

The audience files in, an unholy mix comprised of mainly Johnny Cash fans, men in polyester suits, blondes in beehive bouffants, and some long-haired, acid-eating hippies.

On Johnny Cash's TV show Dylan and Cash sing the haunting duet "Girl from the North Country" (it's the song that opens *Nashville Skyline*). Cash had one of those antediluvian voices that has been described as having "the booming resonance of an Old Testament prophet." Cash, the old country boy, dismissed this as just fancy talk: "We did ['Girl from the North Country'] at rehearsal. I knew my lines, he knew his. I didn't feel anything about it. But everybody said it was the most magnetic, powerful thing they ever heard in their life. They were just raving about electricity and magnetism. And all I did was just sit there hitting G chords."

The line between persona and personality that was long ago eroded in rock 'n' roll is still toyed with in country music. These people know the difference between fantasy and reality. Rather than self-delusion it's part of a hillbilly fairy tale in which a coal miner's daughter or a muffler-shop grease monkey triumphs over life's disappointments. They are carnival figures—the maligned ex, the honky-tonk angel.

Both Dylan and Cash were in states of transition. Cash was rehabilitating himself from his pill-popping hillbilly bad-boy self to Country Music Hall of Fame legend and was beginning to resemble a historical character depicted by the Franklin Mint, the sort of souvenir figure country folk would want to put on their mantelpieces. Ol' Johnny had always been able to do that with no trouble at all.

In country music this was possible because he was an adult, whereas rock stars are perpetual adolescents; you can't go from teenager to American icon overnight. Unlike Dylan, when Johnny Cash, Willie Nelson, and Waylon Jennings (along with Kris Kristofferson) went on tour as the Highwaymen they looked like a singing, traveling Mount Rushmore of country music.

Also interesting to note at the time, Dylan was busy becoming a hillbilly at the same time Cash was reviving his Beat poet muse. In the liner notes to *Nashville Skyline* Cash wrote:

> The man can rhyme the tick of time
> The edge of pain, the what of sane. . . .
> And the creep of blight at the speed of light
> The pain of dawn, the gone of gone.

Dylan and Cash had bonded years earlier, starting with the letter Cash had written to Columbia Records when they were thinking of dropping Dylan. Then there they were, jumping up and down on a bed together at the Newport Folk Festival—out of just sheer joy of finding each other and having like minds and such, despite the obvious gulf between them socially and politically (Cash was a big Nixon supporter). On the other hand they had been taking the same medications to jump-start their celestial machinery for their entire careers. You can see them high as kites singing a haunting version of "I Miss Someone" backstage at Leeds in 1966, a scene recorded in *Eat the Document* and *Something's Happening*.

The *Nashville Skyline* Bob wasn't the first of Dylan's baffling moves, which after all were part of his appeal. Was it a put-on? Was it just a pose? How could this be the same Bob Dylan who sang "Subterranean Homesick Blues"? A scarier thought was that it might *not* be a put-on, that he might be serious. There seemed to be no trace of irony. The eerie sense of an artificial paradise and a *Truman Show* approach to his idyllic family life.

In the mid-'60s, Dylan had reached a kind of perfection of sound and lyrics, and the persona that went along with it was such a spectacular creature, it would mock all his future incarnations and make them seem stagey and counterfeit.

Harder to accept than the parabolic sage of *John Wesley Harding* was Dylan's new persona of Cheerful Rural Gent and Howdy, Neighbor. The new Dylan presented on Johnny Cash's TV show and on the cover of *Nashville Skyline* was problematic on a number of levels: the sunny beamish cover boy—although meant to look reassuringly normal and cheerful—was, in the case of a raving eccentric such as Dylan, disturbing in its just folksiness. This was as close as he was ever going to get to looking country. The good-old-boy pose (the standard country music stance of Cash, Waylon Jennings, Merle Haggard, et al.) was way beyond Dylan's range.

If one were to put into words what was truly disconcerting about *Nashville Skyline*, you might say, "It was the tone, man, the tone!" as a

Rudyard Kipling character said. The idea of Dylan as a lounge lizard at the Nashville Hilton was just a little too jarring an image for most of us. But *Nashville Skyline* turned out to be one of Dylan's best-selling albums, as well as the best-selling country-rock album yet, giving rise to an entire decade of drugstore-cowboy country-rock progeny. Up until *Nashville Skyline*, country music had been viewed by the counterculture as hick stuff, and Dylan's embracing of it might have turned off his fans. But such was Dylan's gravitational pull that *Nashville Skyline* would lead straight to the country-rock fever of the 1970s.

Still, I think I'm just going to put on *Highway 61* if only to remind myself why I bought *Nashville Skyline* in the first place.

It's always a little weird when you see
musicians in a recording studio. Could it
be in this strange industrial space that they
implant those subliminal vocals, those
synaptic whispers? With Charlie Daniels
(right) at Columbia studios, Nashville, May
1969, during the *Self Portrait* sessions.

20   The Amnesia

HAMLET: Why, look you now, how unworthy a thing you make of me! You would play upon me; you would seem to know my stops; you would pluck out the heart of my mystery; you would sound me from my lowest note to the top of my compass; and there is much music, excellent voice in this little organ, yet cannot you make it speak. 'Sblood, do you think I am easier to be played on than a pipe? Call me what instrument you will, though you can fret me, you cannot play upon me.

THE PERIOD FROM *NASHVILLE SKYLINE* THROUGH *NEW MORNing* is the most bizarre and disturbing in Dylan's quixotic career. Bob was in bad shape, the Castalian Spring of inspiration dried up, and his muse ran off with one of those upstart "New Dylans." Words that once zinged through his brain like haywire pinballs had deserted him. "Until the accident," he wistfully told his biographer Robert Shelton, "I was living music twenty-four hours a day... if I wrote a song, it would take me two hours, or two days, maybe even two weeks. Now, two lines..."

During Dylan's free fall—what he calls the Amnesia—his desperation took the form of an eerie cheerfulness. The way he chose to dispel his gloominess was to deliberately infect himself with anodyne forms of pop music: Broadway show-tune sentiments, campfire folk songs, syrupy country standards. Country music, with its odes to down-home rural simplicity, was a sure cure for an overheated brain. Nashville was where the Everly Brothers had come to marry rock and country in an auspicious wedding that begat the Beatles—a source of energy and joy. Nashville—just the sort of place you'd want to go if you were in a funk.

At the heart of darkness during Dylan's Amnesia era lies *Self Portrait*, an album consisting mainly of standards, cloying country songs, and traditional ballads. A Sargasso Sea of undigested, misshapen fragments, it is released in June 1970 and greeted almost universally with incomprehension and hostility. Elaborate explanations are put forward for this baffling album, but the main problem for most people is that there is not enough Dylan in it. Fans soon begin to fall away in droves.

With the release of this double album, Dylan's reputation becomes even more wobbly. Of the twenty-four tracks, only eight of them are by Dylan (and three of these are instrumentals). With its big-production pop songs, sentimental standards, and Bing Crosby–like rendition of "Blue Moon," it seems the antithesis of the fiery disturber of the peace he'd once been. In the past he'd claimed, "Tin Pan Alley is dead. I killed it." Now he seems to be doing it deadpan.

It was the first Dylan album to truly alienate his fans. It was so indigestible that some thought it might be a put-on; the cover shows an art brut painting of a clown by Dylan, perhaps *of* Dylan. A cynical faction felt this might be Dylan's first major miscalculation.

The songs are indifferently performed, badly produced, and often sung in a weary, apathetic voice. It's a collection of sketches, an unformed and shapeless outline. But don't we like to see this kind of thing— dashed off, scribbled, smudged—from the master's hand even when faltering, unsure, beset by doubts? Isn't that why people buy bootlegs, to hear the master in an off moment, a second thought, an aberration that tells you more about the process involved in a great song than the finished product? One of the more appealing theories about *Self Portrait* is that Dylan was trying to reproduce in the studio the magic of *The Basement Tapes*. There is an aborted concept album there—but of what?

Cue *Self Portrait*. All right, track one, side one: What's wrong with "All the Tired Horses"? No Dylan, but, otherwise.... Or "Alberta #1" or "I Forgot More Than You'll Ever Know"—this is so great. Bob *crooning*! And that great old yarn, "Days of 49" (and the allusion to the days of old when he dug up the gold that he now repines). And "Early Morning Rain," the Gordon Lightfoot song he clearly loves and sings with poignant lyricism (see the scene in *Eat the Document* where he plays it in his hotel room), "In Search of Little Sadie"—great rowdy stuff. And "Let It Be Me." Jesus, Dylan doing Elvis, what more could you want? It's all great in a desultory way, not just the obvious plums that wriggling apologists pick out— "Cooper Kettle" and "Belle Isle"—like finding jewels in a Dumpster.

Whatever Dylan's intentions, they were not realized, and on *Self Portrait's* release, reviewers were frothing at the mouth. They ranted, they raved, and in a gruesome feeding frenzy they cursed their onetime messiah without restraint. The man is clearly in bad shape and what do they do? Attack him mercilessly. In the typically self-serving way of critics, they butchered and essentially eclipsed the album. The chief vampire among them was Greil Marcus and his put-down in *Rolling Stone*. The first line— "What is this shit?"—became more famous than the album itself.

Critics took the album very personally. This was the guy who in 1965 had, in Clinton Heylin's words, divided the world into the hip and the unhip. As Greil Marcus's book *Like a Rolling Stone* explores, its namesake had been a conversion experience for many people, among them Marcus himself and Jann Wenner. Now the quintessential hipster was serving up this tripe. *Self Portrait* was an insult. Dylan had betrayed them. He was finished. He was done.

"Unless [Dylan] returns to the marketplace with a sense of vocation and the ambition to keep up with his own gifts," Marcus admonished him with schoolmarmish tut-tuttery, "the music of [the mid-'6os] will continue to dominate his records, whether he releases them or not."

The mob in its fury sealed the hideous thing up in a crate and threw it in the Gowanus Canal—and that's where *Self Portrait* lay, forgotten for four decades. But for all the seething resentment it provoked, *Self Portrait* got to #4 in the United States and #1 in the UK.

The perplexing theories about this album reflect the confusion Dylan was going through as well as the aggravation he put us through. These all amount to explanations of what the unfathomable Bob intended. In other words, since there are no lyrics to decipher, why the hell did he make the record?

REASON #1: Well, the most prevalent theory to this day is that he wanted to undo his own mythology. Even Dylan—especially Dylan— would eventually disown his deformed child through many slippery explanations:

And I said, "Well, fuck it. I wish these people would just forget about me. I wanna do something they can't possibly like, they can't relate to. They'll see it, and they'll listen, and they'll say, "Well, let's get on to the next person. He ain't sayin' it no more. He ain't given' us what we want," you know? They'll go on to somebody else. But the whole idea backfired. Because the album went out there, and the people said, "This ain't what we want," and they got more resentful. And then I did this portrait for the cover. I mean, there was no title for that album. I knew somebody who had some paints and a square canvas, and I did the cover up in about five minutes. And I said, "Well, I'm gonna call this album Self Portrait."

Dylan had first claimed that the album was "to make people go away and follow someone else" in a *TV Guide* interview in 1976. He also repeated the idea while talking to Kurt Loder in the 1980s. However, it's unlikely that he actually meant it.

After all, he had spent three years thinking about it and eleven months on and off working on it, at one point ordering a pile of songbooks brought to the studio so he could study them. If he'd really wanted to annoy us he wouldn't have recorded songs he cared that much about. He'd have cut songs like "Yummy, Yummy, Yummy (I Got Love in My Tummy)" and "The Ballad of the Green Berets."

Additionally, he'd already attempted a similar project, the aborted duets album with Johnny Cash, prior to the *Self Portrait* sessions and made yet another album of covers in pretty much the same vein, doing Joni Mitchell's "Big Yellow Taxi," Elvis's "A Fool Such As I," and "Spanish Is the Loving Tongue." These "outtakes" from *Self Portrait* were released by Columbia as *Dylan*—the so-called revenge album—after Dylan defected to David Geffen's Asylum label. These are considered absolute untouchables in the Dylan canon, but they're not that bad either.

Most important, when *Self Portrait* first came out Dylan told *Rolling Stone*, "It's a great album." Then he added, "There's a lot of damn good music there. People just didn't listen at first." He was right about that.

REASON #2: Maybe he was trying to embrace *all* American music and achieve something even more inclusive than just folk, rock, or country. Dylan is often thought of as a purist, but he's actually madly promiscuous. Just listen to his radio show, *Theme Time Radio Hour*. This music had fed into his life, and it all came from the crazy American song stash. It was noise gushing out of Uncle Sam, Johnny Reb, Yankee Doodle, and Appalachia Americana—another genre he's credited with creating.

In some ways, perhaps Dylan was attempting to become an American HCE (Here Comes Everybody), the protagonist of *Finnegans Wake*. You go out on a Saturday night with him and he drags you through juke joints, folk grottoes, Tin Pan Alley, rock concerts, and Broadway shows, and you end up at a piano-bar sing-along.

REASON #3: Perhaps in his hour of need he was regressing, channeling his young self, traveling back to his teenage years in Hibbing and the traditional folk and country stuff he used to play there. His list of favorite singers, after all, included Al Jolson and Judy Garland. He'd always seen himself as a repository of regional songs, and, having revived so many types of American music, including country, there's no reason why he shouldn't have thought he could send his electric jolt through these standards too. In an interview with *Time* magazine around the time *Biograph* was released he claimed, "My favorite songs of all time aren't anything I've written. I like stuff like 'Pastures of Plenty' and 'That's All' and 'I Get a Kick Out of You.'" The kinds of songs he would have heard growing up in Hibbing on WMFG.

It's said that although Dylan called it *Self Portrait*, he intended nothing of the kind. It reveals nothing about Dylan, unless, as Robert Christgau, a lone voice purring in the wilderness, wrote in the *Village Voice*, it's a sonic picture of Dylan's early history:

> Conceptually, this is a brilliant album, which is organized, I think, by two central ideas. First, that "self" is most accurately defined (and depicted) in terms of the artifacts—in this case, pop tunes and folk songs claimed as personal property and semispontaneous renderings of past creations frozen for posterity on a piece of tape and (perhaps) even a couple of songs one has written oneself—to which one responds. Second, that the people's music is the music people like, Mantovani strings and all.
>
> In other words, you construct your identity through the music you've been exposed to.

But perhaps for Dylan the old radio stations were fading; it was getting hard to tune them in. And the signals were getting muffled by subsequent Dylans. "(How Much Is That) Doggie in the Window?" was starting to mash with Hank Thompson's "The Wild Side of Life."

REASON #4: When I asked Robbie Robertson in the summer of 1970 what he thought Dylan's intention was in making *Self Portrait*, he said he thought Dylan was "appealing to the beer-drinking crowd." But you'd have to have gone more than six rounds with Jose Cuervo to mistake anything on *Self Portrait* for a pop song on the jukebox—although "Wigwam" almost made it into the Top 40 on the charts. When the guy at the end of the bar got to the Isle of Wight version of

"Like a Rolling Stone," where Dylan forgets the words to his own song, he'd probably think he'd wandered into a karaoke bar.

REASON #5: At one point the Byrds were poised to add their liquid hydrogen whine to the album, but there was a mix-up. Somebody didn't tell somebody and the Byrds flew home.

REASON #6: Eric Andersen thinks it was political too—contract obligations—the scaly stuff rock critics don't think about. Another theory is that by making an album of standards Dylan wouldn't have to share publishing with Albert Grossman, with whom he was feuding. This doesn't exactly work either, since Dylan shockingly took credit for rearranging a number of traditional and blues songs on the album.

REASON #7: It was all Bob Johnston's fault. Dylan gave his producer the rough tracks and told him to do something with them. Bob Johnston is fond of saying, "I don't do nothin', I just let the tapes roll." But he's also something of a maniac. In the middle of telling you how he got the studio sound for *Blonde on Blonde* he'll tell you he can get rid of mosquitoes using thirty-seven tones on a CD. It's funny that someone as eccentric as Bob Johnston takes exception to people calling him a maverick. Unfortunately for Dylan (and the apoplectic Byrds—whom he also produced in a bizarre manner) this wasn' true; he was quite capable of diabolical meddling.

REASON #8: It was a response to 1969's *The Great White Wonder*. "I was being bootlegged at the time," Dylan said, "and a lot of stuff that was worse was appearing on bootleg records. So I just figured I'd put all this stuff together and put it out, my own bootleg record, so to speak. You know, if it actually had been a bootleg record, people probably would have sneaked around to buy it and played it for each other secretly. Also, I wasn't going to be anybody's puppet and I figured this record would put an end to that." It's a funny idea with a typical Dylan twist, but unfortunately many of the songs on *Self Portrait* aren't even as good as on that bootleg, *The Great White Wonder*, and artists even as ornery as Dylan don't generally set out to make bootlegs from scratch.

Self Portrait is going to remain a perpetual puzzle, and that's part of its continuing fascination. There is never going to be one answer to this conundrum, especially since we're dealing with someone as complicated as Dylan.

In 2004, prolific alt-country rocker Ryan Adams was asked if he was concerned about burning out and in his darkest hour ending up with the same fate as Bob Dylan, reduced to cutting an album like *Self Portrait*. He said, "I fucking hope so, because it's a great album." Are Ryan Adams and Terri Gross—who frequently uses "Wigwam" as a musical spacer on *Fresh Air*—the only people to have listened to it in the last forty years? Obviously not. There's actually a sizable pack of *Self Portrait* cultists out there.

In an Internet video, a filmmaker asks a number of people their opinion of *Self Portrait* with hilarious results. One of the interviewees says, "Great artists making iffy music (or perceived to be iffy music) is always more interesting than great artists making great music. A twenty-four-minute video on *Highway 61* is not interesting."

In that sense, *Self Portrait*—as an aggravating enigma (as opposed to the Dylan enigmas we like)—is both a joke and an unintentional self-portrait.

FOUR MONTHS AFTER THE RELEASE OF *SELF PORTRAIT* IN OCTOBER 1970, Dylan releases *New Morning*, his most disturbing record yet. Although *Self Portrait* and *New Morning* were recorded around the same time, it was assumed that he had brought out the new album to overcome *Self Portrait*'s bad reception. However, Dylan claims, "I didn't say, 'Oh my God, they don't like this, let me do another one.' It wasn't like that. It just happened coincidentally." Perhaps.

But since Dylan has always needed to create not only the songs but also the characters who sing them, he needed a new Dylan. The doppelgänger he came up with for *New Morning* was that of the Happy Family Man—the scariest form of himself so far—and a nightmare conception for his fans. Like the might-have-been scenes in *It's a Wonderful Life*, it's as though we're seeing a form of what he might have become had he stayed in Hibbing, taken over his dad's appliance store, married early girlfriend Bonnie Beecher or Echo Helstrom, and settled down with a bunch of kids. On "One More Weekend," it's almost as if he woke up one morning and found he'd married Doris Day.

> *We'll go someplace unknown*
> *Leave all the children home*

Dylan's lurch into rural pastoral simplicity, domestic bliss, happily ever afterness, was so extreme you couldn't help wondering (yet again), "Is he putting us on?"

It was as if he'd let Mr. Normal, this new replica of himself, loose and the guy had gotten out of control, liquored up on platitudes, and moved to Montana "where there's fountains in the mountains" or Utah where he was going to build a log cabin. We don't buy these bromides (especially from Bob).

His personal life had become problematic, but, by using his bland New Dylan baritone voice, he distorts the picture. The just-folks character of "Sign on the Window" is pushed almost into caricature:

> *Marry me a wife, catch rainbow trout*
> *Have a bunch of kids who call me "Pa"*

"That must be what it's all about," he says. Keep telling yourself that, Bob.

Dylan had somehow taken whatever was happening in his personal life and created confectionary tales out of it. Of these false positives, the most chilling is "If Not for You" on *New Morning* with its cloud-cuckoo images of romantic devotion. Without you:

> *Winter would have no spring*
> *Couldn't hear the robin sing*

It's so over the top—even for a pop love song—that you wonder if it isn't meant ironically. But read as pure venomous sarcasm it's a devastating taunt. Given Dylan's teetering equilibrium and potent self-contradictory nature, it could well be both sincere and sneering at the same time. Ambivalence runs through the early '70s albums like quicksilver.

Like the scene with the artificial robin at the end of David Lynch's *Blue Velvet*, where the sky is blue, the grass is green, and everything seems right in the world—just before the mechanical bird crunches a bug (and we know where that came from)—there's an ominous overtone to the idyllic scenes he portrays. There's a weariness to the album, especially to "New Morning," a song he sings with leaden enthusiasm. Dylan seems almost remote on this album whereas on, say, *Blonde on Blonde* he seemed preternaturally present, almost inside your head.

New Morning has no connecting theme, and with Dylan we'd come to expect some thread that links all the tracks. It switches abruptly from one scene to another. You're on the podium at Princeton communing with alien insects ("Day of the Locusts"), suddenly you're at a skating rink

("Winterlude," or "Dylan on Ice," as Michael Gray called it), and next you're in a piano jazz bar ("Dogs Run Free"), at the *Highway 61* sessions in 1966 ("One More Weekend"), walking by a Christmas crèche ("Three Angels"), in the third row of an avant-garde play ("Father of Night").

Whether it's getting his honorary doctorate from Princeton or going to see Elvis ("Went to See the Gypsy"), these stories are conversions of incidents into Dylan mythology. Whenever or wherever the meeting with Elvis occurred, they never met again, though Elvis sang "Tomorrow Is a Long Time" and "Don't Think Twice." During his most heavily medicated Las Vegas period, Elvis even used Dylan to explain problems with his vocal cords: "You know what happens to ya when you breathe this [recirculated] oxygen? It dries your mouth out. It feels like Bob Dylan slept in my mouth."

Some of the tracks, especially "One More Weekend" and "Three Angels," seemed to be trying too hard to fulfill the demands of his fans for the old Dylan by reviving the surreal style of his mid-'60s albums— something he'd never deigned to do before.

Musically *New Morning* is inventive, though—the use of jazz on "Dogs Run Free," the Hank Williams-ish "Three Angels," the waltz on "Winterlude," etc. There was a flashback, "Went to See the Gypsy," about Dylan in his youth visiting Elvis in his hotel back in Minneapolis—converted, as with most of his songs, into Dylan mythology. There were the three songs written (though never used) for Archibald MacLeish's play *The Devil and Daniel Webster*, which Dylan in *Chronicles* refers to as *Scratch* ("Time Passes Slowly," "New Morning," and "Father of Night"). The album is fragmented, shifting between country picking, rural-gent songs, and the old flashing images.

But for many reviewers when *New Morning* was released, there was a palpable relief that Dylan had not completely lost his grip on reality after *Self Portrait*. The album was at first embraced as the return of the "real" Dylan. The title itself suggested he was starting over, and the photo of Dylan with Victoria Spivey in 1961 on the back cover suggested he had gone back to his first year in New York. *Rolling Stone* crowed, WE'VE GOT DYLAN BACK AGAIN! The enthusiasm wouldn't last.

We told ourselves we'd gotten Bob back—at least it wasn't Nashville platitudes and the scrappy, halfhearted covers on *Self Portrait*—but as time went on the less convinced we became. Had we just talked ourselves into it? Was the turgid optimism of *New Morning* really what we wanted from Bob?

But even in this grim period, which brought us *Nashville Skyline*, *Self Portrait*, and *New Morning*, Dylan managed several breakthroughs: He had the first rock/country crossover hit with "Lay, Lady, Lay" and virtually invented the covers album. Everyone's done one since: John Lennon, Patti Smith, Brian Wilson, David Bowie, Paul Anka, Rod Stewart.

His other contribution is as the granddaddy of Americana and alt-country music with roots in folk, country, and blues. If the concept of Americana brings distressing images to mind of misplaced nostalgia with a whiff of right-wing patriotism—a garage sale of American junk, including retrieved historical artifacts, rare license plates, antique waffle irons, Franklin Mint plates, and a middle-aged, overweight used-car salesman from Atlanta dressed up as Robert E. Lee—the sound that he unearthed was truly American roots music.

HE LOOKED DIFFERENT. HE WAS A RECLUSE. EXCEPT FOR A FEW LPS, A bootleg, and a handful of appearances, we didn't know what he was up to. But we didn't really notice something had happened to him until *Self Portrait*. It seemed the problems with the albums were related to problems in his life—the Amnesia, his songwriting drought. He was hobbled in some way. Even he thought something strange was going on, and he made that clear in "Nobody 'Cept You":

I know something has changed
I'm a stranger here and no one sees me

He was never going to make albums like *Bringing It All Back Home* again. You couldn't really sing songs like "Highway 61 Revisited" or "Desolation Row" in the chill of the early '70s anyway—not that it stopped people from trying. All this music had been sucked back into the ether and "Bob Dylan" along with it.

Dylan thought he'd killed off Dylan with the motorcycle accident, but then when that didn't work he tried to kill himself off again with *Self Portrait*.

In doing so, "the risk is that Dylan would destroy his myth, which is exactly what he intended to do," Ellen Willis wrote in *Cheetah* in 1974, "but that in the process he would lose his old audience without gaining a new one."

He'd forgotten (and wanted to forget). "It's like I had amnesia all of a sudden.... I couldn't learn what I had been able to do naturally—like *Highway 61 Revisited*. I mean, you can't sit down and write that consciously because it has to do with the break-up of time."

He'd mislaid himself, an incredible lapse of attention. To misplace that precious indelible icon of the '60s—Bob Dylan. If *he's* lost, then we're sunk. He was our Moses, supposed to lead us out of Sinai, out of the Valley of Death and the military-industrial complex of the sinister Amerikan reich. He was the one we expected to carry the ark of the 1960s into the new dispensation. And when he wouldn't or couldn't be our savior we would become resentful of him. That would take a while, but by 1970 the unraveling had begun.

Dave Van Ronk had said that naturally "people stuck in the last period would feel betrayed" when Dylan moved on from agitprop ranter to symbolist poet. He meant *those people*, the folkies and peaceniks who just didn't get the new neon Stratocaster Bob whom we had embraced with stereophonic ecstasy. We didn't realize that one day he would turn on us too.

He had escaped the maelstrom. We didn't begrudge him that, but what happened next was unforgiveable. Bob took an entire imaginary world down with him. He was abandoning us, giving up *everything*—the polka-dot shirts, the shades.... He had been our pied piper, and now he's telling us he's just a guy who writes songs?

Your head is spinning. What just happened? We all knew he was one of the great escape artists—but this! We'll never entirely forgive him. No one's saying he didn't produce some great records, write amazing songs after *Blonde on Blonde*. That's beside the point. We're not denying that; we're not denying anything. We're just saying....

The hipsters from "Visions of Johanna" were all melting into thin air, along with the night watchman and his flashlight, the girls out on the D train. Dylan's gorgeous hallucinatory kingdom was dissolving. An entire universe—ours!—was being demolished with Dylan's withdrawal. The sets had been struck, the dioramas crumbling! The entire population of Desolation Row—gone! Its fantastic collection of freaks evacuated. What would become of Desolation Row now that he had abandoned it? Would it become a tourist destination? Experience the frenzy of the jealous monk! Hear Einstein play his electric violin! Interact with animatronic re-creations of the characters—Casanova, Cinderella, Romeo, Ophelia on her twenty-second birthday, Doctor Filth, and the Phantom of the Opera.... The haunted localities, gone! An entire world of oddness and menace, vanished.

We'd held up his album covers like Russian icons. Behind those images we believed he was still out there somewhere doing fantastic things. He was in the Kettle of Fish with Peter Stampfel discussing whether a diminished seventh could summon up the ghost of Memphis Minnie, or in a garret somewhere compiling a chromatic alphabet with Allen Ginsberg.

The change in Dylan was so extreme that it encouraged bizarre theories, including one that suspected that the CIA, the FBI, or some other acronym had kidnapped him and was siphoning off his thoughts. Or he'd been abducted by aliens—or assassinated by the mob. They pointed out that this is what happened to Jimi Hendrix. There are books, full-length documentaries about it. Crackpot theories. What if someone had come along and taken his place? Think about it—an imposter. That's it! The only possible explanation. Every year there are these look-alike competitions where 137 Dylan imitators show up. And at least half of them look and sound exactly like Bob circa 1966.

We have our own crackpot theories. Had we become victims of the deadly Capgras syndrome, a delusional disorder brought on when a patient believes that a friend or relative has been replaced by an imposter? This mental aberration is generally provoked by witnessing aspects of the person that you don't like, so you imagine someone else has taken his place. You get case histories like, WHEN YOUR BROTHER BECOMES A "STRANGER," or MS. X CLAIMS "IMPOSTORS" POSING AS FAMILY MEMBERS HAVE INVADED HER HOUSE.

Those under this misapprehension may even view themselves as a double, believing they are more than one person—a state of mind that would, of course, fit Bob's own theory of the multiple Dylans. Bob Dylan has been replaced! No one has generated more conspiracy theories than Bob—confirming that the infamous garbologist A. J. Weberman—whether as Dylan adversary, subsequent contrite idolater, or more recently perpetrator of right-wing-Bob rumors—is a true believer. When Weberman claimed at the screening of *Eat the Document* in 1971 that the current Dylan was a fraud who had replaced the noble Dylan in the film we were about to see, we knew what he meant.

The bearer of the vibe had just vanished, gone into red shift. We wanted him back. Dylan's reluctance to be Dylan began to madden a section of his more rabid fans. As much as they'd idolized him when he was on the beam, they now poured all their energy into their rage. In 1971, Country Joe McDonald ranted in *Rolling Stone*:

I heard *New Morning*, and I just couldn't take the fact that he still hadn't learned how to play the harmonica or how to sing. His mark of distinction was his intensity and funkiness. And when he was really on, it didn't matter that he couldn't sing or play—he was so present. Now he's like a ghost of his former self, and it drives me up the wall. I don't know where the real Bob Dylan went, but I don't believe this one, I haven't since *Nashville Skyline*. I don't know what happened to him, but something did—and he disappeared. He stopped being a rebel and started being a nice guy, a family man. He don't fool me, man.

Richard Meltzer just wrote an obituary:

Then there's the unreported deaths of Dylan and Lou Reed, both of them dead TO THIS WORLD but for very different reasons. Bob is just a stiff, pure and simple, he's been that way since the mishap with the bike.

This dismal period has been compared to Rimbaud's self-imposed exile in Abyssinia, but unlike Rimbaud, who was virtually unknown during his lifetime, Dylan had a generation to contend with, a generation who obsessively confused the messenger with his message, and waited patiently at the foot of the mountain for his next commandment. Unlike the anonymous hero/victim of "Like a Rolling Stone," Dylan was no longer invisible. A million eyes watched him even in retreat and waited for the secrets they felt he was hoarding.

By the 1970s there was a major shift in the culture, and with it, attitudes toward Dylan changed too. In some ways his psychic revolution had been too successful. As Dylan noted himself in 1985, "If you want to defeat your enemy, sing his song."

He'd begun as an agitprop activist in the folk movement, and then, as a ranter against corruption and phoniness, he'd become the guiding spirit of the underground. But by the early '70s his integrity was being called into question. When he released "George Jackson," his first political song in years, skeptics called it opportunistic.

Doubt crept into the Dylan flock. He'd been a rock star for almost a decade but, unlike the Beatles, he had not etherealized himself into some untouchable dimension. And when he began building his mansion in Malibu with its giant copper onion dome, he seemed more like Kubla Khan than one of us.

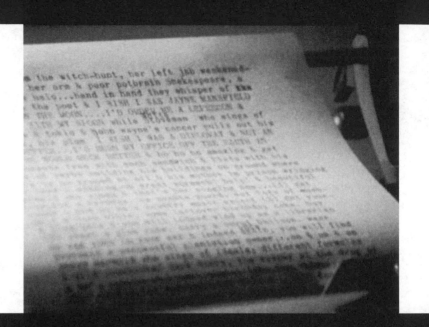

Perhaps, as William Burroughs claimed,
language is a virus and Dylan's typewriter,
like a mutant other, was proliferating,
breeding, metastasizing words like crazy.
Not just any words, these are freaked
ideas—witches, Jayne Mansfield (he wants
to be her), lexical leprechauns, and
Shakespeare as a verb—jammed up
against each other, throwing off little
mental sparks.

21 How Dylan Became Dylan, Sort Of...

A S FAR BACK AS 1969, PIRATED COPIES OF DYLAN'S NOVEL
Tarantula had been floating around for a while. Rabid fans
would do anything to get their hands on it. A Dylan novel—
what fantastic thing might that be? The mind reeled. Then in
May 1971 *Tarantula* was published by Macmillan. There it was, a relic of
the old Dylan in full flashing-chains-of-images mode.

Questions about the viability of *Tarantula* had long preceded its publication. The *New Musical Express*, one of the two leading English music
newspapers, reviewing a bootleg copy, stated that it was the first crack in
Dylan's facade. The unthinkable had happened: He was capable of a
foolish move. Once in the hands of the Dylanoscenti, reactions to this
fabled work ranged from disappointing to dismal to outright rage.

Bob Markel, Dylan's editor at Macmillan, wasn't crazy about the
book. His (unsigned) introduction to *Tarantula* is defensive, even outright
dismissive: The editors, he says, "weren't quite sure what to make of the
book—except money." Ouch! His introduction comes with a disclaimer:
"This is Bob Dylan's first book ... the way he wrote it." In other words,
"We didn't touch a thing, so don't blame us." Markel nevertheless says he
found Dylan's symbolism "earthy, filled with obscure but marvelous imagery." Even Macmillan's poetry editor found it "inaccessible"—no kidding! But wait, isn't that what we expect of modern poetry?

Then came Robert Christgau's brutal review of *Tarantula* in the *New
York Times*. *Tarantula*, he said, "is not a literary event because Dylan is not
a literary figure." He concluded by saying, "It is a throwback. Buy his
records." But as wrongheaded as this was (Robert, I give you a C, and I'm
being generous), there was, as we shall see, some truth to it.

Dylan's hibernation up in Woodstock, or whatever you want to call it,
may have radically changed him, but his output over the next few years
was phenomenal: the 107 songs of *The Basement Tapes, John Wesley Harding,
Nashville Skyline, Self Portrait, New Morning*. Two of the projects he worked

on during this time—*Eat the Document* and *Tarantula*—*are* experimental in the extreme, using nonlinear methods of composition, and are clearly works by the high-sulfate hipster Bob. They were just the sort of thing we'd expect from him, given that mild doses of inscrutability were catnip to his disciples.

There was a belief in the '60s that anything was possible, that like America itself we could reinvent everything. We could even remake the Amerikan reich into *The Peaceable Kingdom.* Bob opted out of this generational delusion by mid-1966, anticipating that as the establishment's most articulate tormentor, he might become a potential scapegoat. Instead he figured he'd try to revolutionize film and the novel in his spare time.

Tarantula, written between 1964 and 1966, is a stuttering liner-note novel interspersed with apocryphal letters. With no music, nothing to anchor them, words appear on the page like restless revenants then drift away, and a new set of apparitions arises. Its plot is missing, lost, forgotten, or probably never existed.

Tarantula—even when you know it's an antic, whimsical work by Dylan—doesn't work in quite the way we would have wanted it to because, like Alice, he had forgotten an essential ingredient: He'd neglected to reinvent the form, something Dylan had been ingenious at accomplishing in a variety of genres. The fact that it didn't make sense was the least of its problems. Actually, we *wanted* Dylan to be indecipherable; we counted on it. We wanted to experience his half-formed spontaneous inventions as they emerged from his seething brain.

His original intention had been to re-create a classic Beat novel—skimming through *Tarantula* by strobe light you might tell yourself that Bob was a budding James Joyce—but *Tarantula,* alas, never quite woke up.

By 1969 even Bob was disowning it, claiming he was told to write it by his imperious manager, Albert Grossman. This was a typically disingenuous Dylan ploy—but who are we talking about it? It's true that Grossman had finagled a deal with Macmillan and gotten Dylan to fulfill that contract, but in fact there were two different books involved and the idea of writing an avant-garde novel had originally come entirely from Dylan. Early in 1964 he began corresponding with Beat poet and publisher Lawrence Ferlinghetti, of City Lights Books in San Francisco, about writing a novel in the high Beat exploding-like-spiders-across-the-stars vein.

On the liner notes to *Freewheelin'* Dylan told Nat Hentoff he was writing three novels:

"Anything I can sing," he observes, "I call a song. Anything I can't sing, I call a poem. Anything I can't sing or anything that's too long to be a poem, I call a novel. But my novels don't have the usual story lines. They're about my feelings at a certain place at a certain time." In addition to his singing and song writing, Dylan is working on three "novels." One is about the week before he came to New York and his initial week in that city. Another is about South Dakota people he knew. And the third is about New York and a trip from New York to New Orleans.

Although *Tarantula* is a tongue-in-cheek version of a Beat epic, Dylan himself knew better than anyone that it was seriously flawed. In 1969 he said:

> *I was doing interviews before and after concerts, and reporters would say things like "What else do you write?" And I would say, "Well, I don't write much of anything else." And they would say, "Oh, come on. You must write other things. Tell us something else. Do you write books?" And I'd say, "Sure, I write books." After the publishers saw that I wrote books, they began to send me contracts. . . . We took the biggest one, and then owed them a book.*

But what he doesn't tell you is that *Tarantula* was the transitive verb in his meteoric career. At first, songs like "Chimes of Freedom" and "Mr. Tambourine Man" seemed to have emerged full-blown out of his head but it's clear that these brain-scan lyrics came out of his experimental fiction. Reading *Tarantula* you can hear embryonic songs starting to materialize, often literally. Since it's assumed that much of *Tarantula* was written in 1964, when you come across phrases like "cowboy angel blues," "subterranean homesick blues," "the vandals took the handles," and "jingle jangle morning" you have to ask which comes first: the chicken, the egg? But, as Clinton Heylin points out, lines from ur-versions of *Tarantula* find themselves decanted virtually unchanged into "Chimes of Freedom":

> *as cathedral bells were gently burnin*
> *strikin for the gentle*
> *strikin for the kind*
> *strikin for the crippled ones*
> *an strikin for the blind*

Tarantula is an archaeological site, but the point isn't the literal transfer of lines from *Tarantula* to the songs. It's the kind of writing that Dylan would use as a template for his new sound and fury. So it was while trying to write the great Beat novel that Dylan first hit on his great chain of flashing images. In other words, how Dylan became Dylan.

This also explains the oddly abandoned state of *Tarantula*. Without the propulsive force of the music, it lacks the traction to pull its freight train of freaked metaphors into the station. But once Dylan had morphed the book into a new sonic language, *Tarantula* had served its purpose. It remains an embryonic work, a kind of midden heap of proto-Dylanisms—one that deserves to be read for a variety of reasons:

13½ REASONS TO READ *TARANTULA*

1. Forget about modernist screeds by Rimbaud, Lautréamont, James Joyce, Ezra Pound, William Burroughs, Ginsberg and Co. You can experience it all just by reading *Tarantula*. This is what Dylan tells you right off the bat:

To my students:
I take it for granted that you've all read
& understand freud—dostoevsky—st.
michael—confucius—coco joe—einstein—
melville—porgy snaker—john zulu—kafka—
sartre—smallfry—& tolstoy—all right then—
what my work is—is merely picking up where
they left off—nothing more—there you have
it in a nutshell—now i'm giving you my
book—I expect you all to jump right in—
the exam will be in two weeks—everybody
has to bring their own eraser
      your professor
      herold the professor

Bob's epitaph is in there too:

here lies bob dylan
demolished by Vienna politeness—
which will now claim to have invented him the cool people can
now write Fugues about him
& Cupid can now kick over his kerosene lampboy dylan—killed by a
discarded Oedipus
who turned
around
to investigate a ghost & discovered that the ghost too
was more than one person

And the letters are all written from Desolation Row.

2. Considering that we live in a fragmented, recombinant Hellenistic culture, and given postmodernism's predilection for sampling, sound bites, cut-ups, pastiche, and put-ons (including personality), isn't it time to reconsider *Tarantula* as ahead of its time? Reissue it on Twitter. What if you got a tweet on your iPhone that would wake you up better than a double latte? Say, something like: "to dream of dancing pill head virgins & wandering apollo at the pipe organ."

3. Since 1964 Dylan has spoken to us in riddles and now you want him to write like John Updike? Objections to the obscurity and impenetrability of *Tarantula* are ridiculous and beside the point. That would be like using *Ulysses* as a guidebook to Dublin. What is this mania for tidiness, anyway, the federal need for narrative structure, the procrustean demand for plots? These you can get anywhere. There's altogether too much of this stuff around. That's why we had such high hopes for Dylan. Any airport or bus station teems with racks of books with plots, nothing but plots— ciphers moving through Sid Fieldsish plot points, writing school graduates with their characters in the round, their observations of daily life, the whole well-behaved Jonathan Franzenian fictional appliance. But what if instead of narrative pabulum you wanted something else? Just sayin'. . . .

4. Compared to Warhol's "novel," *a, Tarantula* is a work of astounding clarity and coherence. But does anyone complain about the (frequently) gibberish speedfreak rants in *a*, taped by a mechanically challenged ninny and transcribed by monkeys? No, it's treated as a treasured artifact. You're at tea in Chiswick and your host reverently brings out the foxed and brittle paperback of *a*; it shows his good breeding and painfully acquired hipness. You bring up *Tarantula* and it's just, "Well, now, that's just silly wordplay, innit?"

5. Set it to music (if Terry Reid and Philip Glass haven't already done so). It's poetry ripe for scoring. The fallacy of rock poetry books, even when quoting Dylan's most sublime lyrics, is that without the music—and without *that voice*—the words are only half dressed. You read a Dylan songbook, same words on the page, but it's as if some demon has siphoned off the mojo. *Tarantula*'s a singing book; it just needs someone to sing it. Click on your Film Score app and orchestrate it. And don't people in India and Yugoslavia still sing books aloud?

6. Think of it as the English-as-a-foreign-language otherwise known as poetry. Rampant loquacity, unstaunchable logorrhea, endemic glossolalia occasionally leading to literary lockjaw. When you read a book stoned the words pull apart from their moorings. Some words will loom and some roll sideways the way they do when you sing them. They change shape. *Tarantula* is essentially a Dylan kit. The reader has to supply his own narrative, and from the Japanese assembly instructions, it's not clear that all the parts are there.

7. You say it doesn't make sense, but how hard could it be to follow? You *listen* to nonsense every day. A pop song—even at six minutes—is a perfect capsule of surrealism. You can't get away from the stuff. Properly ingested while driving, having sex, getting high, drinking, or wandering through the canned food aisle, a pop song puts the listener in a swoon state. The words wash over you, and you don't know what the singer is saying exactly. But you don't need to know. The heart has its own reasons and, giddy in its mood-inducing trance state, wants nothing more than momentary lust-lite frisson (and heavy rotation).

8. If any random set of paragraphs from *Tarantula* had been parceled out as liner notes on the back of an album, we'd have treated it as hip little asides—especially during the lean years. Liner notes were a new literary form brought to a high insolent shine by Dylan. An inspired reanimator, he made disparate fragments come to life: "heterogeneous ideas . . . yoked by a violence together," as Dr. Johnson put it.

9. Consider *Tarantula* as a flawed example of Dylan's use of William Burroughs's cut-up method, which Burroughs described as: "I think of words as being alive like animals. They don't like to be kept in pages. Cut the pages and let the words out." In *Renaldo and Clara* one of the (many) unfilmed scenes proposed was a collaboration between Dylan and Burroughs (as a reincarnated Edgar Allan Poe) doing cut-ups (where words and phrases from newspapers are randomly juxtaposed). It would have been an interesting encounter if only to see Dylan reproducing his alchemical method of songwriting. Did Dylan use cut-ups? Or was it more jump cuts, stop frames, and paranoid montages, as in *Eat the Document*? According to Marianne Faithfull, Dylan, still much in the thrall of Beatitude on his 1965 tour of England, began describing to a journalist how he used Burroughs's cut-up method to write his songs. When the journalist asked him to show her how it was done, he started madly cutting up newspapers, folding them, waving the pieces around—without a clue as to what he was doing—and then in classic Bob fashion, said, "Do you get it? Can you dig it?"

10. The professors all like his book. And here I'm talking hip academics, like Professor Mark Spitzer. Now Dave Itzkoff et al. may have selected this sentence from *Tarantula*—"Now's not the time to get silly, so wear your big boots and jump on the garbage clowns"—as one of the "Top Five Unintelligible Sentences From Books Written by Rock Stars" in *Spin*, but, as Professor Spitzer points out, Itzkoff failed to notice that he was one of the "garbage clowns" himself. "If such bumbling media-mongers juggling rubbish took a moment to consider that the poet might actually be a poet," Spitzer continues, "and have some insight into human nature, they might decode the metaphor." Well, all *right!*

11. Maybe some extraterrestrial entity is trying to get an urgent message through to us—I mean, where else would this mad stream of words come from? And they hit upon this fiendishly clever plan of using Bob to transmit it, implanting alien spore-words in his brain. But we, like foolish earthlings, have willfully ignored it, and so we're all doomed. Unless . . . . Wait! I can make out some words!

12. It's art historical, almost mystical, a little like the automatic writing that mediums and surrealists used to practice—and they weren't even as good at it as Dylan most of the time. But they did it mostly in French—*Les Champs Magnétiques* and so on—and therefore these dudes were *insolite* (they had a word for it, even).

13. And the penultimate reason for the Advancement & Study of *Tarantula* is that it provides food for Dylanologists. Robin Witting has written a sweetly mad pocket guide to *Tarantula, The Meaning of an Orange* (I couldn't bring myself to read his original study, *Tarantula: The Falcon's Mouthbook*). After I finished the *Orange* book I felt I needed a spot of brain detergent. And I say that as a compliment.

13½. Finally, folks, here you are inside Bob's brain! The hum of hypnotic, self-indulgent murmurings—as if some synaptic door has been left open and we can see what is going on inside. Who wouldn't want a peek into that fitful head?

When we first saw Dylan's paintings—on the cover of the Band's first album, *Music from Big Pink*, or the cover of *Self Portrait*—we loved them for their quirky, irrepressible energy. Later on, though, when he got proficient, and did those tourist resort paintings—and then more recently, with the purloined "Asia Series" (what was he thinking?)—we really missed those early brutalist paintings.

22 Under the Rings of Saturn

S INCE DYLAN'S "RETIREMENT" IN WOODSTOCK FOLLOWING THE crash he'd lived happily ever after until the middle of 1973, when it all began to fall apart. He became restless in paradise. The conjurer wished to wander out into the big bad world and reclaim his magic.

By 1973, Dylan was drifting out of focus, and the two Dylan albums released that year didn't help matters: the elegiac soundtrack to *Pat Garrett and Billy the Kid* (consisting mostly of instrumentals) and *Dylan*, an album of reject tracks maliciously put out by CBS Records after Dylan defected to a new label.

When his muse was with him from 1961 through 1969 he could do no wrong; every move was an advance—for him, for us, for salvation. But after 1969 he'd fallen into a slough of despond, unable to function, under some leaden cloud. At the point when we needed him most, our patron saint was off somewhere fighting with a ghost.

But just when people were ready to count Dylan out, he rose again, magnificently. He awoke from his four-year amnesia, and in that instant he seems to have gotten his mojo back. The new songs came from an entirely different source, a direct current flowed through them we hadn't seen since *John Wesley Harding* and *The Basement Tapes*.

But it had taken a terrible turn of events to rouse him. He was a desperate man, and he'd gotten to "the top of the end," he told us. He was "livin' on the edge," and he had to go before he got to the ledge, which all sounded pretty hair-raising. The songs he was beginning to write for his upcoming album, ultimately titled *Planet Waves*, were a seismic register of Dylan's shifting state of mind—hesitant, vacillating, retreating, swearing his devotion, but consumed with rage.

Not only was he having problems at home, but after almost eight years of hibernation he was getting restless and thinking again about touring, something Sara dreaded as she knew this would bring that period of their life—and probably their marriage—to an end. The road is sex and drugs and the disorienting frenzy of renown that will fatally dislocate the peaceable kingdom he's inhabited for the past eight years.

Touring is a guaranteed home wrecker, but even before plans were laid for going on the road, hairy medicated musicians began showing up at the house. Most rock wives assume boys will be boys out on the highway, but now Bob's starting to bring them home—and all the boring muso riffing and diminished-B-flat-minor talk begins, which drives Sara up the wall. In Woodstock the musicians who worked with Dylan had been either neighbors (the Band) or lived in a distant land (the Nashville cats).

Two other unlikely factors also led to the dissolution of their marriage: remodeling and painting classes.

In 1973 Bob and Sara sell their second house in Woodstock and buy a house and twelve acres in Point Dume near Zuma Beach. They want an extra bedroom built. The next day they show up and the architect has torn down the entire house except for one wall (to stay within the remodeling codes). "I want my own fantasy," Bob says, which would include a room he could ride a horse through (or hang the first car he ever owned from the ceiling). The reason for the dome, he said, was so he could recognize his own house when he was driving home. Sara becomes obsessed with redecorating. The costs soon escalate into the millions. The dream house becomes a source of constant aggravation and tension. For the first time the two of them get into violent arguments— over bathroom fixtures, wallpaper, window treatments.

Dylan first caught the art bug up in Woodstock from his neighbor, the painter Bruce Dorfman. This led to his artwork for the Band's *Music from Big Pink* and his own album cover for *Self Portrait*. Then, in the spring of 1974, Dylan takes art classes with a crusty old painter named Norman Raeben. He's a never-heard-of-Dylan kind of guy who appeals to Bob right away. The irascible, cigar-smoking Raeben talks in that gruff old way you'd imagine Rembrandt or Gulley Jimson from *The Horse's Mouth* would talk. He's wild, woolly, a possessed maniac, and he comes with a bag full of all those drawing-from-the-right-side-of-the-brain tricks. He places a vase of flowers in front of Bob and says, "Paint that, kid!" Then, as soon as Bob picks up a brush, Raeben grabs the damn thing and whisks it away. "What're ya waitin' for, lad? *Now* paint the vase!" Aha! The vase is in the mind.

After a few months at the upside-down-Stravinsky school of painting, Bob's point of view changes radically. He begins to see things differently, his perspective on his marriage, for one. Try going home to your wife who's clutching a fan of paint samples and telling her it's all in her mind.

Bob keeps going to his art classes, and Raeben continues readjusting his mental pictures. "I went home after that," said Dylan, "and my wife never did understand me since that day.... That's when our marriage started breaking up. She never knew what I was talking about. And I couldn't possibly explain it."

It's not easy to follow, especially that Raeben thing about putting the past, present, and future together in the same frame and how that helped Dylan write songs *consciously*. All those tenses in one painting, like in T. S. Eliot where he's standing at the end of the street: "And if the street were time, and he at the end of it." What Raeben contributed to Dylan is hard to say, but whatever it was it provoked a radical new direction.

Sara didn't get it and so it became: "My wife doesn't understand me. I think I'll go and have a few affairs." And Bob did just that, sleeping with Columbia executive Ellen Bernstein, actress Ruth Tyrangiel (who later sued him for palimony), and who knows how many others.

Bob and Sara separate, and Dylan spends the summer of '74 on the farm he'd bought in Laredo, Minnesota, on the Crow River north of Minneapolis, just playing with his kid Jakob and enjoying the occasional visit from Ellen Bernstein.

For the time being everything is in suspension. The road would soon change all that.

PLANET WAVES, THE ALBUM THAT CAME OUT OF HIS TURMOIL, WAS done almost as an afterthought, amid preparations for the upcoming tour with the Band. You need to have something to sell out on the trail. While the album wasn't completely realized— "rangy, stray cat music," Robert Christgau called it—Dylan had reemerged fully formed out of his head once again.

In January 1974, Dylan released the album, his first coherent one in three and a half years (since *New Morning*). Recorded the previous November with the Band, the album had been laid down in haphazard, hasty sessions reminiscent of those that yielded *The Basement Tapes*. The atmosphere was so casual that Dylan left the sound of his buttons scraping on his guitar on "Wedding Song."

Here on the original album liner notes was the old Dylan at full poetic power again:

J lit out for parts unknown, found Jacob's ladder up against an adobe wall & bought a serpent from a passing angel. . . . The wretched of the Earth, my brothers of the flood, cities of the flesh—Milwaukee, Ann Arbor, Chicago, Bismarck, South Dakota, Duluth! Duluth—where Baudelaire lived & Goya cashed in his chips, where Joshua brought the house down! From there it was straight up—a little jolt of Mexico and some good luck, a little power over the Grave, some more brandy & the teeth of a lion & a compass.

Bob's past streams through the album's liner notes, a condensed history of the 1950s that includes the "furious gals with garters and smeared lips on bar stools... space guys off duty... all wired up and voting for Eisenhower." In some ways it makes sense that he would go back in his memory because his current turmoil seems to plunge him back into his adolescence. Loss, distance, and memory are equated and used as a form of exorcism. However, the chaos he had perversely summoned up in the past just for kicks now seems to overwhelm him. Where once we followed his progress intimately, here he seems more remote, as if we are hearing some lost soul wailing on the other side of a motel room wall.

Turning to his past, he searches for the flash point where the connections were broken off and for the first time he begins to get nostalgic. In "Something There Is About You," he reminisces about "Rainy days on the Great Lakes, walkin' the hills of old Duluth." In "Never Say Goodbye," he remembers:

Twilight on the frozen lake
North wind about to break
Our footprints in the snow
Silence down below

Generally, the album has an ominous feel. The original title, *Ceremonies of the Horsemen*, has slightly apocalyptic connotations to it, just as the phrase "even the pawn must hold a grudge" from "Love Minus Zero/No Limit" is similarly dark. Ambivalence seeps through the album and bursts into flame. The anthem "Forever Young," written for his son Jakob, and "Wedding Song," his pledge of undying devotion to Sara, are in violent contrast to "Dirge." Whether it's also about Sara, a doomed love affair, or us, his audience, it's chilling:

I hate myself for lovin' you and the weakness that it showed
You were just a painted face on a trip down Suicide Road

The edginess is back. Even on "Wedding Song" there's the foreboding line "What's lost is lost, we can't regain what went down in the flood."

On his hobo-art cover painting, Dylan scrawls: "Cast iron songs and torch ballads." Actually, tormented ballads might be a better description. Eerie, confused, and autobiographical, "Wedding Song" and "Dirge," as different as they are, are two of the most beautiful and terrifying love ballads he has ever written. Both convey his anguish about his marriage to Sara breaking up.

HE'D CALLED IT *PLANET WAVES* BECAUSE SATURN, BRINGER OF MELAN-choly, was no longer obstructing his path. According to the stars, it was time to move, time to reunite with the Band and head back to 1966. But even if you're Bob Dylan, you can't mess with time like that—or turn back the clock. Mick Jagger understood that "time stops for no man," but almost immediately he, too, forgot—then paused and rationalized: "It's a bloody line in a song, innit?"

You can't repeat a scandal either, but that's pretty much what Dylan's 1974 tour with the Band—the so-called Tour '74—set out to do: restage their notorious 1966 world tour, which had provoked violent reactions from Dylan's folk fans from Forest Hills to Perth, Australia.

It was eight years later. Doesn't that mean anything? Almost a decade. Everything is different. Dylan is sanctified, even if that had the unfortunate overtone of making him into a historical figure, a golden oldie of the mythic folk tribe. And no more terrible fate could be imagined for Promethean Bob.

Dylan was still Dylan, the magus of rock, but he no longer had the zeitgeist of the '60s behind him, and the Band, his once-notorious electric backing group, could now hardly be seen as the sinister posse they once were. They were now famous in their own right. Not only was this once-ferocious combination no longer outrageous, but it was also a piece of nostalgia. Besides, no one is booing, so how could it possibly be the same?

The idea for this historical reenactment had hatched in the scaly mind of Dylan's de facto manager of the moment, Bill Graham, and David Geffen, head of Asylum Records, who had briefly lured him away from Columbia. Geffen started out suggesting a few tour dates, but the more he added, the more Dylan said yes to them. Eventually, eighteen million people bought tickets to his concerts, an astounding 2 percent of the American population. This amounted to $95 million in advance sales—a fair price to pay if you could actually bring back the '60s. And if you missed the '60s Dylan was as close as you were going to get to them. The twenty-five-city tour began at the Chicago Stadium on January 3 and ended on February 14 at the Inglewood Forum in Los Angeles.

Onstage the set was a funky living room, designed to make a very nervous Dylan more comfortable. It had the look of an off-Broadway play with a couch, a bed, candles, a washing line, and a Tiffany lamp.

Dylan was anxious about the tour, about performing again after eight years, and he was wary of the press. He deliberately started out in the middle of the country, trying, unsuccessfully, to draw as little attention to himself as possible.

At the first gig, the third of January, Dylan opens defensively with "Hero Blues," a song from 1963, almost as though he hoped to defy the audience's anticipated reaction to him. It's an early version of "It Ain't Me, Babe," one of many Dylan songs that's as ferociously addressed to his audience as it is to the lover in question.

You need a different kinda man, babe
One that can grab and hold your heart

Maybe it was to ward off the criticism that this tour was really about looking back. Either way, Dylan was deliberately playing songs from 1966 and precious few from his current album, *Planet Waves*.

The arenas Dylan and the Band played required more and bigger amps to push the sound, with the intention of underlining the momentousness of the occasion: the Second Coming of Bob. It was sonic hyperbole—the sound trying to live up to the image, to the legend of 1966.

But, because the sound had to be pumped up, the intimacy of the 1966 tour, with its tiny and tinny sound system, was gone. Instead, thunderous sonic ordnance was lobbed at concertgoers with such velocity that the nuances got lost and the songs tended to blend together into a Dylan medley. But big arenas didn't just require a massive sound system; they also needed a bigger persona, readable from the back of the stadium—and that went for the singing too. Dylan needed a new form of semaphore.

In '74 the fans wanted to see the legendary traitor of the folk cult, whatever that was. Back then his attackers had been loud and rowdy, his fans wildly enthusiastic or disgruntled. Now everybody was retroactively cool, flicking their Bic lighters and lighting matches, as if at a memorial service (you can see this on the cover of *Before the Flood*, the double-live album of the tour).

But it was obvious this bunch of nouveau freaks hadn't been given their lines. In 1966 fans knew their roles. This crowd was at a rock concert, and they may have cheered when Dylan sang "sometimes even the president of the United States must have to stand naked," as if it were still mildly inflammatory (this was the Watergate era, after all), but the times had changed. No one believed anymore that songs and protest marches could change the world. That era was over and with it the bite that had made Dylan's songs a stinging indictment of their time.

When he had the lights turned up on the audience, Dylan peered out with alarm. Jeez, who *were* these people? Where was the ragged tatterdemalion crowd he'd played to eight years earlier, folkies, beatniks, college students? These were affluent young hedonists at a rock concert, following the current rituals of hip. "They lit up $40-an-ounce grass, snorted $75-a-gram coke," wrote Lucian K. Truscott IV in the *Village Voice*, "... and shelled out upwards of $100 to scalpers for tickets." Hip lite was to be Dylan's new curse. Anybody with the right gear could be hipper than Bob.

Dylan and the Band in 1974 were essentially for the next generation, the too-late born. You want to see history, children? As if you can recreate this kind of thing! The set consisted of many of the songs they'd done on the 1966 world tour, and no one noticed the irony—of course not—that in '74 audiences were raving over the same songs they had booed eight years earlier.

That these concerts were retro events was confirmed by the fact that people wanted to see the sacred monster, but not necessarily take his music home with them. Despite the huge demand for concert tickets, sales of *Before the Flood* were disappointing.

DYLAN'S BACKUP BAND WAS NO LONGER THE HAWKS. THEY WERE *THE Band*. When the Band's first album, *Music from Big Pink*, came out in

1968 with a Dylan painting of musicians and an elephant on the cover, the reaction was immediate and enthusiastic. An astonishing new voice was heard in the land. With their largo rhythms the Band was like a freight train pulling something weighty out of the past—maybe the past itself.

Despite the fact that only two of their four subsequent albums—*The Band* (1969) and *Stage Fright* (1970)—lived up to the Confederate glory of *Big Pink*, they were virtually a national institution. According to their biographer Barney Hoskyns (*Across the Great Divide*), the core music of the Band and the mystique that emanated from it came from Levon Helm—the ol' Arkansas dirt farmer who seemed to embody the ruminant rural South ("Once you get below Memphis," he says, "the air gets thicker and more resinous")—and Robbie Robertson, a Jewish Indian from Canada who fantasized about that mythical South.

Of course none of this would have had the mythic weight they brought with them without their long apprenticeship with Dylan, the master maker of re-created legends. The members of the Band were essentially anonymous. That was the point. In the Band, each was a character in his own right—somewhat like the Beatles—but the problem was that their characters weren't nearly as defined as those of the Beatles. With their uniformity of black jackets, beards, and studied gravitas, you often have to scan the captions under photographs to tell who's who, with the exception of the elfish Garth Hudson.

They didn't have a figurehead and didn't want one, which was a good thing because none of them really fit the bill. Robbie Robertson would seem to be the obvious choice, and you can see him studying hard for his degree in Dylan iconography in *Eat the Document* (the shades, the clothes, the attitude), but he didn't have the natural-born flash, the minimum requirement for a rock star. Garth Hudson was like a Tolkien wizard. Levon Helm was the only genuinely legendary character in the bunch, but he was the drummer. Richard Manuel was nuts, tied up in knots, and soon developed bad drug habits. Rick Danko, too, was out of control.

The Dylan phenomenon helped launch the Band, but the fame and money that went along with it also helped capsize them. Rock stardom was a lifestyle they couldn't handle. Unlike, say, David Lee Roth or Steven Tyler, they hadn't been rehearsing for wretched excess since adolescence. The Band traveled like rock stars in a Boeing 720, but they weren't rock stars; they were a band of veterans from Appomattox. They were Robert E. Lee's house band.

Libby Titus, Levon Helm's girlfriend at the time, told Barney Hoskyns about the tour: "It was lots of dope and lots of girls. Occasionally the wives and kids were brought in for shows, but it was all so sad and pathetic.... The wives who'd been cheated on, the kids who were destined to be scarred."

As with many other bands, roadies took Polaroid shots of groupies so the members of the Band could choose their favorites before the girls were allowed backstage. It wasn't that Confederate soldiers never visited a whorehouse or got liquored up, but the image the Band projected on their albums and in their photos of traditional values grated uncomfortably against these scenes of hedonism and debauchery.

While Tour '74 put the Band on a crash course with destruction, they (along with Dylan) made a huge amount of money from the tour—"made out like bandits," as Rick Danko said. They were "like Frank and Jesse James getting back together again and hitting a few banks." But Dylan wasn't so happy about it. After the tour he said the songs had been played with "nothing but force." It was "a big circus," he said, "except there weren't any elephants."

As prominent as the '74 tour made Dylan, he remained a figure from the past, a fact that even he understood, playing mostly songs from the mid-1960s. In the '60s, Dylan had been embedded in his persona, but his creature had gotten away from him. That's the trickiest predicament a human can be faced with: to catch up with your own ghost.

Things get serious when you forget who you are. Once a multitude of Dylans buzzed through that fitful head, but it has gotten too crowded in there; time to make a break for it. Time to move back to the Village.

23   The Second Coming of Bob

AFTER THE SECOND FOLK REVIVAL, ROUGHLY 1957–64, THE Village fell into disrepair and squalor. But then it had a second wind in the '70s when people started coming to Bleecker Street to find what was no longer there. All were intent on making it look like the place it was meant to be, but nobody knew quite what that was, even in the '60s. It was somewhat hokey, like Beale Street, Montmartre, or a Renaissance Fair. Reenactments were all the rage. You could relive any period in history: the Civil War, ancient Rome, or the Dark Ages. German businessmen and their wives daubed in woad were spending weekends in thatched huts.

The Village was Folktown, where legions of legendary Frye boots had trodden. Bob Dylan had assassinated Tin Pan Alley right there. You stepped onto hallowed ground, entered into enchanted spaces with candles in Chianti bottles and hot spiced apple cider. It was almost like going to Europe or, at least, somewhere pretty different from Omaha, Ronkonkoma, or the outer boroughs mocked by Pete Seeger in "Little Boxes." Even if it was fake, who cared? The Village was sui generis.

Dylan, during his diaspora, had claimed he had amnesia—an affliction far more common in fiction than in life. He'd forgotten how to be Dylan. The way to find yourself is to retrace your steps, look for the door in the alley where it all began. For Dylan that place was Greenwich Village, the ersatz hamlet in lower Manhattan where "Bob Dylan" was born, sired out of Robert Zimmerman after an out-of-town tryout in Dinkytown.

In the summer of 1975 Dylan was lent a loft in the Village and began hanging out with his old friends. The very day *The Basement Tapes* was released, there was Bob retracing his steps. Had it been ten years since he'd participated in the life of the folk faithful? By God, it had!

The specific gravity of Bleecker and MacDougal Streets pulled him back into its dense orbit. It was folk gravity—heavier than the gravity on Pluto. Incredibly it was all still there, preserved like a fly in amber. Dave Van Ronk was still doing, "You've been a good old wagon, but you done broke down." Ramblin' Jack Elliott still wailed that "the south coast is a wild coast and lonely." It was too good to be true. If Bob had thought twice about it, it might've seemed a little creepy, like an episode of *The Twilight Zone*, but he didn't. When you *want* it all to be just the same as when you left it ten years earlier, none of this bothers you. It's all still there: the Other End, the Kettle of Fish, the Gaslight, Gerde's Folk City.

Bob is back! Quinn the Eskimo's here! Everybody's gonna jump and shout. Bob the reanimator, he's going to bring all the flora and fauna of the Village to life. His presence alone will energize the Village folk scene. But if it had lost its relevance, the folk music field was by now doing a bustling business. What had once been a sacred calling now was a career move for many folksingers. They all had booking agents and managers, lawyers, accountants, and record contracts—even publicists.

Dylan's natural habitat is the world of folk theater. The coffeehouses and bars were like stage sets on the back lot of the Village. The Village itself was a kind of theater and Dylan had earned the right to play any part he wanted.

In Pirandello's play *Henry IV*, an actor falls off a horse and when he comes to, believes he's Henry IV, King of Germany, and out of concern for his sanity his friends and relatives help him maintain the illusion. A somewhat similar thing happened when Dylan returned to the Village.

You fell asleep under a tree in Byrdcliffe, dreamed strange dreams, and when you awoke it was still 1963 in the Village. It was a miracle, like Scrooge in *A Christmas Carol* throwing open his window and discovering he hadn't missed Christmas after all.

However much Dylan wanted the Village to be the same as he remembered it, things outside the gates of the Village *had* changed. For one thing Dylan was now defined by his fame. He was huge—a phenomenon. Dylan had become massively more famous than when he'd left. He'd turned into a legendary character almost like the ones in the old ballads. John Henry or Stackolee. People were now writing ballads about *him*. Tom Pacheco wrote "The Ballad of Bob Dylan" and sang it to him:

> He blew into New York City on a bitter freezing day
> And he drifted to the Village and sang in the cafes
> Hanging out till sunrise sleep till the afternoon
> The Kettle and the Gaslight and the Woody Guthrie tunes

The old folkies said they weren't resentful of Dylan, but come on. You can even hear it in between the wheezy comments of that genial old bear of Bleecker Street, Dave Van Ronk:

> Dylan was one of ours and he had struck gold, and everybody thought that they could get rich, too. There were essentially two reactions. The first was jealousy, variations on "Why him?" and "He copped this from me; he stole that from so-and-so." Of course, we had all been stealing from each other all along, but it had never mattered, because we were all in the same situation. We had been playing for tips and sleeping on floors, and when one of us suddenly could get a suite at the top of the Plaza, naturally that hurt.

The folk revival had started out from its bright morning of discovery and slowly turned into a terrible folk mill. Even if you loved those songs more than your life when you were young, singing them night after night must have become something of a curse. It's nine years later, and Ramblin' Jack Elliott is still out there doing it. *Forty* years later he's *still* doing it.

On other occasions, Bob would have been scornful of consorting with such blatant nostalgia retailers. But now in his moment of confusion and despair he's thrilled they're all there just as they were.

Bob had arrived as a hobo, a loner, an outsider, and the Village had accepted him. It had been the instrument of his fantastic transformation. He'd become part of a community of like minds, the Village folk scene. He'd written songs that had become anthems and made him part of a movement, the spokesman for a generation (his most hated role). He'd escaped from the Isle of Howling Dogs into his own black-lit cave—and then, when even that had not distanced him far enough away from the mob of LP-waving peasants, he faked his own death.

Dylan craved fame, but the fame he desired had taken on a diabolical form. Fame, when it came, involved crowds following him, hounding him, like the goddess Fama in the *Aeneid*—a grotesque monstrosity who never sleeps, and employs her hundreds of eyes, ears, and mouths to see, hear, and spread rumors, slander, and outright lies. Dylan was reclusive and fearful, someone who was afraid to appear on the street in daylight. Like the innocent man who is chased by a homicidal lynch mob in *The Ox-Bow Incident*—one of Dylan's favorite movies—Bob now wished to get as far away from the mob as possible. And he had, for almost eight years. If you're fragile and paranoid and not quite the same invincible character you were when you still had your mojo, the safest place to be is in the past among a group of old mates.

The sense of authenticity, the purity of ancient ballads, hung in the air, and Dylan had been part of that elitist band. The folk revival had come out of clubs, bars, and coffeehouses—places where diverse types of people mingled: musicians, tourists, drug dealers, actors, cops on the take. The irony was that folk music, the province of the serious cognoscenti of the Ye Olde Child Balladry, had bizarrely turned into a scene by the mid-'60s. When it started out it had been tiny, but that original core had been inflated to epic grandeur almost single-handedly by the legend of Bob Dylan.

A new crop of folksingers with clever twists on the old formulas had appeared in the early '70s, satirists like Loudon Wainwright III, George Gerdes, Mark Johnson, and the Roches. And then there was a waiflike, Edith Piaf match girl crossed with Keith Richards: Patti Smith, an edgy, angsty refugee from a girl group.

And most of them are there for Mike Porco's birthday party, October 23, 1975. All those people—including Bette Midler, Ahmet Ertegun, and Tom Waits—squeezed into Gerde's Folk City, the Italian restaurant he'd turned into a club where folk musicians could play and get paid. It was like a fishing boat filled to the gunwales with gawking day-trippers and card-carrying folkniks.

OUR RELATIONSHIP TO BOB BECAME VOYEURISTIC VERY EARLY ON. Many thought the confusion between his personal life and his songs was deliberate. But Dylan consistently claimed that his songs had nothing to do with him, and this confusion of life and art became more problematic with the release of *Blood on the Tracks* in January 1975. Although the album, which included his early autobiography on "Tangled Up in Blue," seemed clearly confessional, Dylan claimed the songs had nothing to do with his marital problems with Sara; instead, he had based them on Chekhov short stories. Which ones would those be? "The Lady with the Dog"? In any case, why put out an album that touches so personally on fresh wounds and dismiss it as an aesthetic pose?

Dylan has always been able to have it both ways—it's his nature—so while denying that *Blood on the Tracks* had anything to do with his personal life he complained, in a radio interview with Mary Travers, that "a lot of people tell me they enjoy that album. It's hard for me to relate to that. I mean, it, you know, people enjoying that type of pain, you know?" This is a bit disingenuous. And anyway we're not enjoying his pain; we're identifying with it. Mostly, we're thinking about our own lives. We could care less about his pain.

Blood on the Tracks is the self-revealing, autobiographical album he seemed to promise us in 1970 on *Self Portrait*. There's a strange, post-humous mood to the songs. He floats over his past like a living ghost, mythologizing his history, dwelling on loss and old memories. As with *Planet Waves* everything is in the past tense, unlike the ferociously present tense songs of the '60s, "Like a Rolling Stone," "Subterranean Home-sick Blues," and "Ballad of a Thin Man."

Perhaps at this stage in his career Dylan began to wonder—having gone through so many different genres—what kind of approach should I take next? What have I overlooked? I've done blues, folk, protests, phantasmagoria, New England transcendentalism, country.... What's left? Reality!

Of course, Dylan's reality isn't going to be the unvarnished truth. It's going to be a simplification, sure, but who would tell such a tale without a little revision? Not Dylan. However minimally recorded—and rerecorded—it isn't going to be anything like reality. While the songs on *Blood on the Tracks* are presented as realistic, if not actually autobiographical, accounts of his life story, the reality they evoke is an even more elusive kind than the surrealistic scenes on *Blonde on Blonde*.

We can't compare *Blood on the Tracks* with the actual events in his life—and who would want to? But clearly the documents in his divorce case present a very different Dylan from the wistful, betrayed character he presents on the album. But then, with any great artist, autobiography is only a half-realized act. It's what happened combined with what should have happened, a dream you had, a story you heard, or something that rhymes.

His approach on *Blood on the Tracks* is the storytelling folksinger, speaking to you directly, telling his tale without guile or artifice. "Tangled Up in Blue" is an autobiographical version of the ramblin' man song beloved by male folksingers. "But me, I'm still on the road/Headin' for another joint" now appended to a why-I-had-to-leave-her divorce song. In performance, Dylan sometimes introduced it as a song that "took me ten years to live and two years to write," even though some of the adventures seem to be updated versions of the shaggy-dog stories he told about his travels when he first came to New York. "I had a job in the great north woods/Working as a cook for a spell" has such a smoky, Jack London–ish ring to it; who cares if he flipped flapjacks in Oregon or not. In any case our voyeurism is aroused by these autobiographical allusions. Is the girl he meets "workin' in a topless place" meant to be Sara when she was a Playboy Bunny?

Either way, Dylan performs a cunning sleight of hand by appearing to reveal the intimate details of his personal life, there being no more convincing way to fabricate your past than by claiming to depict it as the truth. As Rousseau said of another writer of true confessions, "I place Montaigne foremost among the dissemblers who mean to deceive by telling the truth."

Whether truth or Dylan, with the release of *Blood on the Tracks*, the loner intensity missing from his albums since *Blonde on Blonde* has returned. As Dylan exposed the pain of his private life, the separation from his wife, Sara ("Shelter from the Storm," "You're a Big Girl Now"), and the tortured confusion of his early days on the road ("Tangled Up in Blue"), the imagery is no longer all that surreal. He's come up with a simple lyrical style that resembles the storytelling manner of the old ballads, and he employs their figurative language to give an allegorical edge to the songs. But these apparently simple narratives have a hallucinatory quality to them as on "Idiot Wind," where his old fury awakens as he converts his raging anger at Sara into an epic image of national futility.

Crafting the intensely personal feel of the album began as early as the fall of 1974 when he went to check out A&R Studios (the legendary Columbia Studio A, where he'd made "Like a Rolling Stone" and all his LPs up to *Blonde on Blonde*), looking not just for his old recording sound but maybe his old magic too. That was a little harder to locate and he didn't find it there. In September, Dylan tried to record the first versions of songs from *Blood on the Tracks* with Eric Weissberg and his band. He wasn't happy with the results. When he played the tracks for his brother, David Zimmerman, who worked in the music business in Minneapolis, David told him they weren't commercial and he wouldn't get radio play. Dylan then redid half of the tracks on the LP again in Minneapolis. The musicians in Minneapolis were not as accomplished as the New York musicians, but the versions they came up with are rougher and have more energy and immediacy.

One reason Dylan was probably open to his brother's suggestions was because of other problems with the New York tracks: They were all in the same tempo and the same key (open B tuning), so emotional inflection had to be conveyed through his voice, and his voice on *Blood on the Tracks* twists with tension and regret, and then, on "Idiot Wind," erupts in stinging fury. Dylan made some lyrical changes to "Idiot Wind" when he rerecorded it in Minneapolis. The original lyrics had some caustic lines, such as "You can have the best there is/But it's gonna cost you all you love/You won't get it for money." But the more significant shift was from a more insinuating approach to the ranting rock epic he put on the album. Although the lethal venom of "Idiot Wind" is conveyed chillingly on either version.

One day you'll be in the ditch
Flies buzzing around your eyes
Blood on your saddle

. . . .
Idiot wind
Blowing every time you move your teeth
You're an idiot, babe
It's a wonder that you still know how to breathe

In typical Bob fashion, though, he doesn't it make it easy for us to assume any connection between his songs and his breakup—though it's hard to imagine there's no link between the two: "I came pretty close [to revealing too much of my personal life] with that song 'Idiot Wind,'" Dylan told Bill Flanagan with characteristic wiliness in a 1985 interview. "A lot of people thought that song, that album *Blood on the Tracks*, pertained to me. Because it seemed to at the time. It didn't pertain to me. . . . I've read that that album had to do with my divorce. Well, I didn't get divorced 'til four years after that. I thought I might have gone a little bit too far with 'Idiot Wind.' I might have changed some of it. I didn't really think I was giving away too much; I thought that it *seemed* so personal that people would think it was about so-and-so who was close to me. It wasn't."

Regardless of how we interpret Dylan's caginess about the autobiographical nature of the album, it's worth thinking about this album in terms of a recent theory that suggests that personality is merely the story we tell about our past. That's what you get to do when you write songs about yourself and it's pretty much what Dylan does, no matter what he says. Songs are autobiographical by definition. What you make up is you too. Angels and demons are painted by the same hand.

With a narrator as unreliable as Dylan, literally transposing his life into the lyrics is a hazardous business. This turns out to be especially true of "A Simple Twist of Fate," which we assumed—in the context of his breakup album—was about a sordid one-night stand he'd had while married to Sara, but in his notebook of lyrics for the *Blood on the Tracks* album the song is subtitled "4th Street Affair," 4th Street being where he lived with Suze Rotolo during his early days in New York. The disorienting tale is told in atmospheric semaphore, with a keen sense of desperation in the details: the strange hotel, the neon sign, the heat of night that hit him like a freight train. The moment of betrayal and regret is rendered with stinging self-awareness:

> *She looked at him and he felt a spark tingle to his bones*
> *'Twas then he felt alone and wished that he'd gone straight*
> *And watched out for a simple twist of fate*

Despite his ingenuous manner of telling these personal tales, the album resonates with disturbing undercurrents—"someone's got it in for me, they're planting stories in the press" isn't *only* about the media, obviously, or us, or rock critics. It's about Sara telling her friends, or talking to the children ("Ones I love best").

On "Idiot Wind" he turns his own fate into an allegory of a soured American dream, conflating his torment with national turmoil from Grand Coulee Dam to the Capitol (the Watergate hearings had just ended), where a corrupt gargoyle, the sweaty malignant Richard Nixon, broods, thinking his dark thoughts.

However outrageous Dylan's self-martyring poses are, we empathize with him. As on "Like a Rolling Stone," "It Ain't Me, Babe," "Positively 4th Street," and other Dylan kiss-off songs, we identify with his anger and scorn. On "Idiot Wind," we ignore the perfunctory conclusion—"We're idiots, babe/It's a wonder we can even feed ourselves"—as simply an appeasing gesture to the object of his rage, Sara.

On "Shelter from the Storm," his paranoia flares up in startling images of persecution. He's developed a full-blown martyr complex—"Hunted like a *crocodile*, ravaged in the *corn*"—and it reaches an apocalyptic pitch with his identification with Christ:

In a little hilltop village they gambled for my clothes
I bargained for salvation and they gave me a lethal dose

By 1976 he looks the part too. In his beard and Palestinian headdress on the NBC-TV *Hard Rain* special shot at Fort Collins, Texas, he *is* Jesus—and he directs this venom at Sara in the audience with such vehemence it's a wonder she doesn't catch on fire and burn to a cinder before our eyes.

Although the "old Dylan," so often invoked by his fans, is back with a vengeance on *Blood on the Tracks*, the effect of this resurrection has the odd quality of a time warp; it's as if the album with its folk accompaniment belonged somewhere in the past. As he returns to his roots musically and personally, the songs become drenched in memory and loss. He is looking back—even if that is something he told *us* not to do— becoming as wistful about his past self as his fans are. But even he can only revive the lost folk Village of his youth in memory. The thread has been lost, along with the momentum of his generation.

Bob and the Mayflower, straight out of
"Bob Dylan's 115th Dream"—it doesn't get
any more mythic than this. In the local
museum waxwork Indians watch
impassively from behind huge wax leaves
(Sam Shepard tells us), as the Mayflower
lands every fifteen minutes. Dylan in
Plymouth on the Rolling Thunder Review,
1975.

24 Bob's Wild West (Village) Show

EIGHT YEARS OF DOMESTIC LIFE HAD MADE DYLAN RESTLESS. He returned to his old haunts, and the next thought that must have occurred to Bob—or his doppelgänger Neuwirth—was why not bundle up his past, the legendary folk Village, and take it out on the road. Hence the Rolling Thunder Revue, a wagonload of old folkies rumbling down that lonesome road, twangin', pickin', yodelin', and frailin' on guitars, Dobros, and mandolins. It combined Bob's hobo obsession—the wandering minstrel—with the camaraderie of fellow folksingers that loners like Van Gogh always wanted (or thought they wanted). But the road is a tough place—and Bob understands this better than anyone. The only thing you're likely to find out there is ass kissing, adulation, despair, and the one enlightening door he did eventually find: God.

Dylan himself is justification for any tour, for a crusade even, but these are folkies and they need a cause. Along came Rubin "Hurricane" Carter, a boxer allegedly railroaded by corrupt cops on a trumped-up murder charge. Dylan goes to meet him in jail and holds a concert at Madison Square Garden (along with Muhammad Ali and other celebrities) to celebrate Carter's imminent release. Later he will attach his support to more dubious heroes like Joey Gallo.

On the Rolling Thunder Revue Bob is in search of himself, but he'd forgotten just how elusive he was and how fraught this quest is going to be. Everyone turns into a parody of themselves in the end; it's just that with Dylan there are so many selves out there. With Mick it's simpler; he just wants to be Peter Pan. Dylan, seeking the source of his original inspiration, in the process became someone else.

Rolling Thunder would be the last flowering of the Village folk scene. Buffalo Bill Bob's Wild West (Village) Show: miraculously preserved specimens from a more innocent age.

If this caravan, the Rolling Thunder Revue, had taken place in, say, 1963, it would have been a different matter. That would have been more like Ken Kesey and the Further bus. But it never would have happened like that in the past. So, in a sense, Rolling Thunder was a reimagined past cast in a fantasized future, with everybody playing their assigned roles except for Dylan. The old shape-shifter couldn't resist a few new routines—and he wanted to make it all symbolic and bottle it in an epic movie that he would make of these tours, *Renaldo and Clara*.

The Rolling Thunder Revue wasn't the only re-creation of the past going on at the time. There was the Festival Express train trip across Canada, with all the expatriates from Haight-Ashbury on board: Janis, the Grateful Dead, the Riders of the Purple Sage, the Band. Then there were other time warps, such as the *Mad Dogs and Englishmen* tour and the *Rolling Stones Rock and Roll Circus*, not to mention the Beatles' nostalgic fantasy film, *Magical Mystery Tour*. Even the *Let It Be* sessions were a kind of séance, calling up their past. Many of the late '60s festivals were like hippie high school reunions. Woodstock, that bloated, blighted aircraft carrier of fake '60s cargo, was the ghost event of a collective past that never existed.

On the Rolling Thunder tour—unlike folk clubs where everyone who wasn't a tourist was a musician—they were playing to anonymous groups of people whom the usually genial Sam Shepard, taken along to help write the screenplay, describes as dangerous and toxic. He cold-bloodedly dismisses members of the public who managed to get backstage as parasites and hangers-on. Shepard fears the threatening presence of the cannibal crowd: "A strange fear comes over me that the audience might actually devour Dylan and the band. It seems that close. I'm afraid for them. Just the thought that I might be a witness to it. The audience takes on the shape of an animal. It's the crowd Dylan knows about."

Dylan interacts with selected local characters and eccentrics in his characteristic, idiosyncratic prince-in-disguise-as-an-itinerant-peddler manner. He befriends a blind man in a bar. But basically Rolling Thunder was ghosts singing ghost songs to ghost audiences. The closest that most of his demented fans can get to Dylan is through quirky dreams, two of which are quoted in Sam Shepard's *Rolling Thunder Logbook*.

The most famous recluse in all of rock is now followed by crowds. He's *designed* a situation where people are actually encouraged to pursue him. Later, on the Never Ending Tour, due to his aversion to being stared at, his stagehands would be made to sign a contract that they would not look at him when he comes onstage.

Dylan and Baez are also back together on this tour. They had been such a perfect pair in the '60s—the Prince and Princess of Folk—but when you listen to *Baez Sings Dylan*, an entire album of Dylan covers, it's a bit disturbing. Trilling through lines like "In ceremonies of the horsemen/Even the pawn must hold a grudge" as if she were singing, "Alas, my love, you do me wrong to treat me so discourteously," you realize how little she got Dylan's music. But she's no dullard, and never was. Reading the transcription of dialogue on the tour bus you can see how funny and hip she really is. As with any group of musos, the only problem is that everybody is so self-conscious all the time.

From the Roger McGuinn bus tape transcribed in Sid Griffin's *Shelter from the Storm*, Ramblin' Jack doesn't seem to be quite the old folkie fart we thought he was. Although at the end of the tape he starts reciting, *again*, the funny, rambling Peter Ustinov story that he'd already told a few minutes before—and you begin to wonder. Maybe it's a joke. One can only hope. Regardless, the conversations from the McGuinn bus tape are just great as oral voyeurism, even the boring parts. It's like *Interview* magazine. Everybody on the bus—a bus called Phydeaux (Fido)—is an entertainer.

Being part of a group, Rolling Thunder deflected attention from Bob. It was a scary sight, introducing himself in whiteface, a choice he explains in a number of different and contradictory ways (with Dylan, there's never just one explanation):

1. He's Harlequin, a character from the *Commedia dell'Arte*.

2. He's doing it because everyone says he looks so pale that he must be on junk.

3. You can see him better from the back of the arena.

4. It's makeup for his film *Renaldo and Clara*, referencing one of his favorite French movies, *Children of Paradise*, or, some suggest, Wilkie Collins's novel *The Woman in White*.

5. Any disguise will do.

While all this is going on, Phil Ochs hangs himself. The fact that he wasn't invited on the Rolling Thunder Revue may have been the last nail in the coffin, but it wasn't the cause. He had long been a desperate, unstable character, even arriving at the Bitter End with a hatchet. But Dylan's evolution as a songwriter had had a devastating effect on Ochs. Dylan had made the paper he wrote on into smoke, and by 1975 he was an alcoholic overweight ghost.

Scenes from the road: Allen Ginsberg reciting kaddish to a roomful of blue-haired old ladies playing mah-jongg. Dylan and Ginsberg screaming over Jack Kerouac's grave in Lowell. The two men improvising a poem, "To the ground, to the sky, to the day, to Jack, to life, to music, to the worms, to bones, to travel, to the States." Dylan on the phone ordering frankincense and myrrh and royal jelly—like one of the Magi.

They visit Plymouth Rock, a dispiriting experience. The rock is behind iron bars, covered in coins and bottle caps; it's now a creepy, flesh-colored carcass, half buried in sand like a beached, half-eaten sea monster. What's more, the natives claim it's shrinking—as if the original dream of the Pilgrims were contracting annually.

The Rolling Thunder Revue takes place during bicentennial mania. Everywhere there's the feeling that "our present state of madness could be healed somehow by ghosts," Sam Shepard suggests. Costumes, replicas, dioramas—history for sale. In this cultural moment, the looming past swamps the present. We're like a cynical predator, turning our own history into kitsch, baubles, and tchotchkes.

"Dylan creates a mythic atmosphere out of the land around us," Shepard says. He's not just an entertainer; he's the reanimator, bringing the old waxwork corpses to life. The Davy Crockett coonskin caps, the count of no accounts, and damsels of Bleecker Street. His presence is going to bring all this history sleeping in museums to life, which is what he had done to slumbering American folk and blues songs. Now he's going to bring it to cold cinder block auditoriums and dingy bars with card-playing dogs on black velvet.

As the tour proceeds, the mood of shining possibility and hip cynicism have become indistinguishable. "[Dylan] talks about the possibility of discovering America," Shepard writes. "Right here. Right here at the picnic table. 'How 'bout that? We discover America at a picnic! . . . It's the perfect weather for it.'" Dylan lives in his own strange, haunted environment—an outsider, a Jew from the hinterlands—in other words, a double outsider. For Dylan, the past is history as parable, churning up random images. He never doubted his divine vinyl origin.

Dylan had zeroed in on some point, some psychic nexus, the unconscious of the USA. He was extracting the malign and bright dreams of the great continental beast as it slept, the underlying mind swell on top of which is lathered all the rhetoric, the kvelling, the fake, slick surface of the *NEW! IMPROVED!* continent. The grand ol' haywire American mythology of the road.

Dylan's an automythologizer, his project similar to the maniac Ahab's monomania about the whale but now transferred to vinyl and tour buses. America is a monstrous child; like Gargantua it has grown to gigantic proportions, but it has not developed either a morality or cultural maturity to match its size. It's a made-up country, made up of other countries, a collage. It's too big to be any one thing (like Finland or Italy) and too new for its parts to be integrated like an ancient empire (like China). So we need stories—the taller the better. Big as the big-sky country, whatever that is. No way we can all agree on something—or anything. Dylan's quest is to incarnate America itself in the same way he saw someone like Hank Williams or Jack Kerouac or Robert Johnson as an embodiment of the soul of America. Dylan is searching for what is lost in America, but we've always been lost. We supposedly *found* the place; we just didn't know what to do with it.

That had been the big problem with the New World. We have always been babes in the woods, which is why we are so good at wailing (and whaling). The blues, the cry of Charlie Parker's alto sax, the crack in Hank Williams's voice is like a fissure down to hell. And the eerie wail of Dylan's voice on "All Along the Watchtower" is an uncanny warning of we know not what—which is why pop music has been our true testament. Our dreams, like Dylan's, were beyond control. They were epic. The geography was vast. But we, ourselves, were diminutive, tiny figures in a landscape. We *needed* to distort reality,

EVERYONE IS WAITING, ANTICIPATING BOB'S NEXT MASTERPIECE. BUT Dylan is in a funk. His thoughts are buzzing like flies, and they won't stay still long enough for him to catch them and put them on paper. Or if by chance he does manage to get a few words down, they wriggle and writhe. They refuse to be herded into stories, and Dylan is in a rage to tell stories.

Song inspiration is the bulldog at the gate, according to Dylan in *Chronicles*. You *want* to see him there. If you don't, you're out of luck. He also tells us that songs are very touchy: An embryonic song in its quivering half-formed state is something you shouldn't stare at too hard; if you do, it will run away.

So there he was, the greatest songwriter in all of rock, stumped. And then along came Jacques Levy, Jack Syntax, who knew how to storyboard a song. Levy directed *Oh! Calcutta!* and designed the sets for many plays. He also cowrote many of the songs on Dylan's next album *Desire*. He was an impressionistic storyteller; he'd written "Chestnut Mare" with Roger McGuinn, a mystical horse saga with sidewinders, moons, bottomless canyons, and ghosts—just the sort of stuff Dylan now wanted to try to write. Levy also wrote "I'm So Restless," a song supposedly about Dylan (there's a Mr. D. in the lyrics but that's about it), also with McGuinn.

When we first heard that Dylan was writing songs with somebody else, we thought, why would he need anybody to help him write? Could it be that Jacques Levy—amiable, self-effacing, a theatrical boulevardier—helped Dylan become a *writer*? That is how the story goes. But who would want to change a multiphrenic poète maudit into an Iowa Writers' Workshop student? You want to take that kamikaze plunge of the mind and *organize* his thoughts? Give them stage directions, make Dylan hit his mark? As if "Simple Twist of Fate" and "Shelter from the Storm" on *Blood on the Tracks* weren't cinematic enough, he'd written dozens of stories over the summer and fall of 1967 alone. Now he had to learn how to tell stories from Levy? Perhaps it all had to do with the movie Dylan never managed to make, or the one he's already made a couple of times. And if Levy was such a talented director—and an official stage-managing busybody on the Rolling Thunder Revue—why didn't he apply some of his organizing abilities to *Renaldo and Clara*? That would have been something even Bob's most devoted road dwarfs would've appreciated.

Levy's cinematic storytelling was in some ways a disaster to Dylan's songwriting, however raggedy, shapeless, and circular it was—somewhat akin to Roger McGuinn introducing Dylan to the thesaurus and the rhyming dictionary in 1975. If you want to write songs like short stories you need to go to the masters: Joseph Conrad, Anton Chekhov, et al.—and that's what Levy told him to do while they were writing the songs for *Desire*.

Desire, which came out in 1976, is the biggest-selling Dylan album—stylized, cinematic, and with themes of rogues, gypsies, and mythology: "Isis," "One More Cup of Coffee," and "Romance in Durango" are included on its Marty Robbins–ish soundtrack. The reason Conrad's picture is on the back cover of *Desire* is because he wrote stories that were odd and deadpan, and at that point Dylan was interested in storytelling, hence "Black Diamond Bay" and "Lily, Rosemary, and the Jack of Hearts," both great short stories in miniature. Conrad also wrote *Nostromo*, a novel about an earthquake in a fictional South American country that would seem to be the source of exoticism and intrigue in "Black Diamond Bay," with perhaps elements of another Conrad novel, *Victory*. "Black Diamond Bay," with its twist in the last verse—the whole adventure story turns out to be something on television—is often cited as an example of Dylan's newly acquired narrative ingenuity, but in an interview with *Isis* magazine Levy pretty much claims to have written the whole thing himself.

There are two protest songs—if you can call them that—on *Desire*: "Hurricane" and "Joey." But these two, the boxer Rubin "Hurricane" Carter and the gangster Joey Gallo, are dodgy characters to be held up as martyrs. Hurricane, although clearly set up by the police, was hardly a saint. In Dylan's lexicon Gallo qualifies as an outlaw, a sacred category, because Joey was "always on the outside of whatever side there was." However, Gallo, gunned down in a gangland slaying at Umberto's Clam House, was a vicious, sadistic psychopath (even if he did read Nietzsche in jail, as Dylan tells us). When subsequently confronted with the brutal facts of Gallo's criminal career, Dylan has somewhat unchivalrously blamed the whole thing on his cowriter, the late Jacques Levy.

Between 1965 and 1967 Dylan had more or less discarded storytelling, except in a hallucinatory, expressionist manner, but by the end of the '60s and early '70s his songs have already become little movies: "We sat together in the park as the evening sky grew dark." The accompaniment is folkish, storytellerish. *Desire* presented a different musical approach: violin, guitar, bass, drums. And the way he pairs the violin and the harmonica, with its gypsy flavor, is bluesy, Middle Eastern, and mysterious.

Levy says Dylan was not that good at telling coherent stories, and his specific criticism was that Dylan didn't go from A to B to C. But this of course is what we particularly liked about the Dylan of the '60s. Levy, on the other hand, had an off-Broadway theatrical background, and he was clever, crafty, and astute at bringing out the theatrical elements in a song. For example, "Pistol shots ring out" at the beginning of "Hurricane." The songs he wrote with Dylan have a light operetta quality to them: The storm clouds are painted scrim; the hot chili peppers are a south-of-the-border postcard; the demons are from the prop department. He made each song into a playlet. Bright and melancholy-drenched movie shorts with the perfect accompaniment: Rob Stoner on bass, Scarlet Rivera on violin, and Howie Wyeth on drums.

"Sara," which Dylan wrote alone, is one of the two love songs to his wife on *Desire* in a kind of home-movie-as-lament, the other being "Isis," an allegory of his relationship with Sara. They had gotten back together after a brief separation, but their marriage was again rapidly crumbling. And there's that bit of potted mythology in "Isis": Bob on an epic quest for the woman as goddess, his "mystical wife," a "Scorpio Sphinx in a calico dress," as he called her in "Sara."

"This is a song about marriage," Dylan announces at the start of the song in *Renaldo and Clara*. "Isis" is one of the classic songs Levy helped shape, but I'd still like to hear "Isis" before Levy got his hands on it. It's Bob Dylan as tomb raider. Sam Shepard says it's about the voyage of the soul after death—priests, trials by fire, water, sex, the Sphinx—but once you drag ancient Egyptian mythology into it you're off and running; the symbolism has alabaster legs and a bird's head and it talks in hieroglyphics. Dylan says it wasn't about Egypt at all originally but about an adventure in the Grand Tetons; perhaps they couldn't find a rhyme for "Tetons" even in the rhyming dictionary.

> *I broke into the tomb*
> *But the casket was empty*

Of course, if he'd written this song two years later, after his Christian conversion, he'd have *known* why the casket was empty.

From 1976 to 1978 we're on a spooky spur of the Zimmerman line. Dylan and Christ and Billy the Kid (his outlaw prototypes) are like desperados waiting for the (slow) train that will eventually lead from Sara to Jesus.

The way Dylan sings "Idiot Wind" with
such ferocious animus at Sara in the Fort
Worth video it's a wonder she didn't catch
on fire. In *Blood on the Tracks*, Dylan had
allegorized himself as Jesus, but here in
his Palestinian kaffiyeh he *is* Christ.

25   Epiphany in Room 702

I N THE SPRING OF '76 THE ROLLING THUNDER REVIEW, NOW DEDI-
cated to Melville and Rimbaud, resumes. Part of the reason for
the new tour was to raise money for *Renaldo and Clara*, which was
filmed on the tour. *Renaldo and Clara* is part documentary, part
fantasy, and features Dylan, Baez, and Sara, among others, playing assumed characters (Baez, for example, as the Woman in White). It combines concert footage, home movies, and scripted scenes written by Sam
Shepard and Dylan. In some parts "Bob Dylan" is played by Ronnie
Hawkins, while in other parts Baez, Dylan, and Sara act out a ménage à
trois. Kerouac appears symbolically as a leaf.

It's hard enough to make a movie like this without trying to fit it in
while touring—a miscalculation Dylan had already made with *Eat the
Document* in 1966. His temperament is keyed to short bursts of inspiration that are ideal for recording songs but hardly suited to the laborious,
lumbering pace of filmmaking.

Following the tour Dylan begins editing the one hundred hours of
Renaldo and Clara footage as if he could somehow reedit his life—splice
it back together with a mix of fantasy and details—and transmute his
current problems. "Straightening out karmic problems with the empire" is a line of dialogue from the movie. It was to be a form of alchemy
in which everything wrong would be made right again.

When *Renaldo and Clara* (with a running time of almost four hours)
was released in 1977 it was not kindly reviewed. Critics generally used
the occasion to vent their long-held animosity toward Dylan for failing
to live up to his mid-'60s self. His home newspaper, the *Village Voice*,
called it a "coup de grace in his de-adulation campaign" and the spiteful
revenge of "an artist on his groupies." The only good anybody could see
in it was that the performance footage was great.

There was no shortage of people—from Richard Goldstein to his own
backup musicians—to tell him how to fix it. Edit it down to a ninety-
minute concert film, they said. But who are we talking about here: the
man who wrote the longest hit single of all time, and the longest album

track. Come on, could the Life of Bob be told in a ninety-minute concert film?

Dylan insisted it wasn't going to be a concert film with self-indulgent improvised scenes—more like "a cubist painting." Although hardly revealing of his jealously guarded inner core, he claimed it was about identity, when "the mask is more important than the face."

Renaldo and Clara, in other words, was another phase in Dylan's continuing quest to capture a fictionalized identity on film. Consider a play in which a character called "Dylan" is played by Ronnie Hawkins, and, for reasons not entirely clear to us (or him), this character is not to be confused with the "real" Dylan—whoever that is. That's somewhat the idea behind *Renaldo and Clara*. These Pirandellian ploys were not exactly what his fans went to a Dylan movie for. They wanted to see who Dylan was now, not some mystic tease with Dylan juggling identities.

As Bob had experienced throughout his career, Dylans were accumulating faster than anyone could sort them out—on top of which, the Dylan of the Rolling Thunder Revue was a deliberate reprise of an earlier self: late-middle Dylan over early Dylan. And the scripted ménage à trois was a reenactment of a real or imaginary ménage à trois among the actual people involved. These scenes, however, may have been a little too incestuous for Sara. Things between Dylan and Sara deteriorated when one morning she found Dylan having breakfast with a girlfriend, Malka Marom. A violent argument erupted during which Dylan allegedly struck Sara in the face, injuring her jaw, and told her to leave the house. On March 1, 1977, Sara had her lawyer, Marvin Mitchelson, file for divorce, citing adultery, mental cruelty, and physical abuse. The divorce was finalized on June 29, 1977, Sara receiving a ten-million-dollar settlement and moving to Hawaii.

Before long, Dylan was back on the road again—on the so-called Alimony Tour with an eleven-piece band, which included a female gospel group consisting of Helena Springs, Jo Ann Harris, and Carolyn Dennis. In June, *Street Legal* was released, with intimations of his coming conversion.

IN 1979, IN A MOTEL ROOM ON THE ROAD, DYLAN HAD A "VISION AND A feeling" that led to his conversion to born-again Christianity. Dylan began feeling sick in San Diego on November 17, 1978. On the following night in Tempe, Arizona, Dylan recalled:

Towards the end of the show someone out in the crowd . . . knew I wasn't feeling too well. I think they could see that. And they threw a silver cross on the stage. Now usually I don't pick things up in front of the stage. Once in a while I do. Sometimes I don't. But I looked down at that cross. I said, "I gotta pick that up." So I picked up the cross and I put it in my pocket. . . . And I brought it backstage and I brought it with me to the next town, which was out in Arizona [in Tucson]. . . . I was feeling even worse than I'd felt when I was in San Diego. I said, "Well, I need something tonight." I didn't know what it was. I was used to all kinds of things. I said, "I need something tonight that I didn't have before." And I looked in my pocket and I had this cross.

In November 1978, Dylan played a gig at the McKale Memorial Center in Tucson, Arizona, and returned to his hotel room. An hour later, he experienced what he considered his divine revelation. Hotels, motels, and 7-Elevens—that's where things like that happen. They're the most haunted places in the USA. Aliens with tractor beams are sitting out in air-conditioned vans in the parking lot, siphoning off your brain while you're sleeping or brushing your teeth. "There was a presence in the room that couldn't have been anybody but Jesus. . . . Jesus put his hand on me. It was a physical thing. I felt it. I felt it all over me. I felt my whole body tremble. The glory of the Lord knocked me down and picked me up."

Mary Alice Artes, the black actress with whom he was having an affair, introduced him to the fundamentalist church Valley Vineyard Christian Fellowship in Reseda, California, and Bob became born-again. Steven Soles and David Mansfield, who played on *Street Legal*, were also members of the Vineyard Fellowship—they had heard about the church from T-Bone Burnett.

In his essay "What Happened?" written at the time of the first Warfield concerts, Paul Williams theorizes that:

Dylan has always believed, not unreasonably, in the power of Woman. When he finally lost faith in the ability of women to save him (and he seems to have explored the matter very thoroughly, in and out of marriage, in the years 1974 through '78), his need for an alternative grew very great indeed, and he found what people in our culture most often find in the same circumstances: the uncritical hospitality of Jesus Christ.

On the Christian tours that followed his conversion he banned his old "secular" songs from his repertoire, playing only his new religious ones, causing outrage among his fans. On the fall tour of '79 he attacked homosexuals and railed against US foreign policy. When he appeared on *Saturday Night Live* on October 20 of that year he performed only gospel songs.

He then traveled to San Francisco for a series of eight gospel shows that began on November 1, 1979, at the small Fox Warfield Theatre. According to Paul Williams:

> The curtain goes up about 8:20, and Regina Havis, a short vibrant black woman . . . walks up to the microphone and starts telling a story. An old woman wants to go see her dying son, but she has no money and the conductor won't let her on the train. She prays to the Lord for help; the conductor tries to start the train but it won't go; finally he asks the woman to get on the train. "But conductor, you said if I didn't have no ticket I couldn't ride on your train." "Old woman, Jesus got your ticket, now come on this train."

Havis would then be joined by two other black backup singers, and they would sing six gospel songs beginning with "If I've Got My Ticket, Lord, Can I Ride?" and ending with "This Train."

But the train isn't going to start until Bob gets on. And it isn't going anywhere on the map; in songs trains never are. It's a mystical form of transportation bound for glory, even if it's the I-gotta-get-outta-this-place train—the one Robert Johnson, Jimmie Rodgers, Hank Williams, Elvis, Johnny Cash, and Merle Haggard are always yearning to catch. It's imaginary and just taking you away from somewhere, someone—to anywhere but here. And that's just where Bob was headed: *away*. The journey's there in all that train imagery ("It Takes a Lot to Laugh, It Takes a Train to Cry" being the classic transposition of a railway metaphor), in all those train shots in *Eat the Document*.

The last couple of years had been disastrous for Dylan. His marriage had ended in divorce the previous year; his recently released masterpiece, *Renaldo and Clara*, had been trashed; and his world tour had ended in the States to discouraging reviews. Oh, and the world was coming to an end. So what better way to escape one's problems?

By the end of the tour he had substituted passages from the Bible into the verse in "Tangled Up in Blue." But somehow the verse "'Behold, the days come,' sayeth the Lord, 'that I will make a covenant with the house of Israel, and with the house of Judah'" (from Jeremiah) doesn't have quite the same ring as "poet from the thirteenth century." Critics lambasted and ridiculed his three born-again albums: *Slow Train, Saved,* and *Shot of Love,* released between August 1979 and August 1981—although *Slow Train* has some classic songs on it ("Gotta Serve Somebody," "I Believe in You," "Man Gave Names to All the Animals"), and *Shot of Love* had some great tracks ("Every Grain of Sand," "Heart of Mine"). Few had anything good to say about his conversion. His aunt Ethel Crystal put him down for his conversion, saying it was "for publicity," Keith Richards called him the "prophet of profit," and John Lennon wrote a parody of "You've Got to Serve Somebody" called "Serve Yourself."

But these attacks only confirmed his image of himself as some sort of martyr, a Jesus-like figure who was rejected and misunderstood. He began preaching sermons from the stage. Intense, skinny, ethereal, tormented looking, and bearded, he even looked like an early Netherlandish Christ.

John Wesley Harding (he called it "the first biblical rock album") had been apocalyptic, but this was ten times worse:

> *You know we're living in the end times. . . . The scriptures say, "In the last days, perilous times shall be at hand. Men shall become lovers of their own selves. Blasphemous, heavy, and high-minded.". . . Take a look at the Middle East. We're heading for a war. . . . I told you "The Times They Are A-Changin'" and they did. I said the answer was "Blowin' in the Wind" and it was. I'm telling you now Jesus is coming back, and He is! And there is no other way of salvation. . . . Jesus is coming back to set up His kingdom in Jerusalem for a thousand years.*

He was in a desperate state, consumed by regret, rage, and alcohol-fueled self-loathing.

I am broken
Shattered like an empty cup

Getting on that train to glory meant not only denouncing all your old songs (he refused to play them between 1979 and 1980). It also meant renouncing your past, your old self; it was a form of suicide, killing off the old Dylan. He'd tried to do that a few times in the past (as the folk prophet, visionary, etc.) but these were rejections of his former stages as an artist. This was a denial of self.

It was at the small Fox Warfield Theatre that his problems with the press began. Joel Selvin of the *San Francisco Chronicle* called it BOB DYLAN'S GOD-AWFUL GOSPEL. And this view was repeated endlessly. It was easy to believe from what you heard that he had lost his mind. We wanted to think it was a temporary form of psychosis, religious mania brought on by exhaustion, a high fever, and personal disasters of a recent vintage. We knew friends who'd gotten religion (AA itself being a kind of cult involving coffee, smoking, and God) and wished them well. By the end of the '70s, after plagues of cocaine, DMT, ecstasy, angel dust, heroin, amyl nitrate, platform shoes, and glitter, a lot of people needed help. How could the cynical Bob be sucked into this born-again nonsense? It was assumed that he had been manipulated into this cult by some woman friend while he was at a vulnerable point in his life. When it was (erroneously) reported in the *Post* that he had been baptized in Pat Boone's swimming pool . . . well, what were we to think? Perhaps it was a cry for help!

But the audiences at the Warfield concerts were enthusiastic; everyone who attended them said the performances were great. And many people who caught Dylan in concert during this time agreed. "I saw Dylan in Spokane during his born-again period and he was ferocious," says Lenny Kaye, Patti Smith's lead guitarist. Dylan's characteristic disdain for his audiences was gone—unless of course you were a nonbeliever, and then a truly disturbing Dylan awaited you.

His was a mystical train of thought: He was a visionary, a prophet, he made references to the Bible that were thought to be literary allusions. Going to Jesus was a way of standing outside of time and his troubles. For one thing it allowed him to disappear. The gospel singers in the Vineyard Fellowship enfolded him and created a barrier between him and the world in the way the Band had in 1966 and 1974 and the Rolling Thunder Revue did in 1975 and 1976.

With prophets of doom in the '60s and '70s (really just a flaky extension of the '60s), personal confusion and desperation are indiscriminately mixed up with End of Days rhetoric. Hal Lindsey's pop apocalyptic *The Late Great Planet Earth* became the best-selling nonfiction book of the decade precisely because it tapped into the era's mood of exhaustion and confusion.

Dylan is the Jack of Hearts, his fantasy creation, a playing card who lives in his own imaginary world and when that gets shattered he goes into a state of shock. "Son, this ain't a dream no more, it's the real thing." Between 1966 and 1973 he had been cocooned by Sara, but by 1974 he needed shelter from the storm again.

At a concert on November 26, 1979, he sounded like Savonarola, the hellfire-breathing, book-burning fifteenth-century Florentine friar who railed against the political and cultural corruption and decadence of the Renaissance and demanded its lewd pictures and pagan fetishes be burned in the Bonfire of the Vanities—but in the end, he too was burned at the stake. Among the crowd, consisting largely of college kids, some rowdy and obnoxious hecklers respond rudely to the gospel backup singers. Dylan is angry but, for him, unusually patient:

Hmm. What a rude bunch tonight, huh? You all know how to be real rude. You know about the spirit of the anti-Christ? Does anybody here know about that? Well, it's clear the anti-Christ is loose right now. . . . [T]here's many false deceivers running around these days. There's only one gospel. The Bible says anybody who preaches anything other than that one gospel, let him be accursed.

Hecklers shout: "ROCK 'N' ROLL!"

Dylan: "You wanna rock 'n' roll you can go down and rock-n-roll. You can go see Kiss and you can rock 'n' roll all your way down to the pit." Dylan has the lights turned on the audience.

"How many people here are aware that we're living in the End of Times right now? How many people are aware of that?"

"The times they are a-changin'!" someone shouts.

Dylan: "That's right. I told you that. I told you 'The Times They Are A-Changin'" twenty years ago. [*applause*] And I don't believe I've ever lied to you. I don't think I said anything that's been a lie. I never told you to vote for nobody. Never told you to follow nobody."

From the crowd: "Everybody must get stoned!"

Dylan responds to this very earnestly by telling the parable of the woman taken in adultery—"let him who is without sin cast the first stone."

He gets to the point: "Well, let me tell you, that the Devil owns this world. He's called the god of this world. Now we're living in America. I like America just as much as everybody else does. I love America, I gotta say that. But America will be judged."

He now predicts that Christ is returning—literally, *today*. And the urgency with which he says it is intense—and there's always the possibility, however remote, that it might be true. What if?

"He's coming again," Dylan tells them. "You gotta be prepared for this."

Because, no matter what you read in the newspapers, that's all deceit. The real truth is that He's coming back already. And you just watch your newspapers. You're gonna see, maybe two years, maybe three years, five years from now, you just watch and see. Russia will come down and attack in the Middle East. China's got an army of two hundred million people. They're gonna come down in the Middle East. There's gonna be a war called the "Battle of Armageddon," which is like some war you never even dreamed about. And Christ will set up His kingdom. He will set up His kingdom and He'll rule it from Jerusalem. I know, as far out as that might seem, this is what the Bible says.

Dylan became obsessed with the idea of Armageddon; it has an apocalyptic thrill to it. The world was going to end. Life would be thrown into crisis, and we wouldn't need to worry about our silly little personal problems anymore. Predictions of End of Days disaster in the Bible naturally take place in the Middle East. Back then they didn't know about California. But with the Iran-Contra affair going on at the time, the biblical prophecies suddenly seemed to have a special resonance, and Dylan took it all very literally.

His fans found this Christian Bob phase utterly unfathomable, but it wasn't totally unexpected. Although he'd never behaved in so literal a manner before, he'd always been on a quest for mystic deliverance. In some ways his embrace of Christianity was a transcendent extension of his vision of the outsider as saint, with Christ as the champion of the downtrodden, the outcast, and the lost.

BETHEL WOODS
CENTER FOR THE ARTS
★ ★ ★ Bethel, NY ★ ★ ★

FRI AUG 12

IN SHOW & CONCERT!

BOB DYLAN
and
HIS BAND
PLUS

LEON RUSSELL

DON'T YOU DARE MISS IT!

Bethel Woods
CENTER FOR THE ARTS

After all the disheartening accounts you've read
about the Never Ending Tour, here he was, still
sounding just like the old Dylan, even with that
croaky voice, jumpy delivery, growled lyrics,
off-key piano (Dylan does Schoenberg!), thorny
harp solos, and a strange dance thrown in for good
measure (basically just bending one knee, but for
Bob that's colossal). August 12, 2011, Dylan and
Leon Russell perform at Bethel, New York, site of
the original Woodstock festival.

26　Down the Road

The mirror had swung around and I could see the
future—an old actor fumbling in garbage cans
outside the theater of past triumphs.

—BOB DYLAN, *CHRONICLES*

BOB, IN THE '70S, '80S, AND '90S, YOUR CAREER. . . .
But, before you can finish the sentence, you hear Dylan,
in the recesses of your mind, saying, "What career? I've never
had a career."

Well, what would you call it, then—your mission, your quest, your
Fate (what else would it be?)—those three and a half decades of Jack Fate
careening through life, art, dodgy and inspired albums, womanizing,
alcohol, drugs, dazzling and dreadful performances, awards ceremonies, outlandish behavior. It was a terrible roller coaster, all Snakes and
Ladders, creative droughts followed by miraculous recoveries. He's Sisy-
phus rolling Bob Dylan up to the top of the hill and watching him roll
down again, Wile E. Coyote obtaining a new device from the Acme Mail
Order Company that blows up in his face. They cross him off—he's done
for (again)—and then there he is, rising up like the phoenix.

Most performers can only manage one comeback; Dylan, at last
count, has had at least five. Let's see. The first Dylan drought would be
from 1970 to 1974 between *New Morning* and *Planet Waves*. Then there
were the gospel years, roughly from 1978 to 1983, *Street Legal* to *Infidels*—
though this would be considered only a blank period by actual infidels.
He had another dry spell from 1984 to 1989, *Infidels* to *Oh Mercy*. There's
another void from 1989 to 1992, from *Oh Mercy* to *Good as I Been to You*.
And there's another gap between 1994 and 1997, from *World Gone Wrong*
to *Time Out of Mind*. After that it's easy to lose track. In any case it all
becomes irrelevant after his health scare in 1997, after which he is a National Living Treasure, a radio host, and Tex-Mex Santa Claus.

AS OFTEN HAPPENS WITH DYLAN, IN THE END A BAD SITUATION LED TO another rebirth, in this case a solution that would solve the problems in his life and art—for him, at least. First came a series of albums, beginning with the post-born-again (and mischievously titled) *Infidels*.

After the last two not so well received born-again albums, *Saved* and *Shot of Love*, Dylan came back with a great album. A palpable sigh of relief arose that Dylan was back—a popular refrain. A new cycle had begun.

Infidels was recorded in his usual ad hoc manner, coproduced with Mark Knopfler of Dire Straits, who had played on Dylan's classic gospel album, *Slow Train Coming*. *Infidels*, which came out in 1983, included such great tracks as "Jokerman," "I and I," "Sweetheart Like You," and "Don't Fall Apart on Me Tonight." The release of *Infidels* also happened to coincide with the moment when MTV started becoming hugely popular—in part due to the advertising wiz George Lois's "I want my MTV" campaign.

Bill Graham was Dylan's de facto manager at the time and wanted him to capitalize on MTV's growing influence by making a video of one of the songs on the album. Dylan, however, hated videos, despite having inadvertently made a classic one for "Subterranean Homesick Blues" in the opening scene of *Don't Look Back*. However, this video required acting and lip-syncing—two activities Dylan had little talent for.

How, then, did Graham get Dylan to make a video for MTV—a concept he had a special abhorrence for? Larry "Ratso" Sloman—who wrote a great book about the Rolling Thunder Revue—acted as liaison between Dylan and George Lois, the video's director. Lois and Sloman had worked with Dylan on the campaign to free Hurricane Carter in 1975. So Bill Graham called Lois and said, "If you do it, maybe I have a shot. I've been trying to talk him into doing something and he won't do it." Bob signed on—reluctantly.

"Right away I wanted to know if I could do any song on the album [*Infidels*] that excited me," Lois recalls. "When I heard 'Jokerman' I thought, 'Holy fuck, every line is literally biblical.' Right then and there I had half of the visuals in my head. I did the whole board in maybe two days. I call Bill and tell him, 'You are going to love this!' 'What song?' he asks. 'Jokerman!' 'George, are you sure you wouldn't prefer one of the other ones?' he asks. 'Hey, fuck face,' I say."

"George had two main ideas," says Ratso. "Blow up the words because the lyrics are so amazing—put it right in your face, put those words big on the screen—and link them to the art."

Lois storyboarded the entire video and invited Dylan and Bill Graham to come and look at the thing. Lois led them through the video, saying, "Okay, the Michelangelo goes here, see . . . the Picasso we put there," as Ratso recalls the meeting. "It was George's typical way of operating, you know, like a bulldozer."

"The whole side of the room was dark with lights kind of washing on the walls," says Lois. "Bob is sitting there just watching it and by the time I got to about twenty images, maybe half of them, he says, 'You know a lot of the images you have up there I had in my head when I wrote it!' When Bob said that, I knew I had him."

However, Dylan is still hesitant so they decide to shoot him singing just the chorus. That'll be the only time you see him; the first few verses will have the artwork. Lois wants Bob in a white T-shirt and a white sports jacket. Dylan likes the idea but, typically, the next day he's having doubts. He calls Ratso and says he wants to get together and talk about it.

"I suggest this restaurant in Chinatown. I walk in and Bob's already there with Gary Shafner, his road manager. He's sitting there in this little Chinese restaurant in a parka with the hood pulled over his head. He's the only white person there; everyone else is Chinese. No one knows who the fuck he is but he's covered up like he's about to be besieged. He'd gotten into this hooded sweatshirt thing from all those years he was training with the boxer 'Mouse' Strauss."

Ratso reassures Bob that it's going to be great, not to worry. The next day Dylan comes to the studio. They put on makeup, dress him in a white T-shirt and white sports jacket, and get him on the set. George says, "Okay, Bob, we'll play the music and you start lip-syncing." Right away Bob is having problems. "I don't think he had ever lip-synced in a video quite like that before," says Ratso.

"Well he fucking did it six times," says Lois, "and he still wasn't lip-syncing. It was like he was singing 'The Star Spangled Banner.' I said to him, 'You are not leaving this fucking room until you lip-sync this thing. I will lock you in here, I swear to God, I will tie you up. You have to go through the whole song a good four times and concentrate, and out of those four times I will be able to edit something out of it.' He kind of brooded. 'Bob, do I have to tell you how to fucking lip-sync?' Finally he did do it, and then walked away kind of pissed."

But, according to Ratso, Bob's lip-syncing difficulties weren't the only problem: His eyes were shut the whole time. "This goes on for about four takes and George is tearing his hair out. He looks at me and says, 'Tell him,' so I go over and say, 'Bob, you've got to open your eyes.' And he goes, 'I'm trying.' And actually if you watch the video again you will see he has his eyes closed all the way through that last verse and at the very last line he squints—his eyes open a little bit—and stares at the camera, and all the Dylan mystique is captured in that one little gesture. It was unbelievable. He knew exactly what he was doing.

"So we finish the video, cut it, spending days in the editing room with George. We deliver it to Columbia. They love it. They flip out. Well, the next day I get a call from Bob saying, 'I don't know about this video. I mean, me in the studio singing. . . . All I saw was a shot of me from my mouth to my forehead on the screen. I figure, isn't that somethin', paying for that? Why don't we take a hand camera and go to Malibu and just shoot me there.' I said, 'Bob, what are you talking about? It's great.' He goes, 'I could do it better.'

"I have to go tell George that Bob didn't like the close-ups, that he was thinking that maybe we should shoot him on the beach. George goes, 'Columbia paid for it and love it, so fuck him.' Of course it went out the way it was and everybody loved it.

"That summer Bob was playing in Europe, so I flew over just to join the tour and hang out and I remember I got in there and went right to the venue in France, a big outdoor park. There's Bob sitting in front of the trailer before the show and I said, 'Hey, Bob, *Night Flight* just picked the video as number one of the week.' Bob looks at me and says, 'Either I'm crazy or the world's crazy!'"

"Everyone loved it," Lois says, "but Dylan went on complaining about it. I couldn't understand it. Then about maybe ten years later I'm walking by a place called Joe Jr.'s, Twelfth Street and Sixth Avenue. Bob is sitting in the window booth by himself. I look in. He sees me, says to come in, sit down, have a cup of coffee. It's all, 'Gee, how you doin'?' I'm going, 'Yeah, yeah.' Finally Bob says he has to go. As he's leaving he says, 'By the way, George, "Jokerman" was really a great video.'"

WHILE *INFIDELS* RECEIVED CRITICAL ACCLAIM, THE REST OF HIS '80S albums would be seen as the dismal record of a failed artist—the stations of the cross in one of his downward spirals. With his next album, 1985's disco-influenced *Empire Burlesque*, Dylan craved massive commercial success. He wanted to sell albums like Madonna and Prince—said he wanted to *be* them, actually. However, from the much-dissected title to the album cover (with Dylan in his Don Johnson jacket), *Empire Burlesque* was such a wonky idea that it seemed like a *Saturday Night Live* parody. Dylan, with his scrub-board guitar style, was never going to get people up out of their seats. You can't make Dylan into disco, however hard you try. Bob doesn't boogie.

In a quandary, Dylan brought in Arthur Brown, who had made a name for himself making dance floor remixes of Bruce Springsteen and Cyndi Lauper by passing a whiff of amyl nitrate under the noses of their old songs. But Dylan was not going to be another Cinderella kissed awake by technology's cold embrace, with synthesizers, pan scans, MIDI, and other deejayish gimmicks. Neither *Miami Vice* jackets nor parachute pants were going to make someone like Bob fashionable. What's interesting about Dylan's experiment with disco is that his attraction to something that seemed so alien to him was actually part of his nature—one of the most omnivorous, consistently promiscuous artists in rock. Disco just happened to be out of his range.

With his next album, *Knocked Out Loaded* (1986), things got worse. It included "Driftin' Too Far from the Shore"—the same name as the song out of which he claims to have hatched. Perhaps he was trying to touch some totem of his past, but whatever it was it didn't work.

There's one great flawed track—the eleven-minute "Brownsville Girl," written with Sam Shepard—that might have become one of the classic songs of his midcareer, a great electric ballad like "Desolation Row" or "Black Diamond Bay." Unlike Jacques Levy, Shepard didn't try to force Dylan to go from A to B to C in a tidy narrative. "Brownsville Girl" meanders in classic Dylan fashion. It's the kind of tale that needs a storyteller to tell it to you directly, but during this period Dylan was hiding and buried his voice under an overblown production—horns and a girly chorus. The video of "Brownsville Girl" is a visual equivalent of the song's attempt to inflate a tangled tale into a widescreen panoramic epic.

Sam Shepard recounts an interesting instance of Dylan wrangling words into "Brownsville Girl." Bob begins by telling Shepard his idea for the song:

"I was standing in line for this Gregory Peck film," he says.

Shepard asks, "But how the hell are you going to fit this into the melody?"

"Don't worry about it," says Dylan. "It'll work."

"And inevitably it did. The way he squashes phrasing and stretches it out is quite remarkable."

Generally though, Dylan's ingenious talent to make songs out of vernacular phrases was faltering. With *Empire Burlesque* and *Knocked Out Loaded* the words and music were coming apart.

His follow-up to *Knocked Out Loaded* was the meager *Down in the Groove*, an album of covers, scraps collected from six years of playing with different bands, and two collaborations with Grateful Dead lyricist Robert Hunter, which produced one decent song: "Silvio." Then Bob went punk. Well, that would have been interesting if it had worked out. He got Steve Jones from the Sex Pistols and Paul Simonon from the Clash to play on the album, but the production made the different backing groups indistinguishable—all irredeemably "Dylanized," as Robert Christgau put it. But who is this? How much worse could it get? The one redeeming track, "Rank Strangers to Me," a Stanley Brothers song with minimalist instrumentation, would point the way to Americana. He was trying, yet again, to go back to the past to discover a way out. By 1988 he'd given up finding a new identity. But, by then, *Down in the Groove* had fared even worse than *Knocked Out Loaded*, his lowest-selling album so far. People just stopped buying his records.

Another of Dylan's more unfortunate '80s experiments was his involvement with the Grateful Dead. In one sense, the Dead and Dylan would seem to be an ideal pairing. They both came out of the same folk, jug band, bluegrass, country music barnyard. The Dead could almost be said to have come out of the fabric of Dylan's early songs and influences. However, their collaboration turned out to be the biggest mess, by far the worst album, and the absolute nadir of Dylan's career—well, up until then, at least.

After becoming friendly with Jerry Garcia, Dylan toured with the Dead in 1986 (Tom Petty and the Heartbreakers were his backup band). The next year he toured with the Dead again, this time using them as his on the road band. The shows did not do well despite marathon rehearsals that left Garcia bemused by Dylan's approach to playing: "He's funny. He has a chameleon-like quality. He goes along with what he hears.... But he doesn't have a conception about two things that are very important in music: starting and ending a song.... The middle of the song is great; the beginning and ending are nowhere."

Next Bob wants to *join* the Dead. Phil Lesh vetoes it. There are rumors

Dylan and Jerry had similar substance abuse problems, which isn't hard to imagine. In photos from this period, despite his profound kinship with Garcia, Dylan looks affectless, detached, and weary, as if to say, "What the fuck am I doing here?" After Jerry's death he said, "I don't think eulogizing will do him justice. . . . He is a very spirit personified of whatever is muddy river country at its core and screams up into the spheres."

The sets with the Dead create a new criterion for disastrous Dylan concerts: the Least Terrible Show. That would be Giants Stadium, New Jersey, July 12, 1987. This was the original choice for the live album, *Dylan and the Dead*. But Bob for his own perverse reasons chooses tracks from four inferior concerts (of the six they did together). In 1989, *Dylan and the Dead* is released; it's not known how many people ever played it beyond the first track. David Fricke, writing in *Rolling Stone*, titled his review of the album "The Zim & the Grim." But even that album in retrospect is not the travesty it once seemed. Technically the recording isn't very good, Dylan forgets the lyrics half the time, and the Dead aren't the tightest band in the world. But as Bob Hudson points out, "They were both great folk music appreciators, and it's interesting to hear Jerry Garcia playing guitar off Bob's vocals and how the musicians try to resonate with Dylan, their expectations about what the next verse might contain. The interaction between these two giants who emerged out of folk music is fascinating, even if it doesn't fulfill the expectations, and the expectations were huge." However bad the experience with the Dead had been, Dylan saw his playing with the Dead as a turning point. As he told Mikal Gilmore in *Rolling Stone*, "I really had some sort of epiphany on how to do those songs again, using certain techniques. When I went back and played with Petty again, I was using the same techniques and found I could play anything." But that would take a while.

THE NEVER ENDING DYLAN SAGA BEGAN WITH FARCICAL BOB, AN IDIO-syncratic character so off the chart that—even for him—it is hard to believe. But here, at least, he clearly isn't putting us on. Many of his live performances from this period are as bizarre as his records, but in one weird moment of forgetfulness he is unable to even fake himself. Dylan, looking pale and shattered, shows up on January 28, 1985, at A&M Studios in LA to perform at the recording of the "We Are the World" video. It's in support of Live Aid (a concert raising money for famine relief for Ethiopia). You can't have a worldwide charity event like this—the biggest humanitarian intervention ever—without Bob Dylan, who originated protest rock. And if you're Dylan, it's an invitation you can't refuse.

At the taping of "We Are the World," the theme song of the campaign, Dylan approaches the microphone tentatively and begins to sing in a strange little voice. Quincy Jones, the producer, stops the tape. What's the problem? Stevie Wonder explains to him that he doesn't sound—how to put it?—"Dylanesque" enough. And to show him how it's done, Stevie does Dylan, who seems to be going through some bizarre identity crisis. There's an audience of more than a billion people out there, and they want to hear that voice. But he's forgotten how to sing like himself. Quincy coaxes him through his lines, demonstrating the modulation. Dylan gives it another try. "Is that sort of it?" he asks hesitantly.

Things get worse at the Live Aid concert in Philadelphia on July 13, 1985. Dylan is to close the show. Jack Nicholson introduces him with grand eloquence: "Some artists' work speaks for itself. Some artists' work speaks for its generation. It's my deep personal pleasure to present to you one of America's great voices of freedom. It can only be one man, *the transcendent Bob Dylan!*" But Bob wasn't exactly transcendent that night.

They'd wanted him to perform "Blowin' in the Wind" with Peter, Paul and Mary, who had recently gotten back together. Understandably, he refused. He had reason to resent them. When Dylan sang "Blowin' in the Wind" with his mountain twang he could make it sound like an Appalachian Ecclesiastes. Peter, Paul and Mary had brought him immense fortune and fame through their sappy version of his song, but their saccharine treatment had also exposed the song's latent kitsch. He wants to do something funkier, and besides, by now he probably hated the song. He wouldn't even sing it for the pope!

A scruffy-looking Dylan, who has been drinking all afternoon backstage, stumbles toward the microphone. He's like a bug in the spotlight. Dylan doesn't deal well with events of this size—never has. Anything as huge as the Live Aid concert, and his insecurities kick in, just as they did at the Isle of Wight. He performs a ragged version of "Hollis Brown," a morbid tale of a Midwestern farmer who shot himself and his family rather than see them starve to death. His partners are an equally messed-up duo: Keith Richards and Ron Wood, who clearly haven't a clue what's happening.

Well, there were extenuating circumstances—technical problems—

which explain (almost) everything and might absolve Dylan from most of the snarky criticism of his appalling performance. They—Bob, Keith, and Ron—were forced to perform *in front of* their monitors, so they literally couldn't hear one another. Worse, because the rest of the cast was setting up just beyond the curtain directly behind them and making a horrible clatter, they couldn't even hear themselves—which is why, if you YouTube the video, you'll see Keith and Ron exchanging nonplussed looks. Bob, however, simply plows on, singing in a near monotone—which ingeniously solves the problem of what key he's meant to be in—but does not make for a riveting performance.

While the performance is sloppy and embarrassing, Bob's true crime is his impromptu speech in which he says that some of the money raised for Live Aid should go to pay the bank mortgages of American farmers. The reaction is one of shock: Children's corpses are piling up in Ethiopia and he's talking about bank mortgages? Anyway, it's diluting the message, the reason they got him there in the first place. And it's confusing to people (now we don't know *who* to give money to; maybe we won't give at all).

His suggestion, though, does lead to Farm Aid, a concert put together by Willie Nelson, John Mellencamp, and Tom Petty. At the Farm Aid concert on September 22, 1985, Tom Petty and the Heartbreakers are his backup band, and the combination is fortuitous.

Then, while playing Locarno, Switzerland, in October 1987, Dylan has an epiphany: "I'm determined to stand whether God will deliver me or not. . . . Everything just exploded. It exploded every which way."

His revelation is about what to do for the rest of his life. The words written in flames are not exactly apocalyptic along the lines of, say, "And, I John saw a new heaven and a new earth for the former things were passed away." As epiphanies go, Bob's was bluntly practical. It said, "Go forth, Bob, and pursue the Never Ending Tour!"

This was an idea that would utterly change Dylan's life—and even the idea of what a tour is. It would turn out to be an entirely different concept from your basic rock tour—not touring between records or to promote albums (which in Dylan's case were few and far between as it was), but touring as a way of life—or, in Dylan's case, *as* life. If you don't have a life, a family, a home you want to go to—and Dylan didn't—the road was now to be his destiny. Touring provided a solution to his paradoxical demands: exposure without contact, celebrity and invisibility, large sums of money and an odd place to hide—onstage. For someone with a fear of home, touring *was* his home. As Eric Andersen says, "If you were Dylan you wouldn't want to go home either."

AND THEN, AT HIS LOWEST EBB—OR ONE OF THE DOZEN OR SO LOWEST ebbs—fate plucks him out of his misery. Along comes George Harrison, looking for another track to put on his twelve-inch promotional single for his new album, *Cloud Nine*. George's producer, Jeff Lynne, tells him Bob's got a studio in his garage at his house in Point Dume. But first, George has to go and get his guitar, which happens to be at Tom Petty's house. So Tom Petty joins the group. This bunch—George, Petty, Lynne, Bob (and drummer Jim Keltner)—would have made some charming noodling music, but they're a body without a head. Lynne also happens to be producing Roy Orbison, that perfect, trembling, grand ol' operatic baritone with a four-octave range. On top of which Orbison is a truly legendary Nashville guy going back to the mythic Sun Records era—which is as close as you're going to get to rock's Big Bang. And the Traveling Wilburys come into existence. They record the whole album in ten days, and it's full of good-time porch-pickin' and strumming music like "End of the Line."

It was an ideal situation for the reclusive, beleaguered Dylan. He got to cloak himself in a group as one of the pseudonymous Wilbury boys. Bob is "Lucky" Wilbury. The Traveling Wilburys rehabilitated Dylan from the sourpuss character he'd become, reenergized him, pulled him temporarily out of his solitary funk, and made him relevant again—he no longer had to wait for the phone to ring—and it also made him a bunch of money (the album went triple platinum).

Meanwhile the Never Ending Tour went on. It was Dylan's way of dealing with his life. It didn't solve his personal dissatisfaction, his malaise, his songwriting crises, etc., but it did give him a reason for going on.

A lot of people don't like the road, but it's as natural to me as breathing. I do it because I'm driven to do it . . . it's the only place you can be who you want to be. . . . I don't want to put on the mask of celebrity. I'd rather just do my work and see it as a trade. . . . I don't make a record every three years, then go and tour so that audiences will buy it as a souvenir. I'm not that kind of artist and never wanted to be.

The Never Ending Tour wasn't exactly a new idea for Bob. The first inkling occurred to Dylan on the Rolling Thunder Revue. The original idea was a caravan of folk, rock, country, and blues singers, coming and going, a variety show of traditional American music that would just go on and on, trundling down the highways and byways, coming to your town. This was a collective celebration, Dylan appearing now and then simply as the totem figure. But this never evolved because Rolling Thunder Revue Part 2 turned out to be something of a bust.

The gypsy caravan concept dreamed up in 1976 was to be a communal affair. Dylan's Never Ending Tour (1988 to the present) is something else altogether. Aside from the other bands he toured with (he was often unable at this stage to sustain a solo tour on his own), the Never Ending Tour itself was neither communal nor inclusive. His backup bands were paid hands and would come and go. Dylan appeared as an iconic figurehead backed by more or less anonymous groups (except to the Bobcats and the cognoscenti who noted every bass player dropped, every drummer replaced). And, in place of the welcoming troupe of motley musicians envisioned in the Rolling Thunder Revue, Dylan seemed like a man in flight from something—just about everything, as it turned out.

Dylan by this point was, when he felt like it, playing Dylan ("I'm only Dylan when I have to be"). Elvis had become a parody of himself too. As time went on he used his self-caricature to become the first Elvis impersonator. It was a form of armor, a tactic Dylan would follow almost literally. "There's a lot of gypsy in me," he tells *TV Guide*. Motorcycle boots, earrings, he's starting to look like a gypsy himself. Once Elvis had gone, he *was* the Gypsy, even sartorially. With white suits and World Wrestling Federation belts, he looked like he'd been dressed by a wardrobe mistress from a bad provincial production of *Jailhouse Rock*.

Adrian Deevoy, reviewing a Dylan concert in Q magazine, caught the Elvis-on-Dylan effect:

On the opening night, he speaks, laughs and persistently performs a peculiar hip-swinging trouser maneuver that owes as much to Elvis Presley as Shakin' Stevens [who played Elvis in a musical]. . . . It's one of many surprises—some verging on treatable shock—that Dylan springs during his triumphant six-night residency at the punter-friendly 3,500 capacity theatre . . . of course, as is always the case with Dylan, anything could happen next.

Hotel rooms and buses are now his home. When asked, "Do you miss your home?" he says, "This *is* my home." You never have to go home, especially if home is where the heartache is and all the other headaches in your life. There are selected rehearsals and song sets, but once you're out *there*, it's "all the same fuckin' day," as Janis Joplin put it. And, according to Bob:

> *It's all the same tour—the Never Ending Tour—it works out better for me that way. You can pick and choose better when you're just out there all the time, and your show is already set up. You know, you just don't have to start up and end it. It's better just to keep it out there with breaks . . . extended breaks.*

Being part of the successful, chart-climbing, much-beloved Traveling Wilburys is one thing, but where is the new, long-awaited *Dylan* album? By 1989 it had been fifteen years since *Blood on the Tracks*, seven years since *Infidels*, and Dylan is praying for rain. He hears the Neville Brothers' voodoo-drenched *Yellow Moon* (on which they did a spooky version of "Ballad of Hollis Brown"), produced by Daniel Lanois, who had also produced U2's *The Joshua Tree* with Brian Eno in 1987. Bono introduces Bob to Lanois and the drought is over—the result is Dylan's great 1989 album, *Oh Mercy*. And where better to come back from the dead than the hoodoo capital of the world, New Orleans?

Using a mobile studio, Lanois creates a stage set, environments in which the songs can hatch. In order to get "that Louisiana swamp sound," he rents a house at 1305 Soniat Street in New Orleans. Dylan had built any number of houses out of songs since the beginning of his career—"House of the Risin' Sun" on his first album, the house that's not a home on *John Wesley Harding*—but now you had the odd situation of a producer creating a make-believe stage set for Dylan's hoodoo bash, furnishing it with stuffed animals and alligators and moss and generally turning it into a bordello-like environment, like the house of the risin' sun, in fact. Not a haunted house like you'd find at a fairground, but more like a séance of the blues and folk music—and rock 'n' roll. The originators, Little Richard and Fats Domino, had recorded here.

Now he was in a place where the spirits of New Orleans could be summoned up, a polyglot port—exotic sounds poured in from the Caribbean, along with scary magic. Hoodoo and voodoo stirring up a bitches brew of American music. Jazz, that imp of rhythm, was born here.

Okay, not that much actual hoodoo got stirred into the gumbo. Maybe "Man in the Long Black Coat," his spooky tribute to Johnny Cash. But there is the Reverend Bob sermonizing on the "Political World," "Disease of Conceit," and "Ring Them Bells." The denunciations are pretty generic, but Dylan's croaky swamp voice rusts up these incantations and gives them a jagged edge. I'm not sure I know who this preacherman character is, but never mind—whatever juju spirits got summoned up in that old Victorian house, lucky for us they stirred up the ferocious old memory, regret, and recrimination juices in Bob. "Everything Is Broken" is the true protest song on the album in which he catalogs with great relish everything that's busted—broken strings and broken springs, broken bones and broken phones—everything, that is, except for the underlying malaise.

But no one was calling up unclean spirits—no one was rattling bones or shaking sacks of gris-gris—it was essentially Halloween decorations with appliances in the kitchen, as Daniel Lanois told Michael Simmons: "It was a living-room environment, so we were able to focus on Bob's vocal. . . . We made a record next to the coffee machine. [laughs] It was not a very illustrious setting. Walk in the door, have a seat, there's the coffee machine. When he wasn't recording Bob'd go over to the coffee machine, have a cigarette, touch up some of the lyrics, and that was pretty much it."

The songs on Oh Mercy are somber, ruminating, nostalgic. Dylan was forty-eight years old, his personal life was desolate and empty. The wistful "Shooting Star" where the last fire truck from hell ominously pulls out midverse, the self-questioning "What Good Am I?" the poignant mock-bravado of "Most of the Time," with its soul-eating fiction of "I don't even think about her" (keep telling yourself that). "Where Teardrops Fall" comes on the jukebox—it's two a.m. in the Patsy Cline I-Fall-to-Pieces Saloon when guys start writing notes to their exes on soggy cocktail napkins. Of course it's maudlin—that's the genre he's writing in, it's cryin'-in-your-whiskey time. Nobody can talk to themselves as if talking to someone else better than Dylan—and the third person he's talking to is us, in the sullen, corroding kiss-off of "What Was It You Wanted." He's talking to us again in that old confrontational get-lost mode. He cares!

In his characteristically perverse manner he left off two of the three mysterious and intimate Dylan songs dredged out of his subterranean vault: "Dignity" and "Series of Dreams." They were visitations, he said, the kind of songs that appear in the dark of night when you just want to go back to sleep.

As he toured, Dylan's obsession with privacy was making him moody and paranoid and turning him into a nasty drunk. "He was . . . sort of sneaking around, sneaking up the back stairways of places," as Kenny Aaronson, his bass player at the end of the '80s, described him. His old-school fans still regarded him with guarded awe but subsequent generations were less impressed with this increasingly grouchy, sour old guy. On the May 1989 European tour, with the hood of his sweatshirt pulled over his head, you couldn't even see him.

His indifference to his fans had reached a level of absolute contempt.

"What are they looking for, listening for?" he asked irritably. He meant his audience. His die-hard fans had become "they," an amorphous mob wanting things from him he could no longer deliver.

Ronnie Hawkins caught Dylan's set on June 6, 1990, at the O'Keefe Center in Toronto and was startled by what he saw. Dylan started playing "One More Night" from *Nashville Skyline*, and kicked off the song in the wrong key. "I knew then that we had a monkey act," Hawkins said. "The guitar player showed him what key to go to. But meanwhile Bob was too loud to hear him." Backstage he saw a worn-out Dylan partying hard at an age when he should have known better—and this from a famous old wild man of the past.

Disheveled, wearing the same clothes he slept in, Bob looks like an unmade bed. Backstage he's invisible, and his eccentricities become more and more florid. In 1991, rootless, playing small theaters, small towns, staying in Howard Johnsons and off-ramp motels, he becomes Interstate Bob. He stays in his room—broody, cranky, depressed, and frequently irritated with members of his bands.

He begins wearing that monk-like hoodie adopted from his trainer, Bruce "the Mouse" Strauss. "Mouse could walk on his hands across a football field," Dylan told *Rolling Stone*. "He taught me the pugilistic rudiments back a while ago, maybe 20 or 30 years."

"On one of the early Never Ending Tour shows," Bob Hudson recalls, "the friend I was with nudged me and said, 'Hey, what's going on there?' He was pointing to someone in the shadows in the theater's wings standing on his hands! Whoever it was, was on his hands for quite a while. We watched, sort of mystified. When the man got off his hands, we realized it was Dylan. He stretched, shook himself out, and walked onto the stage. Did Dylan learn the handstand thing from Strauss? At the time we figured it was probably a Yoga move, getting the blood to his head sort of thing. Or perhaps he was drunk or stoned and trying to clear his head."

Onstage Dylan's backlit, and you can't see his face. Sullen, looking like the Invisible Man in his hooded sweatshirt and shades, he talks derisively about his performances. He's become just a freak show people come to see, the man who was famous long ago. All those critics, mutterers, and whiners complain that his shows are shoddy, and that he's drunk most of the time, out of control, and a lousy lead electric guitar player to boot. All that's irrelevant, he says. It doesn't matter what he does. He snarls, "You could hammer a nail in a piece of wood or fry an egg. It doesn't matter what you do up there. They've come to see you. For anyone else to be disappointed in this or that I do, I don't pay much attention to that."

His shows are now more often than not described as train wrecks. He's unhappy. He can't find a role, doesn't have a life, and his records don't stick. He's lying on a Naugahyde couch drinking red wine or brandy straight out of the bottle. Wearing a garish Latin shirt and a greasy leather jacket, he's haunted, like Robert Johnson riding that Greyhound bus to hell.

These disastrous performances continue on until February 1991, when Allan Jones, a stone Dylan fan, writes this hair-raising account of Dylan goin' down slow at the Scottish Exhibition and Conference Centre:

> Dylan now resembles nothing so much as an alcoholic lumberjack on a Saturday night out in some Saskatchewan backwater, staggering around the stage here in a huge plaid jacket and odd little hat. The band, meanwhile, have all the charisma of a death squad in some bandit republic. . . . These people aren't so much under-rehearsed as almost complete strangers to each other, and Dylan's music specifically. Dylan, hilariously, doesn't give a fuck. . . . [Guitar player Caesar Diaz] starts strumming the intro to "Mr. Tambourine Man." After a couple of minutes he pauses, waiting for Dylan's vocal entry. He turns to look for Dylan, but Bob's not at his microphone. He's somewhere at the back of the stage wrestling with his harmonica holder which has come loose and now appears to be attempting to strangle him. . . . [Diaz] looks vaguely panic-stricken, still waiting for Dylan. But Dylan doesn't seem to be in any hurry to bail him out.

Then there's Worst Concert Ever—how many rock stars can lay claim to that title? It's at the Liederhalle in Stuttgart, on June 16, 1991. He mumbles through an eight-minute version of "New Morning" barely able to remember even two lines of the song.

The legendary "Bob Dylan" had unavoidably become a cliché repeated in introductions and newspaper articles, an entity over which he had lost control. It's as if he'd given birth to a medium-size city and its inhabitants now pursued him relentlessly. His curious dilemma was that "Bob Dylan" was both the monster he had created and himself.

David Was, who produced *Under the Red Sky* with his brother Don, described the terrible cost of carting this version of himself around all these years: "There was a weariness about him . . . he looked absolutely beleaguered, doing this stuff. It occurred to me that it was a continuous burden having to be 'Bob Dylan' after all these years."

In the fall of 1991 Dylan has another epiphany, one that that turns him from mean-spirited drunk with disdain for his audiences and indifference to his backup bands into an enthusiastic evangelist of his own crusade. He sees the light and begins taking his quest in earnest: "If you are going to be a performer you have got to give it your all."

"It was important for me," Dylan said, "to come to the bottom of this legend thing, which has no reality at all. What's important isn't the legend, but the art, the work. A person has to do whatever they're called on to do."

Bob Hudson feels that at this point Dylan had found a new model for his onstage persona: "When Dylan did his duet with Ralph Stanley—and then started wearing the big cowboy hats on stage, something clicked in my head and said, 'Bill Monroe!' I wondered if Dylan wasn't trying to emulate the older Monroe throughout the 1990s—doing continual shows, creating a 'grand old man' sort of image, encouraging younger talent. Dylan even *looked* like the older Monroe on stage at times—the suits, the erect posture, the slow movements. In a sense, they were two of only a handful of American musicians who invented entire styles of music (Louis Armstrong being another). Consider this quote by Dylan in his 1987 interview with Kurt Loder in *Rolling Stone*: 'I'd still rather listen to Bill and Charlie Monroe than any current record. That's what America's all about to me. I mean, they don't have to make any more new records— there's enough old ones, you know? I went in a record store a couple of weeks ago—I wouldn't know what to buy. There's so many kinds of records out.'"

BILL MONROE MAY HAVE SERVED AS A BEACON OF LIGHT AND A ROLE model, but Dylan's misery during his years in the wilderness continued to be aggravated by his own demons and disenchantment from his outraged fans. Worse yet, these negative perceptions of him were then perpetuated by the press. Not only does the media reduce everything to clichés, but in Dylan's case, they've often helped turn the tide against him. After all, no entertainer since Brando had so skillfully manipulated the press, had toyed with them and taunted them so remorselessly. A whiff of faltering, and they pounced. *Eat the Document, Self Portrait, Tarantula,* and *Renaldo and Clara* were all suitably flawed creations and available for mauling. They mocked his Christian conversion as the rantings of a deluded monomaniac and dismissed the gospel tours and the three Christian albums out of hand. He didn't play any of his old songs from 1979 to 1980, which made them (and quite a few of his audiences) mad. The critics didn't like *Street Legal,* hated *Slow Train Coming* (and the two subsequent gospel albums). They weren't all that kind to *Infidels* either, and it just got worse from there.

The toppling of idols has always been a popular sport, though. Boccaccio's *De Casibus Virorum Illustrium (On the Fall of Famous Men)* was a best-seller in the Renaissance. *People* magazine weekly gloats or sheds crocodile tears over the shameful or tragic fates of fallen stars. That's the price of admission. You can't just be a celebrity; you need to have something terrible happen to you. In the 1980s the gossip mills increased exponentially along with the public's celebrity obsession. By this point Dylan had become a pathetic and humorous caricature. When things went bad, people had nothing really to zero in on but his florid, though always entertaining, eccentricities.

Along with his eccentricities, people began to focus on the way he behaved toward those around him, which wasn't always pretty. His ruthless way of dismissing people like Kenny Aaronson and other members of his band was chilling, and his treatment of his road manager, Gary Shafner, was even worse. While Shafner was away dealing with a family matter, Dylan just took his girlfriend, Britta Lee Shain. He barely communicated with his backup band members and traveled on his own bus. He was a phantom wandering the streets, looking like a bum.

Furtive and suspicious, Dylan lived like a fugitive and shrouded his voice under muddy soundtracks or gospel choruses. He felt besieged and for much of the '80s surrounded himself onstage (and offstage, frequently) with "the hive," the black backup singers he called the Queens of Rhythm: Regina McCrary, Carolyn Dennis and her mother, Madelyn Québec, and a former Raelette, Clydie King, one of many backup singers who had affairs with Dylan, often secretly. His relationship with them was complicated. They were his backup singers, his harem, his protectors, and, in the case of Carolyn Dennis, a second wife and mother of his child. They cocooned him onstage, and enveloped his voice in their collective harmonies on record. "I had the singers up there," he admitted, "so I wouldn't feel so bad."

Also, according to folksinger Maria Muldaur ("Midnight at the Oasis"), "I think he [dated] some of these black girls because they didn't idolize him. They were real down to earth and they didn't worship him. [They are] strong women who would just say, *cut off your bullshit!*"

Carolyn Dennis gave birth to Dylan's sixth child, Desiree Gabrielle Dennis-Dylan (Gabby), on January 31, 1986. *Under the Red Sky* was essentially written as a children's album for her. But Gabby's birth was a deep, dark secret, and four months later they were married. They bought a house in Tarzana at 530 Shirley Avenue. It was an anonymous area—which is not saying much for the outlaying areas of LA—and sounds like a line from a Tom Waits song where he buys a house in Tarzana so he can exhibit his bowling trophies. But, like Bob, it "didn't quite work out like I thought." Nobody out there knew they were living next door to the legendary Bob Dylan. In August 1990, Carolyn Dennis files for divorce. Apparently, a house is not a home. Bob was rarely there, often out philandering with her fellow backup singers and A&R ladies from the record companies.

Aside from Clydie King and Carole Childs, an A&R woman at Geffen, he was also dating Susan Ross, a onetime road manager. Bob, she says, was at the time a raging bitter alcoholic, and the road was his way of dealing with his rage. Then there are the Wicca women, mystical chicks with patchouli and tarot cards, and the occasional trapeze artist.

AS HE SLID FURTHER DOWN THE CHUTE HE WAS SUDDENLY GETTING all these honors. That's when you know it's over. At the Rock and Roll Hall of Fame in January 20, 1988, Dylan is inducted.

It's a $10,000-a-plate, black-tie dinner. Arlo Guthrie accepts an award for his father but says that he doesn't know where Woody would have been that night if he were still alive, "but I can guarantee you he wouldn't be here."

Bruce Springsteen gave the speech:

Bob freed the mind the way Elvis freed the body. He showed us that just because the music was innately physical did not mean that it was anti-intellectual. He had the vision and the talent to make a pop song that contained the whole world. He invented a new way a pop singer could sound, broke through the limitations of what a recording artist could achieve, and changed the face of rock 'n' roll forever.

Without Bob, the Beatles wouldn't have made *Sgt. Pepper*, the Beach Boys wouldn't have made *Pet Sounds*, the Sex Pistols wouldn't have made "God Save the Queen," U2 wouldn't have done "Pride in the Name of Love," Marvin Gaye wouldn't have done *What's Going On*, the Count Five would not have done "Psychotic Reaction," and Grandmaster Flash might not have done "The Message," and there would have never been a group named the Electric Prunes.

You can't blame Bob for the Electric Prunes. He never wrote "Vanilla Sky"–type lyrics; that's pastiche psychedelia, ersatz Bob. But how many times do you think people have used that line? "If there was a young guy out there writing the *Empire Burlesque* album . . . they'd be calling him the new Bob Dylan." I know that was an observation meant to make him feel better about a lousy album, but actually at this point—having been repeated over and over after every disappointing release—it must've felt to Bob like a rusty nail in his foot.

The accolades continue with a Lifetime Achievement Award at the Grammys on February 20, 1991. Dylan mumbles his way through a very strange speech about his father and defilement: "My daddy once said to me, he said, 'Son, it is possible for you to become so defiled in this world that your own mother and father will abandon you. If that happens, God will believe in your own ability to mend your own ways.'"

Then he sings, or rather grunts, "Masters of War." Dylan says Eisenhower's beware-the-military-industrial-complex farewell speech in 1961 had been the inspiration for this song. He also sang it to the cadets at West Point, marbling the words. And here the Gulf War was going on, another war supplied by warmongers and war profiteers in the White House itself, Halliburton.

He had the flu, he said. His head felt like the Grand Canyon, and he sounded like the Grand Coulee Dam singing. When he sang "Masters of War," it was so guttural that David Hinckley reported that "someone in the press room asked if Dylan were singing in Hebrew."

Is it that "Masters of War" has a curse attached to it? Joan Baez couldn't bring herself to sing the terrible verse that begins, "I hope that you die and your death will come soon," but without that it's just antiwar propaganda. The song is a maledict, a black wish on the heads of war perpetrators: McNamara, Kissinger, and Bush. The singer is the figure in a folktale who enters the great hall of the king and points a bony finger: it's Dylan delivering a biblical curse. It's appropriate that Dylan doesn't articulate the words. It's not a decree to be read aloud; it's a plague on both your houses. It's that point of pure rage when language merges with muttering, a howl so ferocious it becomes inarticulate. Words, obviously, have no meaning when you get this down, when the world is this messed up.

Dylan himself looked on the award-bestowing business askance, as if Blind Pew had put the black spot on him. At the time of the Lifetime Achievement Award, he told two female fans it was like going to your own funeral. Not that he disdained this kind of thing altogether. He'd acquired a sweet tooth for award ceremonies and liked being feted, receiving ribbons and medals. March 15, 1982, he had been inducted into the Songwriters Hall of Fame. In 1990 he was made an Ordre des Arts et des Lettres Commandeur by the French government.

On October 16, 1992, Dylan participates in a thirtieth anniversary celebration concert at Madison Square Garden. This kind of thing is unavoidable if you're Bob Dylan and it's thirty years since you cut your first record. That said, if you're gonna hold a wake in your own lifetime, you couldn't assemble a better group of people: John Mellencamp, Neil Young, the Band, the O'Jays, Emotionally Yours, Willie Nelson, and George Harrison appear, among others. Bob sings three songs alone, "It's Alright, Ma," "Girl from the North Country," and "Song to Woody," and two others backed up by guests, "My Back Pages" and "Knockin' on Heaven's Door," although you probably don't want everybody singing "Knockin' on Heaven's Door" at one of these "lifetime achievement" type of shows.

SALVETE, O ROBERTUS, NOBILIS MUSICUS! TIBI
CANTABIS ME, "BLOWIN' IN THE WIND"?

The Pope loves "Blowin' in the Wind" but
Bob, contrary as ever, refuses to sing it.
As he once asked Paul McCartney, when
asked to sing the dreaded song at the
Concert for Bangladesh, "Are you going
to sing 'I Wanna Hold Your Hand'?"

27   When I Paint My Masterpiece

ROM HIS MORE THAN FIVE HUNDRED SONGS TO HIS LINER notes, interviews, *Chronicles*, and heavily allegorical movies, Dylan is the most prolific writer of musical autobiographies of all time. But these are essentially works of fiction, and behind them there is a man who writes compelling tales about his character in a series of self-portraits that he then peevishly paints over. *That's* who we want to know about.

By 1997, Dylan's autobiography had become a tale from the crypt, and the new millennium Dylan is the story of a prolific ghost. In fact, his albums from this period—*Love and Theft, Modern Times, Together Through Life*, as well as 1997's *Time Out of Mind*—are all ghost stories. *Time Out of Mind*, in particular, is Bob rising up and singing to us from beyond the grave. He's telling us that it's over, but he's come back one more time to haunt us. We wouldn't give up on him when he went soft with country pop on *Nashville Skyline* or became the contented husband on *New Morning*—or when he put out an outrageous fib of an album called *Self Portrait*, a portrait basically of everyone *but* him. We didn't believe him when he said he'd died to this world and was born-again to Jesus. What else could he do? Just get into his tomb and blast off into space?

He decided to make one last trip to where he'd started out. It was the end. There wasn't going to be any future that Dylan could slink into; the only place left to go was the past. After a decade of trying this and trying that and failing to get into a contemporary groove he was at a dead end. "My influences have not changed—and any time they have done, the music goes off to a wrong place. That's why I recorded two LPs of old songs, so I could personally get back to the music that's true for me."

He needed to go back, jump into the Black Muddy River source. These songs weren't only the roots of his music; they possessed a kind of supernatural power and could transform life.

I find the religiosity and philosophy in the music. I don't find it anywhere else. Songs like "Let Me Rest on a Peaceful Mountain" or

"I Saw the Light"—that's my religion. I don't adhere to rabbis, preachers, evangelists. . . . I've learned more from the songs than I've learned from any of this kind of entity. The songs are my lexicon. I believe the songs.

Jeered at by his detractors, pursued by his demons, the spectral Dylan of the early '90s is beset by doubts. He delves back into the folk song hoard for his albums, mining it for memory and resonance. Folk songs are sacred texts in which you could divine the mythic past of America and its fate. Rock and pop had stripped lyrics of their archaic meanings by the '90s, but Dylan is still on a quest for redemption through his séances with folk music. On his folk redux albums, *Good As I Been to You* and *World Gone Wrong*, he goes back to the songs of his youth. Dock Boggs, Mississippi Sheiks. The vision of those songs. As he said to Michael Iachetta of the *New York Daily News* in 1963, "There's mystery, magic, truth, and the Bible in great folk music. I can't hope to touch that but I'm gonna try." The past is a source of glory, wisdom, divination. It's the result of his trip into the mythic past.

He was reconnecting with his roots, remembering who he was, and tapping into his original inspiration: this mythical rural America that seemed as old as the Old Testament itself. Just walking in the cool of the evening you could run into John Henry, Stackolee, or Ezekiel.

Everything—except for greed, industry, politics, advertising, the Pentagon, celebrity tabloids, etc.—was still there where he'd left it in 1964.

Susan Ross, his girlfriend at the time, has said that these albums were contract fillers—he owed Columbia a couple of albums—but even if they were, they created an ideal opportunity for Dylan to recharge his batteries by plugging into the direct current of Appalachian ballads and Mississippi Delta blues. He needed to touch his Book of Common Prayer: Harry Smith's *Anthology of American Folk Music*.

On these albums he sounds like the ghosts he's reviving, and, like the fortune-telling lady, he's taken all his things and gone inside to commune with these songs solo—just vocals and guitar. He cuts them in his garage studio from memory, without lyric sheets or prompts. The fuzzy tracks almost sound like they were recorded on wax cylinders. It's as if he'd transformed that space into a shotgun shack or room 414 in the Gunter Hotel in San Antonio where Robert Johnson cut his tracks for Brunswick Records.

Dylan goes acoustic doesn't quite have the ring that Dylan goes electric had in 1965, and it didn't shock anybody this time around. He's a pretty terrible electric lead guitar player anyway.

He inhabits these songs just the way he did on his first album, channeling the old blues and ballad guys, his croaky, muffled voice lending rusty authority to them. He wanted to *be* them. Wasn't he Mississippi John Hurt when he played his songs? Hadn't that been his method since his first album where he impersonates Woody and the Reverend Gary Davis? It's as if he's become them and then, to prove it, he copyrights their songs in his own name—which got quite a few people riled up. "Why has the rich old has-been copyrighted every damn track as traditional arranged by Dylan?" Ian Anderson fumed in *Folk Roots* magazine.

He immersed himself in the swarming Elizabethan world of the folk hoard:

> *When my songwriting started, all that [music] was kind of left to one side. . . . But it was necessary for me to get back to the stuff that meant so much to me at one time. These people who originated this music, they're all Shakespeares, you know? . . . There was a bunch of us, me included, who got to see all these people close up, people like Son House, Reverend Gary Davis, or Sleepy John Estes. . . . Those vibes will carry into you forever, really, so it's like those people, they're still here to me. They're not ghosts of the past or anything. They're continually here.*

His skill was to raise up the folk song arcana and let loose its loony, desperate cast and grisly tales. This is the longtime-gone America fantasized by middle-class Northern folkies out of folk balladry—the "Old, Weird America" of Greil Marcus. What we, and Dylan obviously, believe to be profound and mystical in these old songs, anthropologists (and such astute observers as Bob Hudson and Robert Christgau) hypothesize could simply be a case of faulty transmission. Ballads told over centuries—by ship and by land—contain lyrics that have been misheard, forgotten, or cobbled into a line that makes no sense but rhymes. When something rhymes, it confers its own quirky authenticity on an image no matter how odd it is. It forces words into a new otherworldly sense. And in any case misunderstanding is the source of all art: seeing things askew that make sense aesthetically—and create their own worlds.

Not that there isn't profundity in the old ballads as in the sixteenth-century "Nottamun Town" on which Dylan based the tune of "Masters of War":

Not a soul would look up, not a soul would look down. . . .
Come a stark-naked drummer a-beating a drum. . . .
Ten thousand stood round me, yet I was alone. . . .
Ten thousand got drownded that never was born.

Dylan's raging idiosyncratic liner notes to *World Gone Wrong* are by themselves worth the price of admission, with their paranoid word associations and rants: "Before, the Celestial grunge, before the Insane world of entertainment, exploded in our faces, before all the ancient and honorable. . . ."

Old bluesmen and Appalachian hillbillies inhabited Bob's brain, and so did the fantastic archive of old ballads he'd been accumulating since childhood. Everything went in and it was all sacred, even the ookee-dookee Brill Building ditties.

Good As I Been and *World Gone Wrong* got good reviews in *Rolling Stone* and *Newsday* and in much of the press, which was a good thing because they appeared during Dylan's second great song drought, from 1989 to 1997. As he described it:

There was a time when the songs would come three or four at the same time, but those days are long gone. . . . Once in a while, the odd song will come to me like a bulldog at the garden gate and demand to be written. But most of them are rejected out of my mind right away. You get caught up in wondering if anyone really needs to hear it. Maybe a person gets to the point where they have written enough songs. Let someone else write them.

ON AND ON THE TOURS WENT, EACH WITH ITS OWN TITLE AND "ITS own character & design," says Dylan. There is the Never Ending Tour (May '88 to '91 when guitarist G. E. Smith left), the Money Never Runs Out Tour (fall '91), Southern Sympathizer Tour (early '92), Why Do You Look At Me So Strangely Tour (European '92), the One Sad Cry of Pity Tour (Australia and West Coast America '92), Principles of Action Tour (Mexico–South America '92), Outburst of Consciousness Tour ('92), Don't Let Your Deal Go Down Tour ('93), among many others.

And on and on Dylan goes, reawakening and mangling his old songs (it's up to you), and on and on went the cries of "We want the old Dylan!" But there wasn't going to be a Nostalgia Tour.

Godlike as he is, Dylan, like everybody else in the entertainment business, was subject to the three-year cycle of fame. In the '60s and on through the '70s, Dylan reinvented himself brilliantly, along with revolutionary new musical genres. But you can only reinvent yourself (and the music) when you're on the beam; then you can multiply yourself as often as you like. Otherwise it's just changing sets and costumes—and the outfits of the last three and half decades have left a lot to be desired: funny getups, top hats, plastic cowboy hats, gloves, hoodies, fake beards, and wigs.

"It's either your time or it isn't your time," he said, but that didn't stop him. One time or another he's wanted to be Elvis, Neil Diamond, Madonna, and Prince. He tried disco, swamp rock, alt-country; he played with the Sex Pistols, New Wavers, the Dead. He had a misguided wish to be contemporary that often bordered on desperation and made him look as foolish and grotesque as an old hooker on Seventh Avenue. You just can't teach an old dog like Bob new tricks.

And, to add to his woes, all his ups and downs were observed with raking scrutiny by fans, critics, and the press. He'd become the totem animal of his generation, the two-headed snake; the baby boomer's destiny is obscurely tied to him. Our ongoing obsession with Bob has created this thirty-odd years of lip-biting apprehension as we watched Dylan self-destruct and then sit up again like a magnetic pharaoh popping up out of a magic store coffin. His continual denying of it only further fueled our belief that he was our only authentic voice.

After being awarded the Kennedy Center Honors in December 1997, he's at a ceremony at the White House with Bill Clinton. Bob stands there in his thick Boston strangler gloves with an uncomfortable expression, and the president of the United States is about to give a little speech before conferring the award. Dylan, patiently waiting for the inevitable platitude, thinks, "Oh, no, he's not going to say *that*, is he?"

And out Bill comes with the tombstone tag: the man who "probably had more impact on people of my generation than any other artist." At least he didn't say "voice of his generation." That line and "Blowin' in the Wind" will follow Dylan to his grave. The fate of all celebrities after their initial flash is to become curators of their past. Being buried alive in Bob is something Dylan has shunned like the plague, but roughly since 1983 he's been confused as to what exactly to do with his totemic image.

Always frail, almost ethereal, by 1997, he now looks pale and ill, as if the slightest thing could knock him down. The cynical frequently put him on the rock star death watch—along with Eric Clapton and Keith Richards—but it's a shock when Dylan falls ill on May 25, the day after he turns fifty-six. Dire headlines began to appear: DYLAN COULD BE IN THE FIGHT FOR LIFE! A fungal infection called histoplasmosis, which affected the fibrous sac around his heart, was found. BOB DYLAN HEART MYSTERY, proclaimed the cover of the *New York Post*. Inside were two pages showing the various Dylans, from his beginnings as the chubby-faced folksinger to the scary-looking Dylan of the late '90s. It must have been eerie reading his own obituaries. In June, he says, "I'm just glad to be feeling better. I really thought I'd be seeing Elvis soon." And then, five years later, Dylan has an Elvis sighting in a diner out West.

The telltale sign that Dylan had left the planet came with the release of *Time Out of Mind* in September 1997. How could he have made an album that so uncannily anticipated his own near-death experience that same year? Even the disease itself—histoplasmosis—was so exotic and rare it was as if Dylan had caught it on one of his forays into the past. It was a mysterious disease that had to do with bird droppings, bayou swamps, and airborne spores—the kind of archaic illness old blues guys died of. He might as well have caught it hanging out in a rickety old one-room shack in Lula, Mississippi, with Son House. However, according to Dylan, he'd got it riding on a motorbike from something blowing in the wind.

For years people had been saying uncharitable things about his long and dwindling career. If only he'd have died from that motorcycle accident in 1966, or even as late as 1978, his brilliant creations would have been unsullied by his later fumblings. Like Jimi, Janis, and others, he would have died a true saint and we wouldn't have had to deal with his subsequent messy, confusing final decades. America is not kind to stars who outlive their welcome.

But suddenly there is a chance he might not pull through, and we see the error of our ways. Here we were living in the same world as one of the great geniuses of our age—as if Shakespeare had been alive in our time and we'd ignored him, crossed him off. All the papers and the TV stations begin summing up his career: what he'd done, what he meant to his generation, what other famous people had to say about him.

He recovers, though, and the world showers him with more honors. *Time*, his old nemesis, calls him "one of the most important figures of the 20th century." He's nominated for a Nobel Prize in Literature. The eminent scholar Christopher Ricks compares "Visions of Johanna" to *The Waste Land*. Then there are the more commercial accolades—Sheryl Crow, Billy Joel, and Garth Brooks cover his songs. He gets himself on the cover of *Newsweek*: DYLAN LIVES!

Time Out of Mind gets rave reviews. Journalists and critics reach for their Dylan redux files, with adjectives reserved for the anticipated return of the real Dylan in place of the usurper who parades up and down the land in his name. He's "allegorical," "mystical," his "old intensity renewed." Exclamation marks and italics—that had all been kept handy for the inevitable comeback—pepper reviews proclaiming that he's "back in top form." It is the return of Dylan, but what's really scary is that it's not clear who that is at this point. "It is a spooky record," he tells *Newsweek*, "because I feel spooky. I don't feel in touch with anything."

Time Out of Mind is a work of relentless morbidity, dwelling almost ghoulishly on mortality and death. It's a terrifying psychic landscape, a world where everything has vanished and things are closing in; he's in some desolate space, "a place worse than anyone could have guessed," Nick Hasted wrote in the *Independent*, "made by a man in limbo." Consumed by regret and resentment, spectral lovers haunt him. "Not Dark Yet" is a profound and disturbing meditation, and "Tryin' to Get to Heaven" sounds as if John Donne had picked up a solid-body guitar.

With *Time Out of Mind* he began to work in a patchwork manner, grabbing traditional lines and mixing them with his own idiosyncratic images, magpie lyrics from the Harry Smith anthology, and old songs. The multiphrenic imagery on *Blonde on Blonde* he'd just sucked out of the air. Now he was a kind of gleaner with his cloth sack wandering the cotton fields and hollows picking up a ballad phrase from here, a blues line from there. That's the way traditional music was composed as were epics like *The Odyssey* that use stock lines and phrases. He uses a Charley Patton riff on "Highlands" and borrows the "my heart is in the Highlands" bit from Rabbie Burns, who got it from some itinerant peddler.

Daniel Lanois had produced Dylan's successful 1989 album, *Oh Mercy*, and he again worked with him on *Time Out of Mind*. The idea was to try to create the sound Dylan heard on the old King Records before digital recording. They did everything they could to re-create that old sound, including using twenty-four-track analog tape and ribbon mikes to get the feel of the old blues records, an acoustic depth of field that producers had managed to bottle on mono records. But then when you played it, it didn't exactly sound like an old Cowboy Copas or Hawkshaw Hawkins record. A layer of indelible acoustic varnish had been laid over the whole album. It had somehow been Daniel Lanois–ized. And, despite their otherwise glowing reviews, some reviewers felt that the album was the "most artificial sounding album" in his career.

Still, Dylan won three Grammys that year: Best Contemporary Folk Album, Best Male Rock Vocalist, and Album of the Year. At the ceremony on February 25, 1998, after nervously fidgeting during the speeches, fiddling with his gloves—what is it with those gloves?—and pulling his hat on and off, he gave a strange and moving speech about how a glance from Buddy Holly had anointed him:

> I just want to say, one time when I was about sixteen or seventeen years old I went to see Buddy Holly play at the Duluth National Guard Armory. . . . I was three feet away from him . . . and he looked at me.

Dylan's sense of apostolic succession was intense. It was as if the singers in the 1950s had heard Ezekiel or Isaiah, as if they could still call on that Angeltown sound, the Pentecostal fire of rock 'n' roll:

> Singers in the fifties and sixties were [still] just one step removed from the early ones, and you could hear that. But you can't hear it anymore, it's so polluted and unclean we're on the other side. . . . Even World Gone Wrong is a step or two removed. People should go to those old records and find out what the real thing is, because mine is still second generation.

ON SEPTEMBER 27, 1998, DYLAN PLAYED FOR POPE JOHN PAUL II—A former actor and playwright whom Bono once called "the first funky pontiff"—in Bologna, Italy, while hundreds of thousands of Italians watched, both live and on TV. According to Nigel Williamson, he wore "an embroidered suit that made him look like a riverboat gambler," and opened with "Knockin' on Heaven's Door." It was a bit of a literal choice, maybe, but appropriate. That's as close as you're going to get, anyway. Dylan's singing lulled the old man, which led to the famous picture of the pope dozing off during the performance.

Dylan tried to get away with sticking to "Hard Rain's A-Gonna Fall" and "Forever Young," but that darned "Blowin' in the Wind" was determined to follow him wherever he went (including, probably, the first paragraph of his eventual obituary). Still, he wouldn't sing it and the pope was a little disappointed. He'd written a whole homily around it.

"You say the answer is blowing in the wind, my friend," said His Holiness, "and so it is. But it is not the wind that blows things away. It is the wind that is the breath and life of the Holy Spirit. . . . You ask me how many roads must a man walk down before he becomes a man. I answer: there is only one road for man and it is the road of Jesus Christ." Jesus, Bob must have thought, the pope's turned into another Dylanologist.

Apparently there was a bit of a brouhaha before Dylan's appearance. According to the *Times* of London, the pope's chief aide, the former cardinal Joseph Ratzinger (now Pope Benedict XVI), was "so appalled at the prospect of the pontiff sharing a platform with the 'self-styled prophet of pop' that he tried his utmost to stop the spectacle."

According to Benedict, he "doubts to this day whether it was right to let this kind of so-called prophet take the stage in front of the Pope." He thinks that rock music is the work of Satan. Forget Dylan, the pope has even ordered guitars banned from all masses. We always *hoped* rock music was dangerous, but who knew the guitar itself could threaten to overthrow Christianity?

IN THE 2000S DYLAN ENTERED HIS AFTERLIFE. FOLLOWING THE NEAR-fatal illness he had become untouchable and had already done everything he possibly wanted to do. He didn't even need to read his obituaries; he'd already done that. What he became interested in, instead, was what history was going to say about him, and he stage-managed his entry with characteristic subtlety and guile. Like Andy Warhol he was granted a second life and he used it brilliantly.

The mock misanthropic "Things Have Changed," which he wrote in 2000 for the movie *Wonder Boys*, bridged the gap between *Time Out of Mind* and his next album, *Love and Theft*. Mixing gallows humor— "Standing on the gallows with my head in a *noooooose*"—with whimsy— "Gonna take dancing lessons, do the jitterbug"—the song seemed to say, "Now, about all that death and gloom stuff, I was only kidding. They were *songs*." It won him a Golden Globe and an Oscar, which he took on tour with him and displayed on his amp.

In 2001 (on 9/11), he released *Love and Theft*, his first album of original songs since 1997. Featuring a fantastic assortment of styles from blackface ("Po Boy") to vaudeville ("Floater") to rockabilly ("Summer Days"), the album proved, once again, that Dylan was a one-man repository of American song. Ladies and gentlemen, it's the Bob Dylan Revue of Melody—Two Hundred Years of American Popular Music on One CD!

"One thing about his brain," Eric Andersen says, "he's a serious music maven. I always joke, if the CIA ever had to debrief anybody, and get a whole lot of stuff on Americana, folk music, I think Bob would be the guy to do it. Put him in room for like three years and let him cough up everything he knows. He's like an encyclopedia!"

Now he really was the "song and dance man," the minstrel boy he'd claimed to be in the 1966 press conference in San Francisco. But this aging Dylan—the one with a straw hat and cane doing the hoofer shuffle with that nutmeg grinder of a voice—was also a bit spooky.

When you get to the last two tracks, "I Was Young When I Left Home" and an alternate version of "The Times They Are A-Changin'," you're in Gerde's Folk City back in 1964, and you suddenly realize, "Oh, yeah, this is *Bob Dylan*," and you remember why you're listening to this album in the first place.

In 2003, Dylan's third movie, *Masked and Anonymous*, came out. An allegorical tale about Jack Fate (Dylan) in a corrupt and fallen world, the low-budget movie was shot in three weeks for seven million dollars. It's the most professionally done of all the Dylan movies and made with a bunch of movie stars, including John Goodman, Val Kilmer, Bruce Dern, Jessica Lange, and Ed Harris. With all the inside jokes and self-referential allusions, you'll need a Dylanologist or a semiologist to really get every wink in this movie. But even if you don't get all the references, you can enjoy the hipster dialogue:

> CHEECH MARIN: Where you headed?
> DYLAN: That way.
> CHEECH: That's a good direction, it's one of my favorites.

These lines pretty much mimic the "code-talk" Rudy Wurlitzer wrote for *Two-Lane Blacktop*, in which Dennis Wilson and James Taylor swap similar Beatnik Beckett lines like:

"Here we are on the road."

"Yup, that's where we are all right."

Wurlitzer, of course, also wrote the screenplay for *Pat Garrett and Billy the Kid* with its cowboy hipster dialogue. After *Masked and Anony-*

mous came Dylan's memoir, *Chronicles*, in 2004. It's put together in the same intuitive manner Mark Twain wrote his memoirs: putting down what came to his mind as he remembered events and places without paying too much attention to chronology or coherence.

Composed as it is, *Chronicles* performs a mesmerizing feat. It puts you under the hum of his voice—like the drone of a plane on a summer afternoon, or a voice talking to you as you fall asleep in front of the fire. You are listening to the rhythm of his voice as if it's coming unfiltered from him into your head, but this is yet another Dylan illusion.

Eric Andersen, who has known him since the days they played together in the Village, says of *Chronicles*, "I thought he was kind of ingenuous. Everything was like, 'Wow, this guy is great,' and 'Man, I loved hanging out with that one.' This kind of posed innocence. He's a little more complicated than that. He's plainspoken; he's a regular type of Midwestern guy. I come from there too and I'm familiar with that direct-talking style. But he, of course, could spin surrealistic twists of images at will. Plainspoken stuff and then all of a sudden he'll go into phrases full of whirling dervishes. . . . I mean, he had a good drug connection in London; there's no question about that. A simple guy, on the one hand, but with a very complicated circuitry."

In 2005, the Martin Scorsese documentary *No Direction Home* was released, covering Dylan's life up to 1966. Although made by Scorsese, who never met Dylan during the making of the documentary, we sense it's carefully crafted and edited by Dylan himself. All the footage was selected by Dylan, the interviews were conducted by his manager, Jeff Rosen, and the contributors chosen with an eye to the story Dylan wanted to be told (such as the sacred booing at Newport).

Among many other things in *No Direction Home*, Dylan comes clean as he can about the name game. At home his parents used to call him by his first two given names, Robert Allen, and he initially thought about using this as his stage moniker, but it didn't have the right ring. Then he read a book of Dylan Thomas's poetry and—as he finally confirms after a bit of fiddling—out came his improbable Other, Bob Dylan, who would go on touring and touring, slipping in and out of characters who would all have the same name. Like the word shark that we know he is, if he ever stops swimming he'd die.

2011.4.4
2011年 第14期
www.lifeweek.com.cn

三联生活周刊

迪伦的现实与我们的梦想

答案依然在风中飘

He looks like a character who's just walked out of
an Edgar Allan Poe story, the villain from a silent
movie, a riverboat gambler. Who is this dude? It's
the most unexpected and spooky incarnation of
Dylan yet. Has this wily, wizened old coot—
straight out of American folklore—been there all
along, the enigmatic face behind Dylan's many
disguises? Cover of a Chinese magazine from
when he performed at the Worker's Stadium Arena
in Beijing in 2011.

28   The Enigma Variations

> **fan** contraction of fanatic (fa-nat'ik) [from Latin *fanum*,
> "temple," i.e., a priest or priestess of a cult] an insane
> person, mad, enthusiastic, inspired by a god, a zealot,
> characterized by excessive enthusiasm, especially in
> religion (c 17th applied to zealous religious Nonconform-
> ists in England). "A fanatic," Churchill said, "is someone
> who can't change his mind and won't change the subject."

DYLAN'S SYMBIOTIC RELATIONSHIP WITH HIS FANS IS THE most intense in all of rock; it's as if he has somehow insinuated himself into our brains. Day and night, entire albums are running subliminally in our heads. We can repeat lyrics line for line without even trying. It's those lyrics, those *words* that have carved a groove in our synapses. The mental jukebox is always playing: punch A17 and up comes "Subterranean Homesick Blues." Even in his most rational fans, Dylan's songs induce a kind of fugue state.

We are constantly on the lookout for information about him, and there's always the occasional sensational item in the paper. If you happened to live in Australia at the end of the last millennium, your eye might have caught an article in a tabloid while you were waiting in the check out line: I WAS BOB DYLAN'S SEX SLAVE! claims a fan. Now the truth comes out! We always suspected Dylan had a kinkier side.

Dylan apparently didn't remember the incident quite the same way she did—or their past life experience together. But this is a fairly common occurrence between Bob and his more ardent admirers. Really he's driven us all a little mad, even—especially—his most devoted biographers and exegetes.

Dylan's absence from the scene after his motorcycle accident induced a further sort of mania in his extreme fans, and he had good reason to be afraid. The fan represents the mob in miniature, a personification of the churning wells of desire, resentment, and envy. Then there's that scary point when your biggest fan turns on you.

In June 1981, a rabid twenty-eight-year-old fan named Carmel Hubbell appears at Rundown Studios where Dylan had been recording (he's not there at the time; he's on tour in Europe). She claims she's had an affair with Dylan. In fact, they're married; she's Mrs. Dylan. That they've never met is beside the point.

She's clearly unbalanced, but her obsessions with Bob could turn lethal. Dylan's songs have done something to her brain, given her a case of the Zimmerman syndrome, a cortex-eating, synapse-infesting sickness. She leaves notes addressed to "sweetheart" and "dear dreamboat," then abruptly turns into Ms. X, a.k.a. Ms. Manson: There are threats from the KKK, death devices planted around the studio. She brings up the name of David Chapman, John Lennon's murderer. Lennon's death on December 8, 1980, had unsettled Dylan and ramped up his paranoia.

Acknowledging this phenomenon, the Slovenian philosopher Slavoj Žižek has coined the term "subject supposed to enjoy" to refer to vicarious daydreams in which the mind insinuates itself into the presence of another. According to Žižek, a follower of a famous, admired individual fantasizes obsessively about their idol, becoming fixated on the star who is enjoying all the things they feel they lack. In Bob's case, it's him in his gold-domed palazzo in Point Dume or in a hotel suite with champagne, with the choicest foods, the most beautiful women, the finest clothes. Adulation, yes men, his every wish fulfilled. This inevitably provokes seething resentment: Who does he think he is?

Given the intensity of Dylan's fans, his security has a list of more than five hundred names of people to watch out for. Fans, let's face it, are out of control. They're in a state of hive arousal; it's a condition rock stars try their best to provoke in their audiences. But because they are in an unstable state, they are quite capable of irrational and malevolent behavior. There's the horrifying episode of Richard Dickinson in Hobart, Australia, in 1987. After Dickinson played *Desire* over and over all night long, his mom complained and the enraged Dickinson trampled her to death to the accompaniment of "One More Cup of Coffee."

But, of course, not *everyone* knows who Dylan is. You open up your morning paper—or news blog—and there he is! It's Hobo Bob, Dylan enjoying an afternoon stroll in the rain. He's pulled his hoodie up over his head and is standing on someone's lawn, possibly looking for the house where Bruce Springsteen wrote *Born to Run*. (Okay, he'd once gone to see John Lennon's house in disguise too, but that was on a bus tour.) A neighbor calls the police and he's picked up for vagrancy. Just when he needs it, no one knows who he is.

"I wasn't sure if he came from one of our hospitals or something," a certain Officer Buble told ABC News. "He was acting very suspicious. Not delusional, just suspicious."

Dylan fails to produce adequate ID and she doesn't recognize his name; he's invisible. Officer Buble orders him into the back of her police cruiser and, to check out his story, drives him to the hotel where he claims to be staying. It's only when she radios her senior colleagues back at the precinct that she realizes who she's picked up.

"She is 22 and unfortunately she had no idea who Bob Dylan was," police spokesman sergeant Craig Spencer later says. "He was on a walk-about but she wasn't entirely convinced of his innocence. She took him back to the hotel to check his papers, then she called us to check who Bob Dylan was. I'm afraid we all fell about laughing. If it was me, I'd have been demanding his autograph not his photo ID."

Then there's the occasional weird old man sightings:

KINDERGARTEN kids in ritzy L.A. suburb Calabasas have been coming home to their parents and talking about the "weird man" who keeps coming to their class to sing "scary" songs on his guitar. The "weird" one turns out to be Bob Dylan, whose grandson (Jakob Dylan's son) attends the school. He's been singing to the kindergarten class just for fun, but the kiddies have no idea they're being serenaded by a musical legend—to them, he's just Weird Guitar Guy.

But it's not just fans and frightened kindergarteners who are unhappy with Bob. In the *New York Times*, Maureen Dowd is complaining about Dylan performing in China in April 2011. She objects to the fact that Dylan didn't come right out and protest, either verbally or in his choice of songs. She wanted him to sing "Blowin' in the Wind" (as evasive a protest song as he's ever sung) and "The Times They Are A-Changin'" (an almost manufactured-for-the-occasion anthem) or write new lyrics to "Hurricane" to support the cause of detained Chinese dissident artist Ai Weiwei. Worse, she implied that the songs themselves had been censored by Chinese officials. Not only did this turn out not to be true, the songs he did sing were far more subversive: "Gonna Change My Way of

Thinking," "A Hard Rain's A-Gonna Fall," "Highway 61 Revisited," and "Ballad of a Thin Man."

I may still be stuck at *Blonde on Blonde,* but the usually astute Maureen Dowd apparently doesn't realize that Dylan hasn't been a protest singer for almost fifty years. What her objections really showed was which image of Dylan was going to stick down the road, regardless of what Dylan had done to shape his own legacy. Despite his brilliant mid-'60s albums—reverently referred to as the holy trinity—and half a century of inspired songwriting and endless performing, his indelible image would be that of protest singer, and "Blowin' in the Wind" the song he would be most remembered by.

SO WHO IS HE? WHICH ONE IS HE? HIS AMBIVALENCE, HIS MADDENING evasiveness is essential to maintaining the quicksilver life of his creature. He's like Schrödinger's cat—you don't really know what's going on inside the box—but it doesn't matter, because it's somehow connected to the way he works. His ambivalence, keeping everything in suspension, is part of his magic. He's become a phenomenon, an entity. Even he isn't quite sure who he is some of the time.

> *Sometimes the "you" in my songs is me talking to me. Other times I can be talking to somebody else. . . . It's up to you to figure out who's who. A lot of times it's "you" talking to "you." The "I," like in "I and I," also changes. It could be I or it could be the "I" who created me. And also, it could be another person who's saying "I." When I say "I" right now, I don't know who I'm talking about.*

To his ongoing dilemmas about his identities you have to add his occasional inability to distinguish between fantasy and reality, the most spectacular example being Dylan's injecting himself into a performance of Sam Shepard's *Geography of a Horse Dreamer.* At one point in the play a fat doctor is about to shoot up the protagonist with a hypodermic needle. Dylan, sitting in the back row, suddenly stands up. He's outraged, his sense of injustice has blurred the line between the stage and the audience. "Wait a minute!" he yells. "Wait a second! Why's he get the shot? He shouldn't get the shot! The other guy should get it! Give it to the other guy!" His companions manage to pull him back into his seat. But the end of the play with its shotguns and fake blood is all too much for

Bob. "I DON'T HAVE TO WATCH THIS!" he shouts. "I DIDN'T COME HERE TO WATCH THIS!"

"It's a perfect ending," Shepard writes in his *Logbook*. "An explosion in the audience to match the one on stage.... The play comes to an end and Dylan is hurtling over the aisles, looking for the exit. The critics don't know what to make of it. Have they missed something? Who was that masked man that just flew by them in a red coat and a gaucho hat, yelling at the top of his lungs? Is the play over already?"

Many of those curious as to who Dylan really is think, "What the hell, I'll just interview Bob and ask him." You have to be up for it, the business of interrogating Dylan, because it's one of the most infuriating, exasperating, self-deluding, pointless, and masochistic exercises in all of pop music. And with whatever wily ploy we plan to spring on him, he's going to be as slippery as an eel, a Talmudic twister, a syntactical snake. Besides, he's the Jack of Diamonds, he holds all the cards, and he's been turning the tables at this game for fifty years now. We know what we're up against.

Jonathan Cott, the most metaphysical interrogator of the Bard of Bleecker Street, in his 1978 *Rolling Stone* interview focused on the film *Renaldo and Clara*, a movie that Dylan claimed would reveal all, allegorically speaking. We know we're in for a bumpy ride when, at one point in the interview, Dylan tells him "it's about naked alienation of the inner self against the outer self-alienation taken to the extreme." Undaunted, Jonathan delves into the mystery: "Who is Bob Dylan?" he asks. "Who is Renaldo?" and "What is the relationship between them?" Here's Cott going mano a mano with Dylan:

> "There's Renaldo," says Dylan. "There's a guy in whiteface singing on the stage and then there's Ronnie Hawkins playing Bob Dylan. Bob Dylan is listed in the credits as playing Renaldo, yet Ronnie Hawkins is listed as playing Bob Dylan."
>
> "So Bob Dylan," I surmise, "may or may not be in the film."
>
> "Exactly."
>
> "But Bob Dylan made the film."
>
> "Bob Dylan didn't make it. I made it."
>
> "'I is another,' wrote Arthur Rimbaud."
>
> "Yeah, way back then, I was thinking of this film. I've had this picture in mind for a long time—years and years. Too many years... Renaldo is oppressed. He's oppressed because he's born. We don't

really know who Renaldo is. We just know what he isn't. He isn't the Masked Tortilla. Renaldo is the one with the hat, but he's not wearing a hat. I'll tell you what this movie is: it's like life exactly, but not an imitation of it. It transcends life, and it's not like life."

And at that point your brain is beginning to curdle. It's the Bob Dylan Möbius strip that you will be rolling around in for all eternity. You're up against the begrudging, defensive, squirmy-making, bloody-minded Bob who'll stop you in your tracks. After all, hipsters don't answer direct questions. Well, at least he makes interviews fun, a game of conundrums, puns, and double takes perfected by Groucho Marx. He turns direct questions on their heads, a manner taken to a stylish high finish by the Beatles, notably John and Ringo. But that was playful, a put-on. With Dylan, it's who he is.

Besides, it's the American way. Abe Lincoln did it. Muddy Waters did it. Elvis did it. Even Walt Whitman—who you'd swear was always that guy in the beard and rumpled felt hat who said, just like Bob might have, "Do I contradict myself? Very well then I contradict myself"—wasn't, according to Borges, any more Walt than Bob is Bob:

> He came up with a strange creature we have not yet fully understood, and he gave this creature the name Walt Whitman. The creature has a biform nature; it is the modest journalist Walter Whitman, a native of Long Island, whom some bustling friend might greet on the sidewalks of Manhattan, and it is, at the same time, the other man that Walt Whitman wanted to be and was not, a man of loves and adventures, the loafing, spirited, carefree traveler across America. Thus, on one page of the work, Whitman is born on Long Island; on others, in the South. Thus, in one of the most authentic sections of "Song of Myself," he relates a heroic episode of the Mexican War and says he heard the story told in Texas, a place he never went. Thus, he declares that he witnessed the execution of the abolitionist John Brown. The examples could be multiplied dizzyingly; there is almost no page on which the Whitman of his mere biography is not conflated with the Whitman he yearned to be and that, today, he is in the imagination and affections of the generations of humanity.

With Dylan the put-on, the pose, was a convenient way of dealing with the messy issues of personality and identity; just adopt a persona, and if the literal minded insisted he stick to whatever identity he'd assumed for his most recent album, too bad, they didn't get the joke. They weren't meant to.

Dylan's ambition—like that of all other possessed egomaniacs—Sinatra, Bogart, Einstein, Picasso—was to implant an indelible image of himself in our heads. This he did only too spectacularly. A hologram of Bob Dylan—that hair, the shades, that affectless hipster cool—came spontaneously to life as soon as the needle touched the vinyl, the laser scans the polycarbonite.

"HOW MANY ROLES CAN I PLAY?" DYLAN ASKED ON THE LINER NOTES TO Biograph. "Fools, they limit me to their own unimaginative mentality."

All Dylan's songs are scenes from the life of his character, a series of novels—romans-fleuves—linked together with psychic goo, the way some logorrheic maniac like Balzac might have done. Dylan is the protagonist among an ongoing and increasingly unlikely cast of characters. No wonder we can't figure him out. He's the most profuse ghost of all time.

His Theme Time Radio Hour was the perfect solution to Dylan's paradoxical desire to be both present and invisible at the same time. He's the disembodied voice, the carrier of the entire cargo of American music, bringing back the life of the obscure songs and singers (even if his producer, Eddie G., actually collects them). The ghost voice over the airwaves, a supernatural geography of sound, where everywhere is here, and time is suspended. Covering just about every darn thing under the sun that exists or existed in these United States (and anywhere else, for that matter): coffee, jail, fathers, wedding, divorce, summer, Lefty Frizzell, Blue Hawaii, flowers, people with "Little" in their names, cars, Cool Hand Luke, Prince Buster, the Devil, eyes, dogs, Casablanca, St. Basil, friends and neighbors, People Who Were Cheerleaders (Ann-Margret, George W. Bush), Pee-wee's Big Adventure, radio, the Bible, electric chairs, Charles Bukowski, musical maps, school, the telephone, water, time, Gertrude Stein, guns, sleep, food, Taxi Driver, Thanksgiving leftovers, People Who Died Playing Cards (Wild Bill Hickok, Buster Keaton, Arnold Rothstein), Memphis Minnie, Tennessee, the moon, Snow White, Dylan Thomas, Etta James, women's names, hair, luck, tears, shoes, Texas, trains, Ernest Tubb, spring cleaning, dreams, Lou Reed, the weather, Mother, drinking, Porter Wagoner, days of the week, Cervantes, and baseball—not to mention recipes for making mint juleps and figgy puddings.

Red Grooms was Suze Rotolo's favorite painter, a witty, everything-but-the-kitchen-sink (and that, too) amalgamator of the funky flotsam and jetsam of New York. In *Chronicles*, Dylan described that what appealed to him about Grooms was the ragpicker, beachcomber omnium-gatherum of his paintings, which contained: "old tennis shoes, vending machines, alligators that crawled through sewers, dueling pistols, the Staten Island Ferry and Trinity Church . . . rodeo queens and Mickey Mouse heads, castle turrets and Mrs. O'Leary's cows, creeps and greasers and weirdoes and grinning, bejeweled nude models, faces with melancholy looks, blurs of sorrow . . . figures from history, too—Lincoln, Hugo, Baudelaire, Rembrandt—all done with graphic finesse, burned out as powerful as possible. . . . I loved the way Grooms used laughter as a diabolical weapon. Subconsciously, I was wondering if it was possible to write songs like that." What's interesting about this is not just the epic, almost Homeric lists of stuff, people, books, detritus, and high art, but that his description, it turns out, is itself a collage of reviews about Grooms's paintings—as well as Dylan's own insights—so that Dylan's appreciation is a hodgepodge that mirrors Grooms's art and his own appropriation of that beautiful junkyard into his own songs.

Possessing a maddening capacity for overturning expectations, Dylan has always been the quintessential unreliable narrator of his own life. His predicament was that he had become so identified with the character in his songs he became a walking, talking projection of his own vinyl tales. It's as though Shakespeare had changed his name to Hamlet, dressed in the height of Elizabethan finery—tights, doublet, and poncey hat—and everybody thought that the play he'd written about the prince of Denmark was straight autobiographical stuff (except for the end part). And everywhere he went—the pub, bearbaiting, the nunnery—people would expect him to be broody and gloomy and deliver soul-raking soliloquies, and ask him rude questions about his mum and his uncle and all that. That's pretty close to the situation that Dylan found himself in. And that's what's made him so slippery. "Dylan is definitely an escape artist," Sam Shepard says. "I've never seen the like of it. He vanishes. Just like that." Practically everything about Dylan is paradoxical, if not actually oxymoronic.

His old mentor Dave Van Ronk saw him as someone he conjured up at will—to suit whatever occasion arose—or simply his own willful and devious imagination:

And you could never pin him down on anything. He had a lot of stories about who he was and where he came from, and he never seemed to be able to keep them straight. I think that's one reason Bobby never gave good interviews: his thinking is so convoluted that he simply does not know how to level, because he's always thinking of the effect that he's having on whoever he is talking to.

Like Bob Dylan, the authentic American genius is a synthetic personality. They're all hybrids, hence, inevitably, charlatans. It's the chameleon nature of the American hero—the confidence man, the hustler. His solution to the question of identity is that of the three-card monte player. Anyone looking for the Grand Unifying Theory of Bob is just going to have to keep looking.

Instead, Dylan has become his photographs, and the ones most frequently reproduced—on book covers, album reissues, songbooks—are of the mid-'60s Dylan in shades with that aureole of hair. He's embedded an image in our minds, an autobiographical form of identification so intense that we took it very personally when he abruptly abandoned the high '60s model Dylan. It was an outrage, really.

You've seen the pictures of him recently; it's a disheartening experience. "That can't be him!" we think. Is it because we see our own youth and optimism drained out of that face? His expression used to be that of a perpetually pained Prince Hamlet, contemplating the existential void. His mystique grew, while the person seemed to wither. Now oddly distended, his face seems to express some consuming bitterness. Is it a kind of curse he's brought on himself? Is fame itself a form of revenge that, in the end, eats its victims alive? With that kinky, pencil-thin mustache, he resembles Vincent Price in *The House of Usher*, a doomed aristocrat who has fallen under an ancient curse—in Dylan's case, the weight of fifty years of unreasonable expectations.

THE NEVER ENDING TOUR WAS DYLAN'S SOLUTION TO HIS CRITICAL problem at the end of the '80s. In the same way that Kerouac in 1948 had come to the end of the continent, by 1988 Dylan had come to the end of Dylan. The new all-touring-all-the-time would have seemed to be the beginning of the ongoing collapse of his house of cards, but actually just the opposite has happened.

The key to the Dylan dilemma is that no two people see the shows on Bob's Never Ending Tour the same way. From the lyric altering to the drastic melodic deconstruction to the rhythm changing, it's all somewhat mystifying. But Dylan's live performances are what the devout see as the *whole point*. This mangling of lyrics has been going on since the Band tour in 1974 and has long become an act of faith, at least since the Never Ending Tour began in 1988.

Sure there are all the old fogies, but they're in the minority. In their place are the too-late-born Bobcats, who missed the '60s but for whom that decade was the golden age, and Bob is its avatar and masterpiece. Then there are the youngest fans, who know some of the songs like "Blowin' in the Wind" or "Forever Young" from the iMac commercial. And "All Along the Watchtower" (the Jimi Hendrix version). Dylan's just this mythically cool dude who was famous long ago (a line he sings with biting wit these days).

The occasional nonbeliever will show up at a Dylan concert, like Bob Boilen from NPR's *All Songs Considered*, and venture an opinion. He went to see the Gypsy at a cavernous gymnasium in Washington, DC, on November 13, 2010, and was, well, alarmed:

"One look at the set list and it's easy to think it was an amazing show," he says, and then lists some sixteen classic Dylan songs and covers including "Rainy Day Women #12 and 35," "Señor (Tales of Yankee Power)," "Just Like a Woman," "Desolation Row," "Ballad of a Thin Man," and "Like a Rolling Stone." "But," he concludes, "truth be told, it just wasn't good."

> Usually the melodies are gone, the singing is often staccato, small phrases stripped of their singable signatures. In the gym at George Washington University, it was nearly impossible to make out the words if you didn't already know them. . . . I kept thinking that if any of the classic tunes came out in the form they were performed here, they'd have been long forgotten.

Perhaps Boilen should have read the Dylan Code as set out by Todd Haynes in the Weinstein Company press notes for his film *I'm Not There.*

> THE MINUTE you try to grab hold of Dylan, he's no longer where he was. He's like a flame: If you try to hold him in your hand you'll surely get burned.

Dylan's life of change and constant disappearances and constant transformations makes you yearn to hold him, and to nail him down. And that's why his fan base is so obsessive, so desirous of finding the truth and the absolutes and the answers to him—things that Dylan will never provide and will only frustrate.

Once you've grasped this you can attend a Dylan concert and not sound like Mr. Jones. You can't compare Dylan with anybody else—especially with his old self, much less with other pop stars. He's a living bodhisattva, the carrier of the sacred reliquary of the '60s. His shows are a bit like trundling the image of a saint from fair to fair in the Middle Ages.

Michael Gray, the supreme Dylan exegete (and *not* a big fan of recent Dylan shows), sees him as a sort of effigy of himself, "a little wooden figure not so much going through the motions as being conveyed along them like an object on an assembly line."

The first time I saw the later Dylan was in 1986 at Madison Square Garden. He'd already started his ongoing deconstruction of his old songs, interpreting some as reggae numbers, others sung in an odd Scottish brogue or done in waltz time. Every time he began a song, heads in the audience would swivel around as if to say, "Which one is this?" He sang "Masters of War" the way a wounded bear might have done it, so mumbled and grunted that the following morning the reviewer in the *New York Times* referred to it as "an unidentified song."

I applauded Dylan for all his mischievous contortions—a man should be allowed to torment his old songs, and if this were all he did, who but fools and punters would utter a word against him? But when I saw Dylan in Cooperstown in 2004, I, like many before me, found the spectacle disheartening. The show opened with the theme from the Pepperidge Farm TV show (a.k.a. Aaron Copland's *Fanfare for the Common Man*). Bob's road manager, Al Santos, came out and made a startling announcement:

> Ladies and gentlemen, please welcome the poet laureate of rock 'n' roll. The voice of the promise of the '60s counterculture. The guy who forced folk into bed with rock, who donned makeup in the '70s and disappeared into a haze of substance abuse, who emerged to find Jesus, and who suddenly shifted gears, releasing some of the strongest music of his career beginning in the late '90s. Ladies and gentlemen, Bob Dylan!

The bulk of this he took from a review in the *Buffalo News* by Jeff Miers of a Dylan concert in August 2002 in Hamburg, New York. It was just so odd that Dylan would choose to introduce himself like that.

The performance began and you looked around for Dylan. To the left and almost at the back of the stage was a tiny figure all in black wearing a black plastic cowboy hat hunched over what looked like a toy piano. I wanted to hear Bob ring changes on his famous songs, add new lyrics, alter the melodies to the point where they were hardly recognizable. Instead every song was delivered in an almost identical manner and blasted at arena rock volume with basically no modulation at all, including the insinuating, spookily hissed "Just Like a Woman," which he belted out with his croaky ancient rasp. Here was the once-subtle interpreter of his own and others' songs steamrolling every number, and there I was, standing in the summer rain at the Cooperstown ballpark. All around me were eighteen-year-olds telling me how fucking great he was. I didn't say a thing.

Then last year I went to see Bob at Bethel Woods, the site of the original Woodstock festival from which Dylan had fled in revulsion and terror in 1969. As if this weren't ironic enough, at Bethel Woods there's a museum devoted to the '60s—as if it were fifth-century Athens. Tie-dye T-shirts are displayed with the same historical appraisal as Louis XV furniture.

From the moment we got there the vibe was ecstatic—in a place like this how else would you put it? Everybody seemed blissed out. Dylan songs were playing over the PA system when we arrived. "Well," my wife, Coco, joked, "that's the only time we'll know what song he's singing." But that's not what happened.

I saw an entirely different Dylan at Bethel. To hear Dylan still sounding like Dylan—even with that croaky voice—was astounding. The big white gaucho hat, the black suit with lime piping—as soon he came onstage there was a bizarre surge of energy between Bob and the audience.

There were the original fans and a couple in T-shirts from the Tom Petty tour back in the '80s, but the crowd was predominantly a young one, kids dressed as hippies. Still, everybody hooked into some main-line current. Even the event staff were bopping around (and telling us they, too, had been at the original Woodstock). It was intoxicating, like some spontaneously generated consciousness-raising group.

Everything he did that night was inventive, whimsical. He was Charlie Chaplin again, doing those staccato movements just like he was back at Gerde's Folk City. He sang "Leopard-Skin Pill-Box Hat" like he was riding a horse. "Ballad of a Thin Man" he did to the tune of "I Put a Spell on You" and "Desolation Row" to a kind of samba, syncopated and bonking the syllables as he stretched out the words so that it was a put-on and gothic at the same time.

Nobody's denying that he's given so-called erratic concerts, but you know what, there is no bad Bob. Or maybe these days what's considered "bad Bob" is the most interesting part of Dylan. You wouldn't want him doing a pitch-perfect rendition of "Girl from the North Country" now would you?

Bowie retired to his Weimar lair; he's preserved like a dandy in aspic. So why is Dylan still out there? His voice is shot; he doesn't look so good; he doesn't need the money.

But it's at the shows, the performances the unenlightened have mocked for years, that Dylan comes to life, just as he did in the Village so long ago. Heraclitus said you can't step into the same river twice. Well, with Bob you can't step into the same song twice. He's the only performer of his generation who is still out there experimenting with himself and his material. If all these years he'd put on a greatest-hits show—like the very lucrative 1974 tour with the Band—he would probably have sold out houses, but that's not the way Dylan operates. Many of the uninitiated may strenuously object to his fiendish dismantling of his old songs, but who would not admire his original ambition to recreate and bring them back to life?

FORTY YEARS AFTER GREIL MARCUS INFAMOUSLY ASKED, "WHAT IS THIS shit?" in his review of *Self Portrait* in *Rolling Stone*, he decided to give it another listen. "I thought it was awful then," he wrote in his reevaluation in *Mojo* in 2010, "and looked forward to playing it all and having it come out differently, but it didn't."

> What was painfully embarrassing then . . . is even more insulting now—insulting to the song[s], when [they] deserved more than the equivalent of a tip, insulting to anyone who, buying an album with Bob Dylan's name on it, had a right to expect he would have given what he had to give. What was mediocre then . . . is even more of a throwaway now.

But things have changed. You simply can't apply the same aesthetic criteria to Dylan that you did forty years ago, never mind applying it to a forty-year-old album. Dylan has transcended even his status as Living National Treasure; he's now a psychic entity and has been for almost two decades. To judge whether a specific song, album, or performance by Dylan is critically good or bad is beside the point.

At Bethel, we were all *participating* in Dylan, whatever that is. Given Dylan's mercurial identity, it's not exactly a person you're going to see. It's more an atmosphere that's formed around the idea of "Dylan," a multiphrenic, polymorphous, composite entity. A collective being that magnetizes ideas and identities around it.

Dylan has a psychic membrane so porous he's actually *contagious*. You can get a bad case of Bob after listening to him for a while. And after—what is it?—fifty-odd years, he's part of your genome. Soon the faithful gather, swarm about him—in a sense have *become* him. It's as if his fans have formed a collective organism around Dylan—the hive, the *ummah*. We've become a telepathic entity like the phenomenon Eugène Marais describes in *The Soul of the White Ant*, the fantastic flight of possessed insects in the South African *veld* and on Magnetic Island, Australia, where, tuned into the frequencies emitted by the termite queen, the colony functions as a single being. How can we put it? A group soul!

EVERYTHING DYLAN DOES IS A WORK IN PROGRESS. HE'S A WORK IN progress. He's the great tinkerer. It's Bob in the lab, a sort of wizard's hut with bubbling retorts and potions and sacks of gris-gris. The place is filled to the rafters with stuff—every record ever made in America sort of thing—and he's rummaging. He's taken the flotsam and jetsam of American culture and endowed it with an almost biblical aura. Dylan as the obsessed evangelist of this frothy creed has made us see movies and songs—the most ephemeral and disposable things we've produced—as the truest things about us.

"There's a lot of the junk dealer in Dylan," Bob Hudson says. "He's sifting through the things in his junk shop—Yeats's 'rag and bone shop of the heart.' He's trying to figure out what he can make with a watering can and a monkey wrench, and he's involving us in the process, which is kind of exhilarating to watch."

Anything that's bothered you about Dylan in the past now makes sense. It's not that everything he does comes from some enlightened motive; that alone would be to misinterpret him. He's as perverse as ever. That's the point!

Dylan is the great accumulator. He never abandons anything from his past. He never abandons anything, period. He never says, I used to be this or that, but he also never really repudiates any of it, because it's all him. He's like some great galleon encrusted with barnacles, seaweed, old shoes, tin cans, condoms. It's the same way with his songs. He's everything that preceded him and still sings "Song to Woody." It's all there: everything from Hibbing, his teenage obsessions, Little Richard's hair, the obsessed Elvis fan, earnest folkie, raging protester, *Blonde on Blonde* hipster. And, if you're lucky, it all happens nightly.

Like most American geniuses he's also a synthesizer. America is a polyglot: a hodgepodge, a crazy quilt pieced together by our imagination. A work of fiction. That's the genius of blues, jazz, folk music, rock, and rap—the genius of Bob Dylan. He's still out there, all these years later, making it up as he goes along—and he's devised the oddest of the recluse's tricks: hiding in plain view onstage for the last twenty-four years.

His approach is to link life and fiction in a heady concoction known as Bob Dylan, a creation so intoxicating we still hold the aging folksinger to account, measuring his current condition against this fantastic doppelgänger. To understand as wildly eccentric and inventive a character as Dylan you have to take his self-mythologizing, tall-tale-spinning, perverse statements, and contrary point of view as seriously as the so-called facts of his life. What other approach would be appropriate for a character who believes he was born in the grooves of a 78 record, and has spent his life—imaginary and actual—dealing with the gap between the two?

Bibliography

Andersen, Karl Erik, webmaster. *Expecting Rain* website (daily updated Dylan news), www
.expectingrain.com.

Avedon, Richard, and Doon Arbus. *The Sixties*. New York: Random House, 1999.

Baez, Joan. *And a Voice to Sing With: A Memoir*. New York: Simon & Schuster, 1989.

————. *Daybreak: An Autobiography*. New York: Avon, 1970.

Barker, Derek, ed. *Isis: A Bob Dylan Anthology*. London: Helter Skelter, 2004.

Bauldie, John. *The Ghost of Electricity: Bob Dylan's 1966 World Tour*. Self-published, 1988.

————, ed. *Wanted Man: In Search of Bob Dylan*. New York: Citadel, 1991.

Beaulieu, Victor-Lévy. *Jack Kerouac: a chicken essay*. Quebec: Coach House Translations, 1975.

Benson, Carl. *The Bob Dylan Companion: Four Decades of Commentary*. New York: Schirmer,
1998.

Bob Dylan, official website (news, discography, videos, tour information and tickets, song
lyrics, official merchandise), www.bobdylan.com.

Calasso, Roberto. *Ka: Stories of the Mind and the Gods of India*. New York: Knopf, 1998.

Cantwell, Robert. *When We Were Good: The Folk Revival*. Cambridge, London: Harvard
University Press, 1996.

Charles, Larry, dir. *Masked and Anonymous*, film and DVD. Columbia Tristar, 2004.

Clinton, William J. *The Bob Dylan CD and CDR Field Recordings Guide* website (discography of unofficial recordings and collectors' compilations), www.angelfire.com/wa
/monicasdude.

Cohen, John. *Young Bob: John Cohen's Early Photographs of Bob Dylan*. New York, Power-
house Books, nd.

Cott, Jonathan. *Dylan*. Garden City, New York: Dolphin/Doubleday & Company, 1985.

————, ed. *Bob Dylan: The Essential Interviews*. New York: Wenner Books, 2006.

Cramer, Daniel. *Bob Dylan*. New York: Pocket Books, 1968.

Day, Aidan. *Jokerman: Reading the Lyrics of Bob Dylan*. Oxford: Basil Blackwell, 1988.

Doggett, Peter. *Are You Ready for the Country: Elvis, Dylan, Parsons and the Roots of Country
Rock*. New York: Penguin, 2000.

Dowley, Tim, and Barry Dunnage. *Bob Dylan: From a Hard Rain to a Slow Train*. London:
Omnibus, 1982.

Dundas, Glen. *Tangled: A Recording History of Bob Dylan*. Thunder Bay, Ont.: SMA Services, 2004.

Dunn, Tim. *The Bob Dylan Copyright Files, 1962–2007*. Bloomington, Ind.: AuthorHouse, 2008.

Dylan, Bob. *Chronicles: Volume One*. New York: Simon & Schuster, 2005.

———. *Drawn Blank*. New York: Random House, 1994.

———. *Lyrics, 1962–1985*. New York: Knopf, 1985.

———. *Lyrics, 1962–2001*. New York: Simon & Schuster, 2004.

———. *The Songs of Bob Dylan: From 1966 Through 1975*. New York: Knopf/Cherry Lane, 1979.

———. *Tarantula, Revised Edition*. New York: Scribner, 2004.

———. *Writings and Drawings*. New York: Knopf, 1973.

Egan, Sean. *The Mammoth Book of Bob Dylan*. Philadelphia and London: Running Press, 2011.

Engel, Dave. *Just Like Bob Zimmerman's Blues: Dylan in Minnesota*. Amherst, Wis.: Amherst Press, 1997.

Epstein, Daniel Mark. *The Ballad of Bob Dylan: A Portrait*. New York: HarperCollins, 2011.

Faithfull, Marianne, and David Dalton. *Faithfull: An Autobiography*. New York: Cooper Square Press, 2000.

Fariña, Richard. *Been Down So Long It Looks Like Up to Me*. New York: Dell Publishing Co., 1966.

Feinstein, Barry, Daniel Kramer, and Jim Marshall. *Early Dylan: Photographs*. Boston: Bullfinch/Little Brown, 1999.

Fiedler, Leslie. *Love and Death in the American Novel*. Champaign, Illinois: The Dalkey Archive, 1998.

Gill, Andy. *Classic Bob Dylan 1962–69: My Back Pages*. London: Carlton, 1998.

Gill, Andy, and Kevin Odegard. *A Simple Twist of Fate: Bob Dylan and the Making of Blood on the Tracks*. Cambridge, Mass.: Da Capo, 2004.

Gilmour, Michael J. *The Gospel According to Bob Dylan: The Old, Old Story of Modern Times*. Louisville, Ky.: Westminster John Knox Press, 2011.

Ginsberg, Allen. *Howl*. San Francisco: City Lights, 2001.

Goodman, Fred. *The Mansion on the Hill: Dylan, Young, Geffen, Springsteen, and the Head-on Collision of Rock and Commerce*. New York: Vintage, 1998.

Gray, Michael. *The Bob Dylan Encyclopedia: Revised and Updated Edition*. London and New York: Continuum, 2008.

———. *Song & Dance Man III: The Art of Bob Dylan*. London and New York: Continuum, 2000.

Gray, Michael, and John Bauldie, eds. *All Across the Telegraph: A Bob Handbook*. London: Futura, 1987.

Griffin, Sid. *Million Dollar Bash: Bob Dylan, the Band, and* The Basement Tapes. London: A Jawbone Book, 2007.

———. *Shelter from the Storm: Bob Dylan's Rolling Thunder Years.* London: A Jawbone Book, 2010.

Guralnick, Peter. *Last Train to Memphis: The Rise of Elvis Presley.* New York: Back Bay Books, 1995.

Guthrie, Woody. *Pastures of Plenty: The Unpublished Writings of an America Folk Hero.* Dave Marsh and Harold Leventhal, eds. New York: HarperCollins, 1990.

Hackett, Pat, ed. *The Andy Warhol Diaries.* New York: Random House, 1991.

Hadju, David. *Positively 4th Street: The Lives and Times of Joan Baez, Bob Dylan, Mimi Baez Fariña and Richard Fariña.* New York: Farrar, Straus and Giroux, 2001.

Halberstadt, Alex. *Lonely Avenue: The Unlikely Life and Times of Doc Pomus.* Cambridge, Mass.: Da Capo Press, 2007.

Harvey, Todd. *The Formative Dylan: Transmission and Stylistic Influences, 1961–1963.* Lanham, Md.: Scarecrow Press, 2001.

Hedin, Benjamin. *Studio A: The Bob Dylan Reader.* New York and London: W.W. Norton & Company, 2004.

Helm, Levon with Stephen Davis. *This Wheel's on Fire: Levon Helm and the Story of the Band.* New York: William Morrow and Company, 1993.

Herdman, John. *Voice Without Restraint: Bob Dylan's Lyrics and Their Background.* New York: Delilah/G. P. Putnam, 1981.

Heylin, Clinton. *Behind the Shades, 20th Anniversary Edition.* London: Faber & Faber, 2011.

———. *Bob Dylan: A Life in Stolen Moments.* New York: Schirmer Books, 1996.

———. *Bob Dylan: The Recording Sessions, 1960–1994.* New York: St. Martin's/Griffin, 1997.

———. *Revolution in the Air: The Songs of Bob Dylan, 1957–1973.* Chicago: Chicago Review Press, 2009.

———. *Still on the Road: The Songs of Bob Dylan, 1974–2006.* Chicago: Chicago Review Press, 2010.

Hoskyns, Barney. *Across the Great Divide: The Band and America.* New York: Hyperion, 1993.

Hudson, Bob. *A Complete Bob Dylan Discography and Sessionography, 1957–2011.* Unpublished manuscript.

Humphries, Patrick, and John Bauldie. *Oh No! Not Another Bob Dylan Book.* Brentwood, Essex: Square One Books, 1991.

Irwin, Colin. *Bob Dylan: Highway 61 Revisited.* New York: Billboard Books, 2008.

Jackson, Blair. *Garcia: An American Life.* New York: Penguin, 1999.

Kerouac, Jack. *Book of Sketches: 1952–57.* New York: Penguin Poets, 2006.

————. *On the Road.* New York: Penguin, 1999.

Krogsgaard, Michael. *Positively Bob Dylan: A Thirty-Year Discography, Concert and Recording Session Guide, 1960–1991.* Ann Arbor, Mich.: Pop Culture, Inc., 1991.

————, ed. *Bob Dylan: The Recording Sessions* website (extensive research into Bob Dylan recording sessions), www.punkhart.com/dylan/sessions.html.

Landy, Elliott. *Woodstock Visions: The Spirit of a Generation.* London: Continuum, 1994.

Lawrence, D. H. *Studies in Classical American Literature.* New York: Penguin, 1990.

Ledeen, Jenny. *Prophecy in the Christian Era: A Study of Bob Dylan's Work from 1961–1967.* St. Louis, Mo.: Peaceberry Press of Webster Groves, 1995.

Leland, John. *Hip: the History.* New York: Ecco, 2004.

Lee, C. P. *Like a Bullet of Light: The Films of Bob Dylan.* London: Helter Skelter Publishing, 2001.

————. *Like the Night: Bob Dylan and the Road to the Manchester Free Trade Hall.* London: Helter Skelter Publishing, 1998.

Lerner, Murray. *The Other Side of the Mirror: Bob Dylan Live at the Newport Folk Festival, 1963–1965,* DVD. Sony, 2007.

Marais, Eugène. *The Soul of the White Ant.* Harmondsworth, Middlesex, England: Penguin Books, 1973.

Marcus, Greil. *Bob Dylan by Greil Marcus: Writings 1968–2010.* New York: PublicAffairs Books, 2010.

————. *Invisible Republic: Bob Dylan's* Basement Tapes. New York: Henry Holt, 1997.

————. *Like a Rolling Stone: Bob Dylan at the Crossroads.* New York: PublicAffairs Books, 2005.

Marquise, Mike. *Wicked Messenger: Bob Dylan and the Sixties.* New York: Seven Stories Press, 2003.

Matteo, Steve: *Dylan.* New York: Metro Books, 1998.

McGregor, Craig, ed. *Bob Dylan: A Retrospective.* New York: Morrow, 1972.

Mellers, Wilfrid. *A Darker Shade of Pale: A Backdrop to Bob Dylan.* New York: Oxford University Press, 1985.

Muir, Andrew. *Razor's Edge: Bob Dylan and the Never Ending Tour.* London: Helter Skelter, 2001.

Mojo magazine, eds. *Dylan: Visions, Portraits, and Back Pages.* London: DK Publishers, 2005.

Miles, Barry. *The Sixties.* London: Jonathan Cape, 2002.

Olson, Charles. *Call Me Ishmael.* Baltimore: Johns Hopkins Press, 1997.

Osborne, Jerry. *Elvis—Word for Word: What He Said Exactly as He Said It.* New York: Gramercy/Random House, 2006.

Pagel, Bill, webmaster. *Bob Links* website (concert information, set lists, and links to Dylan sites), www.boblinks.com.

Patchen, Kenneth. *The Journal of Albion Moonlight*. New York: New Directions, 1961.

Partridge, Elizabeth. *This Land Was Made for You and Me: The Life and Songs of Woody Guthrie*. New York: Viking, 2002.

Pennebaker, D. A. *Bob Dylan:* Don't Look Back: *A Film and Book*. New York: Ballantine, 1968.

———, dir. *Don't Look Back: 1965 Tour Deluxe Edition*, DVD. New Video Group, 2007.

Pickering, Stephen. *Bob Dylan Approximately: A Portrait of the Jewish Poet in Search of God: A Midrash*. New York: David McKay, 1975.

Polizzetti, Mark. *Bob Dylan's Highway 61 Revisited*. London: Continuum, 2006.

Ricks, Christopher. *Dylan's Vision of Sin*. New York: Ecco/HarperCollins, 2003.

Riley, Tim. *Hard Rain: A Dylan Commentary*. New York: Knopf, 1992.

Rimbaud, Arthur. *Oeuvres Completes*. Paris: Livre de Poche, 2004.

Rogovoy, Seth. *Bob Dylan: Prophet, Mystic, Poet*. New York: Scribner, 2009.

Rolling Stone magazine, eds. *Knockin' on Dylan's Door: On the Road in '74*. New York: A Rolling Stone Book/Pocket Books, 1974.

Rotolo, Suze. *A Freewheelin' Time: A Memoir of Greenwich Village in the Sixties*. New York: Broadway Books, 2008.

Rowley, Chris. *Blood on the Tracks: The Story of Bob Dylan*. London: Proteus Books, 1984.

Sandburg, Carl. *The Complete Poems*. Boston: Houghton Mifflin, 2003.

Scaduto, Anthony. *Dylan: An Intimate Biography*. New York: New American Library, 1973.

Scherman, Tony, and David Dalton. *Pop: The Genius of Andy Warhol*. New York: HarperCollins, 2010.

Scobie, Stephen. *Alias Bob Dylan*. Red Deer, Alb.: Red Deer College Press, 1991.

Scorsese, Martin, dir. *No Direction Home*, DVD. Paramount, 2005.

Sheff, David. *All We Are Saying: The Last Major Interview with John Lennon and Yoko Ono*. New York: St. Martin's Press, 2000.

Shelton, Robert. *No Direction Home: The Life and Music of Bob Dylan*. Revised, updated edition. Milwaukee, Minn.: Hal Leonard, 2011.

Shepard, Sam. *Rolling Thunder Logbook*. Cambridge, Mass.: Da Capo Press, 2004.

Sloman, Larry. *On the Road with Bob Dylan*. New York: Three Rivers Press, 2002.

Sounes, Howard. *Down the Highway: The Life of Bob Dylan*. New York: Grove Press, 2002.

Spitz, Bob. *Dylan: A Biography*. New York: W. W. Norton, 1991.

Taussig, Michael. *What Color Is the Sacred?* Chicago and London: University of Chicago Press, 2009.

Thompson, Toby. *Positively Main Street: An Unorthodox View of Bob Dylan*. New York: Paperback Library, 1972.

Thomson, Elizabeth, and David Gutman. *The Dylan Companion: A Collection of Essential Writing about Bob Dylan.* New York: Dell, 1990.

Trager, Oliver. *Keys to the Rain: The Definitive Bob Dylan Encyclopedia.* New York: Billboard Books, 2004.

Van Ronk, Dave, and Elijah Wald. *The Mayor of MacDougal Street: A Memoir.* Cambridge, Mass.: Da Capo Press, 2006.

Warhol, Andy, and Pat Hackett. *POPism: The Warhol Sixties.* Boston: Mariner Books, 2006.

Weberman, A.J. *My Life in Garbology.* New York: Stonehill Publishing Company, 1980.

———. *Right Wing Bob.* New York. Published in conjunction with The Yippie Museum Press, 2009.

Wenner, Jann S. *Lennon Remembers: The Full* Rolling Stone *Interviews from 1970.* New York: Verso Books, 2000.

Wilentz, Sean. *Bob Dylan in America.* New York: Doubleday, 2010.

———, and Greil Marcus. *The Rose and the Briar: Death, Love and Liberty in the American Ballad.* New York: Norton, 2005.

Williams, Chris. *In His Own Words: Bob Dylan.* London: Omnibus, 1993.

Williams, Paul. *Bob Dylan: Performing Artist: Mind Out of Time, 1986–1990 and Beyond.* London: Omnibus, 2004.

———. *Bob Dylan: Performing Artist: The Middle Years, 1974–1986.* Novato, Calif.: Underwood-Miller, 1992.

———. *Bob Dylan: Performing Artist: The Music of Bob Dylan, 1960–1973.* Novato, Calif.: Underwood-Miller, 1990.

———. *Dylan—What Happened?* South Bend, Ind.: and books/Entwhistle Books, 1979.

———. *Watching the River Flow: Observations on His Art in Progress, 1966–1995.* London: Omnibus Press, 1996.

Williams, Richard. *Dylan: A Man Called Alias.* New York: Henry Holt, 1992.

Williams, William Carlos. *In the American Grain.* New York: New Directions, 2009.

Williamson, Nigel. *The Rough Guide to Bob Dylan.* London: Rough Guides, 2004.

Witting, Robert. *The Meaning of an Orange*: *Pocket Tarantula*: Scunthorpe, South Humberside, England: Exploding Rooster Books, 1996.

Younger Than That Now. New York. Thunder's Mouth Press, 2004.

Notes

1: Creation Myths

7 "A few toughnecks are still getatable": James Joyce, *Finnegans Wake* (New York: Viking, 1959), 149.

8 "I like the way the hills tumble": Douglas Brinkley, "Bob Dylan's Late-Era, Old-Style American Individualism," *Rolling Stone* 1078 (May 14, 2009), www.rollingstone .com/music/news/bob-dylans-america-20090514?page=7.

8 "I never knew my father": Bob Dylan, in Robert Shelton, *No Direction Home: The Life and Music of Bob Dylan* (Cambridge, Mass.: Da Capo Press, 1997), 58. Taken from *No Direction Home: The Life and Music of Bob Dylan* by Robert Shelton, revised and updated edition, edited by Elizabeth Thomson and Patrick Humphries. Text copyright © 1986 and 2010 by the estate of Robert Shelton. Backbeat Books (USA); Omnibus Press (UK).

9 "As I waited till I heard": Bob Dylan, LP liner notes, *Joan Baez in Concert Part 2* (Vanguard VSD-2923), stereo recording, November 1963. Copyright © 1963 by Bob Dylan. Renewed 1984 by Special Rider Music. Used by permission.

9 "Okemah was one of the singiest, square dancingest, drinkingest": Woody Guthrie, *Pastures of Plenty: The Unpublished Writings of an America Folk Hero*, Dave Marsh and Harold Leventhal, eds. (New York: HarperCollins, 1990), 3.

9 "What's dear to me are the Fifties": Bob Dylan, interview with Alan Jackson, "Bob Dylan Revisited," *Times on Saturday* (November 15, 1997).

10 "Well, in the winter": Bob Dylan, interview with Ron Rosenbaum, Burbank, California, November/December 1977, in *Playboy* (March 1978). Copyright © 1978 by Playboy. Used by permission.

10 "I was always fishing for something": Bob Dylan, *Chronicles: Volume One* (New York: Simon & Schuster, 2005), 32. Reprinted with the permission of Simon & Schuster, from *Chronicles, Volume One* by Bob Dylan. Copyright © 2004 by Bob Dylan. All rights reserved.

11 "All I did was write and sing, paint little pictures": Bob Dylan, interview with Jules Siegel, in Retro, *Saturday Evening Post* (July 30, 1966).

11 "The sound of his voice": Bob Dylan, LP liner notes, *Joan Baez in Concert Part 2*.

12 "An' my first idol was Hank Williams": Ibid.

12 "Elvis ... walks the path between heaven": Peter Guralnick, *Last Train to Memphis: The Rise of Elvis Presley* (New York: Back Bay Books, 1995), jacket copy.

13 "The mysterious Bob Dylan had a chicken-soup, Yiddishe mama": Allen Ginsberg,

in Sam Kashner, *When I Was Cool: My Life at the Jack Kerouac School* (New York: HarperCollins, 2004), 110. See *No Direction Home*, text copyright © 1986 and 2010 by the estate of Robert Shelton.

16   "I never was a kid who could": Bob Dylan, quoted in *No Direction Home*, DVD, Martin Scorsese, dir. (Paramount), 2005.

16   "The name just popped into my head": Ibid.

16   "usually had a poetry book in his hand": Larry Kegan, in Howard Sounes, *Down the Highway: The Life of Bob Dylan* (New York: Grove Press, 2002), 48.

18   "The important thing is to keep moving": Bob Dylan, in Robert Shelton, *No Direction Home*, 14.

2: The Hall of Early Folk Memories

21   "My grandfather used to say": Franz Kafka, "The Next Village," in *Franz Kafka's Created Stories* (New York: Everyman Library, 1946), 377.

21   "The folk music scene had been like a paradise": Bob Dylan, *Chronicles*, 292.

22   "I thought he was oddly old-time": Suze Rotolo, *A Freewheelin' Time: A Memoir of Greenwich Village in the Sixties* (New York: Broadway Books, 2008), 91. From *A Freewheelin' Time: A Memoir of Greenwich Village in the Sixties* by Suze Rotolo, copyright © 2008 by Suze Rotolo. Used by permission of Broadway Books.

22   "He used to do all sorts of Chaplinesque moves onstage": Peter Stampfel, interview with author, February 11 and 28, 2009.

22   "Back then . . . he always seemed to be winging it": Dave Van Ronk and Elijah Wald, *The Mayor of MacDougal Street: A Memoir* (Cambridge, Mass.: Da Capo Press, 2006), 161. Copyright © 2006 Dave Van Ronk, Elijah Wald. Reprinted by permission of Da Capo Press, a member of the Perseas Book Group.

22   "If you're going to send me something": Bob Dylan, *Tarantula*, rev. ed. (New York: Scribner, 2004), 109. Taken from *Tarantula, Revised Edition* by Bob Dylan. Copyright © 1966, 1994 by Bob Dylan. Used by permission of Scribner.

24   "Even what we didn't believe was often entertaining": Dave Van Ronk and Elijah Wald, *The Mayor of MacDougal Street*, 162.

24   "People listen to his stories": Cynthia Gooding, in Robert Shelton, *No Direction Home*, 67.

25   "The thing about Baez": Dave Van Ronk and Elijah Wald, *The Mayor of MacDougal Street*, 167.

25   "Oh, yeah, in my songs": Bob Dylan, interview with Bill Flanagan, *Telegraph* (October 8, 2011), www.telegraph.co.uk/culture/music/bob-dylan5148025/Bob-Dylan-interview -with-Bill-Flanagan.html.

26   "John Hurt is a really interesting story": Peter Stampfel, interview with author.

26   "There was a difference in the concept": Bob Dylan, *Chronicles*, 86.

29   "all performing the same function": Michael Gray, *Song & Dance Man III: The Art of Bob Dylan* (London and New York: Continuum, 2000), 22.

29   "a folk music purist enthusiast": Bob Dylan, *Chronicles*, 248.

29   "When Phil Ochs came along": Peter Stampfel, interview with author.

31   "Folk music, if nothing else": Greil Marcus, *Bob Dylan by Greil Marcus: Writings 1968–2010* (New York: PublicAffairs Books, 2010), 341.

3: Woody Junior

33   "He seemed attached to his guitar": Coco Pekelis, interview with author, March 17, 2011.

34   "Everybody I seen on the streets": Lyrics from "Talking Subway," by Woody Guthrie. Copyright © 1961 (renewed) by Woody Guthrie Publications, Inc., and TRO-Ludlow Music, Inc. (BMI). Reprinted by permission.

34   "He would withdraw anywhere": Suze Rotolo, *A Freewheelin' Time*, 94.

35   "Woody was my last hero": Bob Dylan, in Anthony Scaduto, *Bob Dylan: An Intimate Biography* (New York: New American Library, 1973), 69.

35   "Pete Seeger is a singer of folk songs": Bob Dylan, quoting Woody Guthrie, in Anthony Scaduto, *Bob Dylan: An Intimate Biography*, 69.

36   "Woody never said anything about": Nora Guthrie, quoting Harold Leventhal, in Howard Sounes, *Down the Highway: The Life of Bob Dylan* (New York: Grove Press, 2001), 82.

36   "I don't think he thought anything": Pete Seeger, in Howard Sounes, *Down the Highway*, 82.

36   "It was an act but only for about two days": Bob Dylan, in Robert Shelton, *No Direction Home: The Life and Music of Bob Dylan* (Cambridge, Mass.: Da Capo Press, 1997), 75. See *No Direction Home*, text copyright © 1986 and 2010 by the estate of Robert Shelton.

37   "Dogs a-barkin', cats a-meowin'": Lyrics from "Talking Bear Mountain Picnic Massacre Blues," by Bob Dylan. Copyright © 1962, 1965 by Duchess Music Corporation; renewed 1990, 1993 by MCA. All rights reserved. International copyright secured. Reprinted by permission.

4: Li'l Abner on Bleecker Street

42   "Back to the starting point": Bob Dylan CD liner notes, *Planet Waves*. Copyright © 1973 by Ram's Horn Music; renewed 2001 by Ram's Horn Music. All rights reserved. International copyright secured. Reprinted by permission.

44   "Bright New Face": Robert Shelton, "20-Year-Old Singer Is a Bright New Face at Gerde's Club," *New York Times* (September 29, 1961), www.nytimes.com/books/97/05/04/reviews/dylan-gerde.html.

45   "Out on the street and in the clubs": Suze Rotolo, *A Freewheelin' Time*, 158.

46 "Performers who had been on the scene": Ibid.

47 "The American public is like Sleeping Beauty": Albert Grossman, in Robert Shelton, *No Direction Home*, 93.

48 "Well, I don't know, I'll have to go home": Evan Jones, in Clinton Heylin, *Bob Dylan: A Life in Stolen Moments* (New York: Schirmer Books, 1996), 36.

48 "consciously trying to recapture": Robert Shelton, "Bob Dylan: A Distinctive Folk-Song Stylist: 20-Year-Old Singer Is a Bright New Face," *New York Times* (September 19, 1961).

5: Folk Messiah

51 "Of course, I knew of him": Bob Dylan, "He Will Never Die or Be Forgotten—Even by Persons Not Yet Born," Friday Review, *Guardian* (September 9, 2004).

54 "I saw a new born baby": Lyrics from "A Hard Rain's A-Gonna Fall," by Bob Dylan. Copyright © 1963 by Warner Bros., Inc.; renewed 1991 by Special Rider Music. All rights reserved. International copyright secured. Reprinted by permission.

55 "Nobody's going to put up with her": Robert Shelton, quoting Bob Dylan, in David Hadju, *Positively 4th Street: The Lives and Times of Joan Baez, Bob Dylan, Mimi Baez Fariña and Richard Fariña* (New York: Farrar, Straus and Giroux, 2001), 276.

55 "She looks like a religious icon": Bob Dylan, *Chronicles*, 254–55.

55 "I consider Hank Williams, Captain Marvel": "Dylan Meets the Press," *Village Voice* (March 3, 1965), transcript of press conference in Woodstock, New York, 1965.

57 "It seems to be what people want": Tony Glover, in Clinton Heylin, *Behind the Shades, 20th Anniversary Edition* (London: Faber & Faber, 2011), xiii.

6: The Zimmerman Letter

61 "It was an old showbiz tradition": Dave Van Ronk and Elijah Wald, *The Mayor of MacDougal Street*, 162.

62 "My job was to mail LPs and PR material": Myra Friedman, interview with author, November 16, 2007.

63 "high school and college students": Emily Coleman, "I Am My Words," *Newsweek* (November 4, 1963), 94–95.

63 "He has suffered": Ibid.

63 "Perhaps he feels it would spoil": Ibid.

64 "My son is a corporation": Abe Zimmerman, in Walter Eldot, "My Son, the Folknik: Youth from Hibbing Becomes Famous as Bob Dylan," *Duluth News-Tribune* (October 20, 1963).

64 "I found out for sure that his name": Suze Rotolo, *A Freewheelin' Time*, 105–6.

64 "The discovery of his birth name": Ibid., 106.

65 "I was just somebody else, some stranger": Jack Kerouac, *On the Road* (New York: Viking, 1957), 17.

65 "It's funny. . . . The revelation that his name": Myra Friedman, interview with author.

65 "The revelation that Jack [Elliott] was Jewish": Dave Van Ronk and Elijah Wald, *The Mayor of MacDougal Street*, 162.

66 "I think Dylan initially denied his Jewish background": Allen Ginsberg, interview with author, September 30, 1992.

7: From a Buick 6

69 "charging restless mute": Jack Kerouac, *Visions of Cody* (New York: Penguin, 1993), 319.

70 "I think it was in everybody's mind": Pete Karman, in Howard Sounes, *Down the Highway*, 148.

72 "I am now famous by the rules": Bob Dylan's letter to *Broadside* 38 (1964).

73 "endorsed it reluctantly": Suze Rotolo, in Robert Shelton, *No Direction Home*, 27.

74 "We hit 46 pool halls from Augusta": Bob Dylan, interview with Chris Welles, March 1964, "The Angry Young Folk Singer," *Life* (April 1964).

74 "Ah, my friends from the prison": Lyrics from "Ballad in Plain D," by Bob Dylan. Copyright © 1964 by Warner Bros., Inc.; renewed 1992 by Special Rider Music. All rights reserved. International copyright secured. Reprinted by permission.

75 "You look like you're ready for anything": Pete Karman, in Robert Shelton, *No Direction Home*, 274.

76 "On the day God made Carl": Edward Steichen, in Richard Kenin and Justin Wintle, *The Dictionary of Biographical Quotation of British and American Subjects* (New York: Knopf, 1978), 652.

76 "the fog comes/on little cat feet": Carl Sandburg, "Fog," *Chicago Poems* (New York: Holt and Company, 1916), 71.

76 "The cruelest thing that happened to Lincoln since": Edmund Wilson, *Patriotic Gore: Studies in the Literature of the American Civil War* (New York: Norton, 1994), 115.

77 "We had a definite feeling": Pete Karman, in Robert Shelton, *No Direction Home*, 274.

77 "Without looking at each other": Pete Karman, in Bob Spitz, *Dylan: A Biography* (New York: McGraw-Hill Publishing Company, 1989), 255.

78 "One of the feelings of it was that you were part": Bob Dylan, in Richard Avedon and Doon Arbus, *The Sixties* (New York: Random House, 1999), 210.

79   "Tolling for the rebel": Lyrics from "Chimes of Freedom," by Bob Dylan. Copyright © 1964 by Warner Bros., Inc.; renewed 1992 by Special Rider Music. All rights reserved. International copyright secured. Reprinted by permission.

79   "the countless confused, accused": Ibid.

81   "You could see they were exhausted": Joe B. Stewart, in Robert Shelton, *No Direction Home*, 277.

83   "This guy won't last long": Joe B. Stewart, in Robert Shelton, *No Direction Home*, 279.

83   "this time. king rex": Bob Dylan, CD liner notes, *Another Side of Bob Dylan*. Copyright © 1964 by Warner Bros., Inc.; renewed 1992 by Special Rider Music. All rights reserved. International copyright secured. Reprinted by permission.

85   "Past the Aztec ruins and the ghosts": Lyrics from "Romance in Durango," by Bob Dylan. Copyright © 1975 by Ram's Horn Music; renewed 2003 by Ram's Horn Music. All rights reserved. International copyright secured. Reprinted by permission.

86   "Bob never wanted to stop": Victor Maymudes, in Robert Shelton, *No Direction Home*, 280.

86   "We were driving through Colorado": Bob Dylan, interview with *Rolling Stone*, 1971, in "Bob Dylan, 1971," *The Rolling Stone Illustrated History of Rock and Roll* (New York: Random House, 1980), 212.

87   "Go roll a prairie up like cloth": Anonymous nineteenth-century poem, "How to Write a Splendiferous Poem," *Waterville (NY) Times*, date unknown.

88   "Alph the sacred word river runs": Adapted from Samuel Taylor Coleridge, "Kubla Khan," *Christabel, Kubla Khan, and the Pains of Sleep* (1797).

8: The Hallucinated Alphabet

91   "When I began to read an author": Marcel Proust, "Contre Sainte-Beuve" in *Proust on Art and Literature* (New York: Carroll and Graf, 1997), 265.

91   "Oh the fishes will laugh": Lyrics from "When the Ship Comes In," by Bob Dylan. Copyright © 1963, 1964 by Warner Bros., Inc.; renewed 1991, 1992 by Special Rider Music. Reprinted by permission.

91   "Shut Up . . . and Let Him Sing!": Johnny Cash, "Shut Up . . . and Let Him Sing," *Sing Out!* (March 1964), not paginated.

93   "The ocean wild like an organ": Lyrics from "Lay Down Your Weary Tune," by Bob Dylan. Copyright © 1964, 1965 by Warner Bros., Inc.; renewed 1992, 1993 by Special Rider Music. All rights reserved. International copyright secured. Reprinted by permission.

94   "needless t' say, these people": Bob Dylan, "Advice for Geraldine on Her Miscellaneous Birthday," *Writings and Drawings* (New York: Knopf, 1973), 118–19.

94   "Dylan had a great hunger": Peter Stampfel, interview with author.

95   "I love you, you love me, ookie dookie do": Bob Dylan, spoken introduction to "Blowin' in the Wind," performed at the Finjan Club, Montreal, July 2, 1962, on bootleg CD *Live/Finjan Club* (Yellow Dog YD 010).

96   "It was during the New York blackout": Peter Stampfel, interview with author.

9: Bob Gets Wired

99   "The next thing is: Bob is bigger, bigger, bigger": Myra Friedman, interview with author.

100   "Everything I did was just for a crowd of people": Bob Dylan, in Richard Avedon and Doon Arbus, *The Sixties*, 210.

100   "Folk music was a reality": Bob Dylan, *Chronicles*, 236.

101   "The voice of Dion came exploding out": Liner notes, *King of the New York Streets*, Dion box set (The Right Stuff, 2000).

101   "simple folk changes and put new imagery": Bob Dylan, *Chronicles*, 67.

102   "Both Len [Chandler] and Tom [Paxton] wrote topical songs": Bob Dylan, *Chronicles*, 82.

102   "After I finished the English tour I quit": Bob Dylan, interview with Jules Siegel, *Saturday Evening Post*.

102   "Most of the month or so we were there": Joan Baez, *And a Voice to Sing With* (New York: Summit Books, 1989), 86.

102   "I started putting tunes to their poems": Bob Dylan, interview with Scott Cohen, "Don't Ask Me Nothin' About Nothin', I Just Might Tell You the Truth: Bob Dylan Revisited," *Spin* 1, no. 8 (December 1985), 39.

104   "Maggie comes fleet foot": Lyrics from "Subterranean Homesick Blues," by Bob Dylan. Copyright © 1965 by Warner Bros., Inc.; renewed 1993 by Special Rider Music. All rights reserved. International copyright secured. Reprinted by permission.

105   "My eyes collide head-on with stuffed": Lyrics from "It's Alright, Ma (I'm Only Bleeding)," by Bob Dylan. Copyright © 1965 by Warner Bros., Inc.; renewed 1993 by Special Rider Music. All rights reserved. International copyright secured. Reprinted by permission.

105   "If my thought dreams could be seen": Ibid.

105   "People who came after me, I don't feel": Bob Dylan, interview with Edna Gundersen, "Dylan Is Positively on Top of His Game," *USA Today* (September 10, 2001), www.usatoday.com/life/music/2001-09-10-bob-dylan.htm.

106   "I'm hungry as a hog": Lyrics from "On the Road Again," by Bob Dylan. Copyright © 1965 by Warner Bros., Inc.; renewed 1993 by Special Rider Music. All rights reserved. International copyright secured. Reprinted by permission.

106 "I will go everywhere and do everything": Thomas Wolfe, in Malcolm Cowley, *A Second Flowering: Works and Days of the Lost Generation* (New York: Penguin, 1980), quoted in Richard Kenin and Justin Wintle, *The Dictionary of Biographical Quotation of British and American Subjects*, 652.

107 "The cloak and dagger dangles": Lyrics from "Love Minus Zero/No Limit," by Bob Dylan. Copyright © 1965 by Warner Bros., Inc.; renewed 1993 by Special Rider Music. All rights reserved. International copyright secured. Reprinted by permission.

107 "Pure psychic automatism": André Breton, *Surrealist Manifesto* (1924), quoted in Patrick Waldberg, *Surrealism* (New York: McGraw Hill, 1971), 75.

108 "Ah get born, keep warm": Lyrics from "Subterranean Homesick Blues," by Bob Dylan. Copyright © 1965 by Warner Bros., Inc.; renewed 1993 by Special Rider Music. All rights reserved. International copyright secured. Reprinted by permission.

108 "the basic Legos of pop music": Sasha Frere-Jones, "The Long War: Sade Soldiers On," *New Yorker* (March 22, 2010), www.newyorker.com/arts/critics/musical/2010/03 /22/100322crmu_music_frerejones.

108 "Then take me disappearin'": Lyrics from "Mr. Tambourine Man," by Bob Dylan. Copyright © 1964, 1965 by Warner Bros., Inc.; renewed 1992, 1993 by Special Rider Music. All rights reserved. International copyright secured. Reprinted by permission.

109 "Someplace along the line Suze": Bob Dylan, *Chronicles*, 288.

109 "I read *The White Goddess* by Robert Graves": Bob Dylan, *Chronicles*, 45.

109 "At the very beginning of chapter two of *Chronicles*": Peter Stampfel, interview with author.

110 "The story of those two takes:" Bob Hudson, email to author, September 24, 2011.

112 "I had no idea why they were booing": Bob Dylan, in *No Direction Home*, DVD, Martin Scorsese, dir.

112 "Miles Davis has been booed": Bob Dylan, interview with Robert Hilburn, "How Does It Feel? Don't Ask," *Los Angeles Times* (September 16, 2001), articles.latimes .com/2001/sep/16/entertainment/ca-46189/2. This interview also appeared in Dylan's 2003 official tour program.

112 "The reason they booed is": Al Kooper, in Nigel Williamson, *The Rough Guide to Bob Dylan* (London: Rough Guides, 2004), 54.

112 "If I'd had an ax, I would have cut the damned cable": Story adapted from Seth Rogovoy, "Pete Seeger," *Berkshire Eagle* (June 8, 2001), www.berkshireweb.com/rogo-voy/interviews/feato10605.html; and from Russell Hall, "Pete Seeger Talks Dylan, the Byrds and His Electric Guitar Fascination," *Gibson Lifestyle* online (January 23, 2009), www.gibson.com/en-us/Lifestyle/Features/the-gibson-interview-pete/.

113 "From Dylan's perspective, however": Bob Hudson, interview with author, June 14, 2011.

113 "Yes, I wish that for just one time": Lyrics from "Positively 4th Street," by Bob Dylan. Copyright © 1965 by Warner Bros., Inc.; renewed 1993 by Special Rider

Music. All rights reserved. International copyright secured. Reprinted by permission.

114 "surprised the first time the boos came": Bob Dylan, San Francisco press conference, December 3, 1965; available on CD, *Bob Dylan: The Classic Interviews 1965–1966* (Chrome Dreams, CIS 2004, UK, released April 2003).

114 "That was at Newport": Ibid.

115 "Hipper-Than-Thou": Al Aronowitz, "Let's 'Ave a Larf," *Blacklisted Journalist* online, www.johnlennon.it/al-aronowitz-eng.htm.

115 "By then . . . the multifaceted Bobby Neuwirth": Suze Rotolo, *A Freewheelin' Time*, 285.

10: How Does It Feel?

119 "I think musicians are a strange kind of clergy among us": D. A. Pennebaker, interview with author, in David Dalton, "I Film While Leaping from My Chair," *Gadfly* online (April 1999), www.gadflyonline.com/archive/April99/archive-pennebaker .html.

120 "I was in London and I got news that Dylan was in England": Allen Ginsberg, interview with author.

120 "I want a dog that's gonna collect and clean. . . ." Dylan in *65 Revisited*, film and DVD, D. A. Pennebaker, dir. (Pennebaker Hegedus Films, Inc.), 2007.

121 "I'm glad I'm not me": Bob Dylan, in *Don't Look Back*, film and DVD, D. A. Pennebaker, dir. (New Video Group), 2007.

121 "In 1965, God came to London": Marianne Faithfull and David Dalton, *Faithfull: An Autobiography* (New York: Cooper Square Press, 2000), 40. Marianne Faithfull, interview with author, slightly rephrased in *Faithfull*, April 12, 1993. Taken from *Faithfull: An Autobiography* by Marianne Faithfull and David Dalton. Copyright © 2000 by Marianne Faithfull. Used by permission of Cooper Square Press, a division of Rowan & Littlefield Publishing Group.

122 "I feel like I've been through": Bob Dylan, in *Don't Look Back*, film and DVD, D. A. Pennebaker, dir.

122 "Because of the way Pennebaker shot and edited it": Liner notes, *Don't Look Back*, DVD of film.

123 "There wasn't much to film anyway": Ibid.

123 "If I want to find out anything": Bob Dylan, in *Don't Look Back*, film and DVD, D. A. Pennebaker, dir.

124 "I don't think it matters at all": D. A. Pennebaker, interview with author, in David Dalton, "I Film While Leaping from My Chair," *Gadfly*.

127   "The unspeakable visions of the individual": Jack Kerouac, "Belief and Technique for Modern Prose: List of Essentials," from a 1958 letter to Don Allen, in *Heaven & Other Poems* (Bolinas, Calif.: Grey Fox Press, 1958, 1977, 1983), 47.

127   "Lord if I should hap'n a-die": Fred McDowell, "61 Highway," *I Don't Play No Rock and Roll* (Cema/Capitol, 33919, 1995), originally recorded 1959.

127   "Now the fifth daughter": Lyrics from "Highway 61 Revisited," by Bob Dylan. Copyright © 1965 by Warner Bros., Inc.; renewed 1993 by Special Rider Music. All rights reserved. International copyright secured. Reprinted by permission.

128   "Well, I ride on a mailtrain, baby": Lyrics from "It Takes a Lot to Laugh, It Takes A Train to Cry," by Bob Dylan. Copyright © 1965 by Warner Bros., Inc.; renewed 1993 by Special Rider Music. Reprinted by permission.

128   "down to the crossroads, fell down on my knees": Robert Johnson, "Cross Road Blues," *The Complete Recordings: The Centennial Collection* (Sony/Legacy, 85907, 2011), originally recorded 1936.

129   "Now the rovin' gambler": Lyrics from "Highway 61 Revisited," by Bob Dylan.

129   "He was freaky to me": Bob Johnston, in Richard Younger, "An Exclusive Interview with Bob Johnston," *On the Tracks* 20, www.b-dylan.com/pages/samples/bobjohnston.html.

130   "He came in and played a song": Bob Johnston, interview with Dan Daley, January 1, 2003, "Bob Johnston," willybrauch.de/In_Their_Own_Words/bobjohnston.htm.

130   "As I was to learn, this was a case of": Harvey Brooks, in Clinton Heylin, *Behind the Shades*, xiii.

130   "Dylan did not record everything in one take:" Bob Hudson, email to author, September 27, 2011.

131   "They're selling postcards": Lyrics from "Desolation Row," by Bob Dylan. Copyright © 1965 by Warner Bros., Inc.; renewed 1993 by Special Rider Music. All rights reserved. International copyright secured. Reprinted by permission.

132   "Einstein, disguised as Robin Hood": Ibid.

133   "When you're lost in the rain in Juarez": Lyrics from "Just like Tom Thumb's Blues," by Bob Dylan. Copyright © 1965 by Warner Bros., Inc.; renewed 1993 by Special Rider Music. All rights reserved. International copyright secured. Reprinted by permission.

133   "Because the cops don't need you": Lyrics from "Desolation Row," by Bob Dylan.

133   "Sweet Melinda": Lyrics from "Just like Tom Thumb's Blues," by Bob Dylan.

134   "I wouldn't advise anybody to use drugs": Bob Dylan, interview with Nat Hentoff, *Playboy* (March 1966).

134   "With his ferocious intake of amphetamine": Antonia, interview with author, November 3, 2008.

134   "When your mother": Lyrics from "Queen Jane Approximately," by Bob Dylan.

135   "something is happening here but": Lyrics from "Ballad of a Thin Man," by Bob Dylan. Copyright © 1965 by Warner Bros., Inc.; renewed 1993 by Special Rider Music. All rights reserved. International copyright secured. Reprinted by permission.

135   "Now you see this one-eyed midget": Lyrics from "Ballad of a Thin Man," by Bob Dylan. Copyright © 1965 by Warner Bros., Inc.; renewed 1993 by Special Rider Music. All rights reserved. International copyright secured. Reprinted by permission.

136   "He's a pinboy. . . . He also wears suspenders": Bob Dylan, San Francisco press conference, *Bob Dylan: The Classic Interviews 1965–1966.*

136   "It is through the long, endless": Arthur Rimbaud, "La Lettre du Voyant," May 15, 1871, in Arthur Rimbaud, *Oeuvres Complètes* (Paris: Gallimard, 1972). Translation by David Dalton.

136   "He sits in your room, his tomb": Lyrics from "Can You Please Crawl Out Your Window," by Bob Dylan. Copyright © 1965, 1966 by Warner Bros., Inc.; renewed 1993, 1994 by Special Rider Music. All rights reserved. International copyright secured. Reprinted by permission.

137   "Every album up to *Highway 61*": Anthony Scaduto, in Colin Irwin, *Bob Dylan:* Highway 61 Revisited (New York: Billboard Books, 2008), 228.

12: Godzilla vs. Mothra

141   "Dylan would run into Andy in the nightclubs": Paul Morrissey, interview with author, June 17, 2003.

142   "The joint was atwitter, the denizens agog": Nat Finkelstein, interview with author, December 24, 2007.

142   "Dylan is acting cool": Gerard Malanga, interview with author, September 22, 2003.

142   "The day that Dylan arrived": Billy Name, interview with author, August 19, 2008.

142   "And then after we did a screen test": Ibid.

143   "It was two totally uncommunicative": Paul Morrissey, interview with author.

143   "The circus had come to town": Nat Finkelstein, interview with author.

143   "Their encounter was carefully contrived": Ibid.

144   "Once the screen test was over": Robert Heide, interview with author, October 8, 2008.

144   "Dylan didn't simply commandeer the Elvis painting": Gerard Malanga, interview with author.

144   "It wasn't supposed to be just for the screen test": Billy Name, interview with author.

145 "I get there . . . and who's there": Robert Heide, interview with author.

146 "Edie was taken under a management deal with": Paul Morrissey, interview with author.

146 "There was the prospect of a movie with Bob Dylan": Danny Fields, interview with author, August 2, 2003.

147 "Dylan and Albert Grossman": Gerard Malanga, interview with author.

147 "I never had that much to do": Bob Dylan, interview with Scott Cohen, "Don't Ask Me Nothin' About Nothin'," *Spin*, 80.

148 "There were sparks flying off her brain": Ivan Karp, in Thomas Scherman and David Dalton, *Pop: The Genius of Andy Warhol* (New York: It Books/HarperCollins, 2010), 291.

148 "Dylan . . . was never really real": Pat Hackett, ed., *The Andy Warhol Diaries* (New York: Random House, 1991), 663.

148 "I once traded an Andy Warhol": Bob Dylan, interview with Scott Cohen, "Don't Ask Me Nothin' About Nothin'," *Spin*, 80.

149 "In a way, they're warring sides": Joshua Cicerone, interview with Kevin Johns, http://culturemagazine.ca/art/an_interview_with_joshua_cicerone_creator_of_bob_hates_andy_.html; http://www.bobhatesandy.com.

13: That Wild Mercury Sound

152 "a minority of, you know": Bob Dylan, interview with Klas Burling, Stockholm, Sweden, April 29, 1966, broadcast on Swedish radio, May 1, 1966; available on *Bob Dylan: The Classic Interviews 1965–1966* (Chrome Dreams, CIS 2004, UK, released April 2003).

153 "I told everybody if they quit": Bob Johnston, in Harvey Kubernik, "Bob Johnston on Bob Dylan, Johnny Cash, and *Nashville Skyline*," *Rock's Backpages* (May 2009), www.rocksbackpages.com.

154 "The closest I ever got to the sound": Bob Dylan, interview with Ron Rosenbaum, *Playboy*.

156 "Well, anybody can be just like me": Lyrics from "Absolutely Sweet Marie," by Bob Dylan. Copyright © 1966 by Dwarf Music; renewed 1994 by Dwarf Music. Reprinted by permission.

158 "I was very careful and paranoid": John Lennon, in David Sheff, *All We Are Saying: The Last Major Interview with John Lennon and Yoko Ono* (New York: St. Martin's Press, 2000), 178.

158 "I never asked for your crutch": Lyrics from "4th Time Around," by Bob Dylan. Copyright © 1966 by Dwarf Music; renewed 1994 by Dwarf Music. Reprinted by permission.

158 "We went down there": Bob Johnston, in Harvey Kubernik, "Bob Johnston on Bob Dylan, Johnny Cash, and *Nashville Skyline*," *Rock's Backpages*.

161 "So we took off and I was between Bob:" Al Kooper in Michael Simmons, "Bob Dylan Turns 70: An *L.A. Weekly* birthday tribute," *LA Weekly* (May 12, 2011).

162 "What happened . . . was that I did the interview": Nat Hentoff, interview with author, March 12, 2011.

162 "Carelessness. I lost my one true love": Bob Dylan, interview with Nat Hentoff, *Playboy*.

163 "This was in the days before he became": Nat Hentoff, interview with author.

164 "This should be their religion": Rosemary Garrett, quoting Bob Dylan, in Anthony Scaduto, *Dylan: An Intimate Biography* (New York: New American Library, 1973), 273.

164 "There were these two conflicting points": Rosemary Garrett, in Anthony Scaduto, *Dylan: An Intimate Biography*, 275.

165 "Dylan is LSD set to music": Phil Ochs, in Antony Scaduto, *Dylan: An Intimate Biography*, 271.

165 "I think [Dylan] was frightened": Rosemary Garrett, in Antony Scaduto, *Dylan: An Intimate Biography*, 275.

166 "Using a blowtorch": Richard Fariña, "Baez and Dylan: A Generation Singing Out," *Mademoiselle* (August 1964).

166 "It's about somebody who has come to the end of one road": Bob Dylan, interview with Studs Terkel, live broadcast *Studs Terkel Wax Museum*, WFMT Radio, Chicago, April 3, 1963.

167 "I heard you booing out there": Bob Dylan, in the unreleased film *Eat the Document*.

167 "No, you booed": Ibid.

167 "An image is projected about": Ibid.

167 "I'm not sincere at all": Ibid.

168 "I don't want to talk about protest songs": Ibid.

168 "We were trying to make a story which": Bob Dylan, interview with John Cohen and Happy Traum, Woodstock, New York, June/July 1968, published in *Sing Out!* (October/November).

169 "Someone said, 'You wanna be'": Bob Dylan, in the unreleased film *Eat the Document*.

169 "Frightened as hell": John Lennon, in Jann S. Wenner, *Lennon Remembers: The Full Rolling Stone Interviews from 1970* (New York: Verso Books, 2000), 149. Article by Jann S. Wenner from *Rolling Stone* (February 4, 1971). Copyright © 1971 by Rolling Stone LLC. All rights reserved. Printed by permission.

170 "They had a funny relationship to begin with": D. A. Pennebaker, interview with author, in David Dalton, "I Film While Leaping from My Chair," *Gadfly*.

170 "We ended up in the hotel lobby": David Sheff, *All We Are Saying*, 228.

15: Somebody Got Lucky but It Was an Accident

173 "[My wife] was following me in the car": Sam Shepard, "True Dylan," *Esquire* (July 1987).

174 "Bob said, 'I'd been up for three days'": Al Aronowitz, interview with author, November 20, 2004.

175 "SAM: Did he [Hank Williams]": Sam Shepard, "True Dylan," *Esquire*.

176 "That accident came like a warning and I heed warnings": Bob Dylan, quoted by Al Aronowitz, "My Dylan Papers, Part I: The Woodstock Festival," *The Blacklisted Journalist*, column 48 (August 1, 1999), www.blacklistedjournalist.com/column48 .html.

177 "I had very little in common": Bob Dylan, *Chronicles*, 117.

177 "In the late 1960s, until he began": Michael Gray, *Song & Dance Man III*, xvii.

178 "At Sam's party Dylan was in blue jeans": Andy Warhol and Pat Hackett, *POPism: The Warhol Sixties* (Boston: Mariner Books, 2006), 107.

179 "Many people . . . all felt tremendously affected": Bob Dylan, interview with Jann S. Wenner, *Rolling Stone* 47 (November 29, 1969). Article by Jann S. Wenner from *Rolling Stone* (November 29, 1969). Copyright © 1969 by Rolling Stone LLC. All rights reserved. Printed by permission.

16: Fifty-Four Minutes Inside Bob's Brain

185 "After *Don't Look Back* was finished": D. A. Pennebaker, interview with author, in David Dalton, "I Film While Leaping from My Chair," *Gadfly*.

185 "For Dylan, a real movie meant 'people acting'": D. A. Pennebaker, interview with author, February 10, 1999.

185 "This time Dylan got more involved in the actual filmmaking": Ibid.

185 "There was one scene up in my hotel room": Ibid.

186 "About the second concert I really got": D. A. Pennebaker, in C. P. Lee, *Like a Bullet of Light: The Films of Bob Dylan* (London: Helter Skelter Publishing, 2000), 47.

187 "Albert [Grossman] got pissed": D. A. Pennebaker, in C. P. Lee, *Like a Bullet of Light*, 57.

186 "Dylan told me, 'Why don't you guys'": D. A. Pennebaker, interview with author, February 10, 1999.

187 "They'd made another *Don't Look Back*": Ibid.

187 "But he was very pissed at everybody": D. A. Pennebaker, in C. P. Lee, *Like a Bullet of Light*, 57.

188 "Rick Danko and I are going to snort some methedrine": Bob Dylan, in the unreleased film *Eat the Document*, quoted in C. P. Lee, *Like a Bullet of Light*, 43.

189 "appear to have descended": C. P. Lee, *Like a Bullet of Light*, 41.

190　"Without the strain of having to be a 'public figure'": Carsten Grolin in (Danish magazine) *Ekstra Bladet*, quoted in C. P. Lee, *Like a Bullet of Light*, 55.

191　"Documentary? *Eat* the document!": Al Aronowitz, quoted by D. A. Pennebaker, in David Dalton, "I Film While Leaping from My Chair," *Gadfly*.

191　"What we were trying to do": Bob Dylan, interview with John Cohen and Happy Traum, *Sing Out!*

191　"We cut it fast on the eye": Bob Dylan, interview with Jann S. Wenner, *Rolling Stone*.

17: Who Is Tiny Montgomery?

195　"He had the tradition in him": Charles Olson, *Call Me Ishmael* (San Francisco: City Lights, 1947), 13, 15.

197　"No, they weren't demos for myself": Bob Dylan, interview with Jann S. Wenner, *Rolling Stone*.

198　"We were rebelling against rebellion": Robbie Robertson, in Barney Hoskyns, *Across the Great Divide: The Band and America* (New York: Hyperion, 1993), 165.

198　"contains an alien quality": D. H. Lawrence, *Studies in Classical American Literature* (New York: Penguin, 1977), 7.

199　"You know, that's really the way": Bob Dylan, interview with Jann S. Wenner, *Rolling Stone*.

199　"He damn sure didn't know how it was supposed to sound": Sid Griffin, *Million Dollar Bash: Bob Dylan, the Band, and* The Basement Tapes (London: A Jawbone Book, 2007), 153.

199　"*The Basement Tapes* were incredibly different": Sid Griffin, *Million Dollar Bash*, 317.

199　"Thing's all right and she's all too tight": Lyrics from "I'm Not There, 1956," by Bob Dylan, 1956. Copyright © 1956, 1970, 1998 by Bob Dylan. Used by permission.

200　"I was thinking about Greil Marcus's liner notes": Bob Hudson, email to author, August 4, 2011.

201　"Grady O'lady comes in—gives everybody the nod": Bob Dylan, *Tarantula*, 130.

201　"The next day everybody got up": Lyrics from "Clothes Line Saga," by Bob Dylan. Copyright © 1969 by Dwarf Music; renewed 1997 by Dwarf Music. All rights reserved. International copyright secured. Reprinted by permission.

202　"It was amazing to see him work on a song": Rosemary Garrett, in Anthony Scaduto, *Dylan: An Intimate Biography*, 275.

202　"Buddy Boy Hawkins [a blues singer from the '20s with a dirgelike sound]": J. J. Holliday, in Clinton Heylin, *Behind the Shades*, 559.

203　"They caught lightning in a bottle": Billy Bragg, in Sid Griffin, *Million Dollar Bash*, 308.

18: The Cowboy Angel Rides

206   "All across the telegraph/His name it did resound": Lyrics from "John Wesley Harding," by Bob Dylan. Copyright © 1968 Dwarf Music; renewed 1996 Dwarf Music.

209   "'Frank,' [the first king] began, 'Mr. Dylan'": Bob Dylan, liner notes, *John Wesley Harding*. Copyright © 1968 by Dwarf Music; renewed 1996 by Dwarf Music. Used by permission.

209   "Don't go mistaking Paradise": Lyrics from "The Ballad of Frankie Lee and Judas Priest," by Bob Dylan. Copyright © 1968 by Dwarf Music; renewed 1996 by Dwarf Music. Used by permission.

209   "One should never be where one": Ibid.

209   "A folk song," Woody opined: Douglas Baldwin and Patricia Baldwin, *The 1930s* (Calgary, Alberta: Weigl Educational Publishers, 2000), 39; also the epigraph of the official Woody Guthrie, website: www.woodyguthrie.org.

210   "The age that I was living in didn't resemble this age": Bob Dylan, *Chronicles*, 86.

211   "We were only 15 minutes ahead of our time": Rolling Stones, liner notes, *Between the Buttons* (Decca Records, January 1967).

211   "Outside in the distance a wildcat did growl": Lyrics from "All Along the Watchtower," by Bob Dylan. Copyright © 1968 by Dwarf Music; renewed 1996 by Dwarf Music. Used by permission.

19: The Invisible Man Goes to Nashville

215   "the people who shaped my style": Bob Dylan, interview with *Newsweek*, quoted in Peter Doggett, *Are You Ready for the Country*, 16.

217   "I knew he'd been having some difficulty": Peter Doggett, *Are You Ready for the Country*, 12.

217   "We didn't know what to do": Elliott Landy, *Woodstock Visions: The Spirit of a Generation* (London: Continuum, 1994), www.landyvision.com/The_Sixties_Generation/bob_dylan.html.

218   "These are the type of songs that I always felt like writing": Bob Dylan, interview with Hubert Saal, *Newsweek* (April 14, 1969).

218   "On *Nashville Skyline* you had to read between the lines": Bob Dylan, interview with Jonathan Cott, Portland and New Haven, Oregon, in *Rolling Stone* (November 16, 1978). Article by Jonathan Cott from *Rolling Stone* (November 16, 1978). Copyright © 1978 by Rolling Stone LLC. All rights reserved. Printed by permission.

218   "They are so daringly one-dimensional they seem contrived": Robert Christgau, review of *Nashville Skyline*, "Obvious Believers," *Village Voice* (May 1969).

219   "Now I can go from line to line, whereas yesterday it was from thought to thought": Bob Dylan, interview with John Cohen and Happy Traum, *Sing Out!*

219 "The satisfied man speaks in clichés": Ed Ochs, review of *Nashville Skyline*, in *Billboard* (July 12, 1969).

220 "That was the first live performance Dylan had done": Ken Buttrey, in Howard Sounes, *Down the Highway*, 242.

220 "How hard it was sometimes . . . to be stared at": David Amram, in Clinton Heylin, *Behind the Shades*, 305.

220 "Bob just doesn't really believe who he is": Peter Doggett, *Are You Ready for the Country*, 8.

221 "We did ['Girl from the North Country'] at rehearsal": Ibid.

222 "The man can rhyme the tick of time": Johnny Cash, liner notes, *Nashville Skyline*. Copyright © 1969; renewed 1997 Dwarf Music. All rights reserved. International copyright secured. Reprinted by permission

20: The Amnesia

225 "Until the accident . . . I was living music": Bob Dylan, in Robert Shelton, *No Direction Home*, 424.

225 "Tin Pan Alley is dead": Bob Dylan, in Alex Halberstadt, *Lonely Avenue: The Unlikely Life and Times of Doc Pomus* (Cambridge, Mass.: Da Capo Press, 2007), 167.

227 "Unless [Dylan] returns to the marketplace": Greil Marcus, review of *Self Portrait*, in *Rolling Stone* (July 23, 1970); also in Greil Marcus, *Bob Dylan by Greil Marcus*, 130.

227 "And I said, 'Well, fuck it'": Bob Dylan, interview with Kurt Loder, *Rolling Stone* (June 1984). Copyright © 1984 by Rolling Stone LLC. All rights reserved. Printed by permission.

228 "to make people go away and follow someone else": Bob Dylan, interview with Neil Hickey, *TV Guide* (September 9, 1976).

229 "Conceptually, this is a brilliant album": Robert Christgau, *Village Voice* (July 7, 1970), www.robertchristgau.com/xg/bk-aow/dylan.php.

229 "In other words, you construct your identity through the music you've been exposed to." Ibid.

230 "I was being bootlegged at the time": Bob Dylan, liner notes, *Biograph*, 1985; also in Tim Riley, *Hard Rain: A Dylan Commentary* (New York: Knopf, 1992), 192.

231 "I fucking hope so": Ryan Adams, interview with *Uncut* (January 2004).

231 "Great artists making iffy music": Trott, "Self Portrait," posted March 20, 2005, www.palacefamilysteakhouse.com/2005/03/self-portrait.html.

231 "I didn't say, 'Oh my God, they don't like this'": Bob Dylan, quoted in Clinton Heylin, *Behind the Shades*, 317.

231 "We'll go some place unknown": Lyrics from "One More Weekend," by Bob Dylan.

Copyright © 1970 by Big Sky Music; renewed 1998 by Big Sky Music. Used by permission.

232 "Marry me a wife, catch rainbow trout": Lyrics from "Sign on the Window," by Bob Dylan. Copyright © 1970 by Big Sky Music; renewed 1998 by Big Sky Music. Used by permission.

232 "Winter would have no spring": Lyrics from "If Not for You," by Bob Dylan. Copyright © 1970 by Big Sky Music; renewed 1998 by Big Sky Music. Used by permission.

233 "You know what happens to ya when you breathe": Elvis Presley, Sahara Hotel, Tahoe, May 4, 1976, in Jerry Osborne, *Elvis—Word for Word: What He Said Exactly as He Said It* (New York: Gramercy/Random House, 2006), 246.

233 "We've Got Dylan Back Again!": Ralph J. Gleason, *Rolling Stone* (October 26, 1970). Copyright © 1970 by Rolling Stone LLC. All rights reserved. Printed by permission.

234 "I know something has changed": Lyrics from "Nobody 'Cept You," by Bob Dylan. Copyright © 1973 by Ram's Horn Music; renewed 2001 by Ram's Horn Music. All rights reserved. International copyright secured. Reprinted by permission.

235 "people stuck in the last period" Dave Van Ronk and Elijah Wald, *The Mayor of MacDougal Street*, 198.

236 When Weberman claimed at the screening: Jonathan Cott, "Dylan in the Alley," *Rolling Stone* (March 4, 1971).

237 "If you want to defeat your enemy": Bob Dylan, in Fred Goodman, *The Mansion on the Hill: Dylan, Young, Geffen, Springsteen, and the Head-on Collision of Rock and Commerce* (New York: Vintage, 1998), 351–52.

21: How Dylan Became Dylan, Sort Of . . .

239 "weren't quite sure what to make of the book—except money": Bob Markel, "Here Lies Tarantula," in Bob Dylan, *Tarantula*, vi.

239 "is not a literary event because Dylan is not a literary figure": Robert Christgau review of *Tarantula*, *New York Times* (July 27, 1971).

241 "'Anything I can sing,' he observes, 'I call a song'": Bob Dylan to Nat Hentoff, liner notes, *The Freewheelin' Bob Dylan*. Copyright © 1962 by Warner Bros. Inc.; renewed 1990 by Special Rider Music. Used by permission.

241 "I was doing interviews before and after concerts": Bob Dylan, interview with Jann S. Wenner, *Rolling Stone*.

241 But, as Clinton Heylin points out: Clinton Heylin, *Behind the Shades*, 143.

241 "as cathedral bells were gently burnin": Bob Dylan, from original manuscript of *Tarantula*. Copyright © 1966, 1994 by Bob Dylan. Quoted in Clinton Heylin, *Behind the Shades*, 143.

242 "To my students": Ibid., 126.

243 "here lies bob Dylan": Ibid., 120.

243 "to dream of dancing pill head virgins": Ibid., 2.

245 "heterogeneous ideas...yoked by a violence together": Dr. Samuel Johnson, "Waller, Milton, Cowley," *Lives of the Most Eminent English Poets* (London: 1781).

245 "I think of words as being alive": William Burroughs, "Literary Techniques of Lady Sutton-Smith," *Times Literary Supplement* (August 6, 1964), 27, in Michael Taussig, *What Color Is the Sacred?* (Chicago and London: University of Chicago Press, 2009).

246 "If such bumbling media-mongers": Mark Spitzer, "Bob Dylan's *Tarantula*: An Artic Reserve of Untapped Glimmerance Dismissed in a Ratland of Clichés," *Jack* (2003) http://www.jackmagazine.com/issue7/essaysmspitzer.html.

22: Under the Rings of Saturn

251 "I went home after that...and my wife never did understand me": Bob Dylan, quoted by Pete Oppel, in Andy Gill and Keven Odegard, *A Simple Twist of Fate: Bob Dylan and the Making of* Blood on the Tracks (New York: Da Capo, 2004), 39.

251 Columbia executive Ellen Bernstein: Clinton Heylin, *Behind the Shades*, 371–381.

251 "actress Ruth Tyrangiel": Howard Sounes, *Down the Highway*, 280.

252 "Twilight on the frozen lake": Lyrics from "Never Say Goodbye," by Bob Dylan. Copyright © 1973 by Ram's Horn Music; renewed 2001 by Ram's Horn Music. All rights reserved. International copyright secured. Reprinted by permission.

253 "I hate myself for lovin' you": Lyrics from "Dirge," by Bob Dylan. Copyright © 1973 by Ram's Horn Music; renewed 2001 by Ram's Horn Music. All rights reserved. International copyright secured. Reprinted by permission.

254 "You need a different kinda man, babe": Lyrics from "It Ain't Me, Babe," by Bob Dylan. Copyright © 1964 by Warner Bros., Inc.; renewed 1992 by Special Rider Music. All rights reserved. International copyright secured. Reprinted by permission.

255 "They lit up $40-an-ounce grass": Lucian K. Truscott IV, "Bob Dylan Comes Back from the Edge," *Village Voice* (February 7, 1974).

257 "It was lots of dope and lots of girls": Barney Hoskyns, *Across the Great Divide*, 302.

257 "like Frank and Jesse James getting back together again": Barney Hoskyns, *Across the Great Divide*, 293.

257 "a big circus...except there weren't any elephants": Barney Hoskyns, *Across the Great Divide*, 294.

23: The Second Coming of Bob

260 "He blew into New York City on a bitter freezing day": Tom Pacheco, in Larry Sloman, *On the Road with Bob Dylan* (New York: Three Rivers Press, 2002), 167–68. Copyright © by Tom Pacheco. Used by permission.

261 "Dylan was one of ours and he had struck gold": Dave Van Ronk and Elijah Wald, *The Mayor of MacDougal Street*, 216.

263 "But me, I'm still on the road/Headin' for another joint": Lyrics from "Tangled Up in Blue," by Bob Dylan. Copyright © 1974 by Ram's Horn Music; renewed 2002 by Ram's Horn Music. Used by permission.

264 "I had a job in the great north woods/Working as a cook for a spell": Ibid.

264 "I place Montaigne foremost among the dissemblers": Sarah Bakewell, *How to Live: Or a Life of Montaigne in One Question and Twenty Attempts at an Answer* (New York: Other Press, 2000), 209.

265 "You can have the best there is": Unpublished original lyrics from "Idiot Wind," by Bob Dylan. Copyright © 1974 by Ram's Horn Music; renewed 2002 by Ram's Horn Music. Used by permission.

265 "One day you'll be in the ditch": Ibid.

265 "I came pretty close [to revealing too much of my personal life]": Bob Dylan, interview with Bill Flanagan," *Telegraph*.

266 "She looked at him and he felt a spark": Lyrics from "Simple Twist of Fate," by Bob Dylan. Copyright © 1974 by Ram's Horn Music; renewed 2002 by Ram's Horn Music. Used by permission.

266 "Hunted like a *crocodile*, ravaged in the *corn*": Ibid.

267 "In a little hilltop village they gambled for my clothes": Ibid.

24: Bob's Wild West (Village) Show

272 "To the ground, too, to the day, to Jack": Allen Ginsberg, in Sam Shepard, *Rolling Thunder Logbook* (New York: Da Capo Press, 2004), 90.

272 "Dylan creates a mythic atmosphere out of land around us": Sam Shepard, *Rolling Thunder Logbook*, 63.

272 "[Dylan] talks about the possibility of discovering America": Allen Ginsberg, in Sam Shepard, *Rolling Thunder Logbook*, 145.

276 "I broke into the tomb": Lyrics from "Isis," by Bob Dylan and Jacques Levy. Copyright © 1975 by Ram's Horn Music; renewed 2003 by Ram's Horn Music. Used by permission.

25: Epiphany in Room 702

281 "Towards the end of the show someone out in the crowd": Bob Dylan, speaking to the audience between songs during a performance at the Grady Gammage Memorial Auditorium, Tempe, Arizona, November 27, 1979.

281 "Dylan has always believed, not unreasonably": Paul Williams, *Watching the River Flow: Observations on His Art-in-Progress, 1966–1995* (London: Omnibus Press, 1996), 70.

282 "The curtain goes up about 8:20, and Regina Havis": Paul Williams, *Watching the River Flow*, 166.

282 "'Behold, the days come,' sayeth the Lord": Sleeve notes, *Saved* (Columbia, 1980).

283 "You know we're living in the end times": Bob Dylan, Grady Gammage Memorial Auditorium, Tempe, Arizona, November 26, 1979.

283 "I am broken/Shattered like an empty cup" Lyrics from "Covenant Woman," by Bob Dylan. Copyright © 1980 by Special Rider Music. Used by permission.

284 "I saw Dylan in Spokane during his born-again": Lenny Kaye, interview with author, April 12, 2010.

285 "Hmm. What a rude bunch tonight, huh?": Bob Dylan, Grady Gammage Memorial Auditorium, Tempe, Arizona, November 26, 1979.

285 "How many people here are aware that we're living in the End of Times": Ibid.

26: Down the Road

289 "The mirror had swung around:" Bob Dylan, *Chronicles*, 148.

290 "Right away I wanted to know if I could do any song": George Lois, interview with author, April 18, 2011.

290 "George had two main ideas": Larry "Ratso" Sloman, interview with author, April 14, 2011.

291 "The whole side of the room was dark": George Lois, interview with author.

291 "I suggest this restaurant in Chinatown": Larry "Ratso" Sloman, interview with author.

291 "Okay, Bob, we'll play the music": George Lois, interview with author.

291 "Well he fucking did it six times": Ibid.

292 "This goes on for about four takes": Larry "Ratso" Sloman, interview with author.

292 "Everyone loved it": George Lois, interview with author.

293 "I was standing in line for this Gregory Peck film": Bob Dylan to Sam Shepard, in Howard Sounes, *Down the Highway*, 375.

294 "He's funny. He has a chameleon-like quality": Jerry Garcia, in Blair Jackson, *Garcia: An American Life* (New York: Penguin, 2000), 366.

295 "I don't think eulogizing will do him justice": Bob Dylan on Jerry Garcia, in Blair Jackson, *Garcia: An American Life*, 457.

295 "I really had some sort of epiphany": Bob Dylan, interview with Mikal Gilmore, "Bob Dylan, at 60, Unearths New Revelations," *Rolling Stone* (November 22, 2001). Copyright © 2001 by Rolling Stone LLC. All rights reserved. Printed by permission.

297 "I'm determined to stand whether God will deliver me or not": Bob Dylan, interview with Mikal Gilmore, "Bob Dylan, at 60", *Rolling Stone*.

298 "A lot of people don't like the road, but it's as natural to me as breathing": Bob Dylan, interview with Jon Pareles, *New York Times* (September 26, 1997).

299 "On the opening night, he speaks, laughs and persistently performs a peculiar hip-swinging trouser maneuver": Adrian Deevoy, October 21, 1989, Q 39 (December 1989).

300 "It's all the same tour—the Never Ending Tour—it works out better for me that way": Bob Dylan, interview with Adrian Deevoy, Q, 39 (December 1989).

301 "It was a living-room environment:" Daniel Lanois in "Bob Dylan Turns 70: An L.A. Weekly birthday tribute" by Michael Simmons, May 12, 2011.

302 "I knew then that we had a monkey act": Ronnie Hawkins, in Howard Sounes, *Down the Highway*, 392.

302 "Mouse could walk on his hands across a football field": Bob Dylan, in Douglas Brinkley, "Bob Dylan's Late-Era, Old-Style American Individualism" *Rolling Stone*.

303 "Dylan now resembles nothing so much as an alcoholic lumberjack": Clinton Heylin, *Behind the Shades*, 661.

304 "There was a weariness about him": David Was, in Howard Sounes, *Down the Highway*, 390–91.

304 "It was important for me . . . to come to the bottom of this legend thing": Bob Dylan, interview with Robert Hilburn, "Dylan Now: What Becomes a Legend Most? A Never-Ending Tour, a New Audience and Keeping the Mystery Alive," *Los Angeles Times* (February 9, 1992), articles.latimes.com/1992-02-09/magazine/tm-3235_1_never-ending-tour/2.

305 Clydie King, one of many backup: Howard Sounes, *Down the Highway*, 339, 359.

306 "I think he [dated] some of these black girls because they didn't idolize him": Maria Muldaur, in Howard Sounes, *Down the Highway*, 370.

306 Carole Childs, an A&R woman: Howard Sounes, *Down the Highway*, 369.

306 "Susan Ross, a onetime road manager": Ibid., 369.

306 "Bob freed the mind the way Elvis freed the body": Bruce Springsteen, Rock and Roll Hall of Fame induction ceremony for Bob Dylan, January 20, 1988, rockhall.com/inductees/bob-dylan/bio/.

307 "My daddy once said to me": Bob Dylan acceptance speech, Lifetime Achievement Award, Grammy Awards, February 20, 1991.

27: When I Paint My Masterpiece

311 "My influences have not changed": Bob Dylan, interview with Alan Jackson, Metropolitan Hotel, London, England, October 4, 1997, published in the *Times on Sunday* (November 15, 1997).

311 "I find the religiosity and philosophy in the music": Bob Dylan, interview with David Gates, "Dylan Revisited," *Newsweek* (October 6, 1997), www.thedailybeast.com/newsweek/1997/10/05/dylan-revisited.html.

313   "When my songwriting started, all that [music] was kind of left to one side": Bob Dylan, interview with Gary Hill, San Diego, October 3, 1993, "Bob Dylan Makes a Passionate Record of His Folk Roots," Reuters, printed in *Isis* 52 (date unknown), 29.

314   "Not a soul would look up, not a soul would look down": Sixteenth-century English ballad, "Nottamun Town," Roud Folk Song Index, no. 1044.

314   "There was a time when the songs would come three or four": Bob Dylan, interview with Paul Zollo, "SongTalk Interview," *SongTalk: The Journal of the National Academy of Songwriters* (April 1991).

317   "It is a spooky record": Bob Dylan to Emily Coleman, "I Am My Words," *Newsweek*.

318   "I just want to say, one time when I was about sixteen": Bob Dylan, Album of the Year Acceptance Speech, Grammy Awards, February 25, 1998.

318   "Singers in the fifties and sixties": Bob Dylan, interview with Gary Hill, "Dylan Talks about Religion, Heroism and Elvis," Reuters.

319   "You say the answer is blowing in the wind": Pope John Paul II, World Eucharist Congress, Bologna, September 27, 1997.

319   "so appalled at the prospect of the pontiff sharing a platform": Former cardinal Joseph Ratzinger (now Pope Benedict XVI), *Times* (London) (March 8, 2007).

320   "One thing about his brain": Eric Andersen, interview with author, March 17, 2011.

320   "Cheech Marin: Where you headed?": *Masked and Anonymous*, Larry Charles, dir. (Sony Pictures, 2003).

321   "I thought he was kind of ingenuous": Eric Andersen, interview with author.

28: The Enigma Variations

324   Carmel Hubbell appears at: Howard Sounes, *Down the Highway*, 344–46.

324   "Richard Dickinson in Hobart" Ibid., 394.

325   "I wasn't sure if he came": Chris Francescani, "New Jersey Homeowner Calls Cops on Bob Dylan," ABC News (August 14, 2009), abcnews.go.com/GMA/jersey-homeowner-calls-cops-bob-dylan/story?id=8331830.

325   "She is 22 and unfortunately": Paul Thompson, "Policewoman Escorts Bob Dylan to Hotel after Failing to Recognize Him," *Telegraph* (London) (August 15, 2009), www.telegraph.co.uk/culture/music/bob-dylan/6031615/Policewoman-escorts-Bob-Dylan-to-hotel-after-failing-to-recognise-him.html.

325   "Kindergarten kids in ritzy L.A.": Richard Johnson, "Easily Scared," *New York Post* (May 3, 2007), www.nypost.com/p/pagesix/item_ejX7XCsYvChobq83fuRnJM;jsessionid=FB52E0954EC7D789C981F2C5BE5C7D78.

326   "Sometimes the 'you' in my songs": Scott Cohen, "Don't Ask Me Nothin' About Nothin'," *Spin*.

326 "Wait a minute!": Sam Shepard, *Rolling Thunder Logbook,* 177.

327 "it's about naked alienation": Bob Dylan, interview with Jonathan Cott, "Bob Dylan: The *Rolling Stone* Interview," *Rolling Stone* (January 26, 1978). Copyright © 1978 by Rolling Stone LLC. All rights reserved. Printed by permission.

328 "Do I contradict myself?": Walt Whitman, "Song of Myself," *Leaves of Grass* (1891).

328 "He came up with a strange": Jorge Luis Borges, "Walt Whitman: *Leaves of Grass,*" *Selected Nonfictions,* Eliot Weinberger, ed. (New York: Viking, 1999), 447. Copyright Maria Kodama, 1999. "Walt Whitman, Leaves of Grass," translated by Esther Allen, from Selected Non-Fictions by Jorge Luis Borges, edited by Eliot Weinberger, copyright © 1999 by Maria Kodama; translation copyright © 1999 by Penguin Putnam, Inc. Used by permission of Viking Penguin, a division of Penguin Group (USA), Inc. Excerpt from "Walt Whitman, Leaves of Grass" from *Selected Non-Fictions* by Jorge Luis Borges. Copyright © 1995, 1999 by Maria Kodama, used by permission of the Wylie Agency LLC.

329 "How many roles can I play?": Liner notes *Biograph,* 1985. Used by permission.

330 "Dylan is definitely an escape artist": Sam Shepard, *Rolling Thunder Logbook,* 171.

331 "And you could never pin him": Dave Van Ronk and Elijah Wald, *The Mayor of Mac-Dougal Street,* 179.

332 "One look at the set list and": Bob Boilen, "Nobody Ruins Dylan like Dylan," *All Songs Considered: The Blog* (November 15, 2010), www.npr.org/blogs/allsongs/2010/11/15/131328227/nobody-ruins-dylan-like-dylan.

332 "The minute you try to grab": Todd Haynes, dir., in the press notes for his film *I'm Not There* (Weinstein Company, 2007).

333 "Ladies and gentlemen, please": Al Santos, Bob Dylan's stage manager and announcer, introducing Bob Dylan at the Cooperstown, New York, concert, Doubleday Field, August 6, 2004.

335 "I thought it was awful": Greil Marcus, *Mojo* (January 2010), 55.

336 "There's a lot of the junk": Bob Hudson, interview with author, September 20, 2011.

Acknowledgments

IN THE BEGINNING, THIS BOOK WAS CALLED *BOB'S BRAIN*, A SORT OF manic quest inside the enigmatic head of Bob—*as if!* But even said humorously, I had no idea how daunting a task this might be and that it would require help from far more astute minds than mine.

Had I not been introduced to Bob Hudson by the maverick gadfly John Whitehead, I would have been utterly at sea (and not even realized it!) before even setting sail. Bob Hudson is an eminent Dylan sessionologist (one among many of his talents) who has saved me from misconceptions, errors, and delusions herein. He essentially became my guru. On top of all this he's a fiendish fiddle player.

Without Mark Johnson, songwriter, singer, and possessed maniac, I wouldn't have had a clue about the churning musicological undercurrents streaming through Bob's brain. Who but the obsessed Mark would have guessed what strange and quirky strains lay in that midden heap of half-remembered songs and riffs. Hey, Mark!

I often say in an odd moment that I intend to become a Dylanologist either when I grow up or when I retire (neither seems likely), and that's because at the bottom of my motley heart I feel that the ingenious labors of the dedicated Dylanologist—someone who believes Bob is in the details—are the appropriate response to so vast and labyrinthine a talent. Among that noble band is Mitch Blank, deep-taper, benign and selfless hipster, who at the drop of a hat will share with you any iconic sound or image from his immense collection. If you ever get the opportunity to meet the esteemed Mitch, you may want to ask him to play you the Iglut version of "Quinn the Eskimo."

I am grateful to Kim Tanner for so good-naturedly dealing with the thorny endnotes and permissions, to Nancy Rose who found all the great photos. At Dylan's office I'd like to thank April Hayes, who helpfully shared rare and iconic pictures; Callie Gladman, for making available Dylan's lyrics and writings; and Jeff Rosen for casting a benign eye on this project.

To Paula Cooper, a great copy editor—I had to force myself to stop writing "good catch" on every page of the manuscript.

I AM MORE INDEBTED THAN I CARE TO ADMIT TO MY EDITOR, MATT Inman, who pulled this book into shape and saved me from making a fool of myself through overreaching metaphors. I often thought of him as my parole officer, especially on those occasions when he accused me of trying to give him the slip. I am especially grateful to Hyperion editor in chief Elisabeth Dyssegaard, who believed in this book and whose patience I must have sorely tried. And especially to Bob Miller, from whose fevered head this sprung.

May the celestial nymphs who turn water into words and back again sprinkle their galactic dust on Peter Stampfel and Antonia, who lent me their eyes and ears to see into the murky depths of the candlelit past. And, as the Vedic hymnist Atri hath said, "That something merely happens is pointless. But that something happens and a watching eye gathers it into itself is everything," I am therefore beholden to Larry "Ratso" Sloman, George Lois, Elizabeth Finkelstein, Michael Simmons, Barney Hoskyns, Lenny Kaye, Eric Andersen, Myra Freidman, Danny Fields, Billy Name, Bob Heide, Paul Morrissey, Gerard Malanga, Marianne Faithfull, Nat Hentoff, George Gerdes, Larry Poons, and—wherever you are—Nat Finkelstein, Al Aronowitz, and Allen Ginsberg.

And how could I have dealt with all the travails that arise from putting a book to bed without my smart and comely agent, Eileen Cope? Carilloners, ring them bells loudly for: Linn Prentis, Don and Mosh Statham, Dawn Dickerson, Dorothy Lyman, Ian Kimmet, Anita Hall, Sarah Smith, Simona McCray, and Ken Peterson.

I am extremely grateful to D. A. Pennebaker for generously allowing me to use his iconic images from *Don't Look Back*. It's always a thrill to see our hero in all his prancing, provoking, prevaricating, and street-corner poeticizing glory. And now, with the reissue of the DVD, you get even more of Bob at his most Dylanesque on the bonus disc, *65 Revisited*—containing outtakes that include full performances of songs only seen in abbreviated form in the original film. I'd especially like to thank Frazer Pennebaker for all his genial help in making it possible to use the screen shots reproduced in the book. And, cinematographer, a close-up, please, of the always stylish and sharp-witted Chris Hegedus.

I am thankful to two friends who kindly let me use their photos:

Elliott Landy, for his photograph of Dylan in his lair at Byrdcliffe and for a classic picture of the Band, and to Elizabeth Finkelstein, who gave me two of Nat Finkelstein's iconic pictures from the mythic Dylan/Warhol encounter. Bless you both!

Thanks also to Toby Dalton and Peter Guarino for tech support. Couldn't have done it without you, dudes!

And last but definitely not least, Coco Pekelis, painter of sublime scribbled auras who redecorated the right side of my brain so I could see between the lines.

Index

Page numbers in *italics* refer to picture captions.

Photo and Illustration Credits

Grateful acknowledgment is made to the following for permission to reproduce illustrations in the text: